Educational
Research

Educational Research

The Interrelationship of Questions, Sampling, Design, and Analysis

James B. Schreiber

Center for Advancing the Study of Teaching and Learning
Duquesne University

Kimberly Asner-Self

Department of Educational Psychology and Special Education
Southern Illinois University

WILEY

JOHN WILEY & SONS, INC.

VP and Publisher	Jay O'Callaghan
Executive Editor	Christopher T. Johnson
Acquisition Editor	Robert Johnston
Editorial Assistant	Mariah Maguire-Fong
Marketing Manager	Danielle Torio
Marketing Assistant	Melissa Kleckner
Production Manager	Janis Soo
Assistant Production Editor	Elaine S. Chew
Senior Media Editor	Lynn Pearlman
Cover Designer	Seng Ping Ngieng
Cover Illustration	Laserwords Pvt. Ltd.

This book was typeset in New-Baskerville by Laserwords Pvt. Ltd., Chennai, India and printed and bound by Malloy Lithographers, Inc. The cover was printed by Malloy Lithographers, Inc.

This book is printed on acid free paper.⊗

Founded in 1807, John Wiley & Sons, Inc. has been a valued source of knowledge and understanding for more than 200 years, helping people around the world meet their needs and fulfill their aspirations. Our company is built on a foundation of principles that include responsibility to the communities we serve and where we live and work. In 2008, we launched a Corporate Citizenship Initiative, a global effort to address the environmental, social, economic, and ethical challenges we face in our business. Among the issues we are addressing are carbon impact, paper specifications and procurement, ethical conduct within our business and among our vendors, and community and charitable support. For more information, please visit our web site: www.wiley.com/go/citizenship.

Evaluation copies are provided to qualified academics and professionals for review purposes only, for use in their courses during the next academic year. These copies are licensed and may not be sold or transferred to a third party. Upon completion of the review period, please return the evaluation copy to Wiley. Return instructions and a free of charge return shipping label are available at www.wiley.com/go/returnlabel. Outside of the United States, please contact your local representative.

Library of Congress Cataloging-in-Publication Data

Schreiber, James.
   Educational research : interrelationship of questions, sampling, design, and analysis / James B. Schreiber, Kimberly Asner-Self.
      p. cm.
   Includes index.
   ISBN-13: 978-0-470-13910-3 (pbk.)
  1. Education—Research. 2. Education—Research—Methodology. 3. Qualitative research.
4. Quantitative research. I. Asner-Self, Kimberly. II. Title.
   LB1028.S285 2011
   370.72—dc22
                      2010037939

Printed in the United States of America
10 9 8 7 6 5 4 3 2 1

For Helene, Jakob, Annika, and Fritz.

To Brian, Dylan, and Adrian with all my love.

BRIEF CONTENTS

CONTENTS

CHAPTER TWO
Scholar Before Researcher   30

CHAPTER THREE
Problem Areas and Research Questions   52

CHAPTER FOUR
Participant Sampling and Selection   80

CHAPTER FIVE
Believability in Observation and Measurement   104

CHAPTER EIGHT
Qualitative Design   192

CHAPTER NINE
Analysis Techniques: Descriptive and Inferential Statistics   228

CHAPTER TEN
Data Analysis: Non-Numeric Data   268

CHAPTER ELEVEN
Program Evaluation   302

CHAPTER TWELVE
Writing the Proposal or Final Report   336

PREFACE

Educational Research: The Interrelationship of Questions, Sampling, Design, and Analysis

SCHREIBER AND ASNER-SELF

WHY WE WROTE THIS BOOK

This book is organized around the theme of "The Research Question." Why have we chosen to focus on the research question? We view the research question as the core element around which a research study revolves and evolves. We have many years of experience teaching courses in educational research, sitting on dissertation committees, chairing dissertations, and working with students on research in general. The ability to see the interactive nature of the research question is imperative to us.

Following is a graphic representation we have used with students to remind them that all of these components are integrated. Making changes in one component affects the other components. Your question (s) of interest will be tailored into a research question. For example, "does high school reform do anything?" transition into, after five years after reform, are the students graduating at a higher percentage, going to college, succeeding in college, receiving scholarships, etc. How you word your research question often informs the decisions that will be made in the other areas of the research study.

The Research Question is in the center of the diagram because it is the driving force behind all other decisions made during a research study. We commonly have students come to us and say "I want to do a _____ study." Fill in the blank with qualitative, quantitative, mixed method, ethnography etc. We send them away and tell them to come back when they have a research question they actually want to answer, a question that needs to be answered, and has not been answered.

The research question is intricately connected to each of the areas involved in a research study: the sample, the design of the study, data collection, and analysis of the data. When there is a change in any one of these areas, the other areas are affected. For example, a change in the sample size (from a sampling of 4 people to a sampling of 104 people) or a change in the composite of the sample (students with learning disabilities in an urban environment is changed to students with learning disabilities in urban and suburban environments) can affect what design, data, and analyses are appropriate. Changes in the data collection procedure can affect how many participants are truly possible.

We hope you will make compromises, change direction, adjust research questions, as you progress from research question to final report or manuscript.

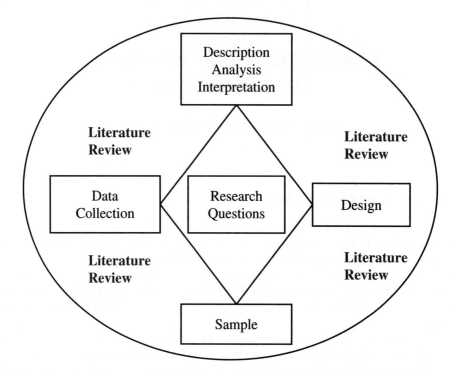

These changes are the mark of a thoughtful researcher who is learning and making important adjustments as they discover more about their research question.

A careful researcher will continue to read the literature throughout the process of her research study. For this reason, the phrase "literature review" appears at every point in the diagram on research design. Often, students believe that their literature review is completed as soon as they have developed their research question. But that is misguided. The sample, design, data collection instruments and procedures, and analyses need to be researched and justified. We often tell our students and colleagues, "the review does not end at Chapter 2 of the dissertation."

As a researcher, you must read extensively to gain the necessary depth of understanding of the area you are researching. This is critical to developing a worthwhile question to research. When you read in a specific area you learn about the types of questions that are asked, the world view of the researchers, the design, data collection, and analyses typically used. And, you learn who has been studied. In depth reading also allows you to critique the area in reference to the strengths, weaknesses, and opportunities for further investigation.

LEARNING TOOLS

Each chapter contains features that will support you in learning about educational research methods. We begin each chapter with a **Key Idea**. Key Ideas act as an organizing mechanism and give you the big picture of that chapter. For example, in

Chapter 2 the Key Idea is: *Reading is fundamental to the development of research problems, questions, designs, and analyses. Good questions come from deep reading and thinking.* We also begin each chapter with a bulleted list of **Points To Know** that serve as a guide to your reading, and a preview of the information you will be reading about in the chapter.

Beginning in Chapter 2, there are opportunities for you to write in the book in response to activities and questions. Many of the writing activities are open-ended questions that allow you to write questions or what you are thinking about the topic at that point. Other activities are designed to help you to think critically or to critique. We chose this path, versus multiple choice questions, or other traditional options because we have observed when students have to write out what they are thinking, they tend to refine their ideas in a more timely and clearer manner.

Throughout the book, we have included **In-Text Activities** where we ask you to write down what you are working on, such as your research question, review of literature, or potential sample. These activities are designed to help you develop your research and act as a running record of your thoughts at that moment.

Each chapter concludes with an **Arm Chair Moment** where we discuss in depth a specific topic that has troubled students in our classes. The Arm Chair Moment is a less formal conversation about a topic in the chapter, and is similar to a conversation you might have with a colleague, professor, or peer. These Arm Chair Moments are based on conversations we had with students and with each other as we have conducted our own research. After reading the Arm Chair Moment, you'll have the opportunity to respond to a question we pose to you, a question that allows you to apply what you learned in the chapter. The Arm Chair Moment allows us to interact with you, to share our experiences in a way we hope will help you to develop your research skills.

Textbooks can feel like a grouping of disparate ideas, definitions, and procedures. In an attempt to solve that within our classes, we created **Case Study** examples that we follow through a semester. For this book, we created one cases for you to follow from chapter to chapter to see how the decisions made, related to the material in the chapter, in a research study affect everything else. These case studies will help you to vicariously experience what our students have experienced as they engaged in the research process.

We have written the book in a very informal tone. Part of that are stems from our personalities and part is it is how we talk to the students so that we do not scare them off. It does not mean that we are not very serious and dedicated to high quality research design. If you were to experience our classes, the language expectation over time switches to more technical language in both conversation and written assignments. We hope you find this book useful and friendly and have attempted to make reading about research design as understandable and approachable as possible. We also try to make as few mistakes as possible, if you notice something please write us, and remember, "nullius in verba", the motto of the Royal Society of the United Kingdom, which essentially means do not take one's word for it.

ACKNOWLEDGMENTS

There are many people who in some way shape or form contributed to the intellectual development of this book. We include our early mentors, our families who let us be us. For Jim, other early mentor include, Ms. Theresa Campbell and Mr. Danforth at Brophy College, Drs. Frenzen, MacInnis, and Nakamoto then at the University of Arizona, Drs. Gryder, Berliner, Middleton, Glass, and Savenye at Arizona State University. A special acknowledgement for the late Dr. Kulhavy who brought me into his lab at ASU and convinced me I needed to be an academic and Don Cunningham for taking me in at Indiana. To my entire NCIC family, this book really would not have been possible without you. Students from GREV 701 at Duquesne whose unvarnished opinions were of great help. Also, Dana Schneider for her dedication to helping get aspects of the book together and her amazing skills at finding articles without our library system. To my colleagues at Duquesne University, thank you for always watching over me and my family and making time to listen to an idea or organization of the material. Finally, a great deal of coffee was consumed during this time, and I must thank, Cindy at Mojo's and Michelle Allen at Aldo's for their constant attention to my coffee needs.

For Kim's acknowledgements: to my early mentors, Drs. Sylvia Marotta and Maria Cecilia Zea at The George Washington University and Sara Nieves-Grafals, all I can say is thank you for your support and help when the going got tough. To my colleagues who have provided ideas, encouragement, and laughter, Drs. Jack Snowman, Lyle White, and Brett Zyromski of Southern Illinois University, thank you. To my university, SIU, thank you for the sabbatical! Thanks to Dave Elam and Alison Wolz for giving me the gifts of time, peace, and energy. Thanks to Helene for many e-mails spent foraging for Howard. Finally, and hardly least, to Jim Schreiber, without whom this book could not have been written, without whose friendship, hard work, dedication, drive, and humor, nothing would have come to fruition.

Introduction to Research Design

KEY IDEA

Being a researcher means thinking and talking like a researcher. Therefore, you must understand the basics and the language.

POINTS TO KNOW

Understand what research is and differentiate among the types of reasoning in research design.

Understand basic philosophical models—the "isms" within research methodology.

Understand the critical importance of research questions in the design process and their relationship with the other components of design.

Understand the basic attributes of qualitative and quantitative methods.

Understand the attributes of the scientific method.

Differentiate among the three basic types of research.

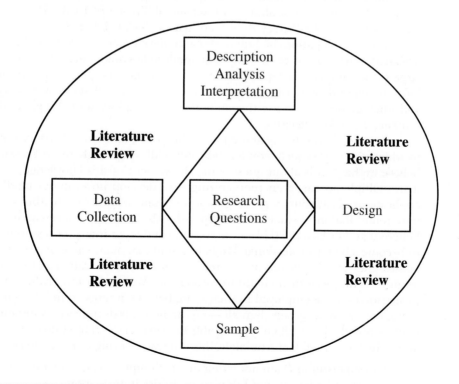

RESEARCH—WHAT IS IT ANYWAY?

We always begin our research courses with a discussion about linguistics. To communicate with other researchers, you will need to learn the language of this community—research methodologists. You have learned many community languages in your life—the language patterns you use at home, with friends, and in school. The language of educational researchers is one more way of thinking and speaking that will allow you to communicate and critique within the educational research community, which can be termed an affinity group.

When we informally surveyed both students' and professionals' first thoughts when they heard the word *research*, we found that some immediately thought of numbers, data, and computers; one thought about needing funding; one imagined a harried scientist, white coat slightly disheveled, scurrying about a laboratory replete with bubbling concoctions of noxious liquids, adjusting drips and flames, while scribbling furiously on a notepad; and others declared feelings such as "stress" and "ack!" These comments are how people generally think about research, but how do researchers think about and discuss research?

Research is a systematic process of active inquiry and discovery through collecting, analyzing, and inferring from data so that we can understand a given phenomenon in which we are interested. Research in all of its forms and procedures really boils down to systematic and disciplined inquiry (Shulman, 1981). Defined in the Health Insurance Portability and Accountability Act of 1996 (HIPAA) within a section known as the Privacy Rule (codified as 45 CFR § 164.501), research is any "systematic investigation, including research development, testing and evaluation, designed to develop or contribute to generalizable knowledge." Research covers a large continuum and is dependent on the questions that peak our curiosity, what information or data we can get access to, what sorts of analyses we want to conduct, and whether we plan to use the study results to explore something, confirm our thinking, or make a decision.

Research is wondering about the world around and within us, developing ways in which to address such wonderings, and adding to the body of knowledge we believe we have. It is about questioning the veracity of this knowledge, evaluating it in multiple arenas, even reorganizing it to develop novel understandings and applications. That sounds pretty good—lofty and worthy of a textbook—but we have found that most students and professionals shy away from research. Students believe that they lack the skills or interest to conduct or interpret research or use it to become a better professional. We have found that many students dread research classes: they avoid, put off, and barely tolerate research, rather than embrace it as an integral piece of their future profession. We've also found that sometimes professionals, once employed in their field, become interested in a technique that seems to work for a certain clientele—say, adolescents dealing with substance abuse issues—but may have difficulty being able to read and critically evaluate the research about the technique. Unfortunately, this can lead to living one's professional life

- in superstition (I am not trying that technique because the other technique worked for before and I don't want to risk it not working),

- inefficiently (inability to adjust to deeper and more comprehensive understanding about adolescent development),
- with unexamined assumptions (this technique just makes sense to me so it must be right),
- and continually reinventing the wheel (wait, isn't this technique just the same as that one we used 20 years ago with a different name?).

Research, as we mean it, is *not* simply summarizing what others have done. Many undergraduate students write research papers for their classes. These narratives are not research; they are simply summaries of what others have done, and in many instances, they are summaries of summaries. It is *not* collecting data for data's sake. Your local, state, and federal governments do this. They collect data without reference to any sort of research question let alone a related methodology. Finally, research is *not* a form of advertising or to be used to end an intense argument. The use and abuse of the word *research* by people is common in commercials and conversations. Our favorite is: "Well, there is research that supports this idea (my personal belief about this phenomenon)." When queried, the person cannot provide one piece of information from the "research."

Designing studies is both an engineering and architectural endeavor. With our students, we typically discuss this endeavor as building a fort. You are building to protect your fort from attacks. Those attacks come from critics of the research: committee members, reviewers, colleagues, and you. Therefore, research design is essentially creating a sound structure. For the structure to be sound, you must understand the relationships among each part of your structure and how each part works together. This is the engineering component and why we drew the diagram you see in the introduction and at the start of every chapter. Your design and the detail involved to make it sophisticated and elegant is the architectural component. We read research manuscripts every day and for some of them we sit back and state, "Wow! That is really a beautiful study."

Reasoning in Research

Reasoning is a critical component of research. As you embark on a research project, you need to know how to reason by making numerous inferences. Reasoning can be defined as the act of making inferences from facts or premises. There are three types of reasoning: abductive,[1] inductive, and deductive. Students and professionals in research and in applied settings use these types of reasoning continuously. We discuss them here and provide an example.

Abductive Reasoning.   Abductive reasoning refers to using the available facts to come up with the best possible explanation. For example, if your friend comes to class coughing and sneezing and carrying a box of tissues, you can infer that she has

---

[1] Others will argue that abduction is analytic induction, i.e., specific to general (Denzin, 1989; Schwandt, 1997). Thomas Schwandt constantly challenged one of us during graduate school about this. Note that researchers argue a great deal with each other. It is a healthy component of the profession—not a dysfunction.

a cold. That's the best possible explanation based on the facts. Or, you might infer that your friend has terrible allergies. Either of these hypotheses could be correct. With further research and reasoning, you can determine the "truth." *"All the ideas of science come to it by way of Abduction. Abduction consists in studying facts and devising a theory to explain them. Its only justification is that if we are ever to understand things at all, it must be in that way"* (Peirce, CP 5.145).

Many professionals, such as counselors and teachers, rely on the process of abductive reasoning, or making inferences, as they search for clues to help them diagnose a client's condition or predict a student's behavior. These explanations are not *empirical*; the counselor is not relying on research studies and collected data. The abductive reasoning a teacher might give for a student's behavior is the culmination of a reasoning process that could be considered the art of being a professional. Facts could lead to any one of several explanations; however, the teacher uses professional knowledge, experience, awareness, and even instinct to determine which of the explanations best describes the facts. Abductive reasoning is generating hypotheses or ideas about the way things are.

For example, Mr. Snowman, an elementary school psychologist, notices that every day the kindergarten teachers complain that at 10:00 A.M. the students are unable to pay attention to their tasks. Some students become irritable, snapping at other children and pushing to get what they want; others withdraw and put their heads on their desks; and still others either wander out of the classroom or ask to go home. He wonders what happens at 10:00 A.M. to create this situation. He gathers information about what is happening and what is not happening. There is no bell ringing, no class change to music or art, no difficult tasks for the students to do. As he looks for clues, he reasons abductively that the students are bored. How will he know that it is because they are bored and not, say, because they are hungry? It has been over two hours since they have eaten anything, and as five-year-olds burn a lot of energy, perhaps they are hungry. It is possible that hunger could explain the students' behaviors. He needs to check out his hypotheses (his abductive reasoning) of boredom or hunger. This will lead to the next type of reasoning: inductive reasoning.

Inductive Reasoning.   Inductive reasoning is the process of coming up with highly probable conclusions.

> *Induction is the experimental testing of a theory. The justification of it is that, although the conclusion at any stage of the investigation may be more or less erroneous, yet the further application of the same method must correct the error. The only thing that induction accomplishes is to determine the value of a quantity. It sets out with a theory and measures the degree of concordance of that theory with fact. It can never originate any idea whatsoever.*

> (CP 5.145)

Mr. Snowman consults with the kindergarten teachers to incorporate either more challenging tasks or a snack time in the classroom at 9:45 A.M. and observe the students' behaviors. For one week, the teachers increase the task difficulty and observe behavior worsening. The next week, the teachers return the task difficulty level to its earlier state and add a snack of milk and cookies. Students' behaviors improved. Mr. Snowman has engaged in inductive reasoning by testing his hypothesis.

Deductive Reasoning.   Deductive reasoning is the act of drawing a logical conclusion based on evidence. Mr. Snowman tells teachers that the kindergarten students need food in the mid-morning to help them pay attention in class. The process Mr. Snowman engaged in is called deductive reasoning. He took the information from his research experiment (inductive reasoning) and made a logical conclusion—he deduced that if students' behavior improved when they were given a snack, then they must have been in need of more energy and nourishment to behave in class.

> *Deduction is . . . the reasoning of mathematics. It starts from a hypothesis, the truth or falsity of which has nothing to do with the reasoning; and of course, its conclusions are equally ideal. The ordinary use of the doctrine of chances is necessary reasoning, although it is reasoning concerning probabilities.*
>
> (CP 5.145)

The kindergarten teachers are critical thinkers and are determined to take a closer look at their research experiment. Children are good mimics and some students' behaviors can influence the whole class. The teachers wonder whether the children's behavior worsened and improved, not because of the addition of challenging tasks or a snack, but simply because a few students worsened and improved. These questions may be enough for some teachers to reject the findings, while others to accept the findings simply because the research made intuitive sense to them or because they like Mr. Snowman. However, Mr. Snowman wonders about the abductive reasoning that some children may influence the classes' behavior and render his findings rather useless. We have returned to abductive reasoning because reasoning is not wholly linear. As evidence comes in, you may need to rethink the inferences, redevelop your hypotheses, and retest the hypotheses. He thinks about how to improve his research design to account for the children's influence. For example, to develop a cleaner study, he decides to ask teachers to use different levels of difficulty at specific times during the days to examine whether it is the students, the task, or the time of day. In research, all three types of reasoning will occur as a sound research design is developed (Table 1.1).

Ways of Knowing

Understanding the different ways in which people come to know the world, the nature of reality, and nature of knowledge is important as a researcher. It not only allows you to understand the language used by other researchers, but also helps you to see how they frame their questions or think about phenomenon. For you, more specifically, it allows you to be aware of your biases and personal beliefs about how

TABLE 1.1
Types of reasoning used in research design

Abductive: Coming up with a plausible explanation: An archeologist notices a flat area in a spot of rolling hills and wonders if this could be George Washington's boyhood home.

Inductive: Testing the hypothesis and coming up with a highly probable conclusion: To test this hypothesis, the archeologist and a team of students begin digging, sometimes sitting on a 20th-century pipe for six hours at a time and begin to find chards of pottery that match the time frame.

Deductive: Coming to a logical conclusion based on the evidence from testing the hypothesis.

Hypothesis: After years of digging and finding the basement of a house and several other artifacts, the archeologist makes an initial conclusion that this was George Washington's boyhood home.

you "know" the world, your personal ways of knowing. A researcher needs to be able to look at all these ways of knowing to see a phenomenon in all its dimensions.

The Basic "Isms".   In addition to ways of reasoning, there are ways of knowing; that is, how we come to understand our world. Let us cover a little history here. It is impossible to cover everything in detail; as such, we are providing a cook's tour (Schwandt, 2000). Table 1.2 provides different epistemological stances along with a defining attribute. It is woefully incomplete, but provides you with a starting point to try to learn about distinct differences in the stances and to begin conversations. We know that people's perception and interaction with culture, family, educational system, and environment have an impact on current issues, the types of questions they ask, and the choice of method(s) to answer those questions (see the interview of George Vaillant, Harvard researcher, in the June 2009 issue of *The Atlantic*). In essence, they have different assumptions about reality and knowledge. Therefore, before we can move forward, we must understand some basic philosophical underpinnings of how we know the things we do.

Modernism.   In the middle of 19th century in Western cultural history, there was considerable political and cultural unrest and change from what had been a traditional way of thought to progressive and modern ideas. This **modernism** rejected traditional thinking that focused on the metaphysical examination of existence, the divine, and universal natural sciences and embraced only those aspects upheld as objective and rational. Thinking and beliefs that could not be objectively authenticated were deemed superstitions and considered to be hampering positive progress.
Modernism embraced two particular philosophies:

- **Positivism:** The only true knowledge is that which can be positively affirmed using sound methodology—the scientific method (see Comte [1855/1974] for greater detail).
- **Rationalism:** The true path to knowledge is through intellectual and deductive reasoning; a doctrine of systematic reasoning to determine that which is true and knowable.

TABLE 1.2
Table of philosophical tradition

Philosophical Category Group/Tradition	Defining Attribute
Empiricism	Knowledge is based on direct (sensory) experience of physical objects or events. See Locke (1974).
Traditional positivism	Knowledge develops through three phases: fictitious, abstract, and then scientific. See Comte (1855/1974).
Logical positivism	Two forms of knowledge are stable, logical-mathematical and natural-scientific knowledge. See Vienna Circle group.
Postpositivism	Set of arguments against positivism; for example, scientific laws being verified because there is no logical reason to argue that a current pattern of events will follow the past pattern of events. See Popper (1959) or Kuhn (1962).
Rationalism	Knowledge, based on reasoning, is determined by the mind and not by our senses as we experience the world. See Kant (1966).
Hermeneutics	In the hermeneutic circle, one uses the interpretation of a piece of text to understand the whole text, and the understanding of the whole is used to interpret parts; this goes in a circular fashion. This part/whole process is systematically and rigorously applied. See Frederick Schleiermacher or Dilthey (1989).
Structuralism	What makes something what it is is its function not its composition. For example, a single block can be considered a car if it is treated like a car. See Ferdinand de Saussure.
Poststructuralism	Reaction to the dogmatism associated with some structuralists.
Critical theory (ideological-oriented inquiry, see Guba (1990))	Critique of the power structures through a variety of perspectives, such as feminist critical theory, economic, political. See McLaren and Giarelli (1995).
Idealism	Knowledge consists only of ideas of representation about reality. See Hegel (1991).
Interpretivism	Reality is assumed to be constructed by the knower based on the interpretation of a particular action. A wink is not always a wink and can have different interpretations. See Ryle (1971) or Geertz (1975).
Constructivism	Many constructions of reality are possible. See Guba (1990) or Schwandt (2000).

Sources: Adapted from Bredo (2006), Guba (1990), and Schwandt (2000).

In modernism, explanations are rational and the analysis of reality is objective. Anything that cannot be observed, measured, and rationally explained is either currently beyond our technological and intellectual ability or rejected as superstitious, impractical, and subverting the inevitable progress of humankind.

Postmodernism. Of course, not everyone agreed or agrees with the totality of the positivist and rationalist views; however, it continues to have an effect on the sciences, both natural and social, and education. Still, it may be that the pendulum of change, from the metaphysical to the rational, has left important elements unacknowledged and unexamined. These elements are the less tangible, less readily observable, more experiential components of human existence. This *postmodern* search for "truth" has more to do with how people make sense of their world. Unlike modernism, **postmodernism** holds that truth is relative, relies on individual meaning making, and evolves as persons do. An example of postmodernism is constructivism, where reality is socially constructed among individuals.

Peirce's Four Ways of Knowing: Pragmatism.   In addition to basic the "isms," we like to provide students and/or colleagues with a different organization of ways of knowing based on the writings of C. S. Peirce. Peirce was a pragmatist, believing that the nature of reality is based on continual reality checks and that for something to be meaningful, it had to be practical. His 1877 article, *The Fixation of Belief*, is devoted to a discussion of how beliefs become fixed or stabilized. According to Peirce, there are four ways that we come to know what we know:

Tenacity: This occurs when we hold on to a belief in the face of doubt in order to preserve a self-identity or a worldview to which we are committed. One kindergarten teacher believes that the 10:00 A.M. misbehavior is an indication of poor parenting and has nothing to do with anything over which the kindergarten teacher might have control. This teacher has always believed that parents are the source of a child's behavior, so this teacher interprets most of what she sees in the classroom as the effects of parenting.

Authority: Authority occurs when we accept the beliefs of authority figures, such as parents, experts, or members of a community with whom we identify or want to identify. The kindergarten teachers who like Mr. Snowman or who believe him are accepting the authority of Mr. Snowman. Or, a school psychologist can be seen as an expert, and teachers may accept his initial findings and provide a snack at 9:45 A.M. "Just tell me what works," the teachers might ask the school psychologist, "so I can get back to teaching my kids."

*A Priori***:** The way of knowing called *a priori* refers to reasoning that occurs before any experience. *A priori* reasoning is when our beliefs are established according to an already existing belief. Sometimes those beliefs are philosophical such as supply-side economics, scientific such as evolution, or cultural such as food preferences. For example, one kindergarten teacher may initially reject Mr. Snowman's findings and attribute the misbehavior in her classroom at 10:00 A.M. as normal for the developmental processes of five-year-olds testing authority and developing autonomy. This kindergarten teacher is using *a priori* reasoning by relying on the scientific information on child development she learned about in a professional development program at the local university. If this kindergarten teacher continues to reason further, beyond her *a priori* knowledge, she may think about how five-year-olds are developing physically and may need nutrition to help them get through the morning. The teacher is revisiting her *a priori* reasoning (her existing internal belief that child development is the reason for the children's behavior). She may integrate these new ideas into her *a priori* thinking.

Experimentation: Mr. Snowman is not convinced that he has found the "truth" about why the children are misbehaving. He continues to test his thinking. He tries to remove any doubts about his conclusion by collecting more observations, generating potential hypotheses, and then reaching a conclusion based on an inferential process. Mr. Snowman will employ several skills as he experiments: skepticism, openness to alternatives, discernment, negotiation, cooperation, and compromise to fix or stabilize beliefs.

The Research Question

Now that we have discussed some of the foundational components of research, it is time to consider the research question. The research question is not an idea or an area of interest. Many times these ideas or areas of interest are simply attitudes or beliefs about some phenomenon. A **research question** has a focus and limits, and allows you to come to some conclusion at the end of your study. In addition, not every question can be researched or is worth researching. We discuss the research question in other areas of the book, but we want to highlight the difference here, so that you are thinking about this throughout the next two chapters. Without a quality research question, you have no idea where to go next.

> *Idea* (belief): Scientific literacy is important.
> *Area of Interest Question:* What affects kids staying in the sciences?
> *Question:* Do social structures reduce students' enrollment in science courses?
> *Research Question:* Does the perception of course difficulty reduce 18-year-old college freshmen's enrollment into science majors?

Even though we have a good start to a researchable question, there are many components that need to be defined, such as perception, difficulty, and science majors (does mathematics count?).

QUALITATIVE AND QUANTITATIVE DESIGN

The two major philosophical schools, modernism and postmodernism, have led to two ways of conducting research in order to "know something": *quantitative* and *qualitative*. A third research approach, a *mixed method*, has evolved over the past 15 years. It does not matter whether the research questions of our students (or of authors sending in manuscripts for journal review!) lead them to a quantitative (numbers), qualitative (not numbers), or mixed method approach. What matters is the soundness of the questions, the methodology, design, instruments, analysis technique, and subsequent discussion and conclusions. As journal editors and editorial board members, we have to tell you: a sound study is a sound study

TABLE 1.3

General tendencies of quantitative and qualitative research

Attributes of Research	Quantitative Research	Qualitative Research
View of reality	Objective social reality exists.	Reality is socially constructed.
Causality	Causality is a mechanical description among variables.	Human intention is involved in explaining causal relationships.
Engagement with participants	As little as possible.	At times, personally involved.
Explanation of the research	The least complicated explanation is the best.	Explanations do not necessarily need to be the least complicated.
Type of primary analysis of the research	Statistical	Abduction/induction
Hypothesizing	Yes	Yes

regardless of the type of data, numbers or not, collected. If the data are used to scientifically test theories, "they fall within the domain of science" because "science involves arguing from methodologically sound data, but science is agnostic on the issue of whether the data need to be quantitative or qualitative" (Mayer, 2000, p. 39). There are gross differences and serious arguments about worldview and procedures that separate qualitative and quantitative research methodologists. We are not focusing on those differences or those arguments—it is not the purpose of this book. A small list of general tendencies or defining attributes between them is displayed in Table 1.3. It also may be better to think about your research along a continuum from quantitative to qualitative. In many of the surveys we have used, the statements are responded to in verbal form and we recode them to numeric form. As you read and synthesize research, you will be abducting, inducting, and deducting, spanning both qualitative and quantitative components.

You may also think about research in a continuum from exploratory to confirmatory. **Exploratory research** is conducted when the researchers have some scenarios about the phenomenon, but need more data. **Confirmatory research** is conducted to provide more support for previous results. The research question you develop will have a more exploratory or confirmatory focus. In the end, we hope you personally explore the differences with others in your research group.

Qualitative Research

Qualitative researchers tend to study things in their natural setting, attempting to make sense of or interpret phenomena in terms of the meaning people bring to them. Denzin and Lincoln (1994) describe **qualitative research** as "multimethod in its focus, involving an interpretive, naturalistic approach to its subject matter"

(p. 2). One can also describe qualitative research as the examination of lived experience, development of alternative criteria for goodness, and tendency toward activist research. A qualitative study may investigate a specific line worker's job satisfaction at Anheuser Busch as it transitions to being owned by InBev.

Interactive and noninteractive methods are two categories within qualitative research methodologies. The main attribute of **interactive inquiry** is the engagement, face to face, with the participants of interest. In **noninteractive inquiry**, there is typically no engagement with participants, but interaction sometime does occur in historical analysis.

Interactive Research.   Researchers use a variety of approaches to interactive research. Here, we discuss ethnography, phenomenology, case study, grounded theory, and critical studies.

Ethnography.   Originally developed in the field of anthropology, **ethnography** is the art and science of describing a group or a culture—such as a kindergarten class, a small business, or returning war veterans. The aim of ethnography is to understand the culture from an ''insider's'' perspective and capture day-to-day life. Bowling (1997) describes ethnography as studying people in the locations where they live and providing a description of their social life and the values, beliefs and behaviors using qualitative methodologies such as observations, unstructured interviews, and review and analysis of documents. This methodology is time intensive in the field. An example of an ethnographic study is an educational researcher who attends kindergarten classes for several months, observing and interacting with the children, the teacher, the teacher's aides, the parent volunteers, the principal, the school secretary, the cafeteria workers, the bus drivers, and the nurse. She might formally and informally interview key contacts, adding to her observations; all helping her to determine what the day-to-day life of a kindergarten student is like.

Phenomenology.   Phenomenology began as a philosophical movement focused on the essence of phenomena as developed within a person's consciousness (see the writings of Edmund Husserl, 1859–1938). A phenomenon is any discreet experience that can be articulated, such as joy, death of a parent, childbirth, parenting a child with autism, friendship. As a research methodology, **phenomenology** is used to study the evolving patterns of meaning making that people develop as they experience a phenomenon over time. This type of research requires the ability to engage a few people in a prolonged and careful description of their experiences, to grasp the essence or meaning they weave. A goal is a deeper understanding of the phenomenon for the individual as opposed to ethnographic research, which focuses on describing a culture or group. Phenomenological work is particularly useful for those in the helping professions (for example, teachers, nurses, doctors, or counselors), so that they can better understand the meanings people may attribute to their experience. The research process tends to be more unstructured in nature as compared with ethnography or case studies. An example could be, What is it like to be a parent with two sons with a rare genetic disability and a daughter without the genetic disability?

Case Study.   The case study is a systematic collection of information about a person, group, or community; social setting; or event in order to gain insight into its functioning. A case is bounded in time and place. Out of all of the qualitative methodologies, this one is the more common and is perceived to be the easiest, but a good case study is not easy to produce. Case studies are common in social sciences such as education, rehabilitation counseling, nursing, and psychology. For example, as a researcher, you may decide to investigate the effectiveness of dual-language programs, where students in a classroom are taught in both English and Spanish. You may collect data through observation, discussion, task completions, standardized tests, and self-report from the classroom participants. A subsequent report would be a case study of one third-grade classroom's experiences in dual-language instruction. Within case studies, there are comparative cases, where cases that are similar in several key elements but different in at least one way are examined. An example is Janel Curry's work on faith-based communities in six farm communities (Curry, 2000). Collective cases are an examination of several bounded cases that are similar in numerous specifically identified ways. Another good example is Peter Miller's work on leadership within homeless centers in western Pennsylvania (Miller, 2009).

Grounded Theory.   A grounded theory study usually captures a process; it answers the question, "What is going on here?" Grounded theory is a systematic and rigorous approach to collecting and analyzing qualitative data for developing an explanation that enhances our understanding of social or psychological phenomena. Grounded theory studies lead to generating a theory, such as identifying the three stages involved in developing a career identity. After the theory is presented, it must then be tested (Glaser & Strauss, 1967).

Critical Studies.   This methodology draws from theoretical views that knowledge is subjective. That is to say, we only know what we know because of our culture, our environment, and our overall experiences. As such, we need to view the data through a prescribed rubric such as critical theory, feminist theory, and race theory. Critical studies employ a wide variety of methodologies, including quantitative and noninteractive qualitative. Essential in critical studies is a fundamental and evolving understanding of the rubric used. For example, "Does Mr. Snowman analyze his observations in the light of the inherent power differentials between and among ethnicities and gender in the U.S. culture?" Critical studies also have the fundamental goal of societal critique, transformation, and emancipation and can interact with other methods such as critical ethnography.

Noninteractive Research.   Researchers also use different approaches to noninteractive research, such as content analysis and historical analysis.

Content Analysis.   Content analysis is a detailed examination of content from a particular body of material. The purpose is to identify patterns or themes in the material. A majority of content analysis occurs with print or film media. A nice example is *The Suspense Thriller: Films in the Shadow of Alfred Hitchcock* by Charles Derry. Derry (2001) uses content analysis to create a working definition of the suspense thriller and examines over 100 films.

Historical Analysis.   Historical analysis provides an in-depth examination of primary documents (see Chapter 2) in order to understand the meaning of events. This method tries to make sense of the ever-growing amount of information as time marches on and as human beings grapple with their understanding of what once was and what now is. For example, prior to the 9/11 attacks on the World Trade Center, our students were amused by stories of World War I name changes for popular foods—frankfurters became hotdogs (Americans wanted to dissociate from Frankfurt, Germany, an enemy in World War I) and hamburgers became liberty burgers. Students also were horrified at the internment of Japanese Americans during World War II. Our students couldn't understand why Americans would be fearful of Japanese people. However, after the tragedy of 9/11 and the attack on the Twin Towers in New York City, our students had more than a theoretical understanding of fearful people who might call French fries "Liberty fries" to distance themselves from the French, who were not supportive of American response to the 9/11 attacks.

Quantitative Research

Interestingly, part of what is commonly termed *quantitative research design* developed from agricultural research. The quantitative research field holds a positivist view of the world. **Quantitative research** focuses on objectivity—there is truth out there—and quantifying the phenomenon under investigation, assigning numbers to ideas or constructs of interest. There are two categories of quantitative methodology: experimental and nonexperimental/descriptive. The field emphasizes outcomes, experimental verification, null hypothesis testing, and generalizing findings from the sample of participants to a population of people. Below we introduce experimental designs underneath the quantitative heading. This does not stop you from designing an experiment and collecting verbal or visual data, which is more commonly associated with qualitative processes.

Experimental Research Design.   Experimental studies include several common components: true experimental, quasi-experimental, single subject, and preexperimental. This widely recognized nomenclature in educational and behavioral research is based on Campbell and Stanley's (1963) true experimental, quasi-experimental, and preexperimental research designs. For single-subject designs, see Kratochwill and Levin (1992). Each of these types of experimental research designs will be examined in this section.

Experimental research manipulates an independent variable that determines what the participants in the study will experience, such as a commercial that has two different versions to it, A and B. This is referred to as an experimental manipulation and participants are grouped into an experimental or nonexperimental/control group.

True Experimental. True experimental designs involve the random assignment of each participant to a group in the study. The primary purpose of random assignment is the limiting of any preexisting differences among the groups. A researcher might randomly assign consumers to different versions of a product or situation and examine the differences in purchasing or likeability in each of the versions. Imagine if Mr. Snowman had randomly assigned kindergarten children throughout the United States to three classrooms where the following occurred at 9:45 A.M.: in one classroom children receive a snack, in the second classroom the tasks increase in difficulty, and in the third classroom nothing is changed. Mr. Snowman would be on the road to designing a true experimental design.

Quasi-Experimental. Quasi-experimental designs do not have random assignment. Quasi-experimental studies occur in the field, or *in situ*. We do not have the opportunity for random assignment of students to a teacher or class. The common term for this type of group of participants is *intact*. Students in two intact classes are given a pretest in math, for example, on some basic algebra problems. Then two different instructional methods are used and a posttest is given. The pretests statistically control for preexisting knowledge differences in order to examine posttest scores and decide whether one instructional method have higher scores as compared with the other.

Single Subject. Sometimes it is impossible to study a large group or groups of participants or the population of participants is not large enough for a true experimental or quasi-experimental design. When this is the case, experimenters use a single-subject design. For example, there would be a limited number of participants available for a study on adolescents who are convicted of arson. This group is not large enough to have traditional experimental and control groups. Like true and quasi-experiments, the researcher can manipulate the intervention variables.

Preexperimental. Preexperimental designs do not have the key defining attributes of experimental studies, random assignment and a direct manipulation of one independent variable. Due to this, preexperimental designs can be termed in the literature as descriptive, exploratory, correlational, or pilot.

Nonexperimental Research Design. Nonexperimental research design includes several types of research: descriptive, comparative, correlational, survey, *ex post facto*, and secondary data analysis. Each of these types of nonexperimental research methods will be examined in this section.

Descriptive.   Descriptive studies simply describe some phenomenon using numbers to create a picture of a group or individual. There is no manipulation of a variable. For example, Mr. Snowman's kindergarten analysis might have stopped at gathering information on the number of kindergarteners, their age, gender, ethnicity, household socioeconomic status, days of attendance, culture of origin, and language use at home to describe what a typical kindergartener in his school looks like. This technique is useful for understudied or underserved groups and groups that are difficult to access, perhaps for fear of reprisal (undocumented aliens, transgender youth, and religious minorities) or historical hostility in interactions with the dominant group (Vontress & Epp, 1997).

Comparative.   Comparative studies examine differences between two or more groups. There is no manipulation of a variable. Comparative research design is an extension of the descriptive studies. The separation of descriptive information across the groups allows for comparison of those numeric values; that is, data that are in number form and not verbal, audio, or video. Mr. Snowman's colleague, Mrs. Hollingsworth, is a school psychologist in a dual-language school where the kindergarteners and the teachers speak Spanish for 90% of the school day. Mrs. Hollingsworth's kindergarteners, as a whole, might be descriptively different in terms of age, gender, ethnicity, household socioeconomic status, days of attendance, culture of origin, and home language use. By collecting the data, Mr. Snowman and Mrs. Hollingsworth can descriptively discuss similarities and differences between their schools and help to broaden our understanding of what constitutes a "typical kindergarten child."

Correlational.   The purpose of correlational research is to assess the magnitude (absolute size between zero and one) and direction of a relationship (positive or negative) between two or more variables. The examination of the magnitude of the relationship occurs with a statistical test. In a correlational study, you might see Mr. Snowman and Mrs. Hollingsworth looking at the relationship between the number of days in attendance and socioeconomic status. Perhaps they find that as the number of days in attendance for the kindergarten children increases, their household socioeconomic status (SES) decreases. That is all they can say about the relationship—that there is a negative (one increases while the other decreases) relationship between attendance and SES.

Survey.   Questionnaires and interviews are the instruments of choice for this method. Though flexible for a wide variety of purposes, a survey is used to describe attitudes, buying habits, voting preferences, and other types of phenomenon or behavior. Traditionally, contact with a large number of participants is necessary for survey research to draw conclusions about the population of interest. During election years, we are often bombarded with poll results, and these results are simply survey research.

Ex Post Facto.   From Latin, *ex post facto* means "that which is done afterward." This methodology allows the researcher to analyze data that is naturally occurring in order to explain what has happened in the past. The comparison of students' state test scores between teacher certification types (major certification in content domain vs. minor certification) is an example. Manipulation of the variables of interest (certification) and random assignment do not occur in this methodology.

Secondary Data Analysis. When a researcher analyzes or reanalyzes previously collected data, we call that a secondary data analysis. Typically, the researcher did not collect the data set. Over the past 30 years, many data sets have become available and have spawned numerous research articles. We included secondary data analysis in the quantitative section because most of the data sets are quantitative, but secondary data analysis is not exclusive to quantitative data.

Mixed Method

Mixed method research is a composite of basic data types and methodological procedures. In a mixed method research study, the researcher collects data based on research questions that will contain numbers and non-numbers along with related methodologies categorized within a qualitative or quantitative framework. For a mixed method study to be acceptable, it must be of high quality for both methodologies as well as the integration of the two methods. Finally, Table 1.4 provides a general research question by design.

Scientific Method

We are hesitant to present the scientific method as it is often presented—as a step-by-step program, such as the four or seven steps of the scientific method. The scientific method is not a recipe, even though many people treat it as such. We take a large view of science as described by the German word *wissenschaft*, which refers to a systematic, rational form of inquiry with rigorous and intersubjectively agreed-on procedures for validation (Schwandt, 1997). Therefore, the **scientific method**, though abundant and popular, is an agreed-on procedure for understanding a phenomenon, not a step-by-step process. For that reason, instead of steps, we present the most defining attributes of the scientific method:

Observation: Observing is a core feature of the scientific method. We observe the phenomenon we are interested in and collect data (information) about it.

Explanation: We use the observational data to create explanations of the phenomenon.

Prediction: We use those explanations to predict the past, present, and future of given phenomena.

Control: Actively and fairly sampling the range of *possible* occurrences, whenever possible and proper, as opposed to the passive acceptance of opportunistic data, is the best way to control or counterbalance the risk of empirical bias.

TABLE 1.4
Design by general research question

Design	General Question Answered
Case study	What are the characteristics of this particular entity, phenomenon, or person?
Ethnography	What are the cultural patterns and perspectives of this group in its natural setting?
Grounded theory	How is an inductively derived theory about a phenomenon grounded in the data in a particular setting?
Phenomenology	What is the experience of an activity or concept from these particular participants' perspective?
Historic	How does one systematically collect and evaluate data to understand and interpret past events?
Content analysis	Is there a theme or set of themes across all of this material?
True	Does the randomly assigned experimental group perform better than the control group?
Quasi	Does the experimental group perform better than the control group?
Single subject	Was there a change in behavior after the intervention?
Descriptive	What do the scores from scale X for the group of people look like?
Comparative	Does group X appear to be different from group Y?
Correlational	Is there a relationship between A and B?
Survey	Does group Z like this idea?
Ex post facto	Does an existing difference between group X and Y explain Z?

Falsifiability: The testing of other explanations in order to falsify the explanation in which you are interested. Interestingly, one of the largest arguments in science is whether string theory, the explanation of how the universe works, is a science because it is currently not testable (subject to falsifiability) (Woit, 2006). As a body of knowledge grows and a particular hypothesis or theory repeatedly brings predictable results, confidence in the hypothesis or theory increases.

Causal explanation: Though some have argued that causality is not "the" goal of science, many researchers in the sciences are trying to make causal explanations.

Replication: The need to replicate observations as a way to support and refine hypotheses is necessary. It is also crucial to falsifiability.

Generalize: In many instances, researchers want to see if their observations in social science research extend beyond the sample of participants or context of that study.

Professional critique: A scientific research study is not a contribution until dissemination and critique by peers occurs. The critiquing process is crucial to the health and vitality of science.

In general, all researchers observe, collect data, examine that data, make hypotheses, test them, and try to draw conclusions. Remember Mr. Snowman wondering about the behaviors in the kindergarten class. He explores and describes that experience. Second, one forms a hypothesis to explain the observations and descriptions of the phenomenon. This sounds remarkably familiar to Mr. Snowman's abductive reasoning process. Third, we use the scenario (hypothesis) to generate predicted behaviors and/or observations (deductive reasoning). Finally, we carefully test the predicted behaviors, trying hard to account for any variations that could cast doubt on our conclusions (remember the kindergarteners) with a solid research design; analyze the results; and offer inferences to our profession. If the testing supports the scenario, then we might argue that our abductive musings were right on target and we truly understand human nature. Should the testing fail to support the scenario, then adjustments are made. In fact, the "failure" to support is rich with information! To paraphrase a quote attributed to Thomas A. Edison (1847–1931) after having tried about 10,000 different filaments to produce an efficient light bulb: You have not failed. You've just found a way that won't work.

Evidence-based research, a currently popular phrase seen in conjunction with the words *scientific research*, is research that focuses primarily on experimental designs that answer outcome questions such as: "Does using dialectic behavioral therapy with emotionally abused adolescents work?" These are predominantly quantitative research methodologies that offer numerical, statistical analyses to verify whether the treatment (in this case) works in comparison to doing nothing and/or using a different treatment. Evidence-based research and evidence-based practice have become important to researchers and practitioners, as the U.S. federal government has enacted legislation such as No Child Left Behind that encourages the use of quantitative methods (Flinders, 2003). Just a reminder: All research is considered science if it. "involves arguing from methodologically sound data, but science is agnostic on the issue of whether the data need to be quantitative or qualitative" (Mayer, 2000, p. 39).

TYPES OF RESEARCH

Research has a few types: basic, applied, and evaluative. Although we discuss the forms as discrete, the reality is that most research is an amalgamation of two or more forms. The types of research differ in their ability to inform different decisions, but each of these types of research collects data.

Basic research is generally exploratory and conducted to add to the theoretical knowledge base and offer a foundation for applied research. Its purpose is to test theories. Basic research will not lead to information for specific policy decisions or social problem solution. Basic research offers practical implications; but application is not part of the design decision. An example of a basic research question might be: "In adults who have anxiety disorder, are there different paths of anxiety development over time?"

Applied research, by contrast, primarily solves practical questions. Fields such as engineering, medicine, education, counseling, and social work are applied fields where the research produced solves a problem. Although it can be exploratory, it is more often descriptive and, unlike basic research, is not used to add to our knowledge simply for its own sake. Applied research is often a derivation of fundamentals established through basic research. In educational psychology, theories of learning are developed from basic research and then tested within schools to determine their efficacy over time or in novel settings, for example, studies examining the use of formative assessment rubrics to help develop self-regulation skills and cognitive activities to increase graduation rates. A strength of applied research is the possibility of an immediate effect from the results. A research question for an applied study might be: "Do partial notes increase retention of material for college students?"

Action research is a form of applied research common in education where practitioners are involved in efforts to improve their work. Qualitative methods are typical, but they are not the only ones that can be used; many action research projects our students have conducted use both qualitative and quantitative components.

Conceptually, **evaluative research** can be thought of as *process evaluation* or *outcome evaluation*. **Process evaluation** research focuses on "how" questions, such as "How do a science teacher and his high school students form an effective and productive working classroom?" In contrast, **outcome evaluation** research measures results, sometimes of the process: "How many high school students involved in a type of science pedagogy scored above the national norms in science?" At the end of an evaluation, a judgment may be made about the merit of a program or project. Did it do what you said it would do? Evaluations also examine whether the cost of the program is worth the observed effect. Evaluations commonly have multiple evaluation components, such as personnel, materials, and locations and use a variety of data collection techniques (e.g., interviews, surveys, historical documents) and types of data (numeric, verbal, pictorial).

General Pattern of Research Study Development

Sound research and research question development begin with a thorough review of the professional literature. This leads the reader on a similar path the researcher walked and then toward the development of a new question (Figure 1.1). This is not *primary research*; it is a review of previous thinking and writing on a particular topic, and something we will cover in detail in Chapter 2. A well-written literature review brings the reader into the researcher's frame of reference, grounds the reader with an overview of the theoretical arguments, critically analyzes and interprets the published information available in support of or contesting said arguments, discusses the implications of the finding, and peaks the reader's interest in what is left unsaid—a hole, if you will, in the literature. This hole represents a developing burning question. That question becomes the research question.

FIGURE 1.1
Graphic display of the process of research study development

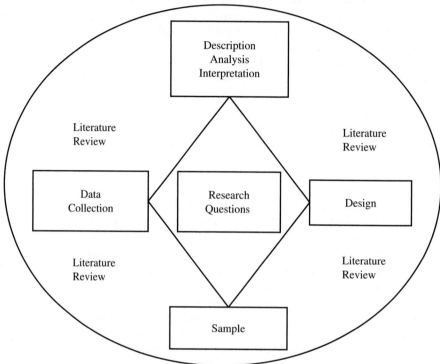

Briefly, a literature review starts with what we like to call "armchair work." This is work best done in an armchair where one can devour and digest large quantities of professional literature. First, the researcher determines what field she is interested in examining. Let us consider a professional mental health counselor who is interested in studying depression (the *problem area*), a topic usually covered by the social, behavioral, and medical fields. She reads about depression, as various experts in these fields understand it. She then moves into her second phase—that of conducting a literature search, tracking down appropriate materials to enhance her understanding of depression. She will find a plethora of sources including but not limited to scholarly books and journal articles, conference proceedings, dissertations, newspaper articles, Internet sites, and government pamphlets. As a rule, in social sciences, a literature review should survey only professionally sound sources—usually this excludes the popular press and many Internet sites. Therefore, our counselor will focus on her profession's books, scholarly articles, conference proceedings, and dissertations.

The third step of the literature review is to determine the quality and usefulness of the materials gathered. Each book, article, proceeding, and dissertation will need to be examined to determine whether it is relevant to the topic and whether it actually contributes to the counselor's (and the subsequent reader's) understanding of that topic. Usually, the literature review will need to provide sources in support of and against a way of conceptualizing the topic and will also cover alternative conceptualizations as well. This process will be covered in detail in Chapter 2. Finally, the counselor will analyze and interpret the authors' findings, interpretations, and discussions. At this point, a researcher has not only sufficient information on a topic, but also an acute recognition of how little she knows. It is not unusual to voice excitement and sometimes frustration: "Oh my goodness, I'll bet this is what is going on!" and "Why hasn't anyone looked at this issue from this point of view?" or "I can't believe all this work has never considered the impact of culture!" This excitement can be a powerful tool when redirected into a passion for discovery. "Someone should study this!" is delightfully followed by the development of a research question.

The research question, as mentioned before, leads directly into the research design. Tashakkori and Teddlie (1998) offer researchers a set of questions for thinking about which research design to use and under what conditions.

- First, is the purpose of the research confirmatory or exploratory?
- Second, what type of data is likely to be available—qualitative or quantitative?
- Third, what sort of analysis and inference are expected—narrative or statistical?

The responses to these questions combine to create categories. For example, if you responded confirmatory, quantitative, and statistical, you are conducting a purely quantitative study, such as a confirmatory factor analysis (Chapter 7). If you chose exploratory, qualitative, and non-numeric analysis, you are conducting a purely qualitative study, such as ethnography.

The research design and data collected drive the type of analyses completed. No analysis used is flawless—as researchers and as editors, we have had to respond to reviewer complaints. Different analyses have their pros and cons. Qualitative data is filtered through the subjective lens of the researcher's own worldview. Quantitative data is rife with mathematical assumptions based on the laws of probability. As a result, each research manuscript ought to discuss these assumptions clearly, and each professional consumer of the literature needs to be aware of and examine logical flaws in the researchers' reasoning, design, and analysis.

In Figure 1.1, we have drawn multiple connections between components for research development design. We chose to draw them in this fashion because the development and design of a study is not a one-way, lockstep path. Information is gathered and preliminary decisions occur. Then as more information is gathered, some decisions hold and others are changed. It is an organic process. One of us used to bring in a crate of different versions of the first three chapters of our dissertation to demonstrate physically how major and minor issues changed what was to become the actual set of studies finally conducted. We also spend a great deal of time developing a study and then asking a colleague to listen and give input to make sure we have not missed something they know, have experienced personally, or have read about.

Theory

A clear definition of theory is important. Novice scientists need to understand how scientists define and use the word *theory*. A **theory** predicts and explains a natural phenomenon. However, it is actually more encompassing. As Kerlinger (1979) states, a theory is "a set of interrelated constructions (variables), definitions, and propositions that presents a systematic view of phenomena by specifying relations among variables, with the purpose of explaining natural phenomena" (p. 64). According to the National Academy of Sciences (1999), a scientific theory is a "well-substantiated explanation of some aspect of the natural world that can incorporate facts, laws, inferences, and tested hypotheses" (p. 2).

A theory is not merely a hypothesis that has been tested many times. Thinking of a theory in this way makes it seem inferior or not factual because it is not a "law." The reality is that a theory can never become a law, because laws are descriptive generalizations about nature (e.g., law of gravity) and theories are explanations (Alters & Alters, 2001). The scientist is therefore interested in confirming, expanding, or rejecting a theory. Those interests lead the scientist to design research studies specifically for that purpose. The emphasis may require more deductive reasoning.

For the public, a theory can be a belief, an ideal, or even an unsupported assumption or opinion with little or no merit. The practitioner, such as a teacher or a mental health counselor, often defines theory in a way that falls somewhere between the public definition and the scientist's definition of theory. Theory to the practitioner is no more than an informational tool for predicting human behavior. A theory is a roadmap that offers considerable flexibility in suggesting possibilities that offer results in any given situation, say in teaching, nursing, or counseling. In many ways, a practitioner is likely to use the word *theory* to imply a stronger focus on process, abductive, and inductive reasoning.

Causality

In addition to research and theory, **causality** is another word that is confused in the literature. To the public, causality comes under the rubric of common sense and experience. If driving to work during morning rush hour takes 90 minutes, it simply makes common sense to assume that driving home in the evening rush hour takes 90 minutes. In this case, the average driver assumes that rush hour causes the 90-minute commute and not that the 90-minute commute causes rush hour. In some disciplines, causality can be rather clear. Biologically, if a person's heart ceases to beat oxygenated blood through his body, barring any intervention, the person dies. This straightforward relationship is observable. Heart beats, person lives.

Heart stops beating, person dies. The person's death occurs because his heart stopped working. In other disciplines, such as education and counseling, cause and effect is not as obvious. It is common to make causal assumptions, but it is imperative to examine those assumptions.

For researchers, a causal statement has two basic components: a cause and an effect (Kenny, 2000). Three commonly accepted conditions must hold for a scientist to claim that A causes B:

- *Time precedence*: For A to cause B, A must precede B.
- *Relationship*: There is a functional relationship between A and B.
- *Nonspuriousness*: A third variable (C), or more variables (D, E, F, and so on), do not explain the relationship of A to B.

Let us look at an example. Exposure to the sun occurs before skin cancer appears. If skin cancer were to appear without exposure to the sun, then the time precedence would fail. The functional relationship between sun exposure and skin cancer is really a truncated statement (Kenny, 2000) of, all things being equal, sun exposure increases the probability of skin cancer. Finally, there is not some third variable C that, when examined in relation to both sun exposure and skin cancer, explains the skin cancer and removes the relationship between sun exposure and skin cancer, such as the amount of pigment in the skin exposed to the sun's rays.

We have many causal assumptions that we use to negotiate our daily lives, such as a door will open when we turn the knob and push or pull on the door. But when engaged in research, we need to pull out those assumptions and examine them. Just as "the unexamined life is not worth living" (attributed to Socrates in 399 BCE by Plato), the unexamined assumption can pervert the research process.

Communicating Effectively

Telling a good research story is the same as telling any compelling story with its exposition, rising action, climax, falling action, and resolution (Freytag, 1894). A good story orients the reader to the setting, the situation, and the main population involved. Once the reader is oriented, the writer introduces some sort of complication that introduces a conflict. That conflict is explored in terms of the setting, situation, and population. The climax occurs when the results of the exploration are beheld, followed by a resolution of the conflict and a commitment to future action.

Beginning researchers are often so passionate about their subject that they jump immediately to the resolution and cannot recognize why or how others do not share their interest. Yet think about the teacher in your past who taught a subject you thought was dull. However, the teacher taught the class in such a dynamic way that you became fascinated. This capacity to engage your readers fully requires that you consider your research as a story—a journey upon which you invite the readers to embark.

Communicating effectively is also critical to getting your research work published. At a recent conference, several journal editors had a chance to discuss publishing in the journals they edit. Two of us made specific statements about writing quality being absolutely critical. The rejection rates at most major journals are quite high—75% and above. As Thompson (1995) stated, ''I am convinced that poor writing will doom even the most significant manuscript..., yet even a trivial report has a reasonable chance of being published somewhere if it is well written.'' Spend the extra time and effort to write clearly and concisely. Then have a true friend read it and give you honest feedback. We both read grammar books, the American Psychological Association publication manual, and instructions to authors before embarking on a writing project just to refresh our skills. We also have friends critique (really rip apart) what we have written.

CASE STUDY TO FOLLOW THROUGH THE TEXT

At the end of each chapter, there will be a case study with a researcher who will be used to highlight information and will be followed throughout the text. This researcher is a composite of all of the people with whom we have worked. This narrative will be used to highlight common issues in research design and display unique challenges we have observed. Read the case study below and think about the research methods and design.

A doctoral candidate in a cognitive science program, Ginette is interested in how people read and interpret graphs in newspapers and magazines. Her interest was peaked by a graphic display in her local newspaper that was overloaded with images and difficult to interpret. She cut out the images and began to ask friends what they would say after looking at the graph.

She is wondering about the following:

1. Do the types of colors used affect interpretation?
2. Would grey scale lead to a different answer?
3. Does the size of the graph affect interpretation?
4. If the scale of the graph is changed, how much does it affect perception?
5. Are graphs similar across papers?
6. Are the graphs even created properly?
7. How do people use (transfer) this information in the graph to educate friends or colleagues?
8. Do they ever use the information in the graph to make a point later?
9. Would the graph interpretation be more accurate with 30 words of text next to it?
10. How much information can be placed in the graph before understanding suffers?
11. Why do people remember graphs at all?

IN-TEXT ACTIVITY

Do you have a general area of interest? If so, start writing questions such as the ones above so you can start thinking about what you may want to research.

[handwritten notes:]

school psychs

Do teachers/admin/ have a preference for/against social skill groups?

Do social skill interventions improve academics?

What're the short + long term effects of teaching social skills?

What children are most likely referred for social skill interventions?

How do s.s. interventions change as students develop?

How can s.s. be more favorable for school professionals?

what're the neg/pos stigmas?

INTRODUCTION TO ARMCHAIR MOMENTS

In these armchair moments, we discuss our experiences conducting research and working with other researchers and students. We discuss specific topics that need a different frame to view them, or we tell a story to highlight some component that sometimes gets lost in the linearity of a textbook. In this first armchair moment, we think about research and what research is like.

At first, a bike rider is lucky if she can stay upright. Slowly, though, the bike rider becomes capable of pedaling, braking, turning, coasting, and changing gears. What is also happening is that as the bike rider's basic skills improve, she spends more of her time assessing the environment around her. She becomes aware of the terrain, traffic, and weather and their impact on her capacity to navigate safely on the bike. She finds that she is scanning constantly and adjusting to the continuous feed of information as she rides the bike. And she *never* stops scanning and assessing while on the bike.

Counselors also learn to continually scan and assess the myriad ecological elements (including but not limited to ethnicity, culture, national origin, gender, age, spirituality, family, socioeconomic status, physical and mental health, legal status, developmental history, regional considerations and economics, and exposure to potentially traumatizing events) present in the environment that may have an impact (positively or negatively) on the client's life, representing either strengths and resources or stressors and the counseling relationship.

Finally, it's pretty important that the counselors account for their own assumptions that exist at all levels of interactions with clients. These assumptions include the counselor's worldview (theoretical orientation, culture, ethnicity, gender, SES, and life experience), the flaws inherent in the instruments used and the research designs, and analyses. Without these assumptions, the mental health professional could not function; however, should these assumptions be unexamined then the biased results they may produce could adversely affect the client.

Sounds inclusive and comprehensive, doesn't it? And all for the benefit of the client who is likely to be under considerable stress and needs another pair of eyes to aid in addressing the stressors and integrating life's experiences productively into his or her daily existence. The good counselor cares deeply about the client's welfare and, as such, considers studying, practicing, and evaluating her counseling, assessment, and appraisal skills; grasp of counseling theory and techniques; and ecological perspective. Becoming a good counselor, just like becoming a good bike rider, does not occur overnight but is a process that happens over time. For counselors and other professionals, the lifelong developmental process affects the manner in which they think, feel, and act.

Now, here's the point: Good research is remarkably similar to biking and counseling, requiring a solid grasp of the fundamentals, consistent curiosity, practice, and evaluation. And being a critical and continual consumer and producer of good research is an essential element of the process of becoming a good counselor (and staying one, too!).

Remember, research is not static—it flows. No two research studies are exactly the same, just as no two interpersonal interactions or people are the same. But we know there can be a general process to counseling, and there is a general process to research, too. We've spent considerable time and energy discussing some terminology and philosophical underpinnings of research. When you look at journal articles that are presenting research findings that you may be interested in learning more about, you will notice that there is a pattern that emerges. This pattern reflects a traditional cadence of research that tends to unfold regardless of the type of research design used.

Take a few moments to think about a phenomenon in which you are interested. At this point in our diagram you are at initial thoughts of a research area, which will lead to the other areas of sampling, analysis, and so forth.

Now, ask colleagues, peers, or your professor what type of designs they predominantly use and why and where they feel they fit from an epistemological stance.

KEY WORDS

a priori	basic research	confirmatory research
abductive reasoning	case study	content analysis
action research	causal explanation	control
applied research	causality	correlational research
authority	comparative studies	critical studies

deductive reasoning

descriptive studies

ethnography

evaluative research

experimentation

explanation

exploratory research

ex post facto

falsifiability

generalize

grounded theory

historical analysis

inductive reasoning

interactive inquiry

mixed method research

modernism

noninteractive inquiry

observation

outcome evaluation

phenomenology

positivism

postmodernism

prediction

preexperimental designs

process evaluation

professional critique

qualitative research

quantitative research

quasi-experimental
 designs

rationalism

replication

research

research question

scientific method

secondary data analysis

single-subject designs

survey

tenacity

theory

true experimental
 designs

wissenschaft

REFERENCES AND FURTHER READINGS

Alters, B. J., & Alters, S. (2001). *Defending evolution in the classroom: A guide to the creation/evolution controversy.* Sudbury, MA: Jones and Bartlett Publishers.

Bowling, A. (1997). *Research methods in health.* Buckingham, UK: Open University Press.

Bredo, E. (2006). Philosophies in educational research. In J. L. Green, G. Camilli, & P. B. Elmore (Eds.), *Handbook of complementary methods in education research.* Mahwah, NJ: Lawrence Erlbaum Associates.

Campbell, D. T., & Stanley, J. C. (1963). *Experimental and quasi-experimental designs for research.* Chicago: Rand McNally.

Comte, A. (1974). *The positive philosophy of Auguste Comte freely translated and condensed by Harriet Martineau.* New York: AMS Press. (Original work published 1855.)

Corbin, J. M., & Strauss, A. L. (1998). *Basics of qualitative research: Techniques and procedures for developing grounded theory.* Thousand Oaks, CA: SAGE Publications.

Curry, Janel M. (2000). "Community worldview and rural systems: A study of five communities in Iowa." *Annals of the Association of American Geographers, 90*(4), 693–712.

Denzin, N. K., & Lincoln, Y. S. (1994). *The SAGE handbook of qualitative research.* Thousand Oaks, CA: SAGE Publications.

Denzin, N. K., & Lincoln, Y. S. (2005). *The SAGE handbook of qualitative research* (3rd ed.). Thousand Oaks, CA: SAGE Publications.

Derry, (2001). *The suspense thriller: Films in the shadow of Alfred Hitchcock.* Jefferson: North Carolina, McFarland & Co.

Dilthey, W. (1989). *Introduction to the human sciences.* Princeton, NJ: Princeton University Press.

Erikson, E. H. (1950). *Childhood and society.* New York: Norton.

Flinders, D. (2003). Qualitative research in the foreseeable future: No study left behind? *Journal of Curriculum and Supervision, 18*(4), 380–390.

Freytag, G. (1894). *Freytag's technique of the drama: An exposition of dramatic composition and art*. An authorized translation from the sixth German edition by Elias MacEwan. *Die Technik des Dramas (Technique of the Drama)*. Chicago: Scott, Foresman, and Company.

Geertz, C. (1975). *The interpretation of cultures*. New York: Basic Books.

Glaser, B. G., & Strauss, A. L. (1967). *The discovery of grounded theory: Strategies for qualitative research*. Chicago: Aldine.

Guba, E. G. (1990). The alternative paradigm dialog. In E. G. Guba (Ed.), *The paradigm dialog*. Newbury Park, CA: SAGE Publications.

Health Insurance Portability and Accountability Act of 1996, 45 CFR § 164.501.

Hegel, G. W. F. (1991). *The encyclopedia logic: Part I of the encyclopedia of philosophical sciences with Zusaetze* (T. F. Garaets, W. A. Suchting, & H. S. Harris, Trans.). Indianapolis: Hackett. (Original work published 1830.)

Kant, I. (1966). *Critique of pure reason*. Garden City, NY: Doubleday. (Original work published 1781)

Kenny, D. A. (2000). *Correlation causation: Revised*. Retrieved from http://davidakenny.net/doc/cc_v1.pdf

Kerlinger, F. N. (1979). *Behavioral research*. New York: Holt, Rinehart and Winston.

Kratochwill, T. R., & Levin, J. R. (1992). *Single-case research design and analysis: New directions for psychology and education*. Mahwah, NJ: Lawrence Erlbaum Associates.

Kuhn, T. S. (1962). *The structure of scientific revolutions*. Chicago: University of Chicago Press.

Locke, J. (1974). An essay concerning human understanding. In R. Taylor (Ed.), *The empiricists*. Garden City, NY: Doubleday.

Marcia, J. (1966). Development and validation of ego identity status. *Journal of Personality and Social Psychology, 3*, 551–558.

Mayer, R. E. (2000). What is the place of science in educational research? *Educational Researcher, 29*, 38–39.

McLaren, P. L., & Giarelli, J. M. (Eds.). (1995). *Critical theory and educational research*. Albany, NY: State University of New York.

Miller, P. M. (2009). Boundary spanning in homeless children's education: Notes from an emergent faculty role in Pittsburgh. *Education Administration Quarterly, 45*(4), 616–630.

National Academy of Sciences. (1999). *Science and creationism—A view of the National Academy of Sciences*. Washington, DC: National Academy Press

Peirce, C. S. (1877). The fixation of belief. *Popular Science Monthly, 12*, 1–15.

Peirce, C. S. (1902). *Application to the Carnegie Institution for support of research in logic, memoir 19, On arguments*. Retrieved from http://www.cspeirce.com/menu/library/bycsp/l75/intro/l75intro.htm

Plato (Jowett, B. 1892). Apology of Socrates from *The Dialogues of Plato, Volume 2*. Translated and with an introduction by Benjamin Jowett. Oxford: Oxford University Press. Retrieved from http://www.law.umkc.edu/faculty/projects/ftrials/socrates/apology.html

Popper, K. (1959). *The logic of scientific discovery.* New York: Basic Books.

Ryle, G. (1971). *Collected papers: Collected essays, 1929–1968. Volume 2 of Collected Papers.* New York: Barnes & Noble.

Schliefer, R. (1997). Saussure, Ferdinand de. In M. Groden & M. Krieswirth (Eds.), *The Johns Hopkins guide to literary theory and criticism.* Baltimore, MD: Johns Hopkins University Press.

Schwandt, T. A. (1997). *Qualitative inquiry: A dictionary of terms.* Thousand Oaks, CA: SAGE Publications.

Schwandt, T. A. (2000). Three epistemological stances for qualitative inquiry: Interpretivism, hermeneutics, and social constructivism. In N. K. Denzin & Y. S. Lincoln (Eds.), *The handbook of qualitative research* (2nd ed.). Thousand Oaks, CA: SAGE Publications.

Shulman, L. S. (1981). Discipline of inquiry in education: An overview. *Educational Researcher, 10,* 5–12, 23.

Tashakkori, A., & Teddlie, C. (1998). *Mixed methodology combining qualitative and quantitative approaches.* Thousand Oaks, CA: SAGE Publications.

Thompson, B. (1995). Publishing your research results: Some suggestions and counsel. *Journal of Counseling and Development, 73,* 342–345.

Vontress, C. E., & Epp, L. R. (1997). Historical hostility and the African American client: Implications for counseling. *Journal of Multicultural Counseling and Development, 25,* 156–166.

Woit, P. (2006). *Not even wrong: The failure of string theory & the continuing challenge to unify the laws of physics.* New York: Basic Books.

Scholar Before Researcher

KEY IDEA

Reading is fundamental to the development of research problems, questions, designs, and analyses. Good questions come from deep reading and thinking.

POINTS TO KNOW

Understand the need to read for your research.

Understand the purpose of a literature search for a thesis or dissertation.

Understand where to obtain research articles.

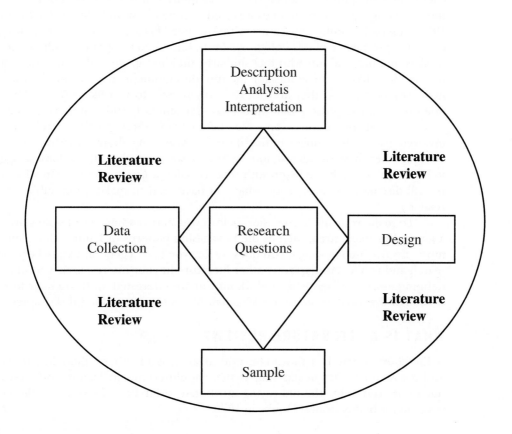

READING—WHY DO IT?

We focus a great deal of our time in class and with our students on the development of good research questions. To develop important research questions, you need to read, read, and read some more. You need to become a well-read scholar before you start your research (Boote & Beile, 2005). Notice in the graphic above that only ''Literature Review'' is boldfaced. That is because you are just starting and are not at the question development stage. So, where or what should you read? Let's get started.

In groups of people (e.g., classroom of students) we have observed that if one person is wondering something, it is likely that some of the other people in the group, as well as some people in the past, are wondering something similar. For example, in Kim's experience, many counseling students and professionals admit to feeling like a fraud, believing that no matter how good they are in classes and with clients, at some point, someone is going to figure out that they do not know what they are doing and should not be entrusted with such responsibility (Clance & Imes, 1978). Jim had a similar experience with Advanced Placement high school students. Given the prevalence of this *imposter syndrome*, Kim often brings up the phenomenon in class, linking students who feel similarly, building group cohesion, and setting the building blocks for counselor identity development. Part of the surprise for many students is that they are not the only person to feel like a fraud. There is often relief in recognizing that others have felt similarly and that there are ways to address the phenomenon—some ways better than others given the circumstances involved. Research is similar in that if we are wondering about something, chances are that others have wondered, too. So how do we learn what others' have struggled to learn? In research, we begin with what is called a *literature review*. (In Chapter 3 we will discuss ways to organize what you have read to make it digestible for the reader.)

To make your life a bit easier, before you start reading you should start with a general problem area, such as the purchasing patterns of Latino adolescents or most effective interviewing techniques, so that you have a general area to begin your search and review. And, as you gather literature in your interest area, you will start defining more precisely what and whom you are interested in. If you want to see a version of that process, go to the Armchair Moment at the end of this chapter.

WHAT IS A LITERATURE REVIEW?

A **literature review** is a thorough, critical analysis of others' thoughts, theories, and research on a particular subject that should eventually lead to your research questions. You know the old saying attributed to Sir Isaac Newton in a letter he wrote to his buddy Robert Hooke in 1676:

> If I have seen further it is by standing on ye shoulders of Giants.

The purpose of a literature review is to find out what others' thoughts are and have been. The focus is *not* on our own thoughts, theories, or research; rather, the focus of a good literature review is our thoughtful summarization and evaluation of the work resting on the shoulders of the giants on which we hope to stand. Most journal articles, dissertations, and theses include an integrated review of the literature. By integrated literature review, we don't mean surveying the finer points of *Moby Dick*, we mean digging through the professional literature, such as peer-reviewed journal articles, books, dissertations, theses, and conference proceedings. Peer-reviewed means that others who know this field or topic area have read the work and agree that it should be published or presented. Of course, before you can do a literature review, you need a general idea of what you are looking for—which leads us to figuring out where you get these general ideas.

RESEARCH IDEA LOCATIONS

What are the sources for subjects to review? Well, we saw in Chapter 1 that one source is very simply the everyday world in which we live and work. A professional counselor wondered whether depressive symptoms might vary for women in shelters who have been battered versus those who have not been battered. She would be interested in reviewing the literature on depression in women with an emphasis on women in shelters and battered women. Another common source for social scientists is the workplace. Marketing executives for movie distributors may be interested in determining what effect the word of mouth of filmgoers has on ticket sales (Moul, 2008). Or what if a kindergarten teacher wanted to know how bilingualism and reading are related (Brenneman, Morris, & Israelian, 2007)? Another example may be a community agency director who is interested in finding out whether using dialectic behavioral therapy (DBT) improves levels of depression in community agency clients with diagnoses of borderline personality disorder (BPD). A literature review in this case would consider not only published work on depression, but also literature on BPD, DBT, and your choice of methodology—program evaluation. Jim recently had a second premature child (27 weeks gestation) and was interested in the more recent research on variables associated with developmental delays. It turns out that a few variables are most associated with developmental delays, such as level of bilirubin.

Another source for subjects is the **theories** we learn in our programs. Each domain of knowledge has theories that drive the research and are tied to large-scale research questions. For example, is cognitive development continuous or discontinuous or something else? Within each theory, there are more specific research questions to be asked. A business marketing student may be interested in how people both accept new technologies and actually purchase the items. Where is the threshold that sends someone across the tipping point from saying, ''Hey, that is neat'' to ''I am going to buy that today.''

A graduate student in a school counseling program who was exposed to Carl Rogers' (1942) thoughts on client-centered therapy through course readings and class discussions is quite interested in the use of client-centered therapy in school counseling with adolescents. Voìla! The student has an idea for a literature review area. The search for information will likely include reading what has been written about client-centered therapy in high school counseling and/or with adolescents.

Finally, another source for ideas is the **published research**. Let's face it, in your career—first as a student and then as a professional—you'll be reading many research articles. This helps you in two ways. One, you may feel, and the authors may tell you, that the way in which the authors conducted their research missed a few essential components and that you can do a better job. For example, the authors might have done research looking at the effectiveness of DBT on community agency clients with BPD but, as they noted, all their clients were Caucasian women. Your agency is situated in a county with a very high Latino population and most of your clientele are Latino. You already know that culture can play a role in treatment and wonder whether DBT would really work with Latino clients. Two, most of the articles have a nice little section that offers suggestions for further research. You may find these sections offer you a source to start your literature review. Or, instead of missing components that caught your attention, you may simply feel that the phenomenon of interest does not work that way and you want to demonstrate that. Within the published research, each domain typically has a few articles that discuss the history of the area, the current understanding, methodological challenges, questions that need to be answered, and data that should be gathered. These review articles are wonderful places to start, so look for specific "Review of X" journals in your content specialty area (e.g., *Educational Psychology Review*).

FINDING LITERATURE

Now that you have a general idea for what you want to look at, your **problem area,** you need to figure out where you are going to find this literature you need to review. Libraries are remarkable places for literature reviews. Yet we've both been astonished by how many of our students, even our colleagues, do not venture forth to the library to peruse the literature aisles. It seems as though cruising the Internet is a far more fashionable alternative to physically entering the hallowed halls of a library. We argue that by limiting yourself to one or the other, you may be limiting yourself to a subset of the literature available to you. Don't limit yourself to a subset of the literature. Without a thorough review and critique (methods, data collection, procedures, analysis) of the body of literature, you leave the reader without **evidence** about the field. Imagine if a couple and family counselor limited himself to talking only to the mother in family counseling sessions, shushing the father, children, and grandmother in the process. Think of the wealth of information he would lose access to that would affect his ability to help the family! Imagine if you limited yourself only to the cheese aisle at the grocery store—you would miss the Oreos!

The Library

As we stated, one great place to go for literature is the library. If you are getting a degree, then you have access to an academic library. If you are already out in the field, you may have variable access to a library or may not know where to find one. Libraries can be **public** (governmental) or **private** entities, **special** (law, medical, military, presidential), and/or affiliated with a university or college (**academic**). Every U.S. state, the District of Columbia, Guam, Puerto Rico, and the U.S. Virgin Islands have academic libraries; all but Guam and Puerto Rico have public libraries, too. Special libraries may house collections related to a particular theme such as the William J. Clinton Presidential Library in Little Rock, Arkansas; the Harry S. Truman Presidential Library in Independence, Missouri; the Folger Shakespeare Library in Washington, D.C.; or the Hawaiian Historical Society Library in Honolulu. You can find a list of libraries in your local yellow pages phone book under ''Libraries—Public.'' You can also find out what academic libraries are around by looking up ''Schools—Academic-Colleges & Universities'' and calling one near you. If you are near your alma mater, you might check at the library there to see what alumni privileges are available to you. Many libraries are equipped with computers and have Internet connections. Many are a part of a library consortium. What that means for you is that if the book or journal article you are interested in is not at your library, you may complete a form (interlibrary loan) and have it sent to your library for a limited amount of time.

Libraries, like universities, schools, and agencies, tend to have ways of doing things—protocols—that are both similar and unique to their system. You may find your access to information to be in a wooden card catalog that you will need to flip through or you may find the catalog computerized. You may find the materials catalogued using the **Dewey Decimal Classification (DDC) system**, the **Library of Congress Classification (LCC) system**, or the **Superintendent of Documents Classification System,** among others. In the United States, you are going to find most libraries using the DDC or the LCC for those documents of interest to you.

Once at the library, you can check with the librarian to orient yourself about what is available. Most librarians will be happy to help orient you to their system—really almost every librarian we have asked is excited to help. Don't drive like our brothers and refuse to ask for directions; if you ask them, they will help you. Some smaller libraries will have volunteers who may walk you through the system. Larger libraries may have free classes and specific content reference librarians with whom you may make an appointment. Almost all libraries have handouts or brochures explaining their system and policies. It is worth your time to get oriented just like getting oriented at your college site or your current employment.

Literature Search at the Library.   There are generally three things you can do when starting your literature search at the library. You can check the catalog for books, articles, and proceedings of interest to you; you can access what are called **databases** or **indexes**—compilations of literature specific to your field; and you can wander through the stacks (if they are *open*). Some libraries, such as the Library of Congress in Washington, D.C., and the Humanities and Social Sciences Library of the New York Public Library system in Manhattan, have what are called **closed stacks,** which means the collections are noncirculating and you can't physically browse through them as you would at a bookstore or open-stack library. This is to protect the collection from loss, theft, and, as much as possible, destruction.

Databases and Indexes

There are several databases and indexes available for you to search. Some of these may come regularly to your library on compact discs. For example, at Kim's university library, U.S. Government Documents Databases and the Indexes of British Parliamentary Papers are only available on the third floor and on CD-ROM. Were she interested in learning how British lawmakers currently consider U.S. business interests, she might find what she's looking for there. Other databases will be accessible online via the Internet for a fee (e.g., JSTOR). Luckily, many libraries have subscriptions to databases and indexes, and you can access these at the library through its computer system. More recently, libraries may allow you to access their databases and indexes from a remote site such as your home or office through your computer connection to the Internet. These libraries are likely to restrict access to their collections to their clientele, so it is a good idea to get a library card or membership.

Common databases and indexes for social sciences are *PsycINFO, Social Sciences Index, ERIC, EBSCO, JSTOR*, and *ProQuest*. **PsycINFO** is a database updated weekly and published by the American Psychological Association (APA). It contains abstracts of psychological books, journal articles, dissertations, and conference proceedings from the 1800s to today. As of August 2006, the majority of the database comes from 2,400 peer-reviewed (97%) journals with 78% of the journals focused on mental health consequence in the fields of business, education, law, medicine, neuroscience, psychiatry, psychology, social sciences, and social work (www.apa.org/psycinfo/about/covlist.html). Almost half the journals (1,018) are indexed cover to cover; however, the rest are reviewed for those articles that have mental health significance.

It is important to understand which documents are included in a database. Some databases include full journals, cover to cover; other databases only include an article if it is deemed relevant to the focus of the database. If the article from a non-cover-to-cover journal is considered psychologically relevant, then it is included in PsycINFO. For example, let's say that you work at an agency whose clientele is predominantly represented by Dominican immigrants. In your social and cultural foundations course you learned that it would be a good idea to read about what stressors might be likely to exist for your clientele. You decide to read what you can about Dominican immigrants in the United States and find an article entitled "Immigrant incorporation and racial identity: Racial self-identification among Dominican immigrants" in a journal called *Ethnic and Racial Studies* (Itzigsohn, Giorguli, & Vasquez, 2005). PsycINFO included this article, but a quick look at the contents for volume 28, issue 1, of *Ethnic and Racial Studies* suggests that although most of the journal articles were included in PsycINFO, the first one, "The 'diaspora' diaspora" by Rogers Brubaker (2005) was not. What is not included could be of interest to you, so as a scholar you cannot simply rely on what shows up on your computer screen. You need to search multiple databases and search engines along with library shelves.

The **Social Sciences Index (SSI)** is published by H. W. Wilson Company and contains citations for journal articles from over 620 journals (since 1983) in a variety of social science journals covering subjects as diverse as addiction studies to urban studies. Social Sciences Abstracts is the same index but with abstracts included, and Social Sciences Full Text offers online access to full texts of the same articles in 210 journals (since 1995). All three are updated daily if your library has an Internet account (WilsonWeb) and monthly through a compact disc (WilsonDisc). The SSI is also in print and may be in your library's reference section. There are journals and articles you may access here that are not in PsycINFO and vice versa.

Since 1966, the **Education Resources Information Center (ERIC)** database, funded by the U.S. Department of Education's Institute of Education Sciences has collected close to 1.2 million citations and 110,000 full-text submissions pertaining to education. Unlike PsycINFO and SSI, ERIC includes both refereed and non-refereed sources and is free to use. The focus of ERIC is education, and the journal list overlaps with PsycINFO and with SSI to a limited extent. For example, both PsycINFO and ERIC include the *Journal of College Student Development* in their databases, but SSI does not. However, ERIC is the only one of the three to include the *Journal of College Student Retention: Research, Theory & Practice*. Were a student getting an MS in college counseling or student affairs, dropping ERIC out of the search equation might be problematic.

Finally, **EBSCO Information Systems** provides access to over 150 databases accessing 14,044 journals worldwide. Most academic libraries will have a subscription to EBSCO, and this is important, EBSCO is generally tailored to fit the unique needs of your library, which means that you may not have access to all the journals in its databases after all. You would want to check with your reference librarian to be sure. We have received preliminary literature reviews both from professionals for journal submission and from students who only used one database and, as a result, missed substantial relevant material to be included in their reviews.

JSTOR is an interdisciplinary archive of scholarly articles from over 1,200 journals in the humanities, sciences, and social sciences. A large number of institutions subscribe to the archive including many academic libraries. ProQuest, like EBSCO is a large database that includes numerous content domains which include over 12,000 titles. ProQuest is also a good starting point for many new researchers.

Some people, and we know this does not apply to any of you, even limit their searches to those databases that will give them access to the full manuscripts right then and there, ignoring those, at times, seminal pieces that may require interlibrary loan or copying a journal article from a bound volume in the stacks. Sadly, their review is as limited as the person who only looks in the cheese aisle and misses the Oreos.

Not to overwhelm you, but there are a considerable number of databases and indexes available, and you are likely to be able to get access to most of them—some more easily navigated than others. We have only discussed a few, but, if you bring the same level of persistence, cleverness, and thought to a literature search as you do to peeling back the layers of life each day, you will be astonished at and proud of your results.

Searching Databases.   Next, we need to discuss the basics of a database or index. Like human beings, each system has similar and unique components. Databases' search engines will only do what you tell them to do, not what you want them to do. Searches can be done using authors' names, the general subject matter, keywords (specialized language to help quickly locate articles), phrases, titles to books, articles, journals, and assigned numbers or labels such as the **International Standard**

Book Number (ISBN) assigned by the U.S. ISBN Agency or the **International Standard Serial Number (ISSN)** for books and journals, respectively. Let's quickly do something. Turn this textbook over and see if you can find the ISBN number on the back cover right above the bar code and write it in the space below. Next, write down the title of this textbook and the authors' names (that would be us, Kim and Jim) and maybe a few key words you think this book might cover.

ISBN: _978-0-470-13910-3_

TITLE: _Educational Research_

AUTHORS: _James Schreiber, Kimberly Asner-Self_

KEYWORDS: _Research, Literature review, Conducting research, Analysis_

Now access your PsycINFO database, and you could find this book by searching under the keyword *research*. That might take a bit of time. You can type in our names—Schreiber, J. or Asner-Self, K.—and in the Select a Field box choose Author, or you could enter the name of this textbook and choose Title. You can even click on more fields and scroll down for other options.

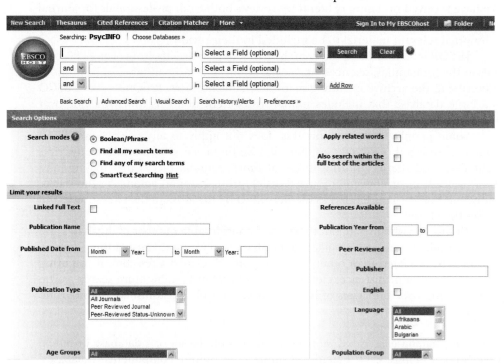

Notice, though, what happens if you type in *research* for a keyword. PsycINFO automatically ties your keyword into a **subject heading**. Each *subject heading* will include a variety of keywords under its umbrella. For example, the keyword *research* brought up the subject heading *Experimentation*. By clicking on Experimentation, we find that Experimentation as a subject heading includes narrower terms such as *qualitative and quantitative methods* and related terms such as *measurement* and *methodology*. Hit the back button on your computer to return to the prior screen. Let's say you aren't sure if this textbook would be under Experimentation or not, but you are sure it has the keyword *research*. If you cast a very large net and select both *Experimentation* and *research*, you will come up with over 300,000 cites—like looking for a needle in a haystack! If you don't include *Experimentation*, you still end up with over 300,000 to go through. If you couldn't remember our names or the title but knew you needed this book to help you conduct some research, you certainly wouldn't want to look through 300,000-plus cites.

Boolean Searches.   In the 1800s, a mathematician named George Boole figured out a way to logically sift through piles of information quickly. Today, most databases can be searched using **Boolean** operators such as AND and OR.

The **AND** operator searches through different piles of information and creates another pile consisting of common information. In our example, the keyword *research* offers us over 300,000 citations. We know we are looking for a textbook so we put it together with another keyword—*textbooks*—and come up with over 6,000 cites. That is still too many to search through in an efficient manner, so we use the Combine Searches option and the Boolean operator AND (which in PsycINFO is the default) and find that we've narrowed down our search to a little over 1,000 cites. Now that's better, but we think we can narrow this down even further. You recall that the book was written specifically for people in social sciences. So you search with the keywords *social science* and *introduction*, generating over 19,000 cites. Combining the above search AND the 19,000+ cites for social science in a Boolean equation of Research AND Methods AND Textbooks, we find that we have narrowed down the number of cites to under 20. We click Display and check out what we have found. Some dissertation abstracts, some book reviews, and some textbooks.

The Boolean **OR** operator combines data and expands your search. An example would be if you worked at a university that has a large community of international students. A student from Gabon has been referred to the counseling center by her resident housing director because her roommate committed suicide. It is not likely that you were exposed to much about Gabon in your graduate classes, and you want to learn more about counseling with clients from Gabon. Therefore, you conduct a search in PsycINFO under Gabonese and find very few cites. An article, written in French, seems interesting, looking at job burnout and Gabonese employees (Levesque, Blais, & Hess, 2004). Another journal article, in English, looks at the cultural context of English textbooks in Gabonese schools. You learn that Gabon is in equatorial Africa and that it is a former French colony. The final article is on Gabonese prosimians and you give it a pass. Not much to go on. So, you do another search, this time under Gabon, which pops up more than 40 cites. A quick look suggests most of the work is on primates (such as mandrills, chimpanzees, and galagos), so you decide to go broader and search under "central African" and get over 30 cites more. You run a search on neighboring countries with a French colonial background, such as Cameroun (4), People's Republic of Congo (0), and Congo (150+). Now you use the Boolean OR to combine the searches and you now have over 200 cites to look through—not bad, going from four cites to over 200 using Boolean logic.

Including Limits.   We have many articles that really don't interest us right now. Let's get rid of the studies on animals by using PsycINFO's limit feature. Scroll down and click on the box that says Human, limiting the articles to human beings. You have slightly over 100 cites now. You can also limit your search by publication date, language, whether you can get access to the full text online, the methodology (click on More limits to see), and intended audience, to name a few. Limits have their good and bad points. They can help you focus, but they can also toss away a cite that you didn't know you needed. Remember: the search engine can only do what you tell it to do, never really what you want it to do. At some point, you will need to go through your list of citations and winnow out some of the articles and books by clicking on the box next to the cite you want to consider. A quick look at the current display shows you that some articles are specific to research on Alzheimer's disease, so you do not click on them. You rapidly go through the list marking only those references that look as though they can help you understand more about being Gabonese and end up with about 60 citations. From these you can read the abstracts and determine which ones can help you. Let's look at what a typical abstract tells us.

Abstracts

A good **abstract** should be a concise description of the article beginning with why the subject matter should entice you, what the problem is, how the authors went about addressing the problem, what their results are, and the conclusions they have. Each journal has limits to abstract length and this will limit how much information from the study the databases you are using will be able to show you. For example, the *Journal for Counseling and Development (JCD)* requires authors to limit their abstracts to 75 words, *Strategic Management Journal (SMJ)* allows 200-word abstracts, and the *Journal of Consumer Behaviour (JCB)* will accept up to 250 words. Note that some authors write terrific abstracts that help you determine what their article is about and whether it is relevant to your search, whereas some do not.

You might be curious how influential some of these articles are and have been. Have they been cited in other people's work (one indicator of importance)? You can search to see whether an article has been cited using either the database you are using or other sources such as Social Sciences Citation Index (SSCI). For example, in PsycINFO, you may click on Other OVID citations to find what other journal articles may have cited the authors' work. There are indices that rank journals in terms of the total number of cites generated by the journal, the impact the journal is said to have on the field, and how close to the cutting edge it is. SSCI calculates a journal's **impact factor** by dividing the number of citations in the current year from the last two years of publication in the journal. The journal's **immediacy factor** is calculated by taking the cites in this current year to articles published in the current year divided by the number of current articles. A journal's cited **half-life** is calculated by taking the median number of citations to the current journal year, whereas the journal's citing half-life is calculated by taking the median age of the citations in the current journal year. You can also check to determine how much the journal cites itself and other sources by looking up the citing journal graph.

TABLE 2.1

Calculating the journal impact factor for 2005

Year	Cites to Articles Published	Number of Articles Published
2004	60	35
2003	68	33
Sum	128	68

$$\text{Journal impact factor} = \frac{\text{Sum of recent cites}}{\text{Sum of recent articles}} = \frac{128}{68} = 1.882$$

Let's take an example of a particular journal, say the *Journal of Marital and Family Therapy (MFT)*, published by the American Association of Marriage and Family Therapy (see Table 2.1). If we look at SSCI's consideration of the journal, we will find that for 2005, using the Journal Citation Report feature, the journal had 698 cites within its 34 published articles. Of those 698 cites, 60 and 68 cites came from 35 and 33 articles published in 2004 and 2003, respectively.

This gives the *MFT* a journal impact factor of 1.882. Hmmm, you might ask, "Is that good or bad? What does an impact factor of 1.882 mean?" Good questions. An impact factor of 1.882 basically means that articles published in *MFT* in the last year or two have been cited, on average, 1.882 times. Let's look at the impact factors, number of cites, and articles published of some different journals you, in social sciences, are likely to use (see Table 2.2). Compared to many of those you might be accessing, *MFT's* impact factor is good. Compared to the *Journal of Academic Management* (5.017), it's a bit behind. In fact, out of 1,747 journals ranked by the *Journal Citation Reports Social Science Edition (2005)* of SSCI, *MFT* ranked at number 203 or in the top quartile in terms of impact. The best practice is to examine these values with reference to the domain area, such as business marketing, counseling, or educational research, and not across domains.

Let's go further and look at the immediacy index and cited and citing half-lives to see what these might mean. Using the *Journal of Marital and Family Therapy* again, we find that out of 34 articles published in 2005, there were six cites to other articles

TABLE 2.2

Journal impact factors, cites, and articles published for selected journals for 2007

Variety of Journals	Impact Factor	Total Citations
Business		
Journal of Academic Management	5.017	9,555
International Journal of Market Research	0.371	102
Education		
American Educational Research Journal	1.930	1,501
Information Science		
Information System Research	2.682	2,146
Journal of American Society for Information Science and Technology	1.436	3,026

Source: Data gathered from Journal Citation Reports (July 4, 2008, 9:17 A.M.).

published in 2005. The ratio of 6 to 34 gives us the immediacy index of 0.176. This index is generally used to compare research on the "cutting edge." *MFT*'s immediacy index is tied with nine other journals at 626 out of 1,747, which put *MFT* firmly in the second quartile in terms of cutting-edge research compared to, say, the number 3 ranked *Counseling Psychologist* with an immediacy index for 2005 of 5.478.

Also reported are the cited and citing half-lives. The cited half-life for *MFT* is 7.5 years. This means that half of *MFT*'s cited articles were published in the last 7.5 years (from 1998 to 2005). The citing half-life of 9.6 means that half of all the articles cited in *MFT* in 2005 were published over the past 9.6 years. The cited and citing half-lives are not considered particularly good indicators of journal quality. Generally, the impact factor and immediacy index are the two measures of quality that people in the field consider worthwhile.

However, the SSCI, like other databases, is not comprehensive and may not include many of the peer-reviewed journals that you might be likely to access. Our counselor, for example, might be looking for information in such journals as *ADULTSPAN Journal*, *Counselor Education and Supervision (CES)*, *Counseling and Values*, the *Journal for Specialists in Group Work (JSGW)*, the *Journal of College Counseling*, the *Journal of Humanistic Counseling Education and Development (HEJ)*, the *Journal of Mental Health Counseling (JMHC)*, or *Professional School Counseling (PSC)*, to name just a few.

IN-TEXT ACTIVITY

Look up the journal immediacy indices and cited and citing half-lives for the *Journal for Specialists in Group Work (JSGW)*, the *American Educational Research Journal (AERJ)*, and the *Journal of Marketing Research (JMR)*. Write down the information below so you get some practice with searching the citations index.

Journal	Immediacy	Cited Half-Lives	Citing Half-Lives
JSGW			
AERJ			
JMR			

Google Scholar

Google Scholar appears to be quite popular with our students—not so much us—but our guess is that you have used Google to search for information or have used Google Scholar to search for scholarly works. **Google** and **Google Scholar** are search engines, not databases. You cannot extract full articles from Google or Google Scholar. But, if you are at a university or a terminal in a university library, many times at the end of the citation you will see Find it at "Y University."

For example, Kim put in the words *Unhappiness and Unemployment* into the Google Scholar search engine. Because of computer Internet access through the university library, the following appeared on the screen:

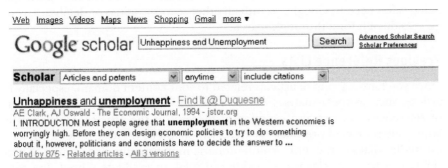

In line 1, key words are provided, telling him that it can be found at her library and information on two possible versions. Line 2 shows the initials and last names of the authors, the journal name, publication year, and electronic database. The third line expands the information in line 2. The final line provides information on how many times the article has been cited (based on articles in Google Scholar index), related articles that can be searched, and an overall Web search option. Note that the number of citations is large for an article. Clicking on the Find it @ Duquesne, this appears:

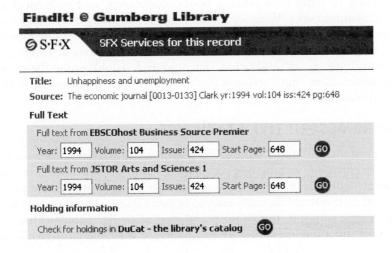

From this point in the search, a search in JSTOR or EBSCOhost Business can be completed to get the electronic version for the complete article. Jim could also check her library catalog to see whether the print version is in his library.

Interestingly, Google and Google Scholar do not provide the same results. Type in *mathematics, regression, achievement,* and see for yourself.

Therefore, you must pay attention to which one you are using and realize that you need to search both if you search one. Overall, the great part of Google Scholar is that it is cross-disciplinary, and books and journal articles are included at one time. You can examine cited references and you can find subjects not well served by your specific library. The problems are the lack of more advanced search features (this is improving), no control for key words, and not all journals participate in being referenced by Google. As with all other search engines or databases, you must go outside of it for a thorough search.

Previous Reference Lists

Once you have a group of articles related to your content domain, especially review articles such as meta-analyses or meta-narratives, you also have a large number of references you can also examine at the end of the articles. Meta-analyses are large-scale reviews of previous research (see Chapter 7). These reviews can be based on studies that are numeric or non-numeric in nature. Jim was trained to read the references from articles while working in a lab in graduate school. Jim took the articles and meta-analyses he had and began to get all of the articles in the reference section. This provided several pieces of information for further searches, such as journals, conferences, authors, edited volumes, and books. It also led him down paths where he obtained reference articles that had not previously been found in his database and library searches. As we stated earlier, you have to be a bit of a detective to really have a truly thorough review.

The Shelves

Finally, be willing to jump into articles, books, collections, and references not directly in your content area. What we mean is that if you study marketing, there are a few journals you should start with, such as the *Journal of Marketing Research.* However, given your area of interest, you might need to also look at psychology, education, anthropology, or evaluation. Each journal could bring theoretical or technical information that increases the quality of your question(s), design, analyses, and discussion.

BACKGROUND DESCRIPTIVE STATISTICS

One of the questions you always want to keep in mind as you are either reading someone else's research or conducting your own research is: "Who and how many people are we actually talking about?" You are not only trying to understand exactly who is included in the research study sample of participants, but also want to be able to generalize findings to the larger population of similar people. There are many descriptive and inference statistics (see Chapter 9) available through a search

Google Scholar gives you:

Google gives you:

on the Internet, in the library, in the popular press, and in advertising, but how do you know the statistics are both accurate and being used in a way that is not misleading? The famous U.S. author Mark Twain (1924) credited British Prime Minister Benjamin Disraeli with having said: "There are three kinds of lies: lies, damned lies, and statistics."

Also, Stamp (1929) provided this example:

> 'Harold Cox tells a story of his life as a young man in India. He quoted some statistics to a judge, an Englishman, and a very good fellow. His friend said, "Cox, when you are a bit older, you will not quote Indian statistics with that assurance. The Government are very keen on amassing statistics—they collect them, add them, raise them to the nth power, take the cube root and prepare wonderful diagrams. But what you should never forget is that every one of those figures comes in the first instance from a chowty dar (village watchman), who just puts down what he damn pleases."' (pp. 258–259)

Well, you have to be a bit of a detective. It's always good to be a little cynical about what might be motivating the authors as they conducted their research. It's also good to wonder what motivates you to do the research you want to do (Best, 2001). For example, what if a counselor in your urban community counseling agency had developed an innovative psychoeducational group counseling program to address acculturative stress among your clientele of primarily immigrants and refugees? At the end of the year, the director is going to want some evidence of the program's efficacy for her annual report to the different state, federal, and private funding organizations footing the bill. She asks the counselor involved for some evidence.

The counselor claims that over 90% of the group participants are now employed compared to over 18% last year, an impressive increase. She goes on to project that the program will lead to higher levels of self-confidence, treatment compliance, and adjustment to life in the United States. A closer look at the data indicates that 10 out of the 11 clients involved in the group are currently employed (90.9%), whereas only two (18%) were employed last year. This change looks clinically very important. The rest of the data are based on **anecdotal evidence**, not systematically or carefully collected evidence. The caseworker claims that the clients involved in these groups are less likely to be no-shows for their appointments than those not involved in the groups. The psychiatric nurse says that she's noted that the group clients are more medication compliant than before. The vocational counselor was heard saying that he liked working with the group clients because they had confidence about getting and keeping a job even though their English was limited. Some of the clients have even approached the director to tell her how much they have enjoyed the groups. If the director believes the program is, in fact, a good one and/or she likes the enthusiasm and verve of the counselor involved, she may inadvertently focus only on the very small number of people on whom the statistics are based and this *anecdotal* information about the program's success, ignoring or devaluing indications otherwise, or not considering other possibilities. The clients, in fact, may be benefiting from what is called the **Hawthorne effect**, responding more to the increased attention and energy directed toward them rather than the actual technique and content of the group. Still, those are nice-sounding statistics.

The U.S. federal government is an accepted source for collected statistics on a wide range of topics. Nevertheless, even this source is not immune to reliability and validity issues (Chapter 5). FedStats is an Internet resource to statistics compiled by over 100 federal agencies (www.fedstats.gov). Each agency collecting statistics is listed alphabetically, along with a description of what sorts of data are of interest to them and whom to contact should you have additional questions. For example, the Administration for Children and Families is described as an agency under the aegis of the U.S. Department of Health and Human Services (HHS) that collects information on a variety of issues of importance to the welfare of children and adolescents. Such information includes data on adoption and child abuse programs that might be of interest to a counselor or counselor-in-training. Clicking on the Key Statistics button will direct you to the Child Welfare Information Gateway (www.childwelfare.gov), where you can access statistics by clicking on the Statistics key under Resources. From there, you may choose to access statistics on child abuse and neglect, where you will be offered the opportunity to peruse data from state, national, and international sources. You can read fact sheets put together by the agencies of specific subjects such as *Child Abuse and Neglect Fatalities: Statistics and Interventions* produced by the Child Welfare Information Gateway (2004). It's always a good idea to look at the data sources from which the fact sheets are drafted as well. Most data sources will have information to let you know how the data were collected. This becomes important because you want to be able to trust the data and can only do so if you know more about it. In the case of child abuse and neglect, data collected are cases that are *substantiated*. A substantiated case is one that has been reported to a social service agency, was investigated, and met the legal definition of child abuse and neglect. This gets even more problematic when you recognize that the legal definition for child abuse and neglect differs by state. This may lead you to suspect that the federal statistics are a conservative estimate of child abuse and neglect cases, not an uncommon suspicion (Jones, Finkelhor, & Halter, 2006).

If you take your search seriously and read the articles in depth, you will be on your path to becoming a scholar. Reading (and critiquing) is fundamental to the development of good, important research questions—it also keeps the field alive and vibrant.

CASE STUDY

In the opening chapter, the student, Ginette, is interested in graphs and interpretations of graphs. At this point, Ginette is still developing the problem area and decides to try to learn about how people learn and remember graphs, and more generally, pictures. Her big-picture question is: How do people interpret graphs they see? Other questions are: How do different components of the graphs (color, scale, type) affect the interpretation? How long before they cannot remember what was in the graph, or remember it incorrectly? Do they ever use the graph information again? Ginette has a more defined problem area, but it could still spiral out of control. A focal point for the search could be based on graphs, understanding, and cognition.

She decides to start with the key words *Graphs Cognition Error* in Google Scholar and gets 36,000 hits. Well, that is too many, but she does notice one article, "Interpretations of Graphs by University Biology Students and Practicing Scientists: Toward a Social Practice View of Scientific Representation Practices," that looks promising. Her university does have the journal in paper form but not a subscription for that year in electronic form. She also notices that the *Journal of Educational Psychology* has several articles on graphs. She is off to the library.

While at the library walking around the shelves, she sees a journal titled *Cognition and Instruction.* She pulls five years' worth of issues from the journal and begins to search for directly and indirectly related articles, information, and citations.

After collecting several articles, she sees a student a year ahead of her in the program and stops to talk. She begins to talk about her concern with the sample of articles she has and that they are really just a convenience sample and she is going to try to complete a bit more prospecting in search of more articles. The student tells her that if she has found an author or two that are cited or have written a few articles in the area, she should get online and search for the researcher's vita. "Researchers," he says, "try to publish in the top journals, but also to a wide readership to increase the potential of their citations. You might be missing something. If you end up looking in education journals, there is the What Works web site at the United States Department of Education."

ARMCHAIR MOMENT

Below is a drawing we have used with our students. The first stage is to have students present a phenomenon or other interest. By phenomenon, we mean the topic you are interested in, such as learning, purchasing habits, relationship development, and so on. After we have the general area, we brainstorm on some basic questions of interest. Notice that we start with a large area, the top of the funnel, and then begin to refine it down to the tip. After a bit of discussion, the students are sent out to search for literature. As a rule, we try to have students search in a variety of journals, because we don't want their review to be myopic or biased with one view of the phenomenon. We reconvene and begin discussing what we have read and begin to refine the questions more. This takes time—so don't get frustrated. Really good questions take a bit of time to develop as a novice—and even as a veteran researcher.

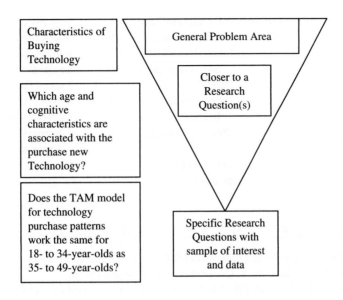

Do you have a general problem area you are interested in? If so, write it out below.

_____

_____

_____

_____

The notion of "scholar before researcher" has been around for quite some time. As our European colleagues say, and Jim's niece Anne found out, you "read for your degree." The phrase, as we were informed, that we chose for this chapter was almost identical to an article title, which Jim should have recognized, so we wanted to give proper acknowledgement to the authors.

KEY WORDS

abstract
academic library
AND
anecdotal evidence

Boolean
closed stacks
database

Dewey Decimal Classifica-
tion (DDC) system
EBSCO Information
Services

Education Resources Information Center (ERIC)
evidence
Google
Google Scholar
half-life
Hawthorne effect
immediacy factor
impact factor
index
International Standard
  Book Number (ISBN)
International Standard
  Serial Number (ISSN)
JSTOR
Library of Congress Classification (LCC) system
literature review
OR
private library
problem area
PsycINFO
public library
published research
Social Sciences Index (SSI)
special library
subject heading
Superintendent of Doc-
  uments Classification
  System
theories

REFERENCES AND FURTHER READINGS

Best, J. (2001). *Damned lies and statistics: Untangling numbers from the media, politicians, and activists.* Berkeley: University of California Press.

Boote, D. N., & Beile, P. (2005). Scholars before researchers: On the centrality of the dissertation literature. *Educational Researcher, 34*(6), 3–15.

Brenneman, M. H., Morris, R. D., & Israelian, M. (2007). Language preference and its relationship with reading skills in English and Spanish. *Psychology in the Schools, 44,* 171–181.

Brubaker, R. (2005). The "diaspora" diaspora. *Ethnic and Racial Studies, 28,* 1–20.

Child Welfare Information Gateway. (2004). *Child abuse and neglect fatalities: Statistics and interventions.* Retrieved from http://www.childwelfare.gov/pubs/factsheets/fatality.pdf

Clance, P. R., & Imes, S. A. (1978). The imposter phenomenon in high achieving women: Dynamics and therapeutic intervention. *Psychotherapy: Theory, Research & Practice, 15,* 241–247.

Itzigsohn, J., Giorguli, S., & Vasquez, O. (2005). Immigrant incorporation and racial identity: Racial self-identification among Dominican immigrants. *Ethnic and Racial Studies, 28,* 50–78.

Jones, L. M., Finkelhor, D., & Halter, S. (2006). Child maltreatment trends in the 1990s: Why does neglect differ from sexual and physical abuse? *Child Maltreatment: Journal of the American Professional Society on the Abuse of Children, 11,* 107–120.

Levesque, M., Blais, M. R., & Hess, U. (2004). Motivational dynamic of burnout and well-being in African teachers. *Canadian Journal of Behavioural Science, 36,* 190–201.

Moul, C. C. (2008). Measuring word of mouth's impact on theatrical movie admissions. *Journal of Economics & Management Strategy, 16,* 859–892.

Rogers, C. R. (1942). *Counseling and psychotherapy.* Boston, MA: Houghton-Mifflin.

Stamp, J. (1929). *Some economic factors in modern life.* London: P. S. King and Son, Ltd.

Twain, M. (1924). *Autobiography.* New York: Sheldon and Company.

Problem Areas and Research Questions

KEY IDEA

Literature reviews synthesize information and allow one to identify a focused problem to investigate.

POINTS TO KNOW

Understand tactics for gathering information from readings.

Understand the basics of synthesizing information into narrative.

Understand how to narrow your research question based on readings.

Understand how to bring literature review to a focused problem
to investigate.

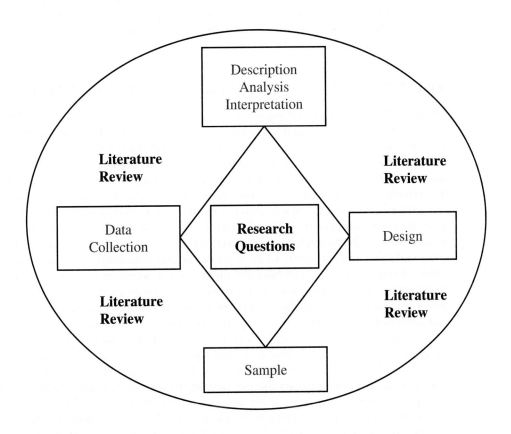

THE NEED TO ORGANIZE

Finding the literature is easy once you have a basic focus. You need to be a good detective sometimes, but the literature is out there. Synthesizing that information is another skill to develop. Students typically become overwhelmed by the massive amount of information available. This feeling decreases over time, as you will develop schemas for what is important and what is not. Therefore, this chapter concerns organizing and synthesizing the research literature, and developing formal research questions from the original content domain. As you read, your problem area will become more and more refined. This is the center of everything you will do for the rest of your study and this book. If you examine the graphic above, you notice we have boldfaced Literature Review and Research Questions. That is the focus of this chapter, helping you get to a question or set of questions you can research. The question may change as you read, and in some research cases, change as you investigate, but you need to start off on a path.

The literature review should synthesize information and allow you to identify a focused problem to investigate. The review should also provide a road map for the reader so that when the reader reaches the research questions, there is no doubt those are the questions to ask.

PRACTICAL TACTICS FOR ORGANIZING YOUR INFORMATION

Many students and even colleagues are quite good at collecting research articles directly and indirectly related to the phenomenon of interest. However, that is really just an initial step along the way to developing and conducting a research study. Articles, reports, dissertations, and so forth, need to be read, critiqued, synthesized, and organized so that they can be useful in the development of a particular study. Therefore, it is imperative that you choose or develop a tactic to organize the information. A great deal of research has been conducted on how to organize information; below we provide a few examples that our students and colleagues have found useful. Organizing your information so it can be categorized, analyzed, critiqued, and written about in an interesting and meaningful way is important. Many of our students do not have the tactical skills necessary to do this when they enter our programs. They can obtain research studies from the library or through electronic means and read them, but they do not truly understand how to transform that information into the academic format of a literature review.

What does a generic empirical article look like (Tables 3.1 and 3.2)? By empirical, we mean a study that collected data, and then analyzed and interpreted that data. Research articles have the same basic format. The abstract leads and provides an overall summary of the article, similar to the first 35 words of a newspaper article. Writing a good **abstract** is almost an art, so don't expect to learn all that you need to know from an abstract. Next is the **body** of the article, which typically has an Introduction and Literature Review sections. This may also be titled Theoretical Framework or Background. The Literature Review provides a synthesis and critique of the research and should lead to the research questions

TABLE 3.1

Example of a quantitative study

Role of Affective Commitment in Organizational Commitment for University Faculty	Title
James B. Schreiber	Author Name
Abstract	Overview of Article
This study examines organizational behavior concepts in a university setting. One-thousand faculty members....	
Theoretical Framework Employees enter and exit organizations for many different reasons. University faculty and the university employment system are somewhat distinct from the traditional turnover issues discussed in the human resources literature. **Research Questions** Does academic rank affect the level of self-perceived commitment to the institution of employment? Does the productivity level of the faculty member affect the self-perceived commitment to the organization? Does commitment affect turnover or intent to leave?	The Theoretical Framework discusses previous research, the area of interest, and the rationale for the current student and focuses the reader on the research problem area and question
Method *Sample* A quota sample of 300 faculty members, 100 for each rank of assistant, associate, and full professor, were participants in this study. *Data Collection* Participants completed a demographic survey that requested information concerning their personal background, educational training, and academic appointments. Next, the participants completed the.... *Analysis* A structural equations model was used to answer the questions. Descriptive statistics are provided in Table 1.	The Method section provides details on the participants, the procedures for the study, how the data will be collected and analyzed, and reliability and validity Chapters 4, 5, 6, 7
Results The results from the model indicate that the assistant and associate professors are more committed to their universities than full professors though this is mediated by the number of published articles and grants the faculty member has received.	The Results section provides basic information on what was observed and how to interpret the results (e.g., a statistically significant t-test) Chapter 9
Discussion The affect of commitment to an academic institution on intent to leave appears to be different among different faculty ranks, number of children the faculty member has and are in school, institutional rank, and perception of the institution by outside organizations. The intent to leave is also mediated by the belief that the faculty member could obtain another academic position with a significantly higher base pay level. These multiple variables that mediate the intent to leave are similar in other research domains.	The Discussion section links the observations from the study to the larger theoretical constructs and previous literature Finally, the Discussion section should have a written narrative on the limitations or shortcomings of the present study Chapter 7

TABLE 3.2
Example of a qualitative article

New Graduate to Full Professor: A Case Study	Title
James B. Schreiber	Author Name
Abstract This study examines one new Ph.D. as she began her career at a Tier 2 university, through tenure, family changes, several job offers, one academic move, and obtaining the rank of full professor.	Overview of Article
Theoretical Framework Employees enter and exit organizations for many different reasons. University faculty and the university employment system are somewhat distinct from the traditional turnover issues discussed in the human resources literature. Research Questions What does the concept of commitment to the institution look like over time for a specific faculty member? What are the personal experiences of being one of only a few women in the academic unit (business school)?	The Theoretical Framework discusses previous research, the area of interest, and the rationale for the current student and focuses the reader on the research problem area and question
Method *Sample* A specific case was chosen to follow over many years in order to obtain an in-depth data set of the successes and struggles, both personal and professional, from new hire to full professor. *Data Collection* Multiple data collection instruments were used, but the main data focus was on interviewing the participant over time. *Analysis* All data were transcribed from notes and audio equipment and then input into Atlas TI, a qualitative research software package. During each phase of data analysis, another researcher reanalyzed the data without knowledge of the study or the researcher's current conclusions. At the end of data collection, I also began to have the participant review my conclusions to see whether there was agreement from the participant.	The Method section provides details on the participants, the procedures for the study, how the data will be collected and analyzed, and issues related to believability and trustworthiness Chapters 4, 5, 6, and 8
Results The first phase of data analysis provided a theme of frustration from the perceived differences in teaching load. As the participant stated, "These teaching loads aren't equivalent. The other young professors have the same numbers of academic units taught, but their class sizes range from 15 to 25, whereas my class size ranges from 50 to 125 with no teaching assistants. On the books, it looks equal, but it isn't. And now I have just learned how much extra tuition money I actually generate in comparison. I am paying for myself and three other faculty members!"	The Results section provides basic information on what has been observed and how to interpret the results Chapter 10
Discussion Though developed from a quantitative survey angle, the concept of psychological contract is appropriate here. Once tenure was granted at the first institution, the participant began to search for other academic positions. The difference in teaching loads, along with other issues such as merit pay and service duty	The Discussion section links the observations from the study to the larger theoretical constructs and previous literature Finally, the Discussion section should have a written narrative on the limitations or shortcomings of the present study Chapter 10

of interest right before the Method section. The **Method section** is composed of several components. The *sample* of participants, study *design, instruments* used for data collection, the *procedure* of the study, and *data analysis* plan are included here. Next, the **Results section** provides the overall observations from the study along with basic inferences from the data. Finally, the **Discussion section** ties the results back to the literature review to explain what the results mean in context and provide a look to the future. The Discussion section should also discuss limitations about the study and typically the importance of the study to the field.

Now generally, **quantitative**, **qualitative**, and **mixed methods** can have slightly different organizations, but all of the categories above will be in the article somewhere. This arrangement, though, is really from the great orator Cicero, who was killed in 43 B.C. His model is an introduction, where you get your audience interested; narration, where you tell the "facts" (i.e., the literature review); then division, where you point out where the others went wrong—why this study needed to be done. Proof is where you give your results and essentially destroy your opponents' arguments. That is, you demonstrate that the other author's theory does not stand up to the data. Finally, a conclusion is where you highlight your best points. For a fun read about all of this, we recommend *Thank You for Arguing* by Jay Heinrichs. It is a practical rhetorical guide and will help you make your argument. By the way, this is what we mean by being willing to read outside your area.

Once you have your articles, you need to read and summarize them. If you are just starting out and have not had further research classes, critiquing the design, analysis, and results sections will be more difficult than the introduction due to lack of experience. Don't worry—that skill develops as the knowledge needed is learned. Right now, you need to read, summarize, and organize first.

Simple Summary

When we introduce students to the literature review component, we start with a task called the **simple summary**: one to two sentences for five key areas. Introducing this task first has appeared to work best versus other summarizing tactics. Students are allowed to write at most 25 words for each section. Many journals, such as *Research in Social and Administrative Pharmacy*, use this model at the start of each article to orient the reader. The five areas are:

> *Background—Basic summary of the study*
> *Objective—Purpose of the study*
> *Method—Sample and design*
> *Results—Key result(s)*
> *Conclusions—Meaning of study in larger context*

The following is an example from the Asner, Schreiber, and Marotta (2006) article:

> *Background*—To study the factor pattern of the Brief Symptom Inventory BSI-18 given previous conflicting results

Objective—Examine factor structure of BSI 18

Method—Survey design (BSI 18) with 100 Central American immigrants

Results—Unidimensional factor structure—different from previous observations

Conclusions—Factor structure appears to vary by sample, so no invariance across groups.

Annotated Bibliography

A more detailed summarization is an **annotated bibliography**. The annotated bibliography is designed to provide an alphabetical list of books, articles, and other documents with a brief (150 to 200 words) description and evaluation of each citation. The main purpose of the annotation is to provide core information about the document's relevance, accuracy, and quality. The quality of the bibliography will be affected by the content quality of the documents you annotate.

The annotated bibliography should answer journalism's core questions of **who, what, where, when, why, and how**. We have used the journalism model with some students and told them to answer these questions about a particular research report and do it in 35 words as if they were writing for a newspaper. The "who" are the participants; the "what" are the procedures of the study—that is, what was done; the "where" is the location, such as school, lab, office; the "when" is the time of year, day of the week, and so forth; the "why" is the rationale for this study; and the "how" is the design of the study (ethnography, experiment, etc.). Included in the annotation is an evaluative component, a judgment on the quality of the work. That means you need to critique the work: did they miss something, do you not believe something, or what did they do wrong?

An annotated bibliography can be formatted differently, depending on a specific academic association's guidelines. We mean that different research and writing groups, such as the American Psychology Association (APA) or the American Sociological Association (ASA), have different formats in which to present information. Following is an example of an APA (2008) annotated bibliography:

Asner-Self, K., Schreiber, J. B., & Marotta, S. (2006). A cross-cultural analysis of the Brief Symptom Inventory-18. *Measurement and Assessment in Counseling and Development, 12*(2), 367–375.

The authors, researchers at Southern Illinois University and Duquesne University, use data collected from a sample of 100 Central American immigrants to test the unidimensionality of the factor structure of the BSI 18 item version. Previous research had indicated multiple factors. Their results indicate one underlying factor using a principal component analysis. If they would have tried a factor analysis with a promax rotation, would they have made the same inferences? The sample size is also small and was a snowball technique (they knew each other), which may be part of the reason they observed a unidimensional model.

The annotated bibliography is *more than* a basic summary. You have abstracts at the start of articles for a summary. The bibliography must have an evaluation component that is descriptive *and* critical. The authors make claims, provide evidence, and draw conclusions. You are deciding whether the evidence warrants the claims and the conclusions.

A common mistake among students first writing a literature review is to write one annotation after another. In doing so, however, you risk losing great information and you will bore your audience. The annotations are a way to summarize and organize information for you, so that you can write a coherent flowing narrative—your literature review—which leads the reader to your research questions and study design. Therefore, annotated bibliographies are not good models for writing a narrative of the information. Finally, the annotated bibliographies are wonderful to have, but they do not allow you to look across all of the studies at once or sort them.

Information Matrix

The **information matrix** is a paper version of a database; therefore, it is easily transferred into Excel or any other database software program. The information matrix we use places the articles in the first column and then information we are interested in the remaining columns to the right. A matrix or database model is the one we currently use most often with students and colleagues. The research question or problem area is addressed at the top of the chart. You can also introduce all of the information—who, what, where, when, and why—from the annotated bibliography into the chart. Table 3.3 is an abbreviated version of one we have used.

We have also integrated the simple summary and annotated bibliography with the matrix below (Table 3.3), where students first answer these questions and then move to a charting/database system that they can more easily manipulate.

IN-TEXT ACTIVITY

Find one or two of your research articles in your area and fill out the table below.

Article	Sample Size	Data Collected (e.g., surveys, interviews, tests)	Main Analysis (e.g., *t*-test, ANOVA, content analysis)	Observations/ Findings

TABLE 3.3
Information matrix example

Differences Between Unique Populations on BSI Study				
Article	**Sample Size**	**Clinical/Nonclinical**	**Country of Origin**	**Observations**
Acosta, Nguyen, and Yamamoto (1994)	153	Psychiatric monolingual outpatients	U.S. residents in Los Angeles	Significantly higher scores on SOM and GSI compared to published norms
Coelho, Strauss, and Jenkins (1998)	39	Psychiatric outpatients	Puerto Ricans in Puerto Rico	Significantly higher scores on SOM, ANX, and GSI compared to 40 Euro-American outpatients
Young and Evans (1997)	60	Refugees	Salvadorans in London, England	No significant differences compared to Anglo Canadian immigrants to England
Ruipérez, Ibanez, Lorente, Moro, and Ortet (2001)	254	University students and community members	Spaniards in Spain	A factor analysis indicated a six-factor model: depression, phobic anxiety, paranoid ideation, obsession-compulsion, somatization, and hostility/aggressivity

With the information in a matrix format, you can begin to look across and down the studies to exam patterns such as sample participants, study design, or analyses. This tactic with a typed or handwritten chart works well when you are looking at a few studies. Many of our students have stated that once you get above 20 studies, putting all the information into an electronic database makes it easier to sort and examine.

Note Cards

We have used different types of information in the charts, such as the one above. A different version of the matrix that can be manipulated on your workroom wall is the note card. A **note card** is typically 3 inches by 5 inches (or 5 × 7) that students use to study for exams, use as prompts for speeches, and use for many other academic and nonacademic activities. Students put the simple summaries, annotated bibliographies, or matrix information on the cards and arrange and rearrange them on the wall or floor, or wherever their research working space exists. This allows you, the researcher, to rearrange them thematically as you look for themes and patterns within the literature. Some have even color-coded parts of the cards in order to see them quickly on the wall. For example, all of the sample sizes (i.e., the number of participants in the study) are in yellow, whereas basic results are in blue. The cards allow you to play with the flow of the information for writing before the first drafts. You can place cards by theme together to see whether that flow of information works for you and hopefully the reader.

Concept Maps

A **concept map** is a technique used to represent information and relationships among information visually. Concept maps come in a variety of flavors, but the purpose of all of the varieties is to understand complexity at a glance. It is much easier to process a large diagram and the relationships within the diagram than it is to read the text related to the diagram. If you are interested in this area, read Paivio's (1990) work in imagery and verbal processing or see Larkin and Simon (1987). That, by the way, is why you have a diagram relating all the core concepts first.

There are four basic types of concept maps (Trochim, 2000):

> *Spider map:* The **spider map** (Figure 3.1) has a central theme or construct and the related material radiates out from that center. Ours is similar to a spider map where the center is the Research Question. We have redrawn ours as a spider concept map.

FIGURE 3.1
Spider map

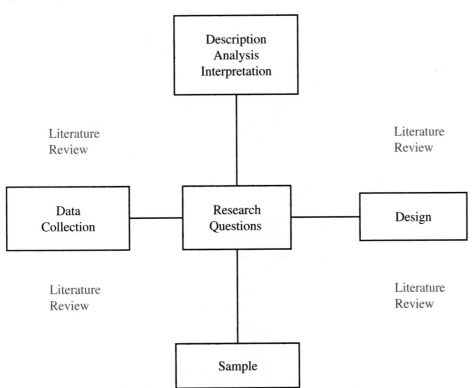

Hierarchical map: The **hierarchical map** (Figure 3.2) provides a central theme or most important topic and then relates that information in a hierarchical manner. By hierarchical we mean that the most important topic is at the top and the different pieces related to that topic are below. The information below is made up of parts or more detailed pieces of that topic. In Figure 3.2, information processing from cognitive psychology is the topic area and components of the model are arranged below (e.g., working memory and long-term memory) along with research areas such as cognitive load. The further down the map, the more detailed it becomes.

Flow Charts: **Flow charts** (Figure 3.3) provide a decision plan system based on how certain questions or patterns within the flow chart are answered. There are several flow charts that can be created for data analysis. Flow charts are quite common, and if you have ever taken a computer programming or informatics-based course, you most likely have completed a flow chart. Here is one related to data and the type of data to use (Chapter 9).

FIGURE 3.2
Hierarchical map

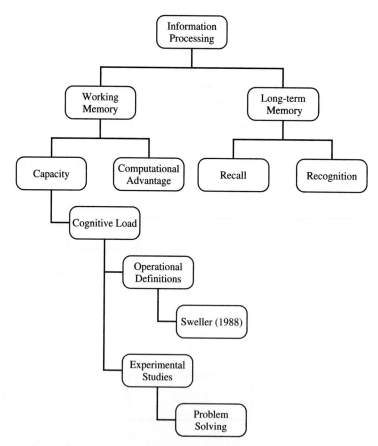

FIGURE 3.3
Flow chart

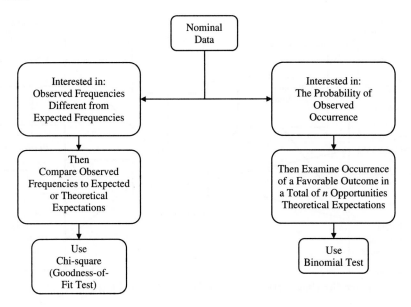

Systems map: The **systems map** (Figure 3.4) organizes information that focuses on inputs, processing, and outputs. The teacher education program where Jim works has a quality assurance group that uses an adapted version of the indicator model by Shavelson, McDonnel, Oakes, Carey, and Picus (1987). The model has three components: inputs, processes, and outputs. The inputs are all of the background characteristics of the students, the faculty, and the school. The processes are the courses and activities students participate in during the program. And the outputs are grades, PRAXIS scores, attitudes, beliefs, dispositions, student teaching reports, employment, and success as a teacher. In the model in Figure 3.4, the underlying causal argument is the background characteristics (inputs), which affect the processes, which affect the outputs.

There is a variety of media avenues to create concept maps. Many students create them on paper first and then transfer them to a software program; others simply start with software programs. Concept map software programs such as SmartDraw, Mind View 3, CMAP, and Inspiration are also available for use. The Web site addresses are at the end of the chapter. You can also use the draw function in Microsoft Word. Most concept maps take a few design iterations before a final map is completed.

Concept maps can work cognitively in the same manner as advance organizers (Ausubel, 1960; Novak, Gowin, & Johansen, 1983). They provide you and the reader with a schema of how information will be organized and discussed. The introduction to this book and the graphic we created are a core representation of the topics

FIGURE 3.4
Systems map

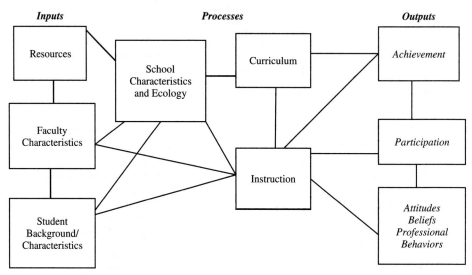

Source: Adapted from Shavelson, McDonnel, Oakes, Carey, and Picus (1987).

for this book and for research in general. Within each major component of that diagram lies more complexity, but the overall picture helps you organiz e and relate the material. For example, when we get to sampling, we will discuss in more detail the different types of sampling processes that you can employ and how sampling affects the other aspects of your study—that is, all of the components to which sampling is connected.

One cautionary note: Watch out for causality in your drawings from the connections you make. If you are trying to make the argument that one phenomenon "causes" another, then that type of picture is acceptable. Except for the systems maps, most organizers are hierarchical or linear in nature (i.e., the information is nested from the top down or moves in one direction).

TRANSITIONING FROM ORGANIZING TO WRITING

You have read many articles, taken notes, and summarized and organized the information. Now, you need to write a coherent narrative that will lead the reader to your research questions of interest. We typically have students outline the information gathered before writing. **Outlining** before writing is an old technique, and we like it, because it still works! Additionally, it is easier to change an outline than rewrite a complete literature review. You can outline chronologically or thematically, such as by type of design or sample participants, just to name a few. At some point, you need to see whether that outline will still read well once you start filling in all of the content. As we write this, we have changed the outline several times because the information did not flow well once the content of the outline was included.

After outlining the material, one tactic is to write a key sentence for each component in the outline and then begin to fill in the full text. This allows you to see how the material is fitting together and then decide how transition sentences and paragraphs will work between topics. Based on social science research, a generic outline, adapted from Jack Snowman (personal communication), that we use with our students is provided in Table 3.4.

The outline allows for a history of the development of the theory and the current state, such as the variables studied and how the researchers define those variables. The history orients the reader to the topic area of interest and sets the stage. The second part provides critical detail about what research has been conducted to date. Next, you critique the research looking for the two types of

TABLE 3.4
Outline for transforming information into narrative form

Critical Analysis Outline for Theoretical Framework/Literature Review

I. Description of Underlying Theory
  a. Origin and Development
    1. When was the theory first proposed?
    2. By whom?
    3. For what reason?
    4. How did the theory develop over time?
  b. Current Status
    1. What are the variables that presently comprise the theory?
    2. How do they relate to one another?
II. Critical Analysis, Synthesis, and Evaluation of Research Literature
  a. Description of Research Literature
    1. What studies have been done?
    2. Why were these studies done?
    3. Who were the subjects?
    4. How were they done?
    5. What did they find?
    6. How could it have been done better?
  b. Evaluation of Research Literature
    1. What weaknesses are evident in the literature?
      i. Errors of commission
      ii. Errors of omission
  c. Synthesis of Research Literature
    1. What does it all mean?
      i. In terms of validity of the theory
      ii. In terms of educational applications
III. Future Directions
  a. New Research
    1. What kinds of studies should be done at this point?
    2. Why should they be done?
    3. How should they be done?

errors: omission—what did they forget to do; and commission—what did they do incorrectly. And finally, what does it all mean? The key is to capture the big picture and transition into the potential set of research questions and subsequent studies that should be completed, of which yours will be one. An example of a full literature review from a published article can be found at the end of the chapter.

The Rationale or Purpose of Your Study

This is where you need to convince readers that this is the study to do based on everything they have just read. To that end, the rationale for your study should be grounded in the literature base that exists or is lacking. Many studies have been designed to answer questions that have either been missed or simply a perspective that has been ignored. If you have used the outline above, your rationale should be derived from the Future Directions section. In the Future Directions sections, you have developed what is out in the literature, what is missing, and what is problematic. You can use the information from this section to transfer your readers from the review of the area to the rationale for your particular study.

Linking Review to Research Questions

The purpose of your theoretical framework is to create a direct link for the reader between the literature and the research questions of interest. Therefore, the literature review should provide the framework for the purpose, and then the purpose should guide your reader to your research questions or problem area of interest. It is like the funnel we brought up at the end of Chapter 2. Your literature review should drive right to the question(s) or problem area of interest. This may read as redundant at this point, but we cannot emphasize how many manuscripts we have read that miss this basic linking component. A well-written manuscript that is moderate in importance has many more publishing opportunities than a poorly written manuscript that may actually be quite important theoretically or empirically.

YOUR RESEARCH INTERESTS

As we stated previously, we like to have students funnel their ideas into more detail. This serves mainly a pragmatic function, in that you can't study everything and every-one in your interest area. Grand global research ideas are not realized—they may be fun to talk about, but they are not reality. Recently, in reference to teacher quality, Lee Shulman (former president of the Carnegie Foundation for the Advancement of Teaching) stated that large policy studies (everything and everyone) should be dropped, because all they do is get a more "precise measurement of failure." Large studies can't really do what they promise to do—answer every possible who, what, where, when, and why combination. Therefore, don't try to research it all; you have a full career ahead of you for that.

Developing your review and research questions from the initial ideas is not as linear as it may appear in text. As you read the literature, you will most likely change major aspects of your interest area and even specific questions you thought you had. There is a general pattern and we use a business marketing example below. We typically have students draw out their big topic area like this:

I want to know who will go buy the newest gadget.

Well, this is where we usually step in to give some direction by asking, What is the technical language for *gadget*? Technology. If we continue refining the word, our big idea is actually:

Technology purchasing patterns.

Now it is important to start asking more specific questions, such as:

1. Do you mean purchase as *intend to purchase, have purchased*, or *am going to purchase* once I am done with this research study?
2. Is the purchase for personal or professional use, or a hybrid?
3. What do you mean by technology (gadget) (e.g., televisions, personal digital assistant, satellite radio)?
4. What groups/population? Adults, toddlers (don't laugh we have seen it), tweens, teens, gender, ethnicity?
5. All adults, or specific age groups (e.g., TV's Nielson rating age groups)?

These are important questions to pose because they help refine the literature search for the future review and assist in examining what has been published in the empirical research literature or other documents. Even with these questions, the study is still open, but it is a good start. Below, write down your general interest area.

Notice at this point, *there is no discussion* of qualitative or quantitative or mixed or anything else. You are still developing and reading. Wait for design issues until you have a more complete understanding of your research area.

Writing the Final Research Questions

We believe that high-quality research questions can only be developed after reading, examining, evaluating, and critiquing the body of research related to the phenomenon of interest. That is why we discussed finding literature and organizing it before we discussed research questions. In Table 3.5, we provide the pattern of development of the technology idea from general to specific.

The more specific the research question, the easier the study is to complete, because you have a focus on the participants (e.g., females in a specific age group), variables of interest (e.g., cost), and a behavior to examine (purchasing). Different study methodologies will have different levels of refinement to their questions.

IN-TEXT ACTIVITY

Write your problem or interest area here:

_____

Now ask yourself some more specific questions about your problem area. Write the questions and answers here:

1.

_____

2.

_____

3.

_____

4.

_____

5.

_____

Now, given the questions posed for the technology study, a starting research question could be:

> *What are the purchasing patterns of young female professionals for personal use technology products, such as personal digital assistants (PDAs)?*

After writing and answering your questions, what is a potential research question for you?

TABLE 3.5
Research question development process

Problem Area (Big Idea)	Question	Refined Question	Researchable Question
Technology Purchasing	What do adults purchase related to technology?	What factors affect purchase of a PDA for females?	Does cost affect the PDA purchasing rates of females aged 35–49?

General ————————————————————————————————→ Specific

Writing Hypotheses

Hypotheses, when appropriate, are derived from your research questions. Quantitative-focused researchers develop their hypotheses early, whereas qualitative-focused researchers may or may not develop all of their hypotheses early. A **hypothesis** is a reasoned belief about what may or may not happen. Jim may hypothesize that if his son pets the beagle, the beagle will wag his tail. He can test this hypothesis and make an inference based on the observation of what happens.

There are two varieties of statistical hypotheses: null and alternative. The **null hypothesis** states that nothing happens, such as no difference between males and females in purchasing behavior or no relationship between x and y. The null hypothesis is not that interesting and has been critiqued as not overly useful for decades (Carver, 1973, 1992). Null hypotheses are associated with statistics, and specifically, inferential statistics (Chapter 9). The **alternative hypothesis** can be categorized as difference or split (Harris, 1997). The *difference alternative hypothesis* would state that there is a difference between males and females in purchasing patterns. A *split* or *directional alternative hypothesis* would state that there is a difference and which direction. The difference is usually stated that the expected value is not zero. The direction indicates that it is greater than zero or less than zero. For example, an alternative hypothesis may be that young male professionals purchase *more* flat screen televisions than young female professionals. The major benefit with split hypotheses is the ability to state that our hypothesis is wrong. There are formal symbols for hypotheses, but those will be discussed and examples provided in Chapter 9.

THE ROAD YOU ARE ON

At this point, if you are reading your research literature along with this chapter, you might have a solid idea of the research patterns used in the domain, the questions you are interested in, and whether your study is moving toward a quantitative, qualitative, or mixed method design. Mainly, you will know this if the majority of research in the area in which you are interested is one of the three. Really, everything is mixed method at some level; some tend to heavily tilt more one way than the other. You will not know your direction until you have completely written your research question, but you should see a path based on the tradition of the area or the types of questions in which you are most interested. Don't let the traditions direct the path though; you are allowed to choose a different path. During your critique, you might observe that the field has been so dominated by one view that it has missed something you feel could provide definitive support or turn the field upside down. By the way, the later one is more fun.

Reminder: The goal of all of this organization is to bring the reader to the question(s) you are interested in trying to answer. By the end of your review, the reader should easily see where you are going with your study and why.

CASE STUDY

Ginette has been reading and summarizing books and articles found to date. The larger issue for Ginette at this point hinges on the direction to focus. Many of the articles are experimental in nature, but some very interesting articles are in the area of meaning making and semiotics of graphs. She is beginning to focus on factors that affect incorrect interpretation, lack of knowledge, experience, or graph construction. The question is beginning to focus on the interaction of several components that appear to cause adults to incorrectly interpret graphs used in everyday life, such as newspapers. At this stage, Ginette is thinking about either a quantitative study where some variables could be manipulated (type of graph) and other variables would have to be included in the analysis (education level, experience with graphs), or a qualitative study with interviews of specific people with specific characteristics.

She is using a charting system and has noticed that a great deal of what she is reading is in the positivist experimental psychology tradition. She has not found much work on the use of graphs from a sociological perspective or everyday use. Ginette has noticed that there are a few articles that seem to be popular, because they appear in article after article (e.g., Larkin and Simon). The majority of studies she has read focus on information processing of pictures, maps, or graphs. Many of these studies have samples from undergraduate students enrolled in a research university. Her desire is still to study people out of school that represent most of the general population.

Right now her main questions are:

Can adults (25–49) correctly interpret everyday (newspaper) graphical information? Can they also identify when data is misrepresented in the graphics?

A friend has suggested she talks to a graphic designer about the work by Edward Tufte in this area. The friend has an internship at the shop and has to read most of Tufte's work on graphical representation.

 ## ARMCHAIR MOMENT

Gathering information, reading the information, and writing a quality literature review takes a great deal of time. You should plan on revisiting a few drafts over time. Jim used to bring in a box of the initial chapters of his dissertation that he had written, reorganized, and so on, during the proposal phase. He used it to highlight that writing is rewriting, and it takes some time even when you are used to writing.

At all times, you should be attempting to make potential readers feel comfortable with the material they are reading, even if they have no background. Not all of your potential readers will have the linguistic experience in your field; therefore, when a word that exists in your research world has other meanings or is essentially unknown in other worlds, you need to provide a brief definition or example for your audience. You will be more or less successful at different times, but it is a good goal to keep in mind.

You also want to provide rich detail. For example, a sentence such as ''The study used a survey to obtain data from the students'' leaves out a great deal of information. A better sentence is, ''The BSI-18 self-report depression survey was used to collect the data from 1,035 females.'' Notice the level of detail with just a few more words (11 vs. 14). The following is another example of poor information from our experience reading dissertations:

Poor information for reader:
Doe (2008) proved that students who see animations do better on statistical information.
Better:
Doe (2008) examined the effect of using animations for conceptual understanding of statistics with 53 graduate students. The observed results indicate that graduate students who saw the animations before the 10-item, multiple-choice test scored statistically significantly higher than those who did not.

Notice that the second write-up actually provides specific information to the reader that the reader can use to evaluate the study. As a reader, I now know that the sample was relatively small and involved only graduate students, and the outcome measure was only a 10-item, multiple-choice test. I also know that the content concerned conceptual understanding and not calculations of statistical values.

Bias: Please review and utilize the guidelines in the APA manual regarding language for disability, race and ethnicity, and sexuality. We would love to include the actual recommendations here, but they take up too much space.

Finally, we highly recommend that you check out the Purdue University Online Writing Lab for a review of APA, MLA, and ASA formatting along with topics on outlining, grammar, and word choice. It is a wonderful resource that we use ourselves and with our undergraduate and graduate students. The Web site is http://owl.english.purdue.edu/owl.

We typically ask students at this point the strength of their writing and grammar skills. Therefore, how strong of a writer are you? Answer this question honestly and then plan accordingly for the time needed to develop your writing skills as a researcher.

KEY WORDS

abstract
alternative hypothesis
annotated bibliography
body
concept maps
Discussion section
flow chart
hierarchical map
hypothesis
information matrix
Method section
mixed methods
note cards
null hypothesis
outlining
qualitative methods
quantitative methods
Results section
simple summary
spider map
systems map
who, what, where, when, why, and how

REFERENCES AND FURTHER READINGS

American Psychological Association. (2008). *Publication manual of the American Psychological Association* (6th ed.). Washington, DC: Author.

Ausubel, D. P. (1960). The use of advance organizers in learning and retention of meaningful material. *Journal of Educational Psychology, 51,* 267–272.

Carver, R. P. (1973). The case against statistical significance testing. *Harvard Educational Review, 48,* 378–399.

Carver, R. P. (1992). The case against statistical significance testing—revisited. *The Journal of Experimental Education, 61,* 278–292.

Harris, R. J. (1997). Reforming significance testing via three-valued logic. In L. Lavoie Harlow, S. A. Mulaik, & J. H. Steiger (Eds.), *What if there were no significance tests?* (pp. 125–174). Mahwah, NJ: Lawrence Erlbaum Associates.

Kulhavy, R. W., Stock, W. A., Peterson, S. E., Pridemore, D. R., & Klein, J. D. (1992). Using maps to retrieve text: A test of conjoint retention. *Contemporary Educational Psychology, 17,* 56–70.

Larkin, J. H., & Simon, H. A. (1987). Why a diagram is (sometimes) worth ten thousand words. *Cognitive Science 11*(1), 65–100.

Novak, J. D., Gowin, D. B., & Johansen, G. T. (1983). The use of concept mapping and knowledge mapping with junior high school science students. *Science Education, 67,* 625–645.

Paivio, A. (1990). *Mental representations: A dual coding approach.* New York: Oxford University Press.

Purdue University Online Writing Lab (OWL). Retrieved from http://owl.english. purdue.edu/owl/resource/560/01/

Shavelson, R. J., McDonnel, L., Oakes, J., Carey, N., & Picus, L. (1987). *Indicator systems for monitoring mathematics and science education.* Santa Monica, CA: RAND Corporation. (ERIC Document Reproduction Service No. ED294738)

Trochim, W. (2000). *The research methods knowledge base* (2nd ed.). Cincinnati, OH: Atomic Dog Publishing.

WEB PAGES FOR CONCEPT MAP SOFTWARE

SmartDraw
http://www.smartdraw.com/specials/concept-map.htm?id=125354

Mind View 3
http://www.matchware.com/en/products/mindview/default.htm

CMAP
http://cmap.ihmc.us/

Inspiration
http://www.inspiration.com/vlearning/index.cfm?fuseaction=concept _maps

LITERATURE REVIEW EXAMPLE: SARAH PETERSON AND JAMES SCHREIBER

Theoretical Framework for Personal and Interpersonal Motivation

Journal of Educational Psychology

Attribution theory seeks to predict expectancy and emotions by examining students' causal attributions in attempting to make sense of their achievement-related performances. Although attributions can include any factors used to explain performance, this study limits attributional information to effort and ability, because they represent the two most commonly perceived causes for performance on school tasks (Weiner, 1986). In individual achievement settings, students are actors who are attempting to understand their performance (Weiner, 2000). Research within this framework has established that three underlying dimensions of attributions are associated in predictable ways with expectancy and emotions. The first dimension, locus of causality, distinguishes between internal and external attributions and is strongly related to the achievement-related emotions of pride and shame following success or failure on tasks (Weiner, 1986). The second dimension, stability, distinguishes between attributions that are relatively stable or likely to vary over time and is associated with expectations for future success.

The third dimension, controllability, distinguishes between attributions that are or are not under the volitional control of the learner. Weiner (1986) claimed that controllability is associated with shame and guilt following individual achievement tasks and that controllability may bear some relationship to expectancy as well. In interpersonal settings, controllability is also related to emotions directed toward others, such as anger and gratitude. Attributional research examining the role of controllability has been conducted in a variety of interpersonal contexts, including perceptions of fairness in achievement evaluation (Farwell & Weiner, 1996), teachers' concepts of punishment (Reyna & Weiner, 2001; Weiner, Graham, & Reyna, 1997), giving help (Schmidt & Weiner, 1988), social approval (Juvonen & Murdock, 1993), and interpersonal attraction (Folkes & Marcoux, 1984). In these contexts, the observer or ''judge'' has a personal interest in others' behaviors and therefore makes judgments of responsibility that lead to emotions concerning the behaviors (Weiner, 1995). However, these interpersonal settings differ from collaborative projects because the observer may not have a personal outcome dependent on the other's behavior. In collaborative projects, in which partners may influence students' grades, each student as judge has a vested interest in the partner's contribution to the project. Therefore, this particular aspect of collaborative projects may result in some modifications of previously developed arguments using an attributional framework.

This summary of theoretical constructs provides a framework within which to examine both personal and interpersonal motivation for collaborative projects. In the following sections, we review in more detail the specific theoretical foundations and attributional predictions for expectancy and emotions within the context of collaborative projects for both success and failure outcomes. Weiner (2000) has made the case that students are most likely to search for causal explanations following failure, and therefore most of the attributional research has focused on failure. However, important achievement outcomes also lead students to engage in causal searches (Weiner, 2000). Furthermore, recent research has also documented the important role that positive emotions play in students' academic motivation (Do & Schallert, 2004; Meyer & Turner, 2002; Pekrun et al., 2002b; Schallert et al., 2004). Because positive emotions and motivational outcomes for successful group tasks are important to students in academic settings, they were examined in this study along with failure outcomes.

Expectations for Success

The expectancy component of motivation has been framed within various theoretical frameworks as students' beliefs about how well they can achieve future tasks (Eccles & Wigfield, 2002), self-efficacy beliefs (Bandura, 1997), and perceived control (Skinner, 1995). From an attributional perspective, Weiner (1986) defined this component as expectancy change or a shift in beliefs about future performance following success or failure. Students who attribute performance to stable causes such as ability will expect similar performance on future tasks, whereas students who attribute performance to unstable causes such as effort may expect a change in future performance (Weiner, 1986, 2000). These linkages for individual achievement motivation lead to the following predictions: Students who attribute failure to lack of ability will expect continued failure, whereas students who attribute success to high ability will expect continued success. Students who attribute failure to lack of effort may expect improved performance given greater effort because effort is unstable and controllable, whereas students who attribute success to high effort will expect continued success only with continuing effort (Hareli & Weiner, 2002; Weiner, 1986, 2000).

Because attribution theory has not been previously tested within the context of collaborative projects, specific linkages between the stability of others' ability and effort with expectancy have not been proposed. One plausible prediction is that similar patterns would be found: Students with a low-ability partner may expect continued failure because their partner's ability is stable and uncontrollable, whereas students with a high-ability partner will expect continued success. Another plausible prediction is that students with a high-ability partner would expect greater improvement, because a failure would most likely be attributed to a cause other than their partner's high ability, and the high-ability partner could help overcome a different attributional cause (e.g., difficult task).

Students with a low-effort partner may expect improved performance given greater effort because effort is unstable and controllable by the partner, whereas students with a high-effort partner will expect continued success only if the partner continues to put forth effort (Hareli & Weiner, 2002; Weiner, 1986, 2000). However, another possibility is that having low-effort partners may also result in expectations for lower future performance because a partner's effort may be perceived as a stable trait or as out of the actor's control.

Emotions

Emotions have been typically defined as brief, intense affective responses to experiences (Do & Schallert, 2004; Linnenbrink & Pintrich, 2002). Although some of the most recent work has considered the emotions that students experience during classroom activities (Do & Schallert, 2004; Meyer & Turner, 2002; Turner & Schallert, 2001), from an attributional perspective, emotions follow from the dimensions of attributions made for success or failure on achievement tasks. In this section, we discuss linkages between attributions and both personal and interpersonal emotions, leading to predictions for emotional reactions following success or failure on collaborative projects.

Shame and guilt

Shame has been characterized as a self-conscious negative emotion arising from a personal failure and focused globally on the self (Covert, Tangney, Maddux, & Heleno, 2003; Gramzow & Tangney, 1992; Lewis, 2000; Turner, Husman, & Schallert, 2002). Guilt is also negative but focuses on a person's behavior or specific actions (Covert et al., 2003; Gramzow & Tangney, 1992; Lewis, 2000). Weiner has proposed that both shame and guilt arise from internal attributions for failure, but low personal ability leads to shame because it is internal and uncontrollable, whereas personal effort leads to guilt because it is controllable and the student could have put forth more effort (Hareli & Weiner, 2002; Weiner, 1986, 1994). Studies examining these relationships have been mixed, however. For example, Van Overwalle, Mervielde, and Schuyter (1995) found that shame was tied to both ability and effort, whereas guilt was tied just to effort, suggesting that shame results from internal attributions regardless of controllability. J. E. Turner et al. (2002) found that students experienced shame for failures following high effort, but they did not report results concerning ability, nor did they address attributional linkages for guilt.

Anger and pity

Anger and pity are other-directed emotions hypothesized to result from judgments about responsibility on the part of another person. Anger follows from judgments that the other person could have behaved differently, particularly when the others' behavior interferes with the student as judge reaching his or her goals (Hareli & Weiner, 2002; Weiner, 1986, 1994). This would be the case in collaborative projects if a student's partner did not contribute appropriate effort to the project and thereby would be judged as causing a lower grade because the partner could have worked harder. However, students' own perceived effort might also affect their judgments of their partner's effort. Specifically, if students themselves do not work hard, they may be less likely to feel anger toward a low-effort partner because they understand that they, too, could have worked harder.

In contrast to anger, pity or sympathy is directed toward another person when failure to reach an achievement goal is caused by lack of ability, because ability is uncontrollable by others (Hareli & Weiner, 2002; Weiner, 1986, 1994). Feelings of pity result in a desire to help the other person (Weiner, 1995). However, in collaborative projects in which students have a vested personal interest in their grade, these attributional linkages are likely to differ. Students are unlikely to feel pity toward a low-ability partner if they perceive that it interferes with their grade. As with effort, there is also a possibility that judgments of a partner's ability will be influenced by the student's own ability. Low-ability students may feel pity toward their partners if they understand that their partner is "stuck" with them because their own lack of ability is stable and uncontrollable for their partners.

Pride and gratitude

Attribution theory posits that the self-directed emotion of pride is experienced when students succeed because of high ability or high effort, because pride is linked to internal causes (Hareli & Weiner, 2002; Roseman, Antoniou, & Jose, 1996; Van Overwalle et al., 1995; Weiner, 1986). However, in one study by Nurmi (1991), pride was more likely to be experienced when success was due to effort rather than ability, suggesting a possible linkage between feelings of pride and controllability.

Gratitude is an other-directed emotion that is experienced for a successful outcome, but only when the other person is responsible for the outcome and intends to effect the outcome (Hareli & Weiner, 2002). Therefore, students with high-effort partners should feel gratitude because effort is controllable and intentional, making the partner responsible for the outcome (Hareli & Weiner, 2002; Weiner, 1986). On the other hand, students with high-ability partners might not necessarily feel gratitude toward their partner, because it is argued that people feel gratitude toward others only when the cause is controllable and the outcome is intended by the other. Because ability is not controllable or intentional, then according to this reasoning, gratitude would not be experienced toward a high-ability partner (Hareli & Weiner, 2002; Weiner, 1986).

All of these potential relationships, including both future expectations and emotions, might be mitigated by circumstances involving collaboration with a partner. Suppose, for example, that a high-ability student who works very hard on a project is paired with a student who does not make a significant contribution. The smart, hard-working student manages to turn out a good product through his or her own efforts and ability. Although attribution theory predicts this student would feel proud of the outcome and have high expectations for future success, the negative effects of working with a noncontributing partner may override the positive motivational consequences. This scenario illustrates the importance of considering both ability and effort within personal and interpersonal motivation.

Overview of the Present Study

In order to examine personal and interpersonal motivation during collaborative projects using an attributional framework, we asked undergraduates to respond to hypothetical scenarios depicting dyads collaborating on projects. On the basis of results from a long-standing tradition of attributional research studies, Hareli and Weiner (2002) recently recommended the use of vignette studies because they have been effective in testing initial attributional assumptions in new settings such as collaborative projects. Motivational variables examined in this study included

TABLE 1
Summary of Research Predictions and Results of Statistical Tests

Attribution	Dependent variable	Prediction	Result
		Failure on project	
Self-ability	Shame	Low-ability students will feel a greater sense of shame than high-ability students.	Not supported
	Pity	Low-ability students will feel more pity toward their partners than high-ability students.	Not supported
	Guilt	Low-ability students will not feel a greater sense of guilt than high-ability students.	Supported
	Future expectations	Low-ability students will not differ from high-ability students in their expectations for future projects.	Supported
Partner ability	Pity	Students with low-ability partners will not feel more pity toward their partners than students with high-ability partners.	Supported
	Anger	Students with low-ability partners will not feel more anger toward their partners than students with high-ability partners.	Supported
	Future expectations	Students with low-ability partners will not differ from students with high-ability partners in their expectations for future projects.	Not supported
Self-effort	Shame	Students with low self-effort will not feel more shame than students with high self-effort.	Not supported
	Anger	Students with low self-effort will feel less anger toward their partner than students with high self-effort.	Supported
	Guilt	Students with low self-effort will feel a greater sense of guilt than students with high self-effort.	Supported
	Future expectations	Students with low self-effort will expect greater improvement on future projects than students with high self-effort.	Supported
Partner effort	Anger	Students with low-effort partners will feel more anger toward their partner than students with high-effort partners.	Supported
	Future expectations	Students with low-effort partners will expect greater improvement on future projects than students with high-effort partners.	Not supported
		Success on project	
Self-ability	Pride	High-ability students will feel more pride than low-ability students.	Not supported
	Future expectations	Low-ability students will not differ from high-ability students in their expectations for future projects.	Supported

(continued)

TABLE 1 *(continued)*
Summary of Research Predictions and Results of Statistical Tests

Attribution	Dependent variable	Prediction	Result
Partner ability	Gratitude	Students with high-ability partners will not feel more gratitude toward their partner than students with low-ability partners.	Not supported
	Future expectations	Students with low-ability partners will not differ from students with high-ability partners in their expectations for future projects.	Supported
Self-effort	Pride	Students with high self-effort will feel more pride than students with low self-effort.	Supported
	Future expectations	Students with low self-effort will expect greater improvement on future projects than students with high self-effort.	Supported
Partner effort	Gratitude	Students with high-effort partners will feel more gratitude toward their partner than students with low-effort partners.	Supported
	Future expectations	Students with low-effort partners will expect greater improvement on future projects than students with high-effort partners.	Not supported

beliefs concerning change in expectations for future success; self-directed emotions of pride, shame, and guilt; and other-directed emotions of anger, pity, and gratitude.

We tested theoretical predictions for expectancy and emotions, given information concerning ability and effort for both self and partner. Predictions are based on comparisons between students with high and low ability and effort. As evidenced in the previous review of the literature, previous attributional analyses sometimes suggest clear predictions for student motivation. However, in other cases, the predictions are more speculative, given the mitigating nature of collaborative projects in which students have a vested personal interest in the outcome of the project. We did not make predictions for possible interactions between ability and effort, although we conducted exploratory analyses to explore these possible interactions. The specific predictions tested in this study are summarized in Table 1.

Participant Sampling and Selection

KEY IDEA

Whom do I want to talk about now or later?

Understand differences among sampling techniques.

Understand that sampling is a process.

Differentiate among populations, samples, and participants.

Understand the relationship between sample technique and research question.

Understand the strengths and weaknesses of each technique.

Understand how each technique affects later interpretations and conclusions.

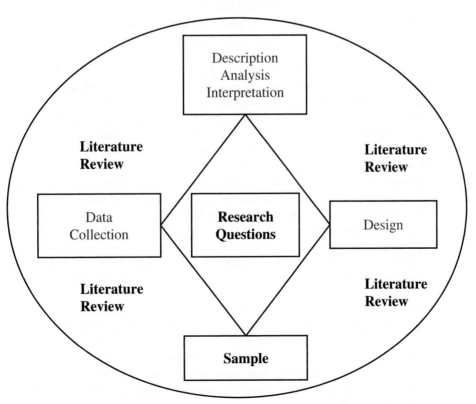

HOW DO WE GET WHO WE WANT?

Finding out what people think is part of human nature. We sample our friends' opinions all the time. The obvious problem is that our friends may not have the best opinion or an accurate representation of all opinions. That lack of representativeness may lead to poor inferences, also known as bad decisions. A commonly provided example of this is the "Dewey Wins" newspaper headline from the 1948 presidential election, which in the end was wrong. There was a sampling error (Dane, 2011).

A more current and funnier example is from Moore and McCabe (1993) and their discussion of Ann Landers, the advice columnist, asking readers to write in and answer the question, "If you had it to do over again, would you have children?" Seventy percent of the almost 10,000 respondents stated "no." A few months after this, a well-designed opinion poll looked at the same issue and over 90% of the respondents said they would have kids. Sampling is important! Clearly, those who are reading Ann Landers' column are not completely representative of the whole parent population—or at least Jim's parents, who had eight children.

In this chapter, we provide descriptions of different sampling approaches. Depending on what you would like to say about your participants with reference to your phenomenon of interest and research question, you will choose one sampling approach versus the others. In our diagram and discussion so far, the research question affects the sampling process you will choose. Some research questions will need a large random sample process in order to be answered, others will not. The sampling process that is chosen (and the one realized) will affect the design of the study, the data collection process as well as the data collected, and the analysis and interpretation of the data. Many studies have started out with an attempt to randomly assign participants, but fell short of that goal. Finally, the sampling process affects the actual question and potentially the design and the results originally envisioned.

Deciding which person or group of people you want to study and potentially discuss or generalize to at the end of the study is a crucial issue, because it will directly affect other components of your designing process. In addition, your actual final sample has the possibility of changing your original research question. In the graphic, this sampling process decision will begin to pull and put pressure on the other components of your design. You may only want to talk about the person you interview and follow for a year, or you may want to discuss thousands of people past the participants in the sample you have, such as all new college graduates. The final sample of participants of a research study will greatly affect analysis techniques and the discussion of the results generated from the data collected. A researcher desiring to make large claims about a population of participants will need to sample accordingly. Another researcher may try to understand the life of one unique person. *Neither of these desires is related to the type of data to be collected, numeric or non-numeric.* We organize research studies into the traditional quantitative and qualitative frameworks, but there is no mathematical proof that you have to collect numeric data with a stratified random sample or verbal (non-numeric) data with a case study.

Compromises are often made in order to obtain a sample of participants to study, and with each compromise the discussion potentially decreases in scope. In this chapter, we describe the traditional sampling techniques and provide personal examples. At the end of the chapter, we ask you to write down your research idea and how the sample chosen would affect your research question and potential conclusions. We would also like to highlight that sampling is not just a participant issue. As we discussed in Armchair Moment in Chapter 2, sampling is also related to the journals and articles you have read. In Chapter 6, we talk about creating instruments for collecting data and the items you use on those instruments. Finally, remember that sampling is a process and method, not simply an end state. Here is to good sampling!

POPULATION, SAMPLE, AND PARTICIPANTS

The **population** in social science research refers to all of your potential participants; think of it as the whole group of people in which you are interested. For example, in business, you might be interested in all females aged 35–39; in education, the population could be third-grade students in the continental United States. The **sample** of participants for your study is part of the population, and all possess some characteristic or characteristics that make them members of the sample group. Those characteristics will have a conceptual or theoretical definition and an operational definition. The conceptual definition uses multiple constructs to create an overall definition, such as socioeconomic status. The operational definition is the specification of that definition, such as income, education level, and job prestige score used as measures for socioeconomic status.

A **sampling frame** is a systematic process to determine the elements from which to sample (i.e., who will be in your final sample from the population). You might initially be interested in all automobile owners as your population; then you might decide to make the first frame female owners and the second frame a specific age group. As sampling frames are applied and the potential sample reduces in size, what one can say about the population as a whole at the end of the study changes. If females aged 35–39 are sampled, at the end of the study the researcher will not be able to talk about males at all or females outside of this age range. If you sample an accessible group of participants from the population of interest, you might have a problem with population validity. **Population validity** concerns how representative of the population your sample is. Your accessible group, many times just a convenience sample (see below), may not be representative of the whole population of people in which you are interested. You can also think about this in terms of your literature review. If you do not try to find a representative body of literature, your review will be lacking and potentially lead you to make incorrect inferences about the field or, more problematic, lead you to the wrong question.

The final sample is actually a subset or portion of the original population for the study (Figure 4.1). A **participant** then is one individual who is in the sample or is the whole sample. Sampling is important in quantitative studies because of the overall desire to generalize from the sample to the population of interest

FIGURE 4.1
Population to sample graphic

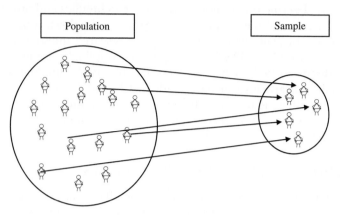

(Henry, 1990). In qualitative studies, this is generally not the overall goal or desire. There really is a purpose difference between sampling for a quantitative study and a qualitative study. In a qualitative or interpretive/constructivist paradigm, the issue is transferability (Stake, 2000; Lincoln & Guba, 2000), that is, letting the reader generalize subjectively from the case in question to their own personal experiences. Though again, this is not telling you which type of data to collect. The separation of the processes below into qualitative and quantitative is simply following tradition and does not stop you from using a stratified random sample while working in a qualitative methodology study.

QUANTITATIVE SINGLE-STAGE SAMPLING PROCEDURES

In research, there are two types of sampling procedures: **nonprobability sampling** and **probability sampling** (Henry 1990). The most common sampling is nonprobability, though it is rarely directly stated in published research. A nonprobability sample is simply a pool of potential participants that preexists or is selected without being able to determine the probability of being sampled. This approach does not use random selection, but instead selects participants who are accessible or represent certain characteristics. For example, if I choose one student out of a group of all students in that grade, we can determine that the probability of being chosen is 1 divided by the number of students ($1/n$). In nonprobability sampling, we have no way to calculate the probability. The key for proponents of probability-based sampling is the ability to estimate sampling error when a random sample is drawn from the population. A sample is truly random when the selection of each participant is not related to or affected by another person in the sample drawn from the population.

Nonprobability Sampling

Nonprobability samples occur due to accessibility issues, costs, desire for a specific sample, and other reasons. The sampling procedures described in this section are considered single-stage sampling, because once the desired final sample is identified, the participants are selected.

The first common nonprobability approach used in social science research is convenience sampling. **Convenience sampling** is used because the researcher has access to the sample, can easily contact the sample, and is often less financially costly than other sampling procedures. Actually, this method is implemented in both quantitative and qualitative studies. Many research studies' samples are a convenience sample because the researcher had access to students in the school, customers of the business, or patients in a hospital. You might be interested in studying novel problem solving with eight-year-old students, but you really only have access to the eight-year-old students at the school down the street and so they become your convenience sample. Many careers in psychology have been made from the convenience sample of the Psychology 101 student pool.

Purposeful sampling occurs when the researcher selects participants because they have specific characteristics that will be representative or informative in relation to the population of interest. A student interested in the development of a new technique for diagnosing clinical eating disorders interviews counselors in this area to determine what the current assessment instruments are missing. The counselors are a purposeful sample; a sample of the general population in this scenario would cost too much from a resource perspective.

Quota sampling allows the creation of a sample that meets some requirement or representation of the population. A researcher may decide that, based on census income data, there is a need for 10% of the sample to have an income less than $20,000, 20% to be between $20,000 and $40,000, and so on. The researcher will sample until all those percentages are met. Once each of these quotas is filled, no more participants will be sampled for that quota category. If you were to examine more requirements (e.g., gender by income), you would begin to create a matrix and fill in the proportions accordingly.

Snowball sampling occurs when participants who are sampled provide the names of other potential participants. As the access to a desired population decreases, this process allows the researcher to obtain a sample size large enough to complete some quantitative analysis. We have used this sampling technique to identify Latin American immigrants in the District of Columbia area. We began with flyers and then asked participants if they knew of friends and acquaintances who would also be interested in participating. This process is helpful when the population of interest is difficult to contact. You might have also used this technique when searching for literature. If you found a review article and then obtained the articles from the review article and then the articles from those articles, you have been snowball sampling your literature.

TABLE 4.1

Strengths and weaknesses of nonprobability sampling methods

Method	Strengths	Weaknesses
Convenience	Requires less time and money Is easy to administer Usually has high participation rate	Is difficult to generalize to other participants Is less representative of a target population Includes results that are dependent on unique sample characteristics Has greater chance of error due to researcher or subject bias
Purposeful	Assures receipt of needed information	Hampers generalizability (gossiping past your sample) Possibly includes bias in the sample actually gathered
Quota	Usually is more representative than convenience or purposeful	Is more time consuming than convenience or purposeful
Snowball	Is easy to collect names of potential participants of interest	Has selection bias because respondents know each other Has potential problem with independence of observations

Nonprobability Limitations.   As wonderful and relatively easy these nonprobability sampling techniques are, important limitations exist (Table 4.1). The first is that the sample may not be representative of the larger population; therefore, making inferences (i.e., generalizations) about the larger population is greatly weakened, if not impossible at times. During undergraduate education, Jim worked on a study that examined sale prices in clothing stores. A convenience sample process was implemented using female-student-based social organizations. After several surveys and interviews, the conclusion was: pick a sale percentage you want, advertise it, and leave it alone because not one of the sample participants could correctly calculate the actual amount saved. Well, that was true for the sample, but we doubt that the observation would hold across all females across the university. That is, the results based on the sample may not generalize to the target population of females aged 18–24.

The second limitation is that the sample may be biased. By biased, we mean the actual statistical values derived from the collected data are incorrect. Someone may call the results not trustworthy or translatable because the mean or average value is incorrect based on our sampling process. Our initial sample responses could have simply been a unique response pattern within the large distribution of response patterns.

Probability Sampling

As stated previously, the most defining attribute of probability sampling is the ability to calculate the probability of being chosen for participation. As you will notice, the researcher must start with a sample selection from a well-defined population and use procedures that allow the researcher to estimate the probability of a subject being included in the sample.

Simple random sampling occurs when all members of the population have the same probability of being selected, also termed *simple random selection*. Figure 4.1 could be viewed as a simple random sample. Jim recently began randomly sampling graduates of his teacher education program to ask them questions about their four-year experience. Each graduate has the same probability or chance of being chosen. If you buy a large bag of M&Ms, shake it, and then close your eyes and pull one M&M out of the bag, you have completed a simple random sample.

The following is the procedure for creating a simple random sample:

1. Define your population of interest—the most current graduates of the teacher education program.
2. Determine the sample size you need (e.g., see Power in Chapter 9 for quantitative or below for qualitative) or desire.
3. Create a *complete* master list of the full set of potential participants and assign a unique number to each potential participant, such as a three-digit number.
4. Find a table of random numbers or go to an online random number generator (e.g., Random.org) and create a random list of three-digit numbers.
5. Close your eyes, point to a number, and write it down (e.g., 757). Repeat this procedure until you have matched the random numbers with the numbers of the participants for the desired sample size number. For example, you would repeat this process 25 times if you wanted 25 participants in the sample.

The major disadvantage is the need for a complete master list that may not be available. Telephone surveys randomly dial phone numbers, which has helped to solve the unlisted number problem from phone lists or an out-of-date paper directory. More recently, though, this random selection of phone numbers is affected by caller identification and the Do Not Call lists. In addition, many people do not answer the phone unless the phone number is recognized or wait until the answering machine starts and the voice is recognized.

Systematic sampling occurs when you choose every nth element (person in our case) from a list (Figure 4.2). Instead of creating the numbers, we could have chosen every fourth student to obtain our sample. You must have a list of all participants in the population, and there cannot be a pattern to the list (e.g., ranked by grade-point average) that is related to what you are studying. If the pattern is associated with the dependent variables (Chapter 7) of interest, then you essentially obtain a stratified sample.

Stratified random sampling (Figure 4.3) is a process where the population is divided into strata or subgroups and samples are drawn randomly from each stratus or group. There are two types: **proportional** and **nonproportional**.

For the proportional sampling, the sample size will be different for each subgroup because the same proportions are used with reference to the size of the

TABLE 4.2
Random number table example

775	570	862	689	309
617	914	317	993	968
598	800	446	589	390
327	484	895	828	640
331	662	984	290	383
827	855	425	981	598
792	418	888	593	350
361	412	596	883	343
190	346	315	217	490
364	522	406	918	259
949	953	996	349	932
595	632	936	430	158
955	418	808	830	925
154	620	406	578	976
732	405	930	167	168
732	840	859	366	318
759	543	639	445	885
215	764	972	288	352
880	879	350	191	149
757	341	355	333	630
668	181	535	642	736
906	704	243	943	511
917	528	669	329	774
639	374	383	244	507
272	624	329	946	624

FIGURE 4.2
Systematic sampling diagram

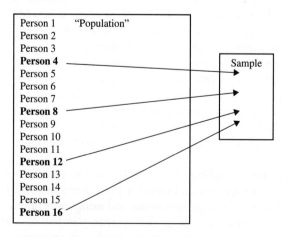

FIGURE 4.3
Stratified random sampling diagram

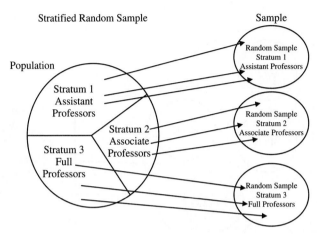

subgroups. The benefit is more precise estimates due to lower sampling error. For nonproportional sampling, different proportions are used in reference to the subgroup's sizes, resulting in a need to adjust or "weight" the results for any analysis. The subgroup sample sizes for nonproportional are the same regardless of the proportion of the subgroup in the population.

In Jim's study of the student teaching experience, the population of graduates was divided into elementary and secondary education majors. From each group of majors, we could stratify again by content area specialty. From this point, we could decide we want 20% of each subgroup, that is, of each stratum. If he has 125 graduates with 75 elementary education and 50 secondary majors and uses 20%, that would provide 15 elementary majors and 10 secondary majors. From here, we could randomly choose 15 and 10, respectively.

Cluster sampling occurs when the population is already divided into natural, preexisting groups (Figure 4.4). A cluster could be a state, district, school, classroom, metropolitan statistical area, city zone area, neighborhood block, street, and so on. A researcher may choose a single street and randomly sample the people who live there. The choice to use a cluster process occurs when the full list of individual units, such as people, does not exist, but the full list of clusters does. The buying power index (BPI) is a cluster based on how much discretionary income inhabitants in a specific area have. If one does not have a full list of residents' incomes but needs to strategically sample an area with high disposable income, BPI is useful because it is readily available in the library reference section or to purchase. The same process is common with large, education-based studies because individual students and teachers are not all known, but states, districts, and schools are.

Cluster sampling is more common with large populations but can occur with small populations, which is commonly observed in theses and dissertations. An example is the use of ZIP Codes as the cluster and randomly choosing 30% of the

FIGURE 4.4
Buying power index cluster example

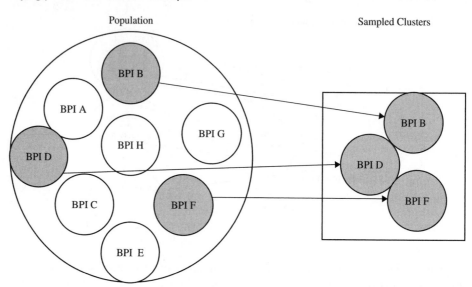

clusters in the geographical area of interest. Then residents in the ZIP Codes could be sent different versions of a product coupon and store sales for the product can be examined after the coupons are mailed.

Multistage cluster sampling occurs when the sampling process takes place in multiple stages and a researcher essentially samples clusters within clusters. For example, first cities are chosen based on a few strata (e.g., size, density), and then school districts are chosen. Next, classrooms are selected in each school, and lastly, students are randomly selected within those classrooms. This type of sampling leads to nested data, where individual units are subgroups of larger units. There are also unique challenges for analyzing this nested data (see Chapter 7). Most large national and international databases in education use this type of technique. Two such large studies are the National Educational Longitudinal Study (http://nces.ed.gov/surveys/nels88/) and the Third International Mathematics and Science Survey (http://nces.ed.gov/timss/faq.asp?FAQType=7). The topic and analyses related to multistage sampling are quite complex, and it is advisable to read in more depth on this sampling process, especially if you decide that a large, previously collected data set could help answer your research questions (Henry, 1990; Hess, 1985).

Probability sampling processes work well because there is obviously the reduction in bias in the sample compared to nonprobability sampling. Some of the processes also are relatively inexpensive as long as you have access to the lists or clusters. Table 4.3 provides a listing of the basic strengths and weaknesses of the probability sampling processes described above.

TABLE 4.3
Strengths and weaknesses of probability sampling methods

Method	Strengths	Weaknesses
Simple Random	Is easy to understand and conduct Requires little knowledge of population Is free of classification error Is easy to analyze and interpret	Requires population list Has larger sampling error than stratified of same size
Systematic	Is easy to understand and conduct Requires little knowledge of population Is free of classification error Is easy to analyze and interpret Does not need a numbered list	Has periodicity in population list Has larger sampling error than stratified of same size
Stratified: Proportional	Is easy to compare subgroups Is usually more representative than simple or stratified Needs smaller n if strata relates to dependent variable Does not require weighting	Must identify subgroup Must have knowledge of population proportion May have costly list preparation
Stratified: Nonproportional	Is easy to compare subgroups Is usually more representative than simple or stratified Needs smaller n if strata relates to dependent variable Ensures adequate n in subgroups	Must identify subgroup May have costly list preparation Must weight subgroups
Cluster	Is low cost Is efficient with large populations Can analyze individual clusters	Is least accurate probability method May be difficult to collect data within cluster Requires unique cluster assignment

Multimixed Sampling

There are times—and it is more common than one thinks—where a multistage multiple mix of sampling processes has been implemented, which we call **multimixed sampling**. For example, the participants are a convenience sample of high school students who are accessed by the researcher. That is one process. Then those students are randomly assigned to different experiences; that is, educational interventions. Or a company develops clusters for marketing purposes and once the clusters are developed, the first process—a random sample of those clusters—is chosen. Next, they interview anyone willing to talk to them by knocking on doors. This is now a convenience process, again. The sampling processes mentioned above are discussed in their purest form when, in reality, researchers often mix them.

Sample Size—Quantitative

In quantitative research where inferential statistics are employed, there are rules for deciding how many participants, **sample size**, one needs to conduct certain analyses. Do not panic and grab your chest in fear of the word *statistics*. Inferential statistics is as much about making a good logical argument and presenting sound evidence as it is about statistical calculations using high-school-level mathematics skills. There are mathematical statisticians, but you do not need to concern yourself with that world; you do, however, need to know the rules that everyone has agreed on. For this type of research, you need a sufficient number of participants who are representative of your population of interest in order to provide your reader with confidence in your conclusions.

To begin, there are published sample size tables and many applets and java scripts (little programs for determining sample size) on the Web that you can use. We recommend using those. The real reason people are concerned about sample size is *power*—do I have a sample size big enough to observe the difference or relationship I think is there? The concept of power is very old but is easily understood from what is called signal detection theory (Green & Swets, 1966). How far apart do two signals need to be before someone can tell they are different? Think about the color red; now think about pink. They are very far apart. Now, think about the color red on a popular soda drink can and the color red you thought of in the above sentence. Are they the same or different? Or is it too hard to answer that question?

General rules of thumb are used in research, and we provide a few in Table 4.4 These are just a general idea and not what you may or may not need for your specific study (Borg & Gall, 1989). There are other factors that will affect the actual size you need.

Another way to think about required sample size is to think about the size of the total population. Krejcie and Morgan (1970) created a sample size guideline based on the number in the population. For example, under 100, you are essentially sampling almost everyone. At 500, you need to sample 50%; at 5,000, you need to sample 357; and at 100,000, you need to sample 384. Remember, these are all guidelines and not absolutes. When you have the ability to obtain a larger sample without overwhelming your resources, you should do so. Again, it is better to research

TABLE 4.4

Basic rules of thumb for sample size

Basic Study Type	Rule of Thumb	
Correlational	30 observations	
Multiple regression	15 observations per variable 100 observations for each subgroup 20–50 for minor subgroups	Size = 50 + 8 × (number of independent variables in regression equation)
Experimental, quasi-experimental, comparative	15–30 observations per group (e.g., treatment/control)	

in detail how many participants you might need from this perspective. Below we talk about a program, G*Power, that can be used, but you need a bit more information.

Factors Affecting Sample Size

The big three related factors to sample size are effect size, alpha, and power (see Chapter 9 also). **Effect size** is how big of a difference you think or the literature has shown between the groups, or how much of an association exists between variables. **Alpha** is the level of statistical significance that must be met to reject the null hypothesis (usually .05). **Power** is typically set at .80 and then sample size is calculated. As you change any one of these three, the sample size requirements will change. Conversely, if you change your sample size, these three will change. If you expect a large effect size, based on previous empirical research, then you will need fewer participants to have enough power to detect differences between the groups.

There are also freeware programs such as G*Power (http://www.psycho.uni-duesseldorf.de/aap/projects/gpower/) that can be downloaded and used to estimate sample size. Below, we provide two examples from the G*Power program. The first example is a correlation (Figure 4.5). For this correlation we have decided to compute the desired sample size needed if we have alpha of .05, $1-\beta$ as .80 (i.e., power), and a test of the null hypothesis. Remember, the null hypothesis for a correlation between two variables is that the correlation is zero in the population. The required sample size is 82 for an expected correlation of .3, alpha of .05, and power of .80.

The second example is a t-test (Figure 4.6). There are two independent groups, such as listened to comedy and did not listen to comedy. For the effect size, we have chosen a medium effect size for t-tests (.5), alpha at .05, and power at .80. We need a sample size of 64 for each group for a total of 128. This provides 126 degrees of freedom (see Chapter 9).

As always, there are financial constraints that affect how big and what type of sample is chosen. A sample of 600 participants, 300 in the United States and 300 in a foreign country, cost Jim and a graduate student a few thousand dollars. The results were great, but it was financially draining.

FIGURE 4.5
G*Power correlation example

_t_-tests - Correlation: Point biserial model		
Analysis:	A priori: Compute required sample size	
Input:	Tail(s)	= Two
	Effect size |r|	= 0.3 (the correlation)
	α err prob	= 0.05
	Power (1 − β err prob)	= 0.80
Output:	Critical t	= 1.990063
	Df	= 80
	Total sample size	= 82
	Actual power	= 0.803305

FIGURE 4.6
G*Power *t*-test example

Analysis:	A priori: Compute required sample size	
Input:	Tail(s)	= Two
	Effect size d	= 0.5
	α err prob	= 0.05
	Power (1 − β err prob)	= 0.80
	Allocation ratio N2/N1	= 1
Output:	Critical *t*	= 1.978971
	Df	= 126
	Sample size group 1	= 64
	Sample size group 2	= 64
	Total sample size	= 128
	Actual power	= 0.801460

The potential importance of the results is also a factor that affects the size of the sample you will need. In exploratory research a smaller sample size is expected, but as the risk increases (such as pharmaceutical research) a larger representative sample becomes increasingly important. As the number of variables that interest you increases, your sample size must increase. Different methods of data collection affect the sample size you desire. For example, if you are interviewing individuals, you are most likely not going to conduct a large sample study because you most likely will not be able to interview all. However, you could still conduct a multistage sampling process. The key is related to how accurate the results must be; as the desired accuracy of your results increases in importance, there is a greater need for you to collect a large representative sample. The 2000 U.S. Presidential Election is an exemplar of the need for a very accurate representative sample in polling to be correct because the sheer vote count was so close.

The size of the desired population will affect the sample size you can attain and eventually the analyses you can conduct. Some populations are not that large (e.g., clinically diagnosed anorexia patients) and can be dispersed (i.e., not centrally located in one major area). Obtaining a substantial number of participants will be difficult to meet for some of the sample size requirements of certain inferential statistics analyses. Therefore, being specific about what you want to be able to say at the end of the study in reference to the population of interest and the sampling process you want to use is important. The sample sizes used in the literature you have read should also give you a range of sample sizes used in the previous studies and the true population size.

QUALITATIVE SAMPLING PROCESS

In qualitative research, the core concept of sampling is the same as in quantitative research—whom do you want to talk about at the end and what story do you want to tell? However, the size of the sample is not the important issue, and in general qualitative research, researchers sample nonrandomly. It is not that potential participants cannot be randomly sampled in qualitative research; it is just not the modal sampling technique. Due to the nature of qualitative research questions, some aspects are potentially more important in the sampling process than random selection. Resampling—collecting another sample—and seeing similar results should be more common in quantitative research. This concept is extremely difficult to accomplish in qualitative research; therefore, care and good thinking *a priori* about sampling in qualitative research is critically important.

Based on the research problem area or question, the site of entry for the qualitative study needs to be developed initially. Where are you going to find the information you desire? In the teacher example, maybe Jim wants to examine what the recent graduates are like as teachers once they are in their own classrooms in comparison to their behaviors as students. The first decision is which schools (sites) to consider. From a list of all possible sites, he chooses an urban school on the academic "watch list" and an urban school considered a model of "excellence."

Site Sampling

In general, we can speak of *purposeful sampling*, which is sampling to find information-rich sites. By *information-rich sites*, we mean **site sampling** where the participants have the information you need and are willing to provide that information. Researchers who collect quantitative data want the same thing, by the way. Information-rich participants will allow for an in-depth study.

More specifically, you are interested in finding sites that will have a high likelihood that information, perspectives, or behaviors which are the focus of your study, will be present. For example, you may choose to study a campuswide initiative at a university because of its particular demographics, such as size, location, or history. You will be required to get permission to collect data at that site and permission to even approach individuals. Finding the site you want is the easy part. Getting access can be more difficult and may require several attempts.

Informant Sampling

At some point, you will be talking to individuals, **informants**, at the site or sites. There is a variety of qualitative participant sampling techniques that you can use; you may also want a random selection as discussed previously. The first traditional qualitative process, **comprehensive sampling**, occurs when you talk to all individuals or groups and in all the settings or events. For example, you may attend faculty meetings at the university, along with the dean's meetings and faculty senate meetings. Clearly, as the number of people, groups, settings, and events increases, the ability to comprehensively sample decreases. Therefore, you can move to a more direct participant sampling technique.

Maximum variation sampling occurs when you choose participants or sites that are very distinct or different. Your choice is based on the diversity as related to your phenomenon of interest. For the university initiative example, you might talk to faculty at different ranks (instructor and full professor) in very different departments (biology, educational psychology, and linguistics). The greatest strength of maximum variation sampling is that it allows you to identify and understand not only issues that distinctly separate the participants, but also commonalities among the participants.

Network sampling is the same as the snowball sampling from the quantitative section, with a comparatively smaller sample size at the end. You ask participants or the person you are interviewing whether there are other specific individuals you should talk to or locations or events you should see.

Informant sampling can be categorized further, that is, participant by participant (Patton, 2002). **Extreme/deviant case sampling** occurs when you choose a participant that is at one end or the other of a continuum related to the phenomenon of interest (i.e., unusual or special in a specific way). For example, you choose to try to interview the faculty member at the university who appears to be the most vehemently against the initiative and the one who is the most for it.

Intense case sampling occurs when the researcher selects people who have had an intense experience or intense feeling related to the topic of interest. Jim is an intense case sample for neonatologists interested in parental experience in neonatal intensive care units, because both of his children were born three months early, with very low birth weight (2.5 lbs) and extremely low birth weight (2.2 lbs). Intense case sampling is often confused with extreme case sampling, but the defining difference is the focus; extreme case sampling focuses on individuals very different from each other, and intense case sampling focuses on individuals who have had more intense experiences than others.

Typical case sampling is looking for individuals who are average in relation to the phenomenon of interest. For our university example, maybe most of the professors on campus have a wait-and-see attitude about the new initiative and only a few are very for or against it—the average professor.

Below we provide a listing with examples of a wide variety of sampling procedures in qualitative research.

- **Unique case sampling** occurs when the choice of the participant is based on what is unusual or rare in relation to the event or phenomenon. For our campus example, maybe it is the only Trinidadian professor on campus.
- **Reputation case sampling** is when the person is chosen or a recommendation is made based on some criteria, such as a professor who specializes in worker-related law or the most famous professor on campus.
- **Critical case sampling** is the person who can illustrate the phenomenon or the one who might matter the most. For our example, the provost who is the academic guard of the campus could be that critical case.
- **Concept/theory sampling** identifies participants or sites that are **information rich** for the situation at hand or are already implementing the concept. The professor who started the idea for the program may be the best for the concept and theoretical background for the idea.

- **Stratified purposeful sampling** combines techniques so that there are purposefully chosen individuals or sites within specific strata of interest. For our example, we may set the strata to be schools, departments, programs, and tenure rank, and then purposefully sample specific people from those strata.
- **Confirming/disconfirming sampling** is most common with grounded theory and is the process of consciously attempting to select participants or sites that fit the theory or do not fit the theory that is developing during the research study.
- **Purposeful random sampling** has been used in qualitative research. Mertens (1996) used this process to randomly select students to be interviewed. It is not a statistically representative sample, but it is a sample that allowed for a potential sampling bias (all good or all bad) to be countered, which can happen by asking for recommendations of whom to interview.
- **Convenience or opportunistic sampling** occurs in qualitative just as in quantitative research. There are times when an opportunity to interview someone becomes available and you make a decision on the spot to interview that person, or survey that group.

Focus Groups

When time, access, or resources are limited, researchers may choose to conduct focus groups. A **focus group** is a small gathering of participants who are related to your phenomenon of interest and can answer questions for one to two hours in general and truly encompasses both a technique for collecting data and a sampling process. A moderator runs the session and may or may not be the researcher. The role of the moderator is to introduce the topic, keep the group focused, and ensure that all participate—no dominators, as we call them. In addition to the saving of resources, focus groups work well when people are more willing to talk in a group than alone, interaction among informants is desired, or there is difficulty in interpreting previous observations to date (Cresswell, 1998; Neuman, 1997). Focus groups can provide a great deal of useful data, as long as you pay attention to the comments and answers of the participants. A company not known for making men's suits tried to jump into the market in the late 1970s. The company ran many focus groups, but only ''heard'' the participants when they stated that the suit looked good, not when they stated that they would not purchase it because of the brand name.

Sample Size—Qualitative

Sample size in qualitative methodology is not typically a topic of discussion, but it should be. Information-rich informants or sites encompass the overall discussion. Other issues related to the sampling in a predominantly qualitative study, such as translatability and credibility, are discussed in Chapter 5. There are some rules of thumb, which we list in Table 4.5.

TABLE 4.5

Rules of thumb for qualitative sample size

Basic Study Type	Rule of Thumb
Ethnography	30–50 interviews
Case study	At least one, but can be more
Phenomenology	Six participants
Grounded theory	30–50 interviews
Focus groups	Seven to 10 per group and four or more groups per each strata of interest

Source: Based on Kruger (1988); Morse (1994).

Qualitatively focused researchers also discuss **data saturation**. Data saturation occurs when the researcher begins to hear the same information from a wide variety of participants or sites on a particular topic or phenomenon. With data saturation, the researcher most likely can stop sampling participants on this topic.

One last note, the sample considerations for many qualitative researchers are made in the light of the researcher's identity—that is, there is a fine line between choosing samples that we know well and are accessible to us (strong advantages to each in several ways) versus a sample that we know too well and will be influenced by our identities (the backyard research dilemma). We want to get access, but researching in our backyard may not tell us what we really need to know.

POTENTIAL HARM TO PARTICIPANTS

People have different schemas of a "research study." We still have participants who have pop culture views of science and will ask us questions such as "Are you going to deny us food?" or "Will we be shocked electrically?" even after they have read the voluntary consent form that outlines the basic study. Because of these schemas or constructions of what social science research constitutes, it is imperative that you make sure your participants have read the consent forms.

Each research organization has a participant statement with rules and regulations that you should read and understand. For us, we want you to focus on the potential perceptions of your participants about the level of potential harm. Imagine a potential-for-harm continuum (psychological and physical) that ranges from very low to very high. Even survey items or questions can be potentially harmful depending on how they are phrased and the participants' past experiences. If you are using a questionnaire that is new or relatively new, you might ask colleagues and friends to rate the questions along this continuum (Chapter 5; Reliability and Validity sections). Universities and research centers have review boards that require your research be cleared before proceeding. They are helpful in determining the levels of risk and how you might be able to adjust your study to reduce the potential risk and still clearly answer your research questions.

More specifically, each institution's employees who conduct research must obtain permission through an **internal review board (IRB)**. The IRB was mandated by the National Research Act, Public Law 93–348. For understanding and training purposes, it is wise to read the federal regulation in Title 45 Code of Federal Regulations Part 46. It can be found in numerous places within your institution (e.g., Office of Research, library). You can also read the **Belmont Report** at http://ohsr.od.nih.gov/guidelines/belmont.html. Another option is to go to the National Institutes of Health Web site at http://www.nih.gov where you can also complete an NIH certificate; most universities will demand that you complete the certificate.

One of the most important components of your research procedures is maintaining confidentiality. It is the law. The Buckley Amendment prohibits access to children's school records without consent. The Hatch Act prohibits asking children about religion, sex, or family life without parental consent. Finally, the National Research Act requires parental permission for research on children.

CASE STUDY

Ginette is struggling with how to obtain the adult population she is interested in. She wants a sample of participants aged 25–54 who read the newspaper most days of the week. She would like a representative sample across economic, education, race, and ethnic levels, but feels this is not possible. She is considering a two-stage study with the first being the undergraduate population she has easy access to because they are there. Then taking those results to malls, libraries, museums, and other locations where she can obtain the sample she really wants. She still has some reading to do but is realizing the constraints of obtaining a sample from the population in which she is interested and is based on her research question:

> What comprehension mistakes do adults make when reading different types of graphs?

A related question is: How do mistakes in the graphs intensify those comprehension mistakes?

To interview people at these potential locations will take a great deal of time and money. Plus there are issues of what time of day to go to these locations. Mornings on Mondays will have one type of person at the museum and most likely a different demographic type at the mall.

Oversampling one day or place will affect how much she can generalize about the larger population. She is also considering a slight change to her question; she is considering examining how people use the information in the graphs in conversations with friends and families as a core focus versus just comprehension mistakes.

ARMCHAIR MOMENT

We want to take a moment and revisit our diagram. Your sample process should be based on your research questions of interest. If you are working on a project as you read, you should know at this point, or have a solid understanding of, the samples of participants the literature has used to date. You can always go back and quickly assign them if you have not based them on what you just read. We recommend you do this; it will help you talk more intelligently to your audience (readers later, committee members for your research thesis or dissertation now).

If you have to make compromises to your originally planned sample process, it will affect what you get to say later. In quantitative terms, this will also bias your parameter estimates. We will discuss this more later, but the basic concept to understand is that your inferential results will not be as exact as you think they are. For qualitative interpretations, it may limit your translatability or credibility. If you were able to talk to the deans but not the provost for the initiative at the university, your story may be woefully incomplete. The sampling process and the final sample matter. The two tend to get brushed to the side many times, and they should not.

IN-TEXT ACTIVITY

Now, take a moment and write your main research question below.

_____

Next, write down how the different types of sampling processes might change your question.

_____

_____

_____

_____

_____

_____

_____

_____

KEY WORDS

alpha
Belmont Report
cluster sampling
comprehensive
 sampling
concept/theory
 sampling
confirming/dis-
 confirming
 sampling
convenience sampling
convenience/
 opportunistic
 sampling
critical case sampling
data saturation
effect size
extreme/deviant case
 sample
focus groups
informant sampling

information-rich sample
intense case sampling
Internal Review Board
 (IRB)
maximum variation
 sampling
multimixed sample
multistage cluster
 sampling
network sampling
nonprobability
 sampling
nonproportional
 sampling
participant
population
power
probability sampling
proportional stratified
 random sampling

purposeful random
 sampling
purposeful sampling
quota sampling
reputation case
 sampling
sample
sample size
sampling frame
sampling process
simple random sample
site sampling
snowball sampling
stratified purposeful
 sampling
stratified random
 sampling
systematic sampling
typical case sampling
unique case sampling

REFERENCES AND FURTHER READINGS

Borg, W. R., & Gall, M. D. (1989). *Educational research*. White Plains, NY: Longman.

Cresswell, J. W. (1998). *Qualitative inquiry and research design*. Thousand Oaks, CA: SAGE Publications.

Dane, F. C. (2011). *Evaluating research: Methodology for people who need to read research*. Thousand Oaks, CA: SAGE Publications

Faul, F., Erdfelder, E., Lang, A.-G., & Buchner, A. (2007). G*Power 3: A flexible statistical power analysis program for the social, behavioral, and biomedical sciences. *Behavior Research Methods, 39*, 175–191.

Green, D. M., & Swets, J. A. (1966). *Signal detection theory and psychophysics*. New York: John Wiley & Sons.

Henry, G. T. (1990). *Practical sampling*. Newbury Park, CA: SAGE Publications.

Hess, I. (1985). *Sampling for the social research surveys 1947–1980*. Ann Arbor, MI: University of Michigan.

Krejcie, R. V., & Morgan, D. W. (1970). Determining sample size for research activities. *Educational and Psychological Measurement, 30*(3), 607–610.

Kruger, R. A. (1988). *Focus groups. A practical guide for applied research*. Thousand Oaks, CA: SAGE Publications.

Lincoln, Y. S., & Guba, E. G. (2000). *Handbook of qualitative research* (2nd ed.). Thousand Oaks, CA: SAGE Publications.

Mertens, D. M. (1996). Breaking the silence about sexual abuse of deaf youth. *American Annals of the Deaf*, *141*(5), 352–358.

Mertens, D. M. (2005). *Research and evaluation in education and psychology: Integrating diversity with quantitative, qualitative, and mixed methods* (2nd ed.). Thousand Oaks, CA: SAGE Publications.

Moore, D., & McCabe, D. (1993). *Introduction to the practice of statistics.* New York: Freeman.

Morse, J. M. (1994). Designing funded qualitative research. In N. K. Denzin & Y. S. Lincoln (Eds.), *Handbook of Qualitative Research* (pp. 220–235). Thousand Oaks, CA: SAGE Publications.

Neuman, W. L. (1997). *Social research methods: Qualitative and quantitative approaches* (3rd ed.). Boston, MA: Allyn & Bacon.

Patton, M. Q. (2002). *Qualitative evaluation and research methods* (3rd ed.). Newbury Park, CA: SAGE Publications.

Stake, R. E. (2000). Case studies. In N. K. Denzin & Y. S. Lincoln (Eds.), *Handbook of qualitative research* (2nd ed., pp. 435–454). Thousand Oaks, CA: SAGE Publications.

Believability in Observation and Measurement

KEY IDEA

Structure stability: Knowing what you have before you use it. Is that cumin or coriander?

Understand the four levels of quantitative data.

Understand that reliability and validity deal with the data from the instruments used and not the instruments themselves.

Understand that reliability and validity scores are based on each administration of the instrument.

Understand conceptual and practical differences between the quantitative and qualitative aspects of reliability and validity.

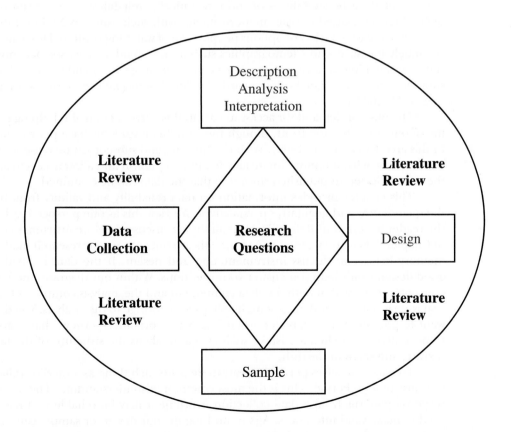

YOU MUST KNOW SO THEY CAN BELIEVE!

If people do not believe your data, nothing can save your study—not an incredible design, not a great experimental stimulus, not a fancy statistical analysis. Therefore, you must understand and determine to a satisfactory level for the reader the quality of your data. The quote in Chapter 2 from Stamp (1929) goes to the heart of observing and measuring—the creation of quality data. The issues about measurement, however, are much older than Stamp's statement. Commercial business and taxation have long dealt with measurement issues (Sears, 1997). For instance, the following is in the Magna Carta, part 35:

> There shall be one measure of wine throughout our whole realm, and one measure of ale and one measure of corn—namely, the London quart;—and one width of dyed and russet and hauberk cloths—namely, two ells below the selvage. And with weights, moreover, it shall be as with measures.

It is essentially a believability—or more technically, reliability—issue. Even now, technology has caused measurement problems with such things as Nielsen ratings because of the wide variety of options people have of watching content. How can one accurately measure who (demographics such as age, gender, race, socioeconomic status) is watching what (live show, download, streaming video) and when (original showing, tape delay, digital video recorder) (NPR *Morning Edition*, Business Section, August 11, 2008)?

The push or demand for access to data in this current era is also helping place measurement at the forefront, though most graduate students have poor training in this area (Aiken et al., 1990). With the Internet and subsequent increase in data structure capacity, it is more financially feasible to publish and allow access to all of the data collected in published studies so that the data can be examined.

This chapter provides information on data reliability and validity from both the quantitative and qualitative perspectives. We view this as one perspective: Does the reader believe you? Reliability and validity are discussed before instrumentation in Chapter 6, because we want you to have these concepts in your research methods memory before we discuss instrumentation and design. If the data is "bad," a good design won't help you answer your questions. Within our diagram, these two concepts are housed in both the data component and the analysis component. The real issue is that if your data is poor, it collapses the bridge to the analysis. You don't want to put cumin in the recipe when it asks for coriander—whew, that is going to be a mess. To a chef, a mistake such as that weakens the structure of the taste, texture, and smell of the dish.

To make ourselves perfectly clear, there is no such thing as a valid or reliable test/instrument. Period. This is the most common misunderstanding. The *scores* or response patterns from a data collection instrument may be reliable and may be used to make valid inferences. Again, nothing in your design or sample can make up for scores that are not reliable.

Researching a phenomenon that you are interested in will lead you to a point where you have to deal with observing and measuring in the most global terms. Whether the focus of your study is quantitative, qualitative, or mixed methodology, you will observe or try to measure something. Luckily, you have a great deal of life experience observing and measuring. Now, you must take that experience and learn to observe systematically.

The data you can collect include a wide variety of numbers, words, pictures, video, audio, and the various versions within each of those. Below is a core separation between quantitative and qualitative data. However, this separation does not preclude taking one type of data and appropriately translating it into another type (Onwuegbuzie & Leech, 2005). For example, when someone chooses Strongly Disagree on a Likert-type scale, that phrase is usually converted to a number.

THE WAYS WE MEASURE QUANTITATIVELY

Quantitatively focused research has four **levels of measurement**—nominal, ordinal, interval, and ratio—each with a defining attribute (Stevens, 1946). These levels are hierarchically arranged. It is important to understand not only each level, but also what type of analysis is best suited for each type of data. For researchers, mismatching the analysis and level of measurement is akin to wearing green plaid pants and a purple striped shirt—just don't do it. These levels, and essentially most of the data we will talk about, are in the form of words or numbers, but we do discuss visual and audio data later.

The first level of measurement is nominal. A **nominal scale** is simply a categorization or label. The most defining attribute of nominal data is the fact that no numbers are associated with nominal data, just a label. For example, male and female are labels for two groups within the construct of gender. By assigning a name or label, we have begun to measure. The measurement or labeling can be extended in many directions, and we have done this throughout our lives and continue to do so. Many times, in quantitative datasets, you will see male assigned the number 1 and female assigned the number 2. This is not a description of better or worse by a higher or lower number, it is simply an assignment to ease some analyses in which the researcher is interested.

As another example, suppose we ride the bus to work and want to collect data on the bus riders. We can label them as Regulars, Newcomers, and One Timers. We can further categorize the Regulars as Thursday Night Happy Hour Riders and Friday Escapers. Though the nominal scale is rather limited, it does separate the data in which you are interested into useful, discrete categories that then can be examined.

We could also collect data on gender and bus ridership to answer the research question "Do Regular riders tend to be female?" We can **operationally define** (a set of guidelines for what counts) the construct of Regular rider as a person who rides the 6:45 A.M. 41G bus at least three times a week. Therefore, we need to ride the bus every day the 41G runs. Notice the level of detail we have to add for our operational definition; it is that funneling we described in Chapters 2 and 3. You must pay attention to the details.

Over the next two months, we see that Regulars, based on our definition, tend to be female and One Timers tend to be men. From a descriptive standpoint (see Chapter 9), we would use the **mode** to describe our data and say the most common riders, or highest frequency, are female. This changed, though, over the past few years. As gas prices have dramatically increased, the mode is still female, but not by much. Two days of the week, there are more males, but for Regulars the mode remains in favor of the females.

Ordinal scale measurements can be thought of as a **rank**. Is X greater or less than Y? If the answer is yes, you may have ordered data. This "orderedness" is the defining attribute. When you are asked your level of education (e.g., did you graduate from elementary school, high school, college, graduate school?), you are answering a question from an ordinal scale. This is not a refined scale and is considered a "gross" indicator, which simply means not very detailed or precise. Though this is easy to interpret, when we rank we lose a great deal of information. For example, law schools commonly rank their students. Five students are ranked first through fifth. The first student has a GPA of 3.97, the second 3.95, the third 3.80, the fourth 3.61, and the fifth 3.0. As you can see, the lower the rank the lower the GPA; however, the difference between rank 1 and 2 is not as great as it is between 4 and 5. That loss of information adds some confusion to how to interpret one rank versus another. Is second really that different from first? Is 21st that different from 20th? Maybe not, but one school gets to say it is in the top 20 and the other has to say top 25. **Percentile ranks** are quite common in education, because they are easy to explain to students, parents, teachers, the community, and politicians, and because people can make quick, but usually poor, comparisons.

With ordinal scale data, the typical descriptive statistic (see Chapter 9) is the median score. The **median** is the middle score of the ordered data. For example, if quiz scores are 5, 4, 7, 8, 3, the middle score of the ordered (ranked) data (3, 4, 5, 7, 8) is 5. Inferential statistics are completed using nonparametric analyses (Chapter 9).

Interval scale measurement is ordered and has two defining attributes—the distance between the ordered numbers are the same and a zero point that is arbitrarily set. Test scores are common interval scales. The difference between 90 and 85 is the same distance as 75 and 70, five points. A score of zero is arbitrary because a zero score indicates the student did not get any test questions correct, not that the student necessarily has a complete lack of knowledge. Celsius and Fahrenheit are both interval scales because the zero value of each is arbitrarily set. Zero degrees Celsius is 32 degrees Fahrenheit.

Likert scales (Chapter 6) are a common system used to evaluate teachers, bosses, products, and so on, and typically ask you to respond to a question or statement using the phrases Strongly Disagree to Strongly Agree. Likert scale data is assumed and typically treated as if it were interval data, but that is not necessarily the case (Fox & Jones, 1998). One can consider this data to be ordered categorical data that exists between ordinal and interval data.

Interval data are described with the mean, median, and mode. The **mean** is the mathematical average of the set of scores. For our law school example, the mean GPA would be 3.66. The median is 3.80—the middle score. There is no mode because there is no GPA that occurs more than once, no most-common GPA. In our law school example, we are treating the data as continuous, that is, an infinite number of possible values along a particular continuum. Depending on the number of decimal places we use, there are an infinite number of GPA values. In contrast, discrete variables have a finite or limited number of possible values. If we were to think about our grades on report cards that become GPAs, we are discussing discrete values 4, 3, 2, 1, for A, B, C, D. Again, these are ordered categorical, similar to the Likert scale data.

These three types of data—nominal, ordinal, and interval—are quite common in social science research. Nominal data are discrete categories. Ordinal data are discrete categories that have an order to them (e.g., highest to lowest). Interval data are continuous across the range of possible values. These words are mixed and matched within research studies, and it is important to understand them now because it makes reading and writing easier.

The most defining attributes of a **ratio scale** are equal measurement units *and* an absolute zero. Interval scales have only the equal measurement units. Because ratio data have both of these qualities, they can be multiplied or divided into fractions. Examples of ratio data include height, weight, degrees Kelvin, and velocity. Ratio scales are rare in social science research. Remember that a zero on a test score does not necessarily mean lack of knowledge; it means none of those items were answered correctly.

Table 5.1 summarizes the information above and provides the type of descriptive and inferential statistics used with each scale, along with a generic research question that would drive this type of data scale collection.

QUALITATIVE DATA

Qualitative data are generally non-numeric and categorized as verbal and nonverbal. **Verbal data** are words such as written personal diaries, letters, press reports, surveys or interviews, and field notes. Within the group of interviews, the data can come from in-depth/unstructured interviews, semi-structured interviews, structured interviews, questionnaires containing substantial open comments, and focus groups, for example. **Nonverbal data**, which is more visually based, include items such as student concept maps, kinship diagrams, pictures, video, film, art, genetic code, or print advertisements. The graphical display of quantitative information can be considered nonverbal (see Edward Tufte's work in this area).

Each type of data and the collection process of that data have different strengths and weaknesses in relation to the research questions and analysis techniques. For example, nonparticipant observations from video collected through surveillance cameras potentially allows the researcher to collect data without influence in the field, but there are ethical and privacy concerns of these observations.

TABLE 5.1
Scale type, analysis options, and research question

Scale Name	Other Names Used	Characteristic	Measures	Descriptive Statistics Example	Inferential Statistics Example	Generic Research Question
Nominal (categorical)	Categories and labels	You can tell objects apart using discrete units of categories (e.g., gender, political affiliation)	Measures in terms of names	Mode, frequency, percentage	Chi-square	Which is the most common?
Ordinal (ordered categorical)	Ranks	You can tell if one object is better or smaller (e.g., school rankings)	Measures in terms of more or less than	Median, percentile rank	Rank correlation	Which is first? What is the middle?
Interval (continuous)	Distance	You can tell how far apart objects are (e.g., test scores or temperature)	Measures in terms of equal distances	Mean, median, mode, standard deviation	Pearson product-moment correlation, inferential statistical analyses	What is the average? Are these statistically different?
Ratio	Magnitude of distance	You can tell how big one object is in comparison to another (e.g., velocity)	Measures in terms of equal distances with an absolute zero point	Geometric mean, median, mode, standard deviation	Almost any inferential analysis	What is the average? Are these statistically different?

"SCORE" RELIABILITY AND VALIDITY

Researchers are consistently concerned about the quality of their measurements, their data. Is it any good? Do I trust it? Can I make any good conclusions from the data I have? You have done this, too. Is my car any good? Can I trust it to start? Do I think I can make it across the country without it breaking down? These questions deal with the reliability and validity of your data.

In the traditional model of classical test theory (CTT), researchers must deal with reliability first. **Reliability** is the consistency or stability of the values, test scores, or weight measurement. Another way to examine reliability is to think about how much error is involved in what you observed. Take someone learning to shoot a gun. Most likely the shots will be all over the target, if they hit it at all. If you were doing the shooting, were your shots reliable? There is a great deal of error, as observed by holes splattered everywhere. This is a reliability problem. As you improve, the shots will hopefully become more centered in one area—not necessarily the center (that is accuracy, which is a validity issue). Are your shots reliable? They are if the holes are in about the same spot, if they are consistent over shot/time. Are they where you want them? No, they are up and off to the left or down and to the right, but not the center. You have reliable shooting, but you really have not obtained accuracy yet—that is validity. In CTT, you must have demonstrated reliability before you can even discuss validity. Therefore, you need to develop evidence you can use to support a reliability argument.

Reliability Typologies

Reliability can be nominally categorized into two major typologies: single administrations and multiple administrations. A summary chart is provided in Table 5.2.

Single Administration. A single administration occurs when data from an instrument has been collected once. When data are collected from a one-time administration, you hope that the data is reliable, that those responses are stable or "accurate." With a single administration, the evidence collected is the **internal consistency** score. A **split-half reliability** coefficient, such as the **Kuder-Richardson 20 (KR-20),** can be calculated in order to examine internal consistency (Kuder & Richardson, 1937) for dichotomously scored items such as test items. That coefficient, or value, can then be used as an indicator of the reliability of the *scores* for the sample who answered the questions or responded to statements. The split-half reliability is calculated by examining the response patterns once the scores from the instrument are separated into two groups (e.g., even-numbered items and odd-numbered items). The KR-20 is essentially the average of all the possible split-half coefficients, or values. The KR-21 is a simpler version for easier calculation and is often inappropriately used

TABLE 5.2
Summary of reliability typologies

Administration	Number of Instruments	Method	Purpose	Technique
Once	One	Split-half/internal consistency	Scores from items on an instrument are similar to each other	KR-20/ Cronbach's alpha
	More than one	Equivalence/ alternate forms	Equivalence of multiform instruments	t-test
One performance	Judges' score sheets	Inter-rater	Examine consistency of judges' scores	Agreement such as A/(A+D)
More than once	One	Test-retest stability	Consistency of scores over time	Correlation between test score administrations
	More than one	Stability and equivalence	Consistency of scores over time and equivalence of alternative instruments	Correlation between test score administrations and forms

due to that. The KR-21 cannot be used if the items are from different constructs or domains or if the items have different difficulty values. In general split-half values closer to one provide evidence of score reliability, and those closer to zero imply no score reliability.

Cronbach's alpha, which is a special case of KR-20, is a second technique that can be used to calculate internal consistency evidence (Cronbach, 1951). It does not tell you if you have created evidence for the phenomenon you are interested in (see *construct validity* below; Schmitt, 1996). The values of alpha can be positive or negative. A value of zero indicates no internal consistency, and a value of one would indicate "perfect" internal consistency. A negative value would indicate a problem (yes, this is mathematically possible). You *can* have negative internal consistency values, but if you get this, you should already know you have some investigative work to complete.

Alternate forms reliability is the examination of the relationship between the scores from two different but equivalently designed forms (such as versions A and B) of an instrument that are administered to only one group. For example, you create two forms, A and B, of a mathematical literacy scale that are same in every way except for the specific information within the individual items. For example, in question 1, you ask elementary students to solve "23 * 47 = "; and in the alternate question, you ask them to solve "34 * 53 = . " Typically, we counterbalance the administration where some of the participants complete Form A and then Form B and the others answer Form B and then Form A.

Each form is administered once and the scores from the forms can be examined with a **correlation**, that is, the relationship between the two scores.. A correlation value close to one would indicate that the alternate form scores appear to be reliable. A correlation value of zero would indicate that they are not. If you are unfamiliar with correlations, see Chapter 9. A correlation value of negative one would indicate that the scores are functioning in completely opposite patterns. If you scored very well on one form, you would score horribly on the other! Note that you can also complete a paired *t*-test or correlation to explore for a difference in the alternate forms.

Inter-rater reliability is examining the consistency of raters watching or grading some phenomenon. The history of scores for Olympic ice skating is a good analogy for discussing inter-rater reliability. We can tell you that unless they fall or stumble, we would score them all as perfect. We have no real business being judges, but we *can* judge the consistency of the scores. In the 1970s and 1980s at the height of the Cold War, the scores for ice skating were not consistent across judges (Weekley & Gier, 1989).

More recently, is there high inter-rater reliability across judges for *Dancing with the Stars* or *American Idol*? One judge may be consistent across time—Paula seemed to love everyone—but are they consistent across each other? One way to calculate this reliability is to determine the number of times the judges agree and disagree, and then divide the number of agreements by the number of agreements and disagreements (A/A+D). Two other methods are calculating the correlations between the judges' scores and the intra-class correlation.

In education, we have this same problem when judging the performances of students and teachers. What identifies exemplary teaching? An amazing amount of detailed work has been completed through the National Board of Professional Teaching Standards, but more is needed to accurately measure and identify varying levels of teaching quality, not just excellence.

Multiple Administrations.   Multiple administrations occur when data from an instrument have been collected multiple times. If the same instrument is administered more than once, then we are interested in the stability of the scores. Are the scores the same over time, given that no intervention has occurred? By no intervention, we mean that nothing happens between the first administration and the next administration that could "cause" those scores to change, such as teaching or studying. Many multiple administration studies are hoping for a change, but in this instance, we want the scores to stay the same over time so we can measure the stability of the scores, their reliability. To examine score stability, a **test-retest method** is used with a correlation between the two groups of scores. A correlation of one would indicate perfect stability. Don't plan on seeing that, however, as all instruments have measurement error that will cause scores to fluctuate. Two types of this error are controllable and uncontrollable. You have control over the quality of the items and format of the instrument. You do not have control over temperature of the room, fire alarms, pen ink leaking everywhere, or participant anxiety.

If you have two or more versions or forms of an instrument and administer them more than once, you are trying to provide evidence for stability and equivalence. **Stability,** as stated above, is the examination of the consistency of scores over multiple administrations. **Equivalence** is the testing of the consistency of the scores from alternate forms over multiple administrations. For example, you create two versions of a test for your class, Form A and Form B. Again, we counterbalance the administration where some of the group members get Form A and then Form B (AB), some get Form B and then Form A (BA), some get Form A and then Form A again (AA), and the rest answer Form B and then Form B again (BB). You administer the test and then calculate the correlations between the test counterbalance patterns. Patterns AA and BB test stability and patterns BA and AB test equivalence. Positive correlation values near one indicate that if you scored well on one form, you scored well on the other form and provide evidence of equivalence.

Validity Typologies

Validity is one of the most misunderstood concepts in research design. We provide this example to students: We can develop a test with questions concerning Advanced Placement Calculus and administer it to you. We are confident that the scores will be reliable, but they are not valid for the purpose of deciding what you learned in a research methods course. At its core, **validity** is an inference made from the data collected from instruments (Messick, 1989). Like reliability, you are developing an argument with validity evidence so that the reader agrees with your inferences.

Face validity provides a very low level of evidence for making inferences. Essentially, face validity occurs if the questions or statements on the instrument appear to be related to the phenomenon of interest. If we look at an English literature exam, for example, we would not expect to see financial accounting questions on it.

Content validity is the extent to which the items on the data collection instrument are sampling the content area or domain of interest in a representative manner. A data collection instrument has high content validity when it reflects the content of interest. An exam, for example, has a high level of content validity if the questions are sampled from and clearly reflect the domain and the responses clearly require skills and knowledge from the domain. An exam for a 20th-century history course that has questions from 18th-century Europe would fail a content validity review.

Construct validity is the extent to which the data collection instrument provides scores that can be used to make inferences about a construct. Constructs cannot be directly observed (that is, they are latent), and as such, the responses to items are used to make inferences about the construct. Achievement, IQ, and love cannot be observed directly, but we collect observable data from instruments or behaviors and make inferences. Items from a test may all appear to have content validity (see previous discussion) and you may have gone through the necessary steps to demonstrate content validity (see Crocker & Algina, 1986), but testing the *construct validity* may indicate that there are more than one constructs being measured. Therefore, construct validity, like all the other validities, is a procedure not an enduring trait.

The traditional testing of construct validity includes the correlation between the instrument of interest and a previously develop instrument or the instrument and a performance. For example, IQ score and job performance is a common combination in both the research literature and the popular media. A second technique, **differentiation between groups**, is the examination of different groups in relation to scores on the instrument. If you expect two groups to score differently in relation to the construct, they can be used to test that difference. For a second language fluency test, you would expect those who have studied the second language to perform at a higher level than those who have not studied it.

Factor analysis is a third technique used to examine whether the underlying construct or constructs are observed within the intercorrelations of the item responses. If you develop several items about "liking snow," you would expect the analysis to indicate that there is one "factor," liking snow. If the items cluster together on more than one factor, problems providing evidence of construct validity exist for a single construct, "liking snow." Note that using Cronbach's alpha does not provide evidence that you have identified a unidimensional latent construct (one factor; Schmitt, 1996). That is, it is not a test of homogeneity of items; it is a test of interrelatedness of items. Scores from a set of items can have a high internal consistency value, yet have multiple latent constructs as Schmitt (1996) clearly demonstrates.

The fourth technique is the **multitrait-multimethod approach**. This approach is composed of convergent and discriminant validation. **Convergent validation** occurs when correlations between instruments measuring the same construct but using different methods are examined. **Discriminant validation** occurs in two patterns. In the first pattern, a correlation between different constructs using the same method of measurement (a Happy Scale and a Sad Scale both using a Likert-type scale) is calculated after respondents have completed both scales. In the second, a correlation between different constructs using different measurement methods is examined. For convergent validation, the correlations should be high; for discriminant validation, the correlations should be small.

Concurrent and predictive validities are the two types of criterion validity. **Criterion validity** concerns whether the respondents' scores meet some level of performance. **Concurrent validation** occurs when the relationship between performance on two or more instruments or tests given at the same time are examined. For example, a paper test on driving is followed immediately by an actual driving test, and those scores are examined. A positive correlation would be evidence of concurrent validity. **Predictive validation** occurs when one instrument is used in an attempt to predict measurements to be taken in the future. For example, the Law School Admissions Test (LSAT) could be examined in relation to the scores on the Multistate Bar Exam (MBE) to see whether the LSAT predicts the scores on the MBE; that is, if students pass the bar exam.

When collecting data using instruments that participants complete, especially belief- or attitude-based instruments, you are asking a participant to self-report about that phenomenon. With respect to reliable and valid scores, self-report is a major concern, especially with social bias. **Social bias** occurs when a participant provides a response that would be valued by the researcher or society, but is not a true reflection of that person's beliefs or behaviors. In the larger picture, that type of response is introducing error into the data, decreasing the quality of the data, and decreasing the validity of the inferences that are made from the data.

AERA/APA/NCME GUIDELINES

The American Educational Research Association (AERA), American Psychological Association (APA), and the National Council on Measurement in Education (NCME) state that you must provide evidence of the reliability and validity of the scores from the instruments you use *from your study* and that you must provide reliability evidence for subscores (AERA/APA/NCME, 1999; Wilkinson & the Task Force on Statistical Inference, 1999). You can report the evidence for reliability and validity from previous studies and the instrument manuals, but you *must* report the reliability and validity evidence for your data.

DEVELOPED INSTRUMENTS

Previously published instruments are quite popular with students and researchers because they save a great deal of time and other resources. The down side is that they may not exactly match the operational definition of your latent construct. Another issue is that reliability and validity evidence have to be reexamined after each administration. The previously developed instrument may have a long track record of high reliability values over several studies and years, but that does not guarantee that you will also obtain high reliability values from your scores. This is especially important when an instrument is administered to a different population than in previous research. This issue becomes even more precarious with translated instruments. As we have stated, just because high internal consistency values were observed once does not mean they will be observed the next 1,000 times; those values could fluctuate every administration (Vaacha-Haase, 1998). In addition to obtaining this information through your literature search, you can find reliability and validity information on instruments in such books as:

- *Mental Measurement Yearbooks (Buros Institute)*
- *Communication Research Measures: A Sourcebook*
- *Socioemotional Measures for Preschool and Kindergarten Children: A Handbook*
- *Handbook for Measurement and Evaluation in Early Childhood Education*
- *Dictionary of Behavioral Assessment Techniques*
- *Research Instruments in Social Gerontology*
- *Tests in Print VII*
- Online resources
  - American Psychological Association (www.apa.org)
  - Buros Institute Test Reviews Online (www.unl.edu/buros)

RELIABILITY AND VALIDITY OF QUALITATIVE RESEARCH

Qualitative researchers discuss reliability and validity in terms of believability. Interestingly, this is what quantitative researchers also mean. Because of the different types that have permeated the language in quantitative research, the concept of believability got lost in the mix. When we read a qualitative-based study, we commonly look to see whether our head is rising up and down or left and right. It is our behavioral believability check. A colleague remarked that this behavior was a "phenomenological nod"—that the authors may have "really gotten it."

The question must be asked, "Is reliability and validity even a proper topic for qualitative research?" Some argue that these two constructs are not useful topics in qualitative research and that discussing them makes qualitative try to "act" like quantitative for acceptance. We understand that argument and agree with it on many levels, but we look at reliability and validity discussions in qualitative research as part of our rhetorical persuasion to guide the reader to a certain understanding of the phenomenon or situation at hand. We feel that the concept of reliability is pertinent to qualitative data (Madill, Jordan, & Shirley, 2000). The reader must trust the narrative we are writing based on our observations (Eisenhart & Howe, 1992; Lincoln & Guba, 1985). If they do not believe us, then we have failed.

Qualitative Reliability and Validity

Inter-rater checks are the extent to which two or more observers "see" or "hear" the same or similar thing. To see really poor inter-rater reliability, go to a museum and listen to people discuss the artwork.

IN-TEXT ACTIVITY

To experience inter-rater reliability or inter-rater checks, go to the Louvre Web site (http://www.louvre.fr/llv/commun/home.jsp?bmLocale=en) and pick four paintings or sculptures and rank them on personal likeability. Next, ask your classmates or friends to do the same. How many times do you and a friend agree? How many times do you disagree? The agreement most likely is quite low. For a good example of poor inter-rater reliability and differing operational definition of a latent construct in a children's book, see *Seen Art?* by Jon Scieszka and Lane Smith.

Diachronic analysis refers to the stability of an observation through time and is similar to multiple administrations of the same test (test-retest reliability) in quantitative research. The greatest problem is that the observations must remain stable over time in an ever-changing world. We tend to watch preservice counselors or teachers over time to see whether the same professional behaviors remain, but they change. The change can be good; for instance, they are more nuanced in their approach and become more effective. Other times, the change is not good. **Synchronic analysis** refers to the similarity of observations within a given time period. This does not mean a perfect replication but the observer sees consistency. **Trustworthiness** is based on the criteria and methodological procedures for determining whether a naturalistic investigation can be trusted (Lincoln & Guba, 1985). The greater the degree of detail and procedural clarity, the more one will be likely to trust the data collected and the inferences drawn from that data. The trustworthiness of a study can be separated into credibility, transferability, dependability, and confirmability.

Credibility is similar to experimental internal validity (Chapter 7) and concerns how close the researcher's representation and the participants' views are in concert. If the researcher provides evidence of this, such as "member checks" where the researcher asks the participant to review his or her inferences, then some assurance is provided. **Transferability,** analogous to external validity in experimental research, is the concern with case-to-case transfer. The researcher must provide enough information on the case studies so that a reader can judge the similarity with another case. **Dependability** occurs when you have provided enough information so that the process of your research study is logical, traceable, and documentable to the reader. This provides your readers the ability to attempt to replicate if desired. **Confirmability** is the notion that you as the researcher provide evidence that can be examined; that you are not simply making it all up like Alfred Dieck. Researchers who work on the bog people had to conclude that the late archeologist Alfred Dieck faked a large number of the 1,800 bog people cases he researched (van der Sanden, & Eisenbeiss, 2006). Behavior such as this not only causes problems for your career, but also is a violation of every research organization's code of ethics, and in the long-run it damages and delays the advancement of the domain of interest you wanted to study.

Triangulation is a methodological procedure for arguing that the criteria of validity, good inference making, has been met. By using multiple pieces of evidence, the researcher can check the integrity or quality of the inferences being made. As Schwandt (1997) wrote, "The central point of the procedure is to examine a single social phenomenon from more than one vantage point" (p. 163). Triangulation provides three pieces of evidence: **convergence**— agreement across data types; **inconsistency**—disagreements across data types; and **contradiction**—different inferences across data types (Denzin, 1978). It is important for the young researcher to realize that multiple pieces of data may lead to no triangulated theme and that the lack of consensus may be more important than the original desired consensus. In addition to triangulation, peer review of your data and participant reading of your inferences are some of the ways to increase the validity of your data. These topics are typically discussed in the analysis component of qualitative work, but they are fundamentally reliability and validity components. Finally, **auditing** your work using such strategies (Chapter 10) as negative case analysis, thick description, peer debriefing, feedback from others, and respondent validation will increase the believability of your research to the reader and the research community as a whole.

Providing evidence of the quality of your data is a crucial component of research. Everything we measure has measurement error associated with it. The official U.S. atomic clock is not even perfect. The National Bureau of Standards has to add a second to the clock about every 100 years. When you fail to take adequate steps in determining the reliability of your data, you not only introduce error into your statistical analysis or written narratives, but also decrease the reader's belief in you work and your ability to make valid arguments. A common mistake made in manuscripts submitted to journals is the failure to discuss the quality of the data and the process used for determining that quality.

CASE STUDY

Ginette is not too concerned about score reliability for the experimental component of her first study with the undergraduate students. The graphs they will see and be asked questions about will be scored the same way and could even be scored by a machine, given the resources. She is most concerned with the open-ended responses (Chapter 6) for both studies. That data scoring will take more planning and some more reading about how others have handled this issue.

The experimental stimuli (the graphical displays) are another issue. For the undergraduates, she wanted to have the students view them on a computer and then answer questions, but that is not how the stimuli will be displayed in the second study. What was nice about the computer was that the stimuli would be seen exactly the same way—light intensity, color, and so on—for each participant. With paper, she is concerned about the quality of the graphs over time and multiple printings. It is a small detail, but is important to deal with as a potential problem that could affect the quality of the responses.

She is also concerned that the inferences she makes from the open-ended responses cannot be checked by the participants and will need to rely on a colleague to review what she has done. It would be too resource intensive to keep track of participants in the second study. The first is possible (having the undergraduate students return for a follow up) but it is still problematic.

ARMCHAIR MOMENT

Jim recently heard Lloyd Bond and Lee Shulman discuss a story about Lee Cronbach concerning reliability and validity and the National Board for Professional Teaching Standards assessments. Dr. Cronbach told them to figure out the assessment (data collection instrument) you want to use and then let him work on the reliability and validity. Don't corrupt the process by choosing the instrument based on desired reliability scores. If you want a portfolio assessment, then design it and test it and work on the score reliability of it.

This is important. Decide what you want, then work on the reliability and validity scores. You may come to see that there are some instruments you want and some you don't want. But do not say, "I am going to go this route because this instrument has a previous reliability or validity score that is good based on past studies." Make sure it really does match what you need. Remember that score reliability and validity need to be reexamined every time.

The believability of the data is one of the first items we look at when we read a manuscript. Jim developed this habit when he was working with Dr. Raymond Kulhavy, who was editor of *Contemporary Educational Psychology* at the time. At one point, Dr. Kulhavy gave Jim a manuscript to read and critique. As he began reading, he realized that the authors did not know what they had from a quality standpoint. Jim walked into Dr. Kulhavy's office and said, "I have no idea if they have cumin or coriander. This is a mess. If I believe this data, then this is really important, but there is no evidence provided so that I can believe it. This reads as if they had data and they analyzed it."

Another issue we run into as journal editors is a misalignment between the operational definition or research questions and the instrument used, actually, the items on the instrument. For example, the author spends a great deal of time discussing a specific aspect of motivation in relation to learning in a specific content area and properly cites well-regarded studies. The research question typically is some aspect of the relationship between motivation and learning in the content area, but the items on the instrument deal with generic academic motivation and learning in general. We see this more often than we expect. If you are a true scholar and working hard to be cognizant of every detail, you should not miss something like this. The items on the instrument need to match the phenomenon you are investigating and the literature you are reviewing.

If there is an instrument you have seen several times in your reading, or one you are interested in, go find out as much as you can about reliability and validity data from articles or one of the yearbooks. Write the information below; we have provided some space, but you may need more. As you search, you might be amazed by how much is out there or shocked by how little.

Name of instrument _____

Author(s) of instrument _____

Year first used _____

Reliability

Type _____ Value _____

Validity

Type _____ Value _____

KEY WORDS

alternate forms
  reliability
auditing
concurrent validation
confirmability
construct validity
content validity
contradiction
convergence
convergent validation
correlation
credibility
criterion validity
Cronbach's alpha
Dependability
diachronic analysis
differentiation between
  groups
discriminant validation

equivalence
face validity
factor analysis
inconsistency
internal consistency
inter-rater checks
inter-rater reliability
interval scale
Kuder–Richardson 20
  (KR-20)
levels of measurement
Likert scale
mean
median
mode
multiple administrations
multitrait-multimethod
  approach
nominal scale

nonverbal data
operationally define
ordinal scale
percentile rank
predictive validation
rank
ratio scale
reliability
single administration
social bias
split-half reliability
stability
synchronic analysis
test-retest method
transferability
triangulation
trustworthiness
validity
verbal data

REFERENCES AND FURTHER READINGS

Aiken, L. S., West, S. G., Sechrest, L., Reno, R. R., with Roediger, H. L., Scarr, S., Kazdin, A. E., & Sherman, S. J. (1990). Graduate training in statistics, methodology, and measurement in psychology. *American Psychologist, 45,* 721–734.

American Educational Research Association, American Psychological Association, & National Council on Measurement in Education. (1999). *Standards for educational and psychological testing* (Rev. ed.). Washington: American Educational Research Association.

Crocker, L., & Algina, J. (1986). *Introduction to classical and modern test theory.* New York: Hold, Rinehart, and Winston.

Cronbach, L. J. (1951). Coefficient alpha and the internal structure of tests. *Psychometrika, I ft*, 297–334.

Denzin, N. K. (1978). *The research act: A theoretical introduction to sociological methods.* New York: Praeger.

Eisenhart, M. A., & Howe K. R. (1992). Validity in educational research. In M. D. LeCompte, W. L. Millroy, & J. Preissle (Eds.), *The handbook of qualitative research in education* (pp. 643–680). San Diego, CA: Academic Press. (Note that this is a good handbook to personally own.)

Fox, C. M., & Jones, J. A. (1998). Uses of Rasch modeling in counseling psychology research. *Journal of Counseling Psychology, 45*(1), 30–45.

Kuder, G. F., & Richardson, M. W. (1937). The theory of the estimation of test reliability. *Psychometrika, 2*, 151–160.

Lincoln, Y. S., & Guba, E. G. (1985). *Naturalistic inquiry.* Thousand Oaks, CA: SAGE Publications.

Madill, A., Jordan, A., & Shirley, C. (2000). Objectivity and reliability in qualitative analysis: Realist, contextualist and radical constructionist epistemologies. *The British Journal of Psychology, 91*, 1–20.

Messick, S. (1989). Meaning and values in test validation: The science and ethics of assessment. *Educational Researcher, 18*(2), 5–11.

Onwuegbuzie, A. J., & Leech. N. L. (2005). On becoming a pragmatic researcher. The importance of combining quantitative and qualitative research methodologies. *International Journal of Research Methodology, 8*(5), 375–387.

Schmitt, N. (1996). Uses and abuses of coefficient alpha. *Psychological Assessment, 8*(4), 350–353.

Schwandt, T. (1997). *Qualitative inquiry: A dictionary of terms.* Thousand Oaks, CA: SAGE Publications.

Sears, S. D. (1997). *A monetary history of Iraq and Iran* (unpublished doctoral dissertation). Chicago: University of Chicago.

Stamp, J. (1929). *Some economic factors in modern life.* London: P. S. King and Son.

Stevens, S. S. (1946). On the theory of scales of measurement. *Science, 103*, 677–680.

Vaacha-Haase, T. (1998). Reliability generalization: Exploring variance in measurement error affecting score reliability across studies. *Educational and Psychological Measurement, 58*, 6–20.

van der Sanden, W. A. B., Eisenbeiss, S. (2006). Imaginary people—Alfred Dieck and the bog bodies of northwest Europe. *Archaologisches Korrespondenzblatt, 36*(1), 111–122.

Weekley, J. A., & Gier, J. A. (1989). Ceilings in the reliability and validity of performance ratings: The case of expert raters. *The Academy of Management Journal, 32*(1), 213–222.

Wilkinson, L., & The Task Force on Statistical Inference. (1999). Statistical methods in psychology journals: Guidelines and explanations. *American Psychologist, 54*, 594–604.

CHAPTER 6

Instruments and Collection

SURVEYS, QUESTIONNAIRES, INTERVIEWS, AND FIELD NOTES

KEY IDEA

To be or not be the instrument.

POINTS TO KNOW

Understand the types of content.

Understand the different types of instruments.

Understand the basics of instrument design.

Understand the different ways to scale the instrument.

Understand the different methods of data collection.

Understand the different types of instruments.

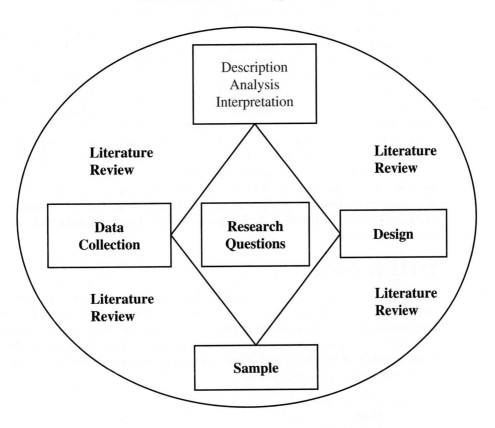

HOW SHOULD I COLLECT DATA?

You need to start making some decisions about how you are going to collect your data. This includes the instruments you will use, such as a survey or yourself, and the tactic for actual collection, such as in person or over the telephone. There are tradeoffs for each type of instrument and tactic. Again, you will be making subjective decisions regarding much of this topic. For example, when Jim studied how people read maps, the choice of map and how much information to put on that map at first was a subjective decision. No mathematical algorithm gave him an exact number.

This chapter covers the major types of instrument designs and data collection tactics. The combination of this chapter and Chapter 5 provide the foundation for data collection. This chapter is not all encompassing. Your research questions and the sample you desire will greatly affect what type of instrument you use, the length of the instrument, the use of multiple instruments, and the analyses possible with the data actually collected. We have previously discussed reliability and validity (i.e., believability), but it is imperative that those concepts and their definitions are in your thoughts as you decide about instrumentation.

Depending on your research questions and study goals, data collection—that is, the use of some instrument to collect data—falls essentially into two categories: you as the instrument or something else (e.g., paper, video camera, PDA) as the instrument. You can also separate instruments into two more categories: those that have been previously prepared and used or a new one developed by you.

We cannot state more bluntly that the *a priori* development of a quality instrument takes time and thought. More studies have collapsed due to poor instrument design than there are printed pages to describe them. A poor instrument will lead to poor data, and as we stated in Chapter 5, you cannot recover from bad data. Below we briefly discuss the common types of instruments that can be used for a research study. We do not provide the rich detail you need to properly develop an instrument. There are books to do that and we suggest that you read a few of them; see the references at the end of the chapter (e.g., Colton & Covert, 2007; Dillman, Smyth, & Christian, 2009; Groves, Fowler, Couper, Lepkowski, Singer, & Tourangeau, 2009).

TYPES OF CONTENT

There are four core types of content that interest social science researchers: demographic, knowledge, behavioral, attitudinal. **Demographic content** asks the respondent (sometimes you) about your background and other aspects of your life, such as gender (male/female), socioeconomic status, job description, education level, number of children, and home ownership, to name a few. In general, the content is formatted similar to this:

> What is your gender?
> ◦ Male
> ◦ Female

Do you have any children?
  - Yes
  - No

What category is your education level in?
  - High school equivalent
  - High school degree
  - Associate degree
  - Bachelor degree
  - Graduate degree

How much do you spend a week on groceries?
  - <$50
  - $50–$100
  - $101–$150
  - $151–200
  - $200

Knowledge content concerns information you know or skills you possess in a particular area (Mertens, 2005). Knowledge questions are quite common on school-based instruments, but can be found in many other domains, such as marketing research. For example:

Please explain the difference between LCD and plasma screen technology.
True or False: The equation for the circumference of a circle is πr^2.
Describe the proper technique for priming a PVC pipe.

Behavioral content typically refers to how often you exhibit a behavior or engage in an activity. Two examples appear below:

How often do you shop at the grocery store?
  - Every day
  - 2–3 times a week
  - Once a week
  - 2–3 times a month
  - Once a month

How much do you study for Class Z in a week?
  - I do not study for this class
  - < 1 hour
  - 1–3 hours
  - 4–6 hours
  - 6 hours

Attitudinal content seeks to determine your current mood, attitude, or long-term belief of some phenomenon or issue. These questions are often formatted to have a range of agreeability options—that is, how much you agree or disagree. In several instances, researchers are interested in whether you endorse or do not endorse an idea even when "agree and disagree" language is used. For example:

The federal government interferes in my daily life too much.
- ○ Strongly Agree
- ○ Agree
- ○ Disagree
- ○ Strongly Disagree

Cable television is just having to pay to watch commercials.
- ○ Strongly Agree
- ○ Agree
- ○ Disagree
- ○ Strongly Disagree

BASICS OF INSTRUMENT CONSTRUCTION

Instrument, questionnaire, and *survey* appear to us to be used interchangeably in the literature and we are guilty of this. Specifically, an **instrument** is anything used to collect data. You could be the instrument through observing and memorizing what is occurring or through writing information down on note cards or field notes. Or you could be administering a test or survey, or having students use personal digital assistants (PDAs). A telephone interview protocol is also a type of instrument. Video recorders, tape machines, and digital video recorders can be data collection instruments. **Questionnaires** are a type of instrument for collecting data where the goal is to look for differences—that is, **variability**—in responses across groups of people. If everyone had the same response, or you believed they would, there is no reason to collect the data. **Surveys**, such as a population census, are designed for descriptive purposes—to observe the current state of the phenomenon.

On a questionnaire you can ask a variety of **questions** or have participants reading your instrument reply or react to **statements**. For example:

A. Do you believe that facts do not change over time?

versus

B. Facts are unchanging.

1 = Agree; 2 = Somewhat Agree; 3 = Somewhat Disagree; 4 = Disagree

The question or statement can be considered open ended or close ended. **Open-ended questions** allow the participant to write, type, or vocalize an extended response such as version A above. Another open-ended example appears below:

How often would you say you read the news on a Web site?

A **closed-ended question** forces the participants to choose among specific responses. For example:

Do you read the daily news from a Web site? Circle one.

Yes   No

How often would you say you read the news on a Web site? Circle one.
> More than once a day
> Once a day
> A few times a week
> Once a week
> A few times a month
> Once a month

Note that these can be rewritten as statements, such as:

> I read the newspaper daily.
> I read the news on the Internet.

Checklists are closed-ended instruments where a respondent is typically marking whether a behavior or attribute is present. Below is an example of a moving-home checklist:

- Day Before Move
  - Transfer bank accounts.
  - Empty water hoses.
  - Defrost refrigerator and freezer; remember to leave doors open.
  - Disconnect major appliances and remove them for move.
  - Pack items you are putting in your car away from other boxes.
  - Check and confirm arrival of moving company.
  - Disassemble bed last.

Checklists can also be used to make sure that the data from your study is collected properly. For example:

- Each survey reviewed for grammar and spelling.
- Each survey printed X number of times.
- Survey packets combined in random order of completion.

You can mix not only the types of questions or statements on any instrument, but also whether they are open and closed. You can have a variety of numeric and non-numeric responses from participants. Do not think that because you are using one type, you cannot add another. Different types of questions and statements can help you answer your questions because the different types of data can be triangulated toward one inference.

When you are creating items for a survey, questionnaire, or interview protocol, you cannot include every item. We sample from the population of items we could ask. The words we choose to use are also a sample of the words possible. We highlight this sampling issue again because sampling is all around, from the questions we choose to investigate (we can't research them all at once) to the words we use (we can't use them all) to the types and amount of data we choose to collect (we can't collect it all). Each choice you make has strengths and weaknesses, will increase or decrease error, and will ultimately affect the believability of your research.

INSTRUMENT DESIGN

The design process of instrumentation has several components that must be carefully considered. Designing your own instrument is popular with students and is perceived as quite easy. However, designing a good instrument is difficult and time consuming if you engage in the task as a scholar. During the design phase, you are balancing the physical layout, the actual behavioral response you want participants to make, and which types of questions or statements are best for the information desired. This is why we stated earlier that the process is subjective. You have to make decisions, and with decisions come tradeoffs and compromises. Below we discuss a few main components that must be considered.

Clarity refers to the discrepancy between how the respondent interprets the question or statement and your intention. For example, you may think that praising someone after he or she does a good job is important, and you create the statement "After he does well, say 'good boy'" as one indicator of praise. However, when the respondent reads that statement, she thinks of her dog and not of working with a person, and she does not endorse it/agree with it. The larger issue is that the respondent does endorse the use of praise, and now you have reliability and validity issues. The reliability issue concerns the fact that if you wrote the statement differently, you would obtain a different response; and the validity issue is that your interpretation of the current response will be incorrect.

Negatively worded statements are popular because researchers are trying to control "response sets" from the participants. A response set occurs when a participant intentionally or unintentionally creates a pattern to his or her responses, such as choosing Strongly Agree every time or C on a multiple-choice test. Many instruments have statements or questions that are all positively worded, which allows the respondent to choose one of the categories quickly without reading the statements. A positively worded statement from a course evaluation may look like this:

I learned a great deal of information in this course.

A negatively worded version would look like this:

I did not learn very much in this course.

Researchers have historically inserted negatively worded items to identify potential response sets. The problems with positive and negative wording have been previously noted (Weems, Onwuegbuzie, Schreiber, & Eggers, 2003; Yamaguchi, 1997). Weems et al. (2003) observed that responses to the positively worded items yielded statistically significantly higher means than did responses to the negatively worded items. Yamaguchi (1997) observed with a survey of clients about their therapist that negatively worded items are easy to deny, or not agree with, whereas positively worded items were harder to endorse, or agree with. The calculated reliability values from this data related to positively and negatively worded items indicated a response bias.

Instrument length must be considered from a participant fatigue, cost, and usefulness perspective. Fatigue occurs when the instrument is too long and participants refuse to respond or stop responding. Nonresponse is a serious issue from a standpoint of both obtaining an appropriate sample and missing data, because it affects your analysis phase (see Allison, 2001; Little & Rubin, 2002). As a survey increases in length, the likelihood of the participant completing the survey decreases. This obviously is worse as the distance between you and the respondent increases. We have been mailed, called, or sent via e-mail many surveys and have not completed the survey due to length. One survey was extremely long, with over 200 closed- and open-ended items. The cost of survey distribution is not just financial, but also time. E-mail and Web-based surveys greatly reduce the financial cost, but many people do not respond. Therefore, you need to balance the length of instrument, the costs, and the potential response rate.

To increase response rates, incentives are quite common now, especially at checkout aisles in retail stores. At the end of the receipt, the company will offer a chance to win cash, products, or a discount on your next purchase if you complete an online survey.

The **format** of your instrument has two main components: the physical layout and how the participants will respond. The physicality of the instrument, even online, has to make completing the instrument easier and not harder. Is it easy to read? Easy to answer the questions? Is there enough space between items? How much of a tradeoff for space to write and production/copying costs is needed? These are all important questions to work through during the design of a survey *and* even choosing a previously developed instrument (see Chapter 5).

The behavior the participants must physically complete after reading or listening to the content is the other consideration. Some of the questions to think about are:

1. Will the participants circle their responses?
2. Will they simply check a box?
3. Will they fill in a bubble (now sometimes a rectangle)?
4. Will they use a computer by clicking, accessing pull-down windows, or typing?
5. Will they be verbally stating their response? If so, how much time is enough?
6. How long or large will the open-ended response section be?

Teachers are notoriously bad at leaving space for the different hand-writing sizes of students.

The order of questions or statements, **ordering**, can ease completion of the instrument or create massive problems. For knowledge- and attitude-based content, you do not want the response to one item to influence the response to the next item. You want each response to be independent of the other responses even when you are looking for similar responses among items. You can randomize the order in an attempt to avoid this problem. If you are using multiple instruments that have similar content, you can counterbalance the instrument administration. **Counterbalancing** occurs when two or more instruments are completed in different orders by the participants. For example, you want students to complete happiness and sadness instruments. The counterbalancing would have one-half of the participants take the happiness scale first and then the sadness scale. The second half of the participants would complete the sadness scale first.

Finally, **instructions** to the respondent need to be clear *to the respondent*, not just you. Ask yourself: Are they informative for the whole instrument? Do you need different instructions for different sections? Can this be completed without assistance? Examining the instructions from a task analysis perspective is helpful here. A **task analysis** examines each step needed to complete a given task.

IN-TEXT ACTIVITY

As a classroom exercise, many people have participated in a task analysis on making a peanut butter and jelly sandwich or how to tie your shoes. Write down each step and then ask a child to read and follow the instructions. See what happens! Another way to handle the instructions is to have a friend who is not a researcher attempt to complete the instrument without your assistance.

_____

_____

_____

_____

_____

_____

SCALING

On instruments, **scaling** is the assignment of numbers to statements based on a rule system (Stevens, 1946). Therefore, scaling is a set of procedures we use to obtain something meaningful from which we can make inferences. The response scale is the collection of responses from participants, such as true or false.

Thurstone Scaling

Thurstone (1929) was the first to develop a scaling procedure. His work led to three types of unidimensional scales: equal-appearing intervals, successive intervals, and paired comparisons (Thurstone & Chave, 1929). Unidimensional refers to measuring only one construct or idea at a time. **Equal-appearing intervals** is the most common and the simplest to implement, and we provide a basic example below. For equal-appearing intervals, first define the area in which you are interested, such as enjoyment of LEGO building bricks. Next, decide whether you want statements or questions. For our example, let us use the following statements:

LEGO bricks are fun to play with.
LEGO bricks are only for little kids.
Building with LEGO bricks is an art form.
Building with LEGO bricks is relaxing.
LEGO bricks are great because you can take them apart and build something new.

Next, you need to develop a large number of statements, around 100, because you are going to select the final scale items from the developed item pool after judges rate the items from 1 to 11, where 1 is least favorable toward LEGO bricks and 11 is most favorable. You can complete the reverse of this and rank as most unfavorable to most favorable. Remember the key is for the judges to rate the item in reference to the scale and not whether they endorse the item or agree with the item.

Once you have the judges' responses, plot each item and obtain the median, values for quartiles one and three, and the interquartile range (see Chapter 9). Once you have these values, you need to order the items based on their median score. What you can do now is choose one to two questions (or more) from each median category (e.g., 1, 2, 3, 4, ... 9, 10, 11) that has a low interquartile range (the closer to zero the better); that is, a small value for the interquartile range indicates that the judges appear to agree. Finally, look at the chosen items. Are there any that are confusing or would be difficult to interpret? If so, choose the next best item from that median category. Finally, choose the scale response you want, such as an agree/disagree system, format the instrument, and administer. In this case, we recommend a pilot test of the instrument with a few conveniently available participants or a full formal pilot test.

Successive intervals is based on having participants place each statement from a group of statements on a continuum that has equally spaced intervals ranging from low strength of sentiment to high (Thurstone & Chave, 1929). **Paired comparisons** asks judges to examine all possible pairs of statements, such as crimes, and judge which is the most serious (Thurstone, 1929).

Guttman Scaling

Guttman scaling is also known as **cumulative scaling** or **scalogram analysis**. **Guttman scaling** is a procedure for developing a one-dimensional continuum for a construct. Guttman (1950) argued for a common content (one-dimensional) scale whereby if a respondent agreed or endorsed an extreme statement, that respondent should endorse every less extreme statement on the instrument. In general, the goal is to obtain items so that if a respondent agrees with one item, he or she also agrees with all the previous items. As with the Thurstone scaling process, we need to choose

TABLE 6.1
Example of Guttman judges' scores

Judge	Item Number				
	1	2	3	4	5
1	y	y	y	y	y
2	y	y	y	y	y
3	y	y	y	n	y

a topic area, develop statements, and have them judged. During the judging, the response scale is simply a yes or no on favorability to the concept (e.g., enjoy LEGO bricks). The judges are deciding whether the statement is related to the concept or construct. Once the judges' yes/no responses are completed, create a spreadsheet of judges by items. Then sort the judges based on those who agreed with the most statements at the top and those who agreed with the fewest statements at the bottom. Next, examine the agreements by consistency. For example, in Table 6.1, judges 1 and 2 agree with all items, but judge 3 did not agree with item 4. That disagreement for item 4 is an inconsistency. With a few items, this is easy; with a large number of items, you need to complete a *scalogram analysis* to determine the best pool of items. The best pool will consist of items with the fewest inconsistencies among judges. Once you have your items, either by hand or scalogram analysis, choose a final pool. Once you have the pool, ask people to simply respond whether they agree or disagree.

Likert Scale

The **Likert scale** (Likert, 1932a) is quite popular due to the ease of use (Edwards & Kenney, 1946). You do not need to develop hundreds of items, and you do not have to worry about whether judges can rate statements independent of their own beliefs, as was needed with Thurstone's process. You will need judges to complete the survey and examine the content. As previously stated, choose a construct you want to measure. You can create items by yourself, but it is quite helpful to ask other experts to examine the items. Likert scaling is a unidimensional scaling procedure, though it is commonly employed in other ways, such as multidimensional instruments. It is important to note that a Likert scale is a set of several items, not a single item, where you can the participants' responses are added and/or averaged to create an overall score.

Once you have your items developed—by you or by the experts—you can have a group of judges rate the items on a five-point scale: strongly unfavorable to the concept to strongly favorable to the concept. Next, you need to compute the correlations among all of the items, called the interitem correlations. If the interitem correlations are very high, >.90, you may not need to keep both items. Then, create a total score for each judge for the instrument by adding up the individual responses of each item for each judge. The total, or summed, scale score is simply the summation (adding) of each items response values for each judge.

Finally, calculate the correlation between each item and the total score. Remove those items with low item-summed score correlations. There is no perfect rule, but you might want to consider removing those with a correlation of less than .7 and probably remove those with less than .6. But, this is a judgment call.

For each item, you can also get the average rating of the top 25% of judges' scores and the bottom 25%. Then run a *t*-test (see Chapter 9) on those mean values for the two groups. Items with higher *t* values are better at separating responses and should be kept. At this point, you are trying for high item-total score correlations and high *t* values for choosing the final group of items.

After you decide which items to keep, you can format your instrument. Begin by choosing the response scale size. The tradition with a Likert scale is 1 to 5, but you will see 1 to 7 or 0 to 4. Notice that these have an odd number of categories. Odd numbers of categories leaves the respondent a middle or neutral choice. This is a design decision that needs to be carefully judged in reference to the research questions, the study design, and analysis. There is no agreement whether a middle category is acceptable. Overall, we like an even number of categories (no middle or neutral category) because it forces the respondent to choose a side and a neutral category does not make sense with many of the constructs in which we are interested.

Finally, in several Likert-type scales we have received in the mail, there is an interesting artifact. Look at this item:

> You recently stayed at Hotel YYZ. How would you rate the accommodations?
>
> Excellent   Good   Fair   Poor

Notice that in this example, from a real questionnaire, there is only one negative response. This arrangement almost guarantees the look of positivity toward the construct or topic of interest. This is a serious problem because it can cause inferences from the averaged data to be incorrect. For example, this version of the statement allows for an equal number of positive and negative options.

> You recently stayed at Hotel YYZ. How would you rate the accommodations?
>
> Excellent   Good   Poor   Horrible

Therefore, if you have a research hypothesis based on your research questions about positive or negative perceptions, data from a disproportionately positive or negative scale will lead to poor inferences.

Semantic Differential

Semantic differentials are created when a statement or question is followed by a set of bipolar, or opposite, adjectives called anchors, and a set of responses placing the individual between these anchors (Osgood, Suci, & Tannenbaum, 1957). Common anchors are composed of bipolar adjectives such as easy/hard or fast/slow. These anchors are grouped into evaluation, potency, or activity dimensions. The bipolar scale traditionally is formatted using seven positions that denote the directionality and intensity of the individual's reaction to the concepts being measured (Osgood et al., 1957). The respondent checks the blank that corresponds to his or her feelings, attitudes, or beliefs. An example from a cell phone survey is below:

Usability: What is your experience using this cell phone?

Easy: _ _ _ ✓ _ _ _ :Hard

Boring: _ _ _ ✓ _ _ _ :Exciting

As with Likert-type scales, the number of points, or blanks, can be changed to include fewer or more response categories.

Multidimensional instruments measure several different constructs in one instrument. For example, the Minnesota Multiphasic Personality Inventory (MMPI) (Hathaway & McKinley, 1940) measures multiple constructs related to mental disorders. Likert-type scaling is popular in multidimensional instruments even though it was originally designed for unidimensional instruments. Researchers develop items for each construct of interest, decide on a scale level (e.g., 1 to 5 or 1 to 7) for endorsement, and administer the instrument. After collecting the data, typically researchers examine internal consistency values with Cronbach's alpha for each set of items for each construct in order to estimate reliability of the scores for each construct and conduct factor analyses to examine the structure of the multidimensions.

Ranking

Ranking occurs when participants are asked to choose which item is considered first, second, third, and so on. The rankings could focus on importance, fairness, desire, or choice, for example. An example of ranking is below:

Which type of magazine do you like to read? Please rank each below and only choose one rank (first = 1, second = 2, third = 3, etc.) for each type.

_____ Style

_____ Sports

_____ Music

_____ News/Politics

_____ Sports

_____ Home

_____ Travel

Rankings are quite popular because respondents are forced to make a choice, though you will have some respondents who double rank two items or statements.

PRETESTING

Whether you create your own instrument or choose to administer a previously developed one, you need to **pretest** or **pilot test** the instrument and the administration procedures you will use. Even asking a few colleagues or friends to help complete the instrument or protocol can help identify how much time it will take or potential problems you may have missed when designing the instruments and study. What appears easy and apparent to you may not be to your participants. Pretesting the instrument and the process of administering the instrument can save you future resources and reduce frustration and stress later.

INTERVIEWS

Interviews, or interview protocols—the face-to-face version of all the instruments we have been discussing—are another form of collecting data, and they have their own typologies and rules to understand. Interviews are traditionally categorized in two formats: structured and unstructured. **Structured interviews** have a set format and question order, whereas **unstructured interviews** do not. In reality, most interviews fall along a continuum from structured to unstructured because in practice at the end of a structured survey many times there is an unstructured component because the interviewer has follow-up questions based on responses from the participants. Depending on the purpose and goal of the study, unstructured interviews may end up with structured questions by the time all of the interviews are done.

Contacting respondents occurs after you have defined your sample. Due to the nature of interviewing, entry into the field of your sample is more complicated than other forms of contacting sample participants. For example, issues related to confidentiality and informed consent are intensified because you are typically meeting one to one or in small groups, so anonymity no longer exists as with a mail-based survey. Once you are conducting the interview, you must develop rapport with the participants. Making the participants feel comfortable and at ease increases your ability to obtain quality data. Without the rapport between you and the interviewee(s), you hinder your ability to answer your research questions and can increase your measurement error. After each interview, you should assess the quality of the interview. Did you feel the participant was honest with you? Do you think you made the respondent feel comfortable? Do you think the participant provided full and complete answers to you? Or was the respondent withholding information? Were you professional? Did you stay on task?

Focus groups are interviews with a larger number of respondents (usually 12 to 15) together in a room who are interviewed about a topic or product. Television networks have historically used focus groups to examine what viewers pay attention to in commercials. With the advent of hundreds of channels and the massive amount of commercial information that viewers see, the need to know what viewers recall is becoming increasingly important. Many retail companies, automobile producers, book publishers, politicians, and even universities use focus groups to gather information about their product or current and future trends. A famous focus group story details how management at Levi Strauss either ignored or misinterpreted the comments from adolescent focus groups in the early 1990s about the desire to have wider jeans and not the slim cut jeans for which Levi Strauss is famous (Munk, 1999). The resulting business decisions put Levi Strauss at a disadvantage during the next few years.

METHODS OF DATA COLLECTION

There are several methods for obtaining respondents to collect data once you have developed your instrument. **Direct administration** occurs when you administer the instrument or interview directly to the respondents. You can use direct administration in classroom research or interviewers at retail shopping malls and even at museums. This method happens most often in experiments, interviews, and focus groups. The respondents have contact with people directly involved in the study. **Indirect administration** occurs when there is distance, both physical and time, between you as the researcher and respondents, such as mailings. However, depending on the actual administration process, it is more likely that the administration of the instrument is somewhere between direct and indirect. For example, you decide to use a telephone survey, but hire a company to make the calls. You are not directly administering the survey, but the company is.

Telephone, Mail, Internet

Telephone surveys and interviews are quite popular, especially during a political election year cycle, because of the ability to reach and use a variety of closed- and open-ended items with the respondent. The downside is that the cost of conducting telephone surveys is high because they are one on one. Also, the telephone survey process needs a great deal of care to obtain the sample you desire in order to obtain the most accurate results.

 Mailing surveys is a relatively inexpensive way to reach your sample of potential participants, but return rates can be problematic. The return rate is the proportion of respondents who returned the survey divided by the number of surveys mailed. Simple things you can do to increase the return rate include making the format clean and not cluttered, making the actual task you want the respondent to complete simple (e.g., fill in a bubble), and including a self-addressed stamped envelope (Dillman, 2000). Making the whole survey process easy is important, because you are essentially asking the respondents to self-administer the instrument.

 E-mail is a wonderfully inexpensive technology to transmit information and collect data. Obtaining e-mail addresses of your population, though, is the greatest challenge for the new researcher. **Web-based surveys** typically start with contact through e-mail, and then the respondent is directed to a Web page to complete the survey. Companies such as Zoomerang, Cvent, SurveyMonkey, or Key Survey allow individuals to create Web-based surveys that can have a Web link sent through e-mail accounts. As with the mailed instruments above, response rates can be problematic so make the process easy for the respondent (e.g., make sure the Web link to survey is actually working).

 A recent data collection device is the personal response system, which allows participants to respond as they watch a show or commercial or a teacher. One version of the system is hand held and allows the participant to dial between 0 and 100 for how much they like, are paying attention, think the person is behaving appropriately, and so on. Other versions of this are now in the classroom where the instructor can post a question to the students during class and the students respond. The data can then be displayed immediately to the class.

Finally, many studies are conducted through the collection of data from a personal computer, whereby participants respond to stimuli on a specialized program on the computer. For example, Jim and a colleague studied response times and pattern behavior of poker players using a program specifically designed to collect certain data, though the program ran just like a computerized poker game (Dixon & Schreiber, 2002).

Though you have just read content concerning how to contact respondents in various ways, we would like to put in our word of warning. You can have planned and planned and still have problems. In Chapter 4, we discussed sampling processes. How you execute that procedure becomes very important as you contact potential respondents. For example, in 1936, the *Literary Digest* conducted a poll to see whether Franklin D. Roosevelt, who was running for re-election against Kansas governor Alfred Landon, would win. After collecting the polling data, the magazine predicted that Landon would win based on a poll of 2.3 million Americans. A poll that large, given the size of the United States at the time, was impressive. Unfortunately, the magazine was wrong. The sample size was great but was based on *voluntary response*. Ten million surveys were sent out, but only 2.3 million came back (Bryson, 1976).

Field Observations

Before you enter the field, you need to decide what you are going to observe and whom. For **field observations**, there are some basic collection decisions you need to make. The first is how to record the observations. Traditionally, many people use paper or journals that have been set up to collect the desired data. Like interviews, the instrument can be more or less structured. This choice is typically based on personal preference or habit from your training. We use blank field notebooks in our research and write extensively as we observe. We are very unstructured and are essentially the instruments. We also use very structured instruments when we observe colleagues teaching because of the rules governing peer observations in our faculty handbooks.

Electronic data collectors (EDCs), such as personal digital assistants (PDAs) — Palm Pilots, iPhones, and other commercially available devices—are beginning to be used more and more to collect data in the field. Jim used Palm Pilots in Rome for students to collect data on schooling, learning, and living in Rome (Schreiber, 2004). Some students created checklists to use for observations and others just took notes. Even the note takers used two different tactics: some ''wrote'' on their Palm Pilots and others used the portable mini keyboard.

Audiotaping or videotaping interviews allows you to review and obtain verbatim all of the interview. Many researchers audiotape the sessions and transcribe the interviews afterward. Videotaping serves the same purpose and adds the ability to examine nonverbal statements (body movements) by the respondents. The down side of this tactic is the cost for the equipment and the massive amount of data that must be dealt with. Transcribing interviews verbatim is extremely time consuming versus just listening to the tape and taking notes from it. Note that when you take notes from the tapes and do not allow readers or reviewers access to the tapes (or transcripts as the case may be) you are most likely decreasing your believability in the eyes of some readers.

Because of the amount of data possible from audio or video, we recommend creating a coding system before you begin listening to or watching the tapes. This does not mean you will not have to change your coding system, but it can reduce the resources devoted to transcribing and coding. Consider how much of the data you truly want to code beforehand; the level of detail should be decided upfront. For example, an audio transcription can be as simple as what was said or as complicated as the length of time for pauses, upticks in speaking at the end of a sentence, or emphasis on specific words spoken by the respondent. Whether you want to develop a protocol for coding before, called *a priori*, or develop it as you review is up to you and is affected by the type of study you are conducting (e.g., grounded theory). Analysis packages such as Transana or Inspiration let you analyze audio and video data in amazing ways, but you still need to complete some transcription along the way.

If you are using **multiple observers**, which we highly recommend, everyone must be trained in observing and recording if you have preestablished coding scheme. If you fail to train everybody well, the differences between your observers may be enormous, which decreases the believability of your data. If you are not using a preestablished coding scheme, then you must set some basic ground rules of how much to code, as discussed earlier. Again, if you have multiple observers listening to and watching audiotapes and videotapes, a large amount of data is quickly generated, and the sheer amount of data to analyze can become overwhelming. At this point, you should realize that a great deal of planning is necessary for your data collection and subsequent analysis.

PAPER-AND-PENCIL TESTS AND INVENTORIES

There are many instruments that have already been developed that you could use for your study, as long as they are appropriately based on your questions and your operational definitions. We did not discuss these in the "Types of Content" section because we wanted to pay special attention to them.

Paper-and-pencil tests are quite common. Their most defining attributes are that a standard question set is presented to each participant and that answering the questions requires some cognitive task. The responses are graded and summarized exactly the same way, and the participants are provided some numerical value indicating how well the participant performed on that test or in comparison to a reference group. For example, if you took the Graduate Record Examination, your score was compared to the participants who took the exam that day. Though we use the phrase paper-and-pencil tests, many of these tests have a computerized version, also known as computer-based testing.

The computer-based testing versions of these instruments tend to take less time to complete, because they estimate your score based on the difficulty of the questions you answered. You have answered many test questions over your life and have probably made statements about them, such as "that one was hard" or "tricky" or "easy" or "not in my notes or the book." Each question has a difficulty level based on how many previous respondents answered the item correctly. The lower the difficulty value, the harder the question. As you correctly answer items on the test, the items become more difficult until you are missing several in a row. The computer models your score until you have hit the highest level (i.e., starting to miss every question at a certain difficulty level). For the remainder of the chapter we use the phrase paper-and-pencil tests.

Below we discuss several types of tests, but the biggest difference among them is how they are used—that is, the inferences people make from the test score. The tests themselves are not truly problematic; some are theoretically and empirically better than others. The real problems occur when the scores from the tests are interpreted past what they actually measure (Nichols & Berliner, 2007).

Standardized tests are administered and scored the same way. Simply, everyone takes the test the same way with the same instructions and the responses are scored using the same procedures. Large testing companies create their tests and create a norm group. A **norm group** is a representative sample of the population of participants, which can be used to compare your score on a test to the average of the group. For example, if you are a graduate student reading this book and took the Graduate Record Examination, you were compared to a group of test takers who have either completed a bachelor degree or will soon and are planning to apply to graduate school. You are not compared to all of the potential and recent graduates.

Criterion-referenced tests, or the more current incarnation **standards-based tests**, are tests designed to examine a participant's performance level as compared to a cutoff value, not a norm group or other group type of comparison. The decision of what the cutoff should be is a professional one made by individuals knowledgeable in the content area. In the United States, the individual states and commonwealths have created different criteria proficiency levels.

With the passage of No Child Left Behind (a revamping of the Elementary and Secondary Education Act of 1965), state testing with standardized tests became the norm. In actuality, though, many states had previously developed criterion tests to see whether students were learning the content within the state standards (Amrein & Berliner, 2002). Though these tests are to be used to see whether a particular student has met a criterion (proficiency), the scores are aggregated by classroom and school using the percentage of who made a specific criterion and are used for comparative purposes, even though that was not their designed purpose. The key is that your instruments can only provide quality information for their designed purpose. Extending the data past the original design will lead to poor inferences—that is, a believability problem.

COGNITIVE TESTS

Cognitive tests are different than the traditional paper-and-pencil tests that typically measure some content. **Cognitive tests** are divided into aptitude, intelligence, and achievement.

An **aptitude test** is designed to predict the learning capacity for a particular area or particular skill(s). Intelligence and aptitude are sometimes used interchangeably in the literature, but they serve different purposes. For example, the SAT I (Scholastic Achievement Test, previously Scholastic Aptitude Test) was originally designed to help selective northeastern states with their admission decisions (Nitko, 2004). The test was developed as a scholastic aptitude test. The (ACT) American College Test was designed to be different from the SAT and help public Midwestern colleges and universities; it was designed to measure educational achievement and development versus aptitude. Aptitude tests are typically given in group form outside of a school setting, but some are individual based. These types of tests are used most commonly in job-hiring situations. The respondents answer questions that are both verbal and nonverbal where the person is trying to apply his or her experience and education to solve problems. The content on these tests can vary greatly.

Multifactor aptitude tests measure several different aptitudes in one test. The Armed Services Vocational Aptitude Battery (ASVAB) is one such multifactor test. The armed forces has a long tradition of testing, such as the Army Alpha test in 1916. The ASVAB currently consists of 10 individual tests of the following subjects: Word Knowledge, Paragraph Comprehension, Arithmetic Reasoning, Mathematics Knowledge, General Science, Auto and Shop Information, Mechanical Comprehension, Electronics Information, Numerical Operations, and Coding Speed.

Intelligence quotient (IQ) tests can be thought of as general scholastic aptitude tests in a multifactor form. IQ tests attempt to measure some form of cognitive ability and are typically administered individually. Aptitude batteries, on the other hand, are administered in group format. There are several intelligence tests available from publishing companies. Three common ones are the Stanford-Binet Intelligence Scale, the Wechsler Intelligence Scales, and the Kaufman IQ Test.

The Wechsler Intelligence Scale for Children (4th ed.) (WISC-IV) is composed of 10 core subtests and five additional subtests. The scores from these subtests can be added to create four index scores and one total score, the full scale IQ score (FSIQ) (Figure 6.1). The typical amount of time to administer the test is between 65 and 80 minutes. If additional subtests are required, the amount of time can be over 100 minutes. The amount of time it takes to administer some instruments creates a major problem for completing a study in a timely manner.

Achievement tests are different because the goal is to determine how well a person has achieved, "learned," in a specific area. Achievement tests, more recently, have been used both for criterion decisions and for norm-group comparisons. Tests such as the California Achievement Test or the Iowa Tests of Basic Skills are large-scale, group-administered instruments with questions that cover several academic content areas, such as reading, comprehension, and addition or multiplication.

FIGURE 6.1
Wechsler Intelligence Scale for Children (WISC-IV)

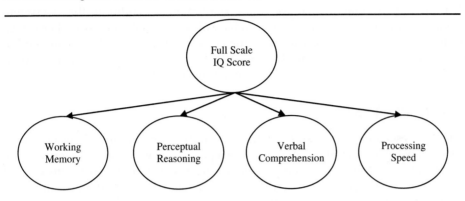

These instruments are called *batteries*, and each content area is considered a *subtest*. These types of achievement tests are standardized instruments used to make a comparison between an individual's score and the norm group. Some achievement tests, such as the Gates-MacGinitie Reading Test is used for diagnostic purposes to identify where students are having difficulty learning to read. Table 6.2 provides examples of paper-and-pencil tests.

    Alternative tests or assessments, also known as *authentic assessments*, are actually alternatives to the traditional tests just discussed, but could have standardized administrations. Examples of alternative assessments include papers, projects, displays,

TABLE 6.2
Paper-and-pencil tests by type

Aptitude Tests	Achievement Tests
Group Intelligence or Ability	*Diagnostic*
Cognitive Abilities Test	Woodcock Reading Mastery Test
Otis-Lennon School Ability Test	Key Math Diagnostic Arithmetic Test
Individual Intelligence	*Criterion-Referenced*
Stanford-Binet Intelligence Scale	Writing Skills Test
Wechsler Intelligence Scale for Children	Most state achievement tests
Multifactor	*Specific Subjects (Content Areas)*
Armed Services Vocational Aptitude Battery	Modern Math Understanding Test
General Aptitude Test Battery	
Specialized	*Batteries*
Law School Admissions Test	Iowa Tests of Basic Skills
Watson-Glaser Critical Thinking Appraisal	California Achievement Test Series

experiments, portfolios, and performances. They are typically not completed in the same manner as traditional tests and generally have specific rules or instructions that are to be followed to complete the assessment. In addition, the assessment cannot be graded by a machine as is possible with traditional standardized tests such as the ACT. One of our favorite authentic tasks is the Rube Goldberg competition each year (http://www.rubegoldberg.com/), because students have to apply their knowledge in unique ways in order to stay within the rules and regulations.

AFFECTIVE TESTS

Affective tests are more than the attitudinal instruments briefly discussed above. **Personality inventories** attempt to measure a person's psychological characteristics. The Guilford–Zimmerman Temperament Survey is a multiple scale instrument and is a structured personality test because it has standardized administration and scoring procedures. **Projective tests** use a different data collection technique in that they ask participants to respond to ambiguous stimuli in an attempt to discover hidden emotions, attitudes, beliefs, or conflicts. Though quite popular at one time, a projective test is completely dependent on the quality of the examiner's skill set. Proponents of this technique argue that the stimuli present allow the examiner to obtain a participant's innermost thoughts and beliefs. Unfortunately, this claim is not often warranted because the examiner has beliefs about the interpretation of the statements and how to interpret them in comparison to some standardized meaning. Many of you might recognize the *Rorschach Inkblot Test* because it is commonly seen on television shows and movies. The participant is asked to examine irregular but symmetrical blots of ink and describe what he or she ''sees.'' The examiner must write down what the person says, response time, and response focus. The responses are then compared to a set of responses about that specific inkblot and interpreted within that context of previous responses. A second commonly used projective test is the *Thematic Apperception Test*. For this test, the participant examines an ambiguous scene with people and is asked to describe it. Next, the participant is asked to describe what occurred just prior the shown scene. Again, the examiner must take a lot of notes and make inferences from those notes. As the focus in psychology has transitioned to a cognitive and neurological model of diagnosis and care, projective tests have declined in use.

Attitude instruments attempt to measure how people feel or think about a certain topic, content area, or product, such as whether the person has a positive or negative feeling about an object, people or person, government, and so on. In education, numerous surveys exist for measuring attitudes about subjects such as mathematics, science, reading, history, and writing. One such instrument is the School Attitude Measure (Wick, 1990). The instrument has items pertaining to five scales: Motivation for Schooling, Academic Self-Concept (Performance), Academic Self-Concept (Preference), Student's Sense of Control Over Performance, and Student's Instructional Mastery and uses a four-category Likert-type scale.

Value instruments measure the level of commitment to an ideal or principle. These can also be described as measuring long-lasting beliefs. A notable value instrument is The Study of Values (Allport & Vernon, 1933). The instrument measured six value areas: Theoretical (e.g., truth), Economic (e.g., useful), Aesthetic (e.g., beauty), Social (e.g., altruism), Political (e.g., power), and Religious (e.g., mystical).

Interest instruments measure your level of interest in a topic area or preference for a specific activity. One example is the Reading Interest Inventory, which asks people to rank the types of reading genre they enjoy. The Strong Interest Inventory, for example, measures occupational preferences, such as farmer, artist, or scientist, along with many other occupations.

If you are considering using any of the predeveloped instruments, such as those discussed above, you need to thoroughly research the instrument concerning reliability and validity scores (Chapter 5) and the operational definition in use for the constructs measured on that particular instrument. Intelligence and achievement tests that are used to make high-stakes decisions are expected to have high, >.90, test-retest reliability or internal consistency values. Affective tests usually have moderately high score reliability values, >.70, but projective tests tend to have lower score reliability values.

LANGUAGE AND BIAS

If you are developing your own instrument, you need to refer to the APA manual discussed earlier in reference to bias, in all its forms, in the content and language used. Bias, from just a pure technical standpoint, introduces error into your scores and therefore reduces the reliability of the scores and quality of the inferences that can be made. From an affective standpoint, it can upset your respondents and cause them to disengage or purposefully provide deviant responses. Jim once witnessed a demonstration of a test for immigrant children of Mexican descent where the first question asked was "What sound does a dog make?" Unfortunately, of the four choices provided, none were correct (in English or Spanish, or one of the many dialects).

OPERATIONALIZING LATENT CONSTRUCTS

Forgotten in the decision to choose an instrument is the meaning of the latent construction and how that will materialize on the instrument. Each question or statement on many of these instruments is meant to represent something else, a latent construct—that which you can't see. Mathematics literacy cannot be seen; but if a student answers mathematics questions correctly, we infer the student is mathematically literate. We don't see love, but we infer from behaviors and statements from people. Therefore, you need to examine the questions or items and how well each aligns with the definition of the construct that you are using.

DATA COLLECTION PATTERNS

There are a few collection patterns that are typically followed in data collection. In addition to the common one-time administration, there are also multiple administrations that can be completed by the same people or by multiple groups of people over time. These multiple administration studies are grouped under developmental studies—cognitive, physical, and social change—over time but can apply to any topic of research. **Longitudinal studies** examine people or topics over long periods of time. There are three types of longitudinal studies. **Trend studies** follow a general population over time. The participants are sampled from the population each year or other time period. Therefore, the sample group changes each administration. These are common in public opinion polling and are cost effective, but because questions or statements change over time, comparisons aren't possible. **Cohort studies** follow the same people who have a common characteristic. These are good when random assignment is not possible, such as smoking studies, but causality is tough to argue. Finally, in **panel studies**, the exact same participants are followed over time but data are collected at different time points. These are good for looking at changes over time and long-term effects, but mortality (people leaving the study; see Chapter 7) is problematic.

Cross-sectional studies examine different groups at the same time and are used for descriptive purposes. For example, if you are interested in rates of technology ownership, you might ask participants in different age groups, such as teenagers, 20- to 30-year-olds, 31- to 40-year-olds, and so on. You can also blend cross-sectional and longitudinal studies where groups are followed for differing amounts of time. Longitudinal studies are wonderful because one can examine a phenomenon over time and see how it changes. The downsides are the cost of tracking all of the participants, instrument changes when publishers create new versions, and for the researcher, a major commitment of his or her career.

IN-TEXT ACTIVITY

Take a moment to answer the following:

1. Write your current version of your research question below.

   _____

   _____

2. How large of a sample are you thinking about? _____

3. Which type of instrumentation (yourself, survey, questionnaire, interview) appears to be the best fit? _____

4. What type of instrument is it (knowledge, attitude, etc.)? _____

5. What scaling system does it use or could use? _____

6. What have previous studies used? _____

7. Are the data from those studies believable? _____

8. Did they create or use previously developed instruments? _____

As you have read, there are a great number of decisions related to instrumentation that need to be considered when designing a study. You should keep your research question and desired sample in mind as you are making the decisions. As you change aspects of your question or your sample, the data collection instrument that will best suit your needs will change. Your question may have originally been moving toward a longitudinal study, but the costs of the instruments over time is too high and you need to adjust.

CASE STUDY

Ginette has decided to attempt two studies with college students and then one with a more general population. She will be using several graphical data displays from newspapers and will also create some in order to manipulate specific variables. These instruments are her study stimuli that will allow her to control some aspects of what is seen by participants and yet still have some data from actual, or what is termed *ecologically valid*, data displays. Ecologically valid displays are those that would be seen out in public and were not created and manipulated for an experiment. Her data collection instrument is currently a structured open-ended questionnaire. One question she has written is: "Do the percentages in the picture need to add up to 100%? Please explain."

This question and the other questions she is writing must be able to be used both in a laboratory setting, where students will complete the questionnaire related to the displays on a computer, and in the field, where people in the mall or library, for example, who agree to be participants, will complete the questionnaire. For the possible responses, she is developing a scoring guide so that she and a fellow student, who has agreed to help score and code the data, can score the questionnaires independently. She enlists the help of a friend in order to obtain some level of reliability of the scores because she is not using a previously developed instrument or an instrument where the responses are forced choices. There will also be a category for statements or comments that do not fit the *a priori* code sheet that will allow for later examination.

ARMCHAIR MOMENT

Researcher questions are well developed at this point in the design phase, though they can change. The desired study population or populations in mind and the number of participants needed are close to being settled. However, the tension or interaction between question, sample, and instrumentation begins. If you are completing a purely experimental study or a case study, the rules and procedures around these appear more linear in nature, but that is not always the case. In fact, we argue that in most circumstances it is not the case at all. An original research question may point to a large sample size in order to obtain a picture of what people think at a moment in time or to make a large generalization about the population. For example, you may hear a newscaster say, "Eighty-three percent of respondents from a representative sample of 1,203 people agreed with the statement that the economy is poor. Therefore, the country clearly is worried about the economy.'' This is a large sample and the representativeness allows for a generalization past the sample. The problematic part is an inference that was not part of the original statement or response. Saying the economy is poor is one thing and is a correct interpretation, but the extension to ''worried'' is not; being worried is different than agreeing with a statement that the economy is poor.

However, to collect such data, you need resources to obtain 1,203 responses. In addition, most of these polls don't readily admit how many people refused to answer or their characteristics. In addition, this type of data collection is expensive and time consuming. Most likely, you will need many telephone interviewers who will need to be trained and paid. Most social science research is conducted on a smaller scale by professors, researchers at think tanks and centers, and some graduate or undergraduate students. Because of this and the resource issues, compromises or tradeoffs are made. For example, I want to answer question A, but in reality I am going to attempt to answer A with a smaller sample because I need to interview participants, or the participants must fill out several instruments and I will need to provide some incentive to get them to participate. Incentives cost money, so I need a smaller sample size than originally desired from my research question. Or, I want to stay one whole year observing the culture change in this school, but will only be able to stay six months. You need to understand that as you design, and sometimes after you start, modifications will occur. You need to take a moment and examine how that affects your actual research question and what you really want to say at the end of the study.

KEY WORDS

achievement test
affective test
alternative test
aptitude test
attitude instrument
attitudinal content
behavioral content
checklists
clarity
closed-ended question
cognitive test
cohort studies
contacting respondents
counterbalancing
criterion-referenced test
cross-sectional studies
cumulative scaling
demographic content
direct administration

electronic data collectors
    (EDCS)
e-mail
equal-appearing intervals
field observations
focus groups
format
Guttman scaling
indirect administration
instructions
instrument
instrument length
intelligence quotient (IQ)
    test
interest instrument
interviews
knowledge content
Likert scale
longitudinal studies

mailing survey
multidimensional
    instruments
multifactor aptitude test
multiple observers
negatively worded
    statements
norm group
open-ended questions
ordering
paired comparisons
panel studies
paper-and-pencil test
personality inventories
pilot test
pretest
projective test
questionnaire
questions

ranking	statements	Thurstone scaling
scaling	structured interview	trend studies
scalogram analysis	successive intervals	unstructured interviews
semantic differential	survey	value instruments
standardized test	task analysis	variability
standards-based test	telephone survey	Web-based survey

REFERENCES AND FURTHER READINGS

Allison, P. D. (2001). *Missing data.* Thousand Oaks, CA: SAGE Publications.

Allport, G. W., & Vernon, P. E. (1933). *Studies in expressive movement.* New York: Macmillan.

Amrein, A. L., & Berliner, D. C. (2002, March 28). High-stakes testing, uncertainty, and student learning. *Education Policy Analysis Archives, 10*(18). Retrieved from http://epaa.asu.edu/epaa/v10n18/

Bryson, M. (1976). The literary digest poll: Making of a statistical myth. *American Statistician,* 184–185.

Colton, D., & Covert, R. W. (2007). *Designing and constructing instruments for social research and evaluation.* San Francisco, CA: Jossey-Bass.

Czaja, R., & Blair, J. (2005). *Designing surveys: A guide to decisions and procedures* (2nd ed.). Thousand Oaks, CA: Pine Forge Press.

Dillman, D. A. (2000). *Mail and internet surveys: The tailored design method.* New York: John Wiley & Sons.

Dillman, D. A., Smyth, J. D., & Christian, L. M. (2009). *Internet, mail, and mixed-mode surveys: The tailored design method.* Hoboken, NJ: John Wiley & Sons.

Dixon, M. R., & Schreiber, J. B. (2002). Utilizing a computerized video poker simulation for the collection of experimental data on gambling behavior. *Psychological Record, 52,* 417–428.

Downing, S. M., & Haladyna, T. M. (2006). *Handbook of test development.* Mahwah, NJ: Lawrence Erlbaum Associates.

Edwards, A. L., & Kenney, K. C. (1946). A comparison of the Thurstone and Likert techniques of attitude scale construction. *Journal of Applied Psychology, 30*(1), 72–83.

Groves, R. M., Fowler, F. J., Couper, M. P., Lepkowski, J. M., Singer, E., & Tourangeau, R. (2009). *Survey methodology* (2nd ed.). Hoboken, NJ: John Wiley & Sons.

Guttman, L. (1950). The basis for scalogram analysis. In S. A. Stouffer, L. Guttman, E. A. Suchman, P. F. Lazarsfeld, S. A. Star, & J. A. Clausen (Eds.), *Measurement and prediction: Studies in social psychology in World War II* (Vol. IV). Princeton, NJ: Princeton University Press.

Hathaway, S. R., & McKinley, J. C. (1940). A multiphasic personality schedule (Minnesota): I. Construction of the schedule. *Journal of Psychology, 10,* 249–254.

Likert, R. (1932a). *The method of constructing an attitude scale: Readings in attitude theory and measurement*. New York: John Wiley & Sons.

Likert, R, (1932b). A technique for the measurement of attitudes. *Archives of Psychology, 140,* 1–5.

Literary Digest, 31 October 1936.

Little, R. J. A., & Rubin, D. B. (2002). *Statistical analysis with missing data* (2nd ed.). New York: John Wiley & Sons.

Mertens, D. M. (2005). *Research and evaluation in education and psychology: Integrating diversity with qualitative, quantitative, and mixed methods*. Thousand Oaks, CA: SAGE Publications.

Munk, N. (1999, April 12). How Levi's trashed a great American brand. *Fortune*, p. 82. Available: http://www.referenceforbusiness.com/businesses/G-L/Strauss-Levi.html#ixzz0YeaXsYpI

National Public Radio. NBC and the Olympic sponsors. Morning Edition Business Section. Retrieved from www.npr.org

Nichols, S., & Berliner, D. C. (2007). *Collateral damage: How high-stakes testing corrupts America's schools*. Cambridge, MA: Harvard Educational Group.

Nitko, A. J. (2004). *Educational assessment of students*. New York, NY: Merrill.

Osgood, C. E., Suci, G. J., & Tannenbaum, P. H. (1957). *The measurement of meaning*. Urbana: University of Illinois Press.

Schreiber, J. B. (2004, April). *Palm Pilots in international research: Advantages, disadvantages, fires, dust, and cognitive overload*. Paper presented at the annual meeting of the National Consortium for Instruction and Cognition.

Stevens, S. S. (1946). On the theory of scales of measurement. *Science, 103*(2684), pp. 677–680.

Thurstone, L. L. (1929). *Theory of attitude measurement*. Washington, DC: American Psychological Association.

Thurstone, L. L., & Chave, E. J. (1929). *The measurement of attitude*. Chicago, IL: University of Chicago Press.

Weems, G. H., Onwuegbuzie, A. J., Schreiber, J. B., & Eggers, S. J. (2003). Characteristics of respondents with different response patterns to positively- and negatively-worded items on rating scales. *Assessment and Evaluation in Higher Education, 26*(6), 587–607.

Wick, J. W. (1990). *School attitude measure*. Chicago, IL: American Testronics.

Yamaguchi, J. (1997). *Positive vs. negative wording: PCA of residuals*. Retrieved from http://www.rasch.org/rmt/rmt112h.htm

Experimental and Nonexperimental Research Design

KEY IDEA

Protecting your fort from attack: A well-thought-out quantitative design.

POINTS TO KNOW

Distinguish between independent, dependent, mediator, and moderator variables.

Explain the limitations of experimental and nonexperimental research designs.

Describe the three components of causality.

Describe the types of experimental and nonexperimental designs with related basic research questions.

Determine the defining attributes of single-subject, longitudinal, preexperimental, quasi-experimental, and true experimental designs.

Identify the main components of advanced techniques.

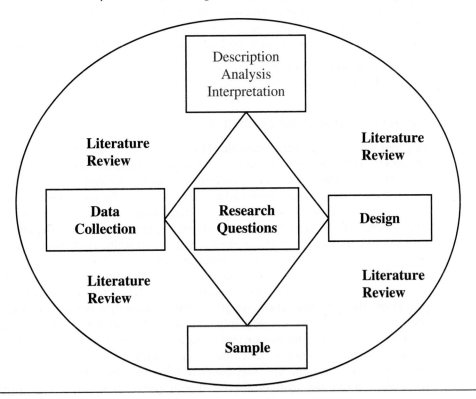

DESIGN FOR STRENGTH AND ELEGANCE

We think of research design as building a strong structure that is resistant to attack. By attack, we mean critics who will look for ways not to believe your observations; the critics of your research will look for weaknesses. Elegance is a bit more difficult to design because it interacts with the instruments or stimuli created for participants. Jim is continually struck by the elegance of the developmental experiments of the 1960s, such as the "visual cliff" study by Gibson and Walk (1960). It is a solid design with a great stimulus.

For this chapter, you should begin to see which of the types of designs examined might align with the research questions or hypotheses you have. To aid in your understanding, we created a chart with basic research designs and the types of analyses that align to different types of designs. This appears in Table 7.15 after the discussion of the experimental designs. Before we look at experimental research design, let's review some material that will help along the way. Although we discuss data in terms of a quantitative perspective, this does not preclude you collecting non-numeric data in an experimental or nonexperimental design.

STUDY DESIGN REVIEW

You probably had a basic statistics course and learned the terms *independent* or *dependent variable*, but the definitions and examples may still be fuzzy in your mind. This is the traditional failure to retrieve information: you forgot what these terms are and what they mean. Before reading further, try to define these terms.

    A. Independent variable _____
    B. Dependent variable _____

Variables: Independent and Dependent

In general, the **independent variable (IV)** is the variable that is argued to cause or be associated with some outcome—the **dependent variable (DV)**. For example, the number of hours you study (independent variable) may increase your performance on an essay exam (dependent variable or outcome) in your research methods course. In each design below, these two variables will have more explicit attributes that separate them, but it is important to begin to separate independent and dependent variables early in the design stage. Naturally, they should easily flow from the literature review and your research question(s). The example above could be rewritten as a research question: Are the number of hours studying (IV) predictive of the essay exam score (DV) in a research methods course? A **moderator variable** influences the direction and strength of the relationship between two variables, such as an independent and dependent variable. A **mediator variable** explains the relationship between the two variables. As an example, consider the relationship between the desire to quit a particular job and being a good company citizen. Age may be a moderator, in that the associate between desire to quit and company citizenship could be stronger for older employees than for young employees.

Education level could be a moderator because it would explain the relationship between desire to quit and company citizenship. When you add education to the analysis, the association between desire to quit and company citizenship ceases to exist (Baron & Kenny, 1986).

Number of hours studying is typically not manipulated by the researcher. The researcher might assign participants to studying different organizations of material. For example, some participants are told to read a story, others to read a story and take notes, and others to read a story, take notes, and predict what happens next. Reading the story has three versions, or levels, where each level is a different manipulated version of the IV.

Random Assignment/Selection

Random assignment occurs when each participant from a sample is randomly assigned to one of the experimental or control conditions. **Random selection** occurs when participants are randomly selected from the population of potential participants. Random assignment of participants is common, but random selection and then random assignment are rare in social science research. The random selection and assignment are an important assumption for null hypothesis testing (see Chapter 9).

DESIGNS AND THEIR LIMITATIONS

This section provides information about traditional single-subject, time series, and pre-, quasi-, or true experimental designs. We discuss them in this order because there is a natural progression in the core designs from single subject through true experimental. These designs are the most common that we see, and therefore, not all encompassing. They set the foundation for understanding.

In addition to understanding how to proceed with each of the basic research designs in this chapter, it's important to understand that each has limitations or weaknesses. We present the limitations of experimental research design first and then discuss the types of experimental designs. We do not tell you each design's limitation as we describe it. Instead, we ask you to try to determine the limitations of each design. After the designs, we provide a table indicating each design's flaws. We have noticed that students understand the flaws in their own experiences with experimental research, and getting students to do that first appears to help make the connection to the research language much stronger. But that is anecdotal, nonexperimental evidence, ironically.

Limitations

Every study and essentially every design has limitations, weak spots. Depending on the type of argument you are trying to make, you are trying to reduce the number of limitations, to reduce the level of error in your conclusions. There are three categories that are crucial to understand during the design phase: internal validity, external validity, and statistical conclusion validity. These three validity topics are traditionally discussed within experimental designs; however, they apply to social science research in general.

Validity is the quality of the evidence we use when we make a claim. Therefore, validity is an inference and is not an all-or-nothing proposition (Messick, 1989). Internal validity concerns causality, or cause and effect (A caused B). Causality, or the ability to make a causal claim or argument, has very specific criteria (Kenny, 1979, 2004):

1. *Temporal Precedence: The cause must precede the effect—we must be able to show this.* Consider the hemline theory, also called the skirt length theory, which states that when women's skirts are short, the stock market booms, whereas longer skirts mean a tough economy. You might think that this would lead our economists and political leaders to urge women to wear mini-skirts exclusively. But, unless the research can show a causal link indicating the relationship between skirt length and the economy, we'd better hold off on dictating economic decisions based on fashion trends.

2. *Covariation of the Cause and Effect: A change—the effect—must occur.* For foreign language education research, the relationship between enrolling in a total immersion language program (e.g., French) and French fluency is a research line of great interest to some. If we were to research this, we may observe a positive correlation between the two. Over time, we are also likely to observe that enrollment in the program increases French fluency. Finally, we are likely to observe that those students who enrolled in the immersion program earliest, say in kindergarten, have a better level of fluency than those who enrolled in high school, as early second-language acquisition leads to better second-language capacity (Lazaruk, 2007). If the pattern always followed this, then we could support a causal argument. However, we suspect that we would observe some students, who started language learning in high school, who have as good or better fluency than some who started in kindergarten. In general terms, effect B must follow cause A, and B must always follow A.

3. *No Plausible Alternative Explanation—there is not a third or fourth or other explanation for the change.* For the depression study example we use for most of the designs below, a change in depression scores must occur after the intervention, must always occur after the intervention, and cannot be due to a third variable such as medication. Yes, it is difficult to argue for causality. Therefore, you are trying to reduce the number of reasons readers have for denying your causal inferences and arguments, also known as **rival hypotheses**.

Internal Validity Threats

Internal validity threats are issues or concerns that develop when problems internal to the study, such as participants leaving, and the data negatively affect the quality of the causal argument. These threats fall into seven major categories. We use a blend of both the more recent names for these threats, as well as the original titles from Campbell and Stanley (1963).

Historical Effects.   Historical effects are unplanned instances or events that occur during a study that could affect the results. For example, Jim has had several fire alarms go off during studies in schools. One occurred while helping a friend complete the final experiment during her dissertation (well, the second to last experiment as it turned out). These events create problems in determining, and arguing for, why the results occurred.

Maturation.   Maturation is the natural developmental patterns that occur due to engaging in everyday life events. As the length of a study increases, the chance of a maturation effect increases. Studies with very young children and long-term, or longitudinal, studies are most susceptible to this validity problem. Change in performance over time could be due to the natural changes in motor skills as children grow. The researcher must show that maturation is not the sole reason for the change. Maturation can include age, experience, physical development, or anything that leads to an increase in knowledge and understanding of the world that is not related to the variables of study.

Testing Effects.   Testing effects occur because the participant has experience with the instrument or activity. For example, scores on the SAT may increase with a second administration simply because the test takers have experience with the test and format. Jim had to help someone practice several IQ test administrations; the person performed adequately on the first, but by the last one, he had increased his score to MENSA proportions. At the end, he didn't feel smarter, just tired and hungry.

Instrumentation Threats.   Instrumentation threats occur due to problems or other inconsistencies with the data collection method. This could be from the actual instrument (typos), the interviewer, observer change, or grader, for example. This is a common problem in longitudinal research, because instruments change over time. One research area where instruments change over time is intelligence tests. For example, the WISC-III to the WISC-IV test changed and the focus of interpretation changed from composite to level of index scores (Weiss, Saklofske, & Prifitera, 2005). It is also a common threat in cross-cultural research. For example, the Brief Symptom Inventory has a statement on it to check for depressive symptoms "feeling blue." When translated into Spanish and used with a group of Central American immigrants, Kim found that the color blue was not used to describe sadness at all (Asner-Self, Schreiber, & Marotta, 2006).

Regression to the Mean.   The regression to the mean phenomenon demonstrates that individuals who score on the outer extremes (either very high or very low) of the score continuum will naturally score closer to the mean when retested. School districts are seeing this problem in repeated mandated testing. Their highest scoring students are "dropping off" on the next round of tests, when in actuality it is best explained by regression to the mean. Extreme group analysis (EGA) is highly susceptible to this problem. EGA occurs when the sample is at either end of the continuum of the phenomenon of interest. For example, you put students who are in the bottom group of reading ability in a reading program, and they show reading ability gains after the treatment. In reality, there is little evidence that the treatment worked, and it is likely that it is just a simple regression to the mean.

Mortality.   In certain types of studies, mortality does mean the death of participants, but for most of social science research, mortality occurs when participants decide to disengage from the study. Depending on which participants leave and how many, their departure can affect the results and lead to incorrect inferences from your data. For example, during data analysis, there appears to be no meaningful change over time for a group of students learning how to solve different volume problems. The lack of difference may be due to the departures because those participants with increasing scores left the study, but those who stayed were hoping that their scores would change. This is also an issue when participants are removed from a study during the data examination or cleaning phase. One should examine the demographics and response patterns of participants who leave the study and examine the types of participants who are removed from the data set.

Selection Threat.   The above internal validity threats are considered single-group threats because the focus is on the sample group of interest. However, multiple-group designs (e.g., experimental and control group) are the norm and are subject to the same threats as single groups. The observed study differences are due to differences between groups that were preexisting or occurred during the study. A selection threat is generated when there are inconsistencies in the comparison groups, a sampling process problem that becomes a rival hypothesis. Within selection there are a few multiple-group threats, which we discuss next (Trochim, 2000).

Selection-history occurs when one group experiences a non-experiment-related event that the other group or groups do not. For example, a group of randomly assigned students in an educational intervention experience a fire alarm during the learning phase that the other groups do not experience. This happens more often than you would think.

Selection-maturation occurs when one group matures faster than the other, for example, a higher proportion of females in one group compared to males during adolescent years for a study on social skill development.

Selection-testing occurs when one group has previously taken the instrument. During an evaluation project, Jim discovered that the control group had been exposed to the content material and the test previous to his entry into the project, and subsequently, the control group outperformed the experimental group.

Selection-mortality occurs when one group has a higher rate of leaving. School-level data is prone to this type of problem based on mobility rate. Mobility rate is a percentage of students that enter and leave a school in a given time period. Students from families with lower socioeconomic status (SES) tend to have a higher mobility rate than students from families with a higher socioeconomic status. Because of this, researchers attempting to conduct studies over a semester, full school year, or longer have a difficult time because the lower SES students leave the school in higher proportions than the higher SES students.

Selection-regression occurs when one group has a larger proportion of very high or very low scorers. An example of selection-regression is two groups of students who are in a summer reading improvement program. The participants in Group 2 started at a much lower initial average score compared to the first group on a reading comprehension test. At the posttest, Group 2 has much greater reading comprehension gains compared to Group 1 because of initial very low scores.

Internal Social Effects

Humans are social creatures. Humans run experiments. Social creatures interact during experiments. It is unavoidable. Jim has tested this during experiments by having the researcher flirt or act overly social as participants enter the lab. The results were different between those who had this extra treatment study versus those who did not. The larger issue is the inferences that cannot be made to the larger population or simply inference mistakes that occur when these social effects occur (Trochim, 2000).

Diffusion or Imitation of Treatment.   The knowledge of the study's purpose or the difference in treatment can lead to diffusion or imitation of treatment. Many years ago, this happened to a friend who had created a behavioral contract with one of her classes, which allowed the class to have a pizza party at the end of the school year, but not with the other class. This was done in order to increase the positive behaviors in the first class. Unfortunately, at an unsanctioned off-school-property event (i.e., house party) near the end of the implementation phase, one student in the pizza group was talking to another student in the pizza group and a third student in the no-pizza group heard. Party over, the deal had been diffused to the other group. You could also consider the house party a historical event.

Compensatory Rivalry or the John Henry Effect.   John Henry supposedly tried to lay railroad track faster than a machine and thus was in rivalry with the machine. In research, when the control group tries to outdo or compete with the experimental group, the control and experimental group may perform in a similar manner. In the pizza example, the no-pizza group could get mad and decide to behave better than the pizza group. Though this is an odd concept, their desire to prove the teacher wrong outweighs everything else. They essentially want to mess up the results of the program, or in this case to cause problems and retribution to the teacher by actually behaving better, and this desire outweighs the fact they are not getting pizza for positive behavior. A **placebo** treatment is often given so that everyone knows they are in the study, but participants do not know whether they are in the experimental or control group.

Resentful Demoralization.   The reverse of the compensatory rivalry is resentful demoralization. For the no-pizza group, individuals or the group as a whole may begin behaving even worse than before the study. Interestingly, the differences between the two groups increases and the intervention appears to be working, when in actuality the difference in the two groups has nothing to do with the study.

Compensatory Equalization of Treatment.   For the no-pizza group, the parents became involved in who receives pizza, and then all the students received a pizza party at the end. Obviously, changes in the research design and methodology have occurred at this moment. Part of being transparent means that the researcher had to then clearly record this change of events as possible threats to the validity of his or her findings. Interestingly, the experimental group still had fewer negative behaviors at the point of the diffusion, for weeks after the diffusion, after the announcement of pizza for everyone, and at the end of the study. The no-pizza group's negative behaviors skyrocketed after the announcement of pizza for everyone! What do you think that was all about? Certainly, that question would lead you to another research project!

Novelty.   Simply being a part of the study causes participants to increase interest, motivation, or engagement. Therefore, the treatment may be effective because it is a novelty and not because it is better than other treatments or no treatment. To deal with this situation, one should conduct the study over a longer period of time, so this effect can wear off.

External Validity

External validity concerns the inferences that can be made to the larger population in general or to other populations. In quantitative-focused research, one of the goals is to make inferences from the sample in the study to the population in general. Unfortunately, problems from the design perspective can reduce the validity of those inferences.

Selection Treatment.   Even with random assignment, external validity can be a problem when the sampling process creates a bias that interacts with the experimental variable of interest and the results do not represent the population as a whole. We see this problem in what we call **convenient random sampling**. For example, you could say that the participants were randomly sampled, but the sample is actually a convenience sample from a Psychology 101 student pool, a grade school by your house, a company where you know the owner, or the train you ride to work. These participants may or may not represent the whole population of interest and may interact with the experimental variable differently than the rest of the population. As a group, the participants are a nonrandom or volunteer group. However, the inferences to the larger population base are greatly limited. After all, what percentage of the U.S. population is similar to the kinds of people who take Psychology 101, who choose to take your study, and who need the points toward their grades? Kim did a study once looking at the mental health of Central American immigrant and refugee community members. She used an acculturation measure that had been normed on immigrant Latinos who were college students. Yet, a full 65.3% of the sample of people she studied had a high school education or less (and 33.7% of the sample had six years of education or less).

Pretest Treatment Interaction.   Pretest treatment interaction occurs when the pretest sensitizes the participants to components of the study, which affects the posttest scores. How much will depend on the sample of participants, the nature of the study, and the nature of the instruments used. The more unique or different the material or the study is from previous experience, the more likely this affect will be seen. If you believe this could happen due to the nature of your study, consider gathering data from other sources, such as school or employment records that are not part of the study but can give you information on prestudy knowledge of the participants.

Multiple Treatment.   Multiple treatment concerns studies where participants engage in more than one treatment. For example, students participate in Reading Programs A, B, and C. The problem occurs when one treatment interferes positively or negatively with the other treatments. An example would be if participants who had treatment A first performed worse on the reading test after treatment B, and those participants who had treatment C first performed better after treatment B. This can be solved in the design so that every possible combination of treatments is covered and any effects can be examined.

Reactive or Participant Effects.   Participants react to knowing that they are being studied or watched. We all do, and we change our behavior. This change in behavior is why reality television is not reality. In general, the term **Hawthorne effect** applies to any situation in which participants' behavior is affected by knowing they are in the study or being watched. The name comes from a study at the Hawthorne Works plant of the Western Electric. The company was studying productivity and light intensity. As light intensity increased, production went up; and as light intensity decreased, production went down. The researchers, being good at observing and thinking, realized that it was not the light level that affected productivity, but the fact that attention was being paid to the workers.

Specificity of Your Variables.   In addition to developing stable measures as stated in the previous chapters, you must be specific about the definition of your variables and the details of how you had collected data that match that definition. You must give rich detail to the setting and the procedures you used, so that researchers can attempt to replicate or compare your study to other studies.

Experimenter Effects (aka Rosenthal).   As the researcher, you present a potential limitation. You can consciously, or unconsciously, affect the results by your engagement with the participants. Your gender, age, race, or outgoingness can affect the participants. The expectations for the study can also affect the participants when you engage with the experimental and control group differently and how you score their responses. For these reasons, the "blind" study or scoring is popular, where a third party not familiar with the study is executing the study or scoring the data. Many graduate students have begun their research careers as the third party in a set of studies.

Finally, there are externalities that can affect the outcome of programs, and the ability to design a project that limits outside factors is crucial. Therefore, having a clear understanding of the threats during the design phase of your program can help you strengthen the structure of the study and avoid negative comments from critics who review your work.

Ecological Validity

Ecological validity is related to the "realistic" nature of the material or context used in the experiment. The specificity of variables, multiple treatments, pretest effect, and any Hawthorne effect can also be considered an ecological validity problem. After a decade of map and text studies, the research group Jim participated in finally conducted one that was similar to how students see maps and related text material in textbooks. The results supported the previous basic research work, but this series of studies needed to be completed from an ecological validity perspective.

Statistical Validity

Statistical validity concerns using the most appropriate statistical analysis in relation to the design, data, and of course, the research question. This requirement seems obvious when one reads it, but it is a common mistake. There must be systematic connections between your research questions, your sample, the design, collected data, the analysis, and the discussion. All of it has to make sense together. Not surprising, studies without the clear link are likely to languish unpublished, unwanted, or ignored by the savvy consumer of research (i.e., you).

Now, if you want a challenge, try to identify all of the validity issues in Schuyler Huck's poem concerning the limitations of experimental designs. The poem can be found where it was published in the *Journal of Experimental Education* in 1991. The full reference can be found at the end of the chapter. Dr. Huck provides the answers in the article, so don't worry.

EXPERIMENTAL DESIGNS

Experimental designs have one thing in common: an independent variable (or variables) that is manipulated by the researcher. Each design can be described symbolically/graphically using a group of letters based on Campbell and Stanley (1963), where R = random assignment; O_i = observations (the subscript tells which time period); G1, G2, G3, etc., = which group the participants are in; and X_i = the treatment (i.e., the activity in which the participants are engaged in).

We use X_c (others use X_o to indicate no treatment) to indicate a control group. R indicates *random assignment* only of participants to one of the groups. You will also see this discussed as the ROX system. We present the types of designs by single-subject, pre-, quasi-, and true experimental because we feel that there is a natural flow in this order and it appears to have been acceptable to our students. After each design, you are asked in a table to answer five core questions and sometimes a few others. The five core questions are:

1. What are the weaknesses of this type of design? What bothers you?
2. What is the greatest internal validity threat? External?
3. What does this mean for the participants not discussed in the study? Think of Chapter 4 on sampling.
4. What about Chapters 5 and 6? What information is pertinent here?
5. What about the instrument used to gather the data? What are your concerns? What should your concerns be? Think "trustworthiness."

Single-Subject and Single-Subject Time Series Designs

The **single-subject design** is the study of one participant over time. In general, the participant is observed before an intervention or activity occurs and then observed after to determine whether the intervention made a difference.

Simple Time Series or A-B Designs. The simple time series or A-B design is the simplest of time series designs where a participant is observed multiple times during the **baseline period** A and then observed multiple times after the **experimental treatment period** is started, B. The general research question associated with this design is: Does the implementation of an experimental treatment decrease (increase) the observed behavior? For example, an educational psychology student wonders, "What are the number of daily positive statements before and after implementation of reflective journaling?" In our alphanumeric symbols from above it looks like

$$O_{11}O_{12}O_{13}O_{14}O_{15}O_{16}X_TO_{21}O_{22}O_{23}O_{24}O_{25}O_{26},$$

where the subscript indicates whether the observation is before or after intervention and the order of the observation (e.g., O_{12} means pretreatment second observation). The basic analysis for this design is descriptive by time point. A graphical descriptive statistic example is shown in Figure 7.1. The independent variables are time (days) and treatment (reflective journaling). The dependent variable is the number of positive statements.

The experimental reflective journaling was implemented after day 5 and, as can be seen, the number of positive comments are higher for days 6 through 10. In addition to the graph, the mean and standard deviation values before and after the implementation can be calculated and displayed.

FIGURE 7.1
Simple time series graph

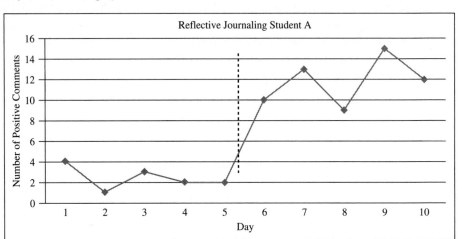

A-B-A and A-B-A-B Designs.   Extending the A-B design can be accomplished by removing the intervention and observing again (A-B-A design) and then implementing the intervention again (A-B-A-B design). Clearly, this can be extended over a long period of time. The A-B-A format is termed *reversal* and the A-B-A-B is termed *alternate time series.*

Preexperimental Designs: Beginning to Examine Groups of Participants

Preexperimental design is not experimental at all and clearly does not have random assignment or selection. More recently, some of these designs have been discussed as quasi-experimental (see below) (Shadish & Lullen, 2006). Personally, we view it as nothing more than examining and describing a group of participants. The **one-shot group case study** is the examination of a single group of participants after some experimental treatment or intervention. Symbolically, it looks like

$$X\ O,$$

where the X indicates that there is an intervention and the O indicates that some observation was made for the group. In our example, the research question may read as such: What are the scores on the Beck Depression Inventory-Short Form after participants listen to comic Denis Leary? The independent variable is the intervention of listening to comedy and the dependent variable is the BDI-Short Form score for each participant. The basic analysis is the mean and standard deviation of the individual participant scores from the instrument. This study could have just as easily collected open-ended responses with an analysis of the responses written into a narrative. Again, the design is one component; the actual type of data collected needs to align with the research questions and sample process chosen.

One Group Pretest-Posttest Design.   The one group pretest-posttest design adds an observation of the group before the intervention—so it is a simple extension of the previous design. Symbolically, it looks like

$$O_1 \; X \; O_2,$$

where the subscripts 1 and 2 indicate a pre- and postobservation (test), respectively. In this design we have added a pretest in order to determine the pre-intervention score of each individual. The student's research question is different: Does listening to the comedian Denis Leary change depression scores on the BDI-Short Form? The basic analysis is a paired or dependent t-test (Chapter 9) to see whether a statistically significant change occurred.

Static-Group Design.   The static-group design (nonequivalent comparison group without a pretest) is simply the one-shot case study with a separate group serving as a control. The second group of participants, G2, acts as a comparison to the experimental group on the outcome measure. For our continuing example, the research questions is: Do participants have different scores on the BDI-Short Form after listening to Denis Leary compared to a group that does not listen to Denis Leary? Symbolically, it looks like

$$
\begin{array}{lcc}
G1 & X_E & O \\
G2 & X_C & O \\
& \text{or} & \\
G1 & E \quad X & O \\
G2 & C & O,
\end{array}
$$

where G indicates the participants in the experimental (E) treatment and listening to Denis Leary and the participants that are in the control (C) group. The X indicates the group that experiences the treatment, and O indicates that an observation occurred for each group (the BD-Short Form scores). For this design, the basic analysis is an independent t-test to compare the mean values of the two groups.

Quasi-Experimental Designs

Quasi-experimental designs are a reaction to the traditional messy world of insitu research where groups of participants are preexisting or random assignment of individual participants is not possible. They are experimental designs because a variable is manipulated. Again, by manipulated we mean that one group engages in the treatment and one does not. Or, the groups receive different levels or activities related to that treatment. We have seen quasi-experimental designs used as precursors to full experimental designs, that is, pilot studies. Pilot studies are small-scale versions of a full study to test different components in order to examine the viability of the larger study. It's like making a 10-inch chocolate cake for the first time before you decide whether to make a three-level monstrosity for your friend's wedding. Major examples of quasi-experimental designs are diagrammed and discussed below. For more designs, see Shadish, Cook, and Campbell's (2002) quasi-experimental design book. There is a large body of literature written about quasi-experimental designs, and we have seen all of the true experimental designs below in quasi form because the participants were not randomly selected or assigned. We begin with the three generic forms of quasi-experimental designs.

Nonrandomized Control Pretest-Posttest Design.   By adding a pretest to a static-group design, one creates the nonrandomized control pretest-posttest design. Symbolically, it looks like

$$G1 \quad O_1 \quad X_T \quad O_2$$

$$G2 \quad O_1 \quad X_C \quad O_2,$$

where G_i indicates the group the participants are in, O_i indicates the observation time period, and X indicates the group of participants that received the treatment, or part of the treatment (X_T), and which group that received no treatment (X_C).

The student's research question has two distinct possibilities. The first is: Do scores on the BDI-Short Form change at different rates for the Denis Leary group and no-Denis Leary group? Clearly, the researcher would hope that the change in scores is much larger for the group who received the treatment. The second research question is: After controlling for initial depression scores, on the pre-intervention test based on the BDI-Short Form, is there a difference in BDI-Short Form scores between the Denis Leary group and the no-Denis Leary group? Obviously, the independent variable with two levels is treatment and no treatment, and the dependent variable is the score on the BDI-Short Form.

The pretest score can be considered a covariate. A *covariate* is a variable that the researcher believes needs to be controlled for or at least examined before the final analysis is done. The covariate is associated with the second research question above.

Extended Group Time Series and Cohort Design.   The extended group time series design is a group version of the single-subject design previously discussed. The participants in the group are observed multiple times, then a treatment is implemented, and then observations occur once again. Using our symbols,

$$G \quad O_{11}O_{12}O_{13}O_{14}O_{15}O_{16}X_TO_{21}O_{22}O_{23}O_{24}O_{25}O_{26},$$

where the subscript indicates whether the observation is before or after intervention and the order of the observation. The research question is: After determining a stable baseline score on the BDI-Short Form based on multiple administrations, is there a change in scores after the intervention and does that change last over time? Actually, there are multiple questions here that could be broken down, but this one is the all-encompassing picture. The participants who are followed over time could also be considered a cohort.

Note that the extended group time series design can be expanded with multiple groups, for example

$$G1 \; O_{11}O_{12}O_{13}O_{14}O_{15}O_{16}X_TO_{21}O_{22}O_{23}O_{24}O_{25}O_{26}$$

$$G2 \; O_{11}O_{12}O_{13}O_{14}O_{15}O_{16}X_CO_{21}O_{22}O_{23}O_{24}O_{25}O_{26},$$

where X_C (G2) is the control group.

Counterbalanced Design. The counterbalanced design is a reaction to multiple intact groups and multiple experimental treatments. Instead of one intervention, multiple comics could be used, such as Denis Leary, Tim Allen, and Jerry Seinfeld. Yes, all three are men, but we are controlling for a gender variable, while manipulating three types of comic genres. The counterbalanced design is also recommended for survey designs where participants must complete several surveys. The overall research question is: Are there differences in BDI-Short Form scores after listening to comedy? A more detailed question is: Are there differences in BDI-Short Form scores between participants who listened to each type of comic genre?

A partial version of all possible combinations in this design is

$$G1 \quad X_{T1}O_1 \quad X_{T2}O_2 \quad X_{T3}O_3$$

$$G2 \quad X_{T2}O_1 \quad X_{T1}O_2 \quad X_{T3}O_3$$

$$G3 \quad X_{T3}O_1 \quad X_{T2}O_2 \quad X_{T1}O_3,$$

where X_{Ti} indicates which treatment (comedian) the participants received and O_i indicates the observation time period. Therefore, $X_{T2} O_2$ indicates comedian number two, second observation.

Nested Data and Quasi-Experimental Designs. The participants in many quasi-experimental designs have a data problem: they are nested. Actually, many studies we read have **nested data**. There are many times when a whole classroom is assigned to treatment or control, yet the students are the actual observation unit. The students are nested within the assigned group. Historically, researchers just analyzed the student data, but the problem was that the class/teacher was assigned so the teacher was the unit of experimentation and the students were the unit of observation. Analyzing just the student data will give you the wrong estimates, or results. Aggregating that student data to the teacher/class level will do the same thing. The issue has easily been handled from an analysis perspective since the work on nested data by Hopkins (1982) and multilevel modeling by Raudenbush and Bryk (2002). This issue has been incorporated into most statistical packages or multilevel statistical packages.

Levin (1992) provided several alternatives to alleviate the nesting problem. From his suggestions, a readily implementable design alternative is to use six or more classrooms that are randomly assigned to the experimental condition and control/alternative condition. Therefore, you would have three classrooms for the experimental group and three for the treatment.

True Experimental Designs

True experimental designs have random assignment of participants to experimental/treatment and control groups. Random assignment is a very important component in reference to error and the assumptions of the statistical tests used to analyze the data (Chapter 9).

Posttest-Only Control Group Design.   In the posttest-only control group design, participants are randomly assigned to one or more experimental groups or control group and only one observation, after the treatment, occurs. Symbolically it looks like

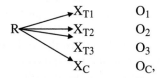

where X_{Ti} indicates the treatment (comedian) the participants are receiving, X_C is the control group, and O_i indicates the observation time period. Therefore, X_{T2} O_2 indicates comedian number two and observations from that group. Here, the research question would be: Do BDI-Short Form scores vary among the different participant groups?

Pretest-Posttest Control Group Design.   In the pretest-posttest control group design, the participants are randomly assigned to one of the experimental or control groups.

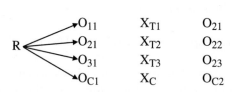

In the above design, we have three experimental groups and one control group. Each group is observed before and after the treatment. In the study, the global research question is: Do the scores on the BDI-Short Form differ between participants who listen to comics versus those who do not? A second question could be: After controlling for initial scores on the BDI-Short Form, do the scores differ between participants who listen to comics versus those who do not? In the second question, the pretest (initial scores) is considered the covariate.

Solomon Four-Group Design.   The Solomon four-group design is an advanced version of the other true experimental designs and can solve many of the internal validity problems, yet it is not very common as a design in social science research.

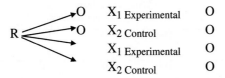

$$
\begin{array}{llll}
 & O & X_1\ \text{Experimental} & O \\
R & O & X_2\ \text{Control} & O \\
 & & X_1\ \text{Experimental} & O \\
 & & X_2\ \text{Control} & O \\
\end{array}
$$

We now have two experimental groups, but four groups, and two of the groups have a pretreatment observation. This is a combination of two basic designs: pretest-posttest control and posttest-only control. The major advantage to the researcher of the Solomon four-group design is the ability to determine whether a difference in the dependent variable is due to an interaction between the pretest and the treatment. The student now can ask these questions: Overall, do scores differ between those who listened to Denis Leary and those who didn't? And, were those participants' scores who saw the instrument before treatment different than those who only saw the instrument later? This second question is quite important to understand and test.

Factorial Designs.   Factorial designs are typically thought of as true experimental designs, but we have seen quasi-experimental factorial designs with intact classrooms. The most defining attributes of factorial designs are main and interaction effects. A main effect is the examination of differences between experimental groups, such as listening to comedy or not listening to comedy. An interaction effect is between the main effects (the independent variables), such as listening to different comedian genders (male/female) and comic content (comedic genre). In our ROX symbols, for a study of three types of genres (dark, improvisation, character) by gender it would look like

$$
\begin{array}{lll}
 & X_{DM} & O_{DM} \\
 & X_{DF} & O_{DF} \\
R & X_{IM} & O_{IM} \\
 & X_{IF} & O_{IF} \\
 & X_{CM} & O_{CM} \\
 & X_{CF} & O_{IF} \\
\end{array}
$$

where M = male, F = female, D = dark, I = improvisation, and C = character.

Factorial designs are typically drawn with blocks or squares though, so that people can more easily identify the levels of main effects and interactions. For example, the main effect for comedy genre has three levels—that is, three types. Comedian gender has two. There is one interaction, genre by gender. Main effects are related to the overall research questions: Are the scores different among participants based on hearing a male or female comedy? Are the scores different among the different genres? The third question is: Do scores among participants

FIGURE 7.2
Block drawing of a factorial design

	Main Effect Genre Dark, Improvisation, Character		
Main Effect Gender Male/ Female	DM	IM	CM
	DF	IF	CF

vary based on the interaction between gender and genre? In the third question, you want to see whether the two variables are interacting, thereby producing different score patterns among the groups. Figure 7.2 provides a graphical representation.

The design is a 3 (comedy genre) × 2 (gender) factorial design. A common extension of this would be adding a control group that only completes the BDI-Short Form. As stated earlier, the participants could be randomly assigned intact groups such as classrooms. Remember, one can collect numeric or non-numeric data; this is just the design not the data choice.

Latin Square Design. The Latin square design does not appear to be as well known or utilized in social science research as it could be. Mathematician Leonhard Euler worked on it (circa 1780), but it was known only in ancient periods of China and India (Armstrong, 1955). You probably have seen a Latin square and even used one if you have tried a Sudoku puzzle. The Latin square is a wonderful alternative to factorial designs when there is a limited number of potential sample participants and many treatments (independent variables) of interest. For example, let us say we have our three comedic genres, three marital status categories of our participants (single, married, divorced), and three age groups (20–34, 35–49, and over 50). For a factorial design, we would need 27 group combinations (3 × 3 × 3). With a Latin square, we need only nine combinations (Table 7.13). Wow, what a saving of resources!

Take a moment to write down your research question or questions based on the designs above. Use a separate piece of paper or the space provided at the end of the chapter. Then examine the differences among them, how your study would change, and potentially the conclusion you would make.

In Table 7.15, we have a basic experimental design chart with the types of analysis traditionally associated with each design and provide the answer to the threats and even potential threats that we asked you to think about above.

After reading about all of the internal, external, and statistical validity issues, you can easily see why people inherently like random assignment of participants to experimental groups. Many research problems are solved with random assignment. In reality, random assignment does occur but random selection does not. Therefore, you still potentially have a problem with your sample participants that were randomly assigned because they were not randomly selected.

NONEXPERIMENTAL AND DESCRIPTIVE DESIGNS

Nonexperimental designs do not have a manipulated variable or assignment of participants to groups. The researcher does not have the ability to manipulate (i.e., create levels) the independent variables or to randomly select or assign participants. For example, the researcher may not be able to decide ahead of time, *a priori*, how many milligrams of aspirin certain individuals take on a daily basis for a headache study. Also, in most instances, the researcher is using a preexisting data set. With all of these studies, you should be thinking about the limitations and how they reduce your ability to make believable inferences. You should especially focus on the sample and the quality of the data. Always ask: Do I trust this? Do I think I can make that inference? Finally, you should attempt to answer the five core questions for each. When you answer the questions, you should see a large number of potential limitations.

Ex Post Facto Designs

Ex post facto **designs** essentially "look back" in time to see why the variability or differences exist (e.g., drop-out rates, purchasing patterns, test scores). The researcher is typically looking "for a cause." In the comedy example, the researcher has current BDI scores and begins to interview all the participants in her group therapy sessions and notices that the ones who seem to be improving discuss how they used to love to go to comedy clubs.

A general research question for this type of design is: Do between-group differences explain the variability in BDI scores? Another example is: What is the proportion of dropouts at age 16 who also failed one or more classes in sixth grade compared to those students who have never failed a course? Or, how many of item X were sold on the aisle shelf versus at the checkout counter?

Comparative Designs

Comparative designs use naturally occurring groups. Note that this has historically been called *causal comparative*, but the ability to make a causal argument is really not the case with this design. Again, no variables are manipulated in order to examine differences. The researcher is interested in examining relationships among current variables. In the depression study, the research could examine the BDI scores by gender, education level, or occupation. For a comparative study, education level could be the independent variable with five levels (no high school, GED, high school graduate, bachelor degree, graduate degree) and the dependent variable is the BDI score.

Survey Studies

Survey studies are based on trying to obtain a description of where a population of interest and subpopulations are on a phenomenon of interest. You have filled many surveys in your life, such as the ones at the retail shopping malls, the ones that come with new product warranties, the ones done over the phone, and so on. Each of these techniques is used to determine how people think, feel, or behave. The consumer confidence index is a monthly survey examining how confident U.S. consumers are about the state of economic conditions.

Correlation Designs

Correlation designs examine the linear relationships between two or more variables of interest, such as professional development opportunities and job satisfaction. For the depression study, the examination of the relationship between the number of minutes per day listening to comedy and depression scores is one example. Correlation-based studies are quite common and typically are based on survey or questionnaire data (Chapter 6) and answer the basic research question: "Is there a relationship between variable X and variable Y?" For example, is there a relationship between the numbers of hours playing Guitar Hero III on the Nintendo Wii game system and the amount of housework that is not completed?

Observational Studies

Observational studies occur when the researcher observes and/or describes a phenomenon of interest. This is what Piaget did early on with his children. He observed and described their cognitive solving behaviors using different tasks. This design is more commonly thought of within qualitative methodologies, but many of us use observational techniques and collect numeric data. An example would be observing first-year teachers and indicating the number of times they ask students conceptual and procedural questions in a secondary school mathematics course.

Developmental Studies

Developmental studies are similar to time series, but without intervention. The researchers collect the same data over time in an attempt to see how the phenomenon develops. For example, K. Warner Schaie has conducted developmental studies on intelligence (Schaie, 1994). The data, when displayed over time, provide a path or trajectory of the phenomenon. Developmental studies typically use cohort, panel, and cross-sectional groups of participants for the study (Chapter 6). Developmental studies attempt to answer large questions, such as "Is the development of X continuous or discontinuous?"

Design/Analysis Blended Techniques

Many "designs" are really a blend of a design and an analysis technique, or they are not clearly separated in the literature. Below we discuss several techniques that are common and not so common in the social science literature. Note that most of these analyses can be used with experimental and nonexperimental quantitative data.

TABLE 7.1
Time series design questions

1. Answer the five core questions.

TABLE 7.2
One-shot group case study questions

1. Answer the five core questions.

TABLE 7.3
One group pretest-posttest questions

1. Answer the five core questions.

2. What does this simple pretest addition allow us to say later?

3. Compared to the previous design, what can we say about the effect of the intervention on scores?

4. How is this design an improvement over the previous one? Why?

TABLE 7.4
Static-group design questions

1. What does this simple addition allow us to say later?

2. Compared to the previous design, what can we say about the effect of the intervention on scores?

3. How is this design an improvement over the previous one? Why?

4. Answer the five core questions.

TABLE 7.5
Nonrandomized control pretest-posttest design questions

1. What does this simple addition allow us to say later?

2. Compared to the previous design, what can we say about the effect of the intervention on scores?

3. Is this design an improvement over the previous one? Why?

4. What do you think about the quality of a causal argument with this design? Is it good, poor, or mediocre with this design?

5. Answer the five core questions.

TABLE 7.6
Extended group time series and cohort design questions

1. What are the strengths and weaknesses of this design?

2. What can be said in comparison to a single-subject version of this?

3. What might happen to the scores given that the BDI is administered so many times?

4. Answer the five core questions.

TABLE 7.7
Extended group time series design with multiple-group questions

1. Is this better than the previous design? Why?

2. What do you get to say at the end about the participants or population?

3. Answer the five core questions.

TABLE 7.8
Counterbalanced design questions

1. What are the strengths of this design?

2. Answer the five core questions.

Regression.   Regression is quite popular in student theses and dissertations. Typically, the data used in **regression analyses** are from survey data that have been completed by participants in a study and typically involve a large number of participants. Therefore, the design is typically a survey and the analysis is regression. In a regression, there are one or more independent variables and one outcome or dependent variable. Using technical language, the dependent or outcome variable is regressed on the independent variables. The independent variables in regression are not typically manipulated, though they can be. The desire of the researcher is to have the independent variables strongly related to the dependent variable and

TABLE 7.9
Posttest-only control group design questions

1. What are the strengths of this design?

2. What do you think makes this design better than the quasi-experimental design?

3. What about the sample? Even with random assignment, does that solve the potential limitations?

4. Answer the five core questions.

TABLE 7.10
Pretest-posttest control group design questions

1. What do you think makes this design better than the posttest-only control design?

2. What are the strengths of this design?

3. What do you think makes this design better than the quasi-experimental design?

4. What about the sample? Even with random assignment, does that solve the potential limitations?

5. Answer the five core questions.

unrelated to each other. The depression researcher may be interested in regressing the new BDI score (the DV) on the IVs of the gender of the participant, the original BDI score, the number of months in counseling, and the average number of minutes listening to comedy per week.

Regression Discontinuity.   Regression discontinuity is quite similar to a time series (interrupted time series) design. The core difference is that the treatment (i.e., interruption) is not researcher implemented. Typically, an historical event or policy is implemented and the researcher wants to see whether there is a difference before and after that implementation. For example, what if the student had been collecting BDI-Short Form scores in Washington, D.C., for a few weeks before the attacks on 9/11 and kept collecting scores from the same people after 9/11? The most recent Supreme Court decision on handguns in Washington, D.C., is a time point where the number of gun-related crimes can be compared before and after the decision.

TABLE 7.11
Solomon four-group design questions

1. What do you think makes this design better than the pretest-posttest control design?

2. Given that this design can be expanded to more experimental groups, why is it better than the other designs?

3. What do you think makes this design better than the quasi-experimental design?

4. What about the sample? Even with random assignment, does that solve the potential limitations?

5. Answer the five core questions.

Meta-analysis.   Meta-analysis in quantitative research concerns the creation of effect sizes or review of effect sizes for a number of quantitative studies. Meta-analysis is generally described as the analysis of analyses and is associated with quantitative methodologies, but does have qualitative analogs (e.g., **meta-ethnography**). This technique is distinctly different from secondary analyses where the original data from a study is reanalyzed.

Quantitative meta-analysis mathematically reviews a collection of analyses from related individual studies in order to provide a summarization or integration of the results. The core of this review is the calculation of an effect size. The effect size can be based on the difference between two groups divided by their pooled standard deviation or a correlation between two variables. Quantitative meta-analysis, in its current form, became a popular integrative methodology with the work of Gene Glass (1976,

TABLE 7.12
Factorial design questions

1. What is better about factorial designs compared to the other designs?

2. What do you think makes this design better than the quasi-experimental design?

3. What about the sample? Even with random assignment does that solve the potential limitations?

4. There is a hidden question that we hope you would see. Is there an interaction between the gender of the participant and the gender of the comedian or the comic genre?

5. Answer the five core questions.

TABLE 7.13
Latin square example

Age Group	Marital Status		
	Single	**Married**	**Divorced**
20–34	Dark	Improvisation	Character
35–49	Improvisation	Character	Dark
Over 50	Character	Dark	Improvisation

TABLE 7.14
Latin square design questions

1. What about the sample? Even with random assignment does that solve the potential limitations?

2. Answer the five core questions.

2002). Others have used different quantitative techniques to summarize results before Glass, such as Schramm (1962) and Dunkin and Biddle (1974) to name two.

One reason for Glass's development of the effect size for meta-analysis was due to his frustration with hypothesis testing. Hypothesis testing in quantitative research methods leads to the determination of a statistically significant observation, or not. But, statistical significance is greatly affected by sample size and fails to indicate how large of an "effect" was observed.

Procedurally, quantitative manuscripts are gathered and examined to determine whether enough information is available to calculate effect sizes. Jacob Cohen (1992) provided basic guidelines for effect size interpretation such that .3 is a small effect size, .5 is moderate, and .8 is large. Those calculated effect sizes can then become dependent variables, and characteristics of a specific study (e.g., true or quasi-experimental) can become independent variables in a predictive regression equation. More recently, multilevel modeling analysis has advanced the traditional regression models by allowing the modeling of within and between study variance of calculated effect sizes (Raudenbush & Bryk, 2002).

There are numerous critics of quantitative meta-analysis both within the quantitative research community and outside of it. A common concern is the quality of the study included in the meta-analysis. A poorly designed and implemented study can lead to large effect sizes. Yet, a moderate effect size can be quite important if the manipulation of the independent variable is weak.

Design Experiments

Since Brown (1992) **design experiments (DEs)** have been increasing in the literature. DEs developed, as with many new ideas, out of a realization that the previous patterns of work did not assist in helping to solve the current problem. Many learning theory researchers had been working on quite complex learning environments and the traditional paradigms of research experimentation did not fit this research setting. Essentially, researchers are developing theories as they are systematically experimenting or instituting different learning programs, or software, on communities. Collins (1999) states that DEs examine learning in real-life, messy situations—not in the laboratory; they include many dependent variables, describe all of the variables and do not attempt to control them as in traditional experiments, acknowledge that the study design is flexible and can change and develop profiles, and do not test hypotheses.

To us, the most important part of design-based research is the ability to redesign as we move forward—a "test bed of innovation" as Cobb, Confrey, diSessa, Lehrer, and Schauble (2003, p. 9) stated. Schoenfeld (2006) provides the example about course development to explain DEs. He states, "Anyone who has taught knows full well, first versions of courses never come out right (nor do second or third versions although they may come closer to what one wants). Therefore the design process is iterative" (p. 197). As you watch your course over time, you see what works and make changes, you modify theories as the students react, and if you do this systematically, you collect all of this information in design or implementation cycles. Jim's teaching schedule is rarely the traditional semester length and so he has been systematically testing different components of the course within certain learning theories to examine the level of learning by students. It is messy and difficult, but it is enlightening and exciting because each new implementation is putting a theory in front of a firing line as students react and learn. It is important to note that the design experiment field is evolving and there is a great deal of work ahead for those who are engaged in this area.

BRIEF DISCUSSION OF ADVANCED DESIGNS/STATISTICAL TECHNIQUES

Advanced statistical analysis techniques are more and more common. In fact, from the perspective of the number of research articles that use the technique, they are no longer advanced. Below, we discuss some of the more current techniques you might encounter as you read. As with all of the designs, these are scholarly areas of research and as with your literature review in your topic area, you should also be a scholar of the design and statistical techniques you choose.

TABLE 7.15

Experimental design by analysis and validity threats

Name of Design	ROX Setup	Typical Analysis Continuous Quantitative Data	Threats	Potential Threat	Controlled
One Group Posttest-Only	*X O*	*Measures of central tendency and variability*	HI, SEL, MAT, SX	SR, INST, ATT, EE, TR, SE	
One Group Pretest-Posttest	*G O X O*	*Paired (dependent) t-test*	HI, PRE, MAT, TX, SX	SR INST, EE, TR, SE, SC, SEL, ATT	
Nonequivalent Group Posttest Only	*G1 X O* *G2 O*	*Independent t-test*	SEL	EVERYTHING BUT PRETESTING	
Nonequivalent Groups Alternate Treatment Posttest Only	*G1 X1 O* *G2 X2 O*	*Independent t-test*	WITHIN GROUP HI, ATT	SR, INST, MAT, DOT, EE, SE, TR	
Posttest-Only Control Group	**R G1 X O** **R G2 O**	**ANOVA**		HI, INST, ATT, DOT, EE, TR, SE, SC	SEL, MAT
Pretest-Posttest Control Group	**R G1 O X O** **R G2 O O**	**ANCOVA or one within/one between (repeated measure)**		ATT, DOT, EE, TR, SE, SC	HI, INST SEL, SR, PRE, MAT
Pretest-Posttest Control/Comparison Group	**R G1 O X1 O** **R G2 O X2 O** **R G3 O X3 O** **R C' O O**	**ANCOVA or ANOVA with one between (repeated measure) 4 levels**		HI, INST, ATT, DOT, EE, TR, SE, SC	SEL, SR, PRE, MAT
Solomon Four-Group	**R G1 O X O** **R G2 O O** **R G3 X O** **R G3 O**	**ANOVA or ANCOVA**		HI, MAT ATT, DOT	Protects against the remaining threats
<u>Nonequivalent Groups Pretest-Posttest</u>	G1 O X O G2 O O	ANCOVA or one within/one between (repeated measure)	SEL, MAT	HI, SR, INST, ATT, DOT, EE TR, SE, SC	
<u>Nonequivalent Groups Pretest-Posttest Comparison</u>	G1 O X1 O G2 O X2 O G3 O X3 O	ANCOVA or ANOVA with one between (repeated measure) 3 levels	SEL, MAT	HI, SR, INST, ATT, DOT, EE TR, SE, SC	
<u>Single-Group Time Series; also ABA or ABAB</u>	G OOOXOOOO	Averaged dependent t-test	HI	SEL, PRE, INST, ATT, TR, SE, SC	SR, MAT, EE
<u>Single-Group Time Series with Control</u>	G1 OOOXOOOO G2 OOOX$_c$OOOO	Averaged dependent t-test		SEL, INST, ATT, TR, SE, SC, EE	HI, SR, PRE, MAT

Italics are preexperimental designs.
Boldfaced are true experimental designs.
Underlined are quasi-experimental designs.

ATT	= ATTRITION		RE	= REACTIVE
DOT	= DIFFUSION OF TREATMENT		SC	= STATISTICAL CONCLUSION
EE	= EXPERIMENTER EFFECT		SE	= SUBJECT EFFECTS
HI	= HISTORY		SEL	= SELECTION
INST	= INSTRUMENTATION		SR	= STATISTICAL REGRESSION
MAT	= MATURATION		SX	= SELECTION INTERACTION
MT	= MULTIPLE TREATMENTS		TR	= TREATMENT REPLICATION
PRE	= PRETESTING		TX	= TESTING INTERACTON

Structural Equations Modeling and Its Family Members

Structural equations modeling (SEM), or latent variable analysis, is a family of techniques that is typically separated into two components: the measurement model and the structural model. The measurement model is essentially a confirmatory factor analysis (discussed below). The structural model tests the relationships among theoretical variables and is also termed the path-analytic component or path analysis.

SEM is a flexible analysis technique because a wide variety of data, research designs, and theoretical models can be analyzed. Many social science researchers are interested in measuring and understanding the relationships among variables that are not observable or "able to be seen," such as patient satisfaction, organizational functioning, or doctor empathy, but must be inferred from observations or other data. These unobservable variables are termed *latent variables, latent constructs*, or *factors*. To measure these latent variables, a participant may be asked to respond to several statements or questions about that latent variable, such as "Did the doctor understand your concern?" The score, from answering such questions, is a representation of the latent construct.

For structural equations modeling, you should learn to interpret the common graphical representations of theorized models presented along with the final model discussed. There are two basic types of variables: unobserved and observed. Unobserved variables, called latent factors, factors, or constructs, are graphically depicted with circles or ovals (Figure 7.3). *Common factor* is a less utilized term for latent factors because of the shared effects in common with one or more observed variables.

Observed variables are termed measured, indicator, or manifest, and a square or rectangle is traditionally used to designate them graphically (Figure 7.3). In Figure 7.3, the ovals represent the latent constructs and the small circles represent the unique factors—measurement errors—in the observed variable or disturbances in the equation, measurement, or both. Errors are the variance in the responses that are not explained by the latent construct. This is a major strength of SEM because measuring the error in the observed individual items separately allows for a theoretically error-free measure of the latent construct.

Single-head and dual-head arrows are called *paths*. Single-head paths represent directional effects from one variable (latent or observed) to another, and dual-head paths represent a correlation or relationship. In the example, we have created a model where three latent constructs—physical health, level of exercise, and life satisfaction—are measured using three items from three instruments. We are also stating by the direction of the arrows from the latent constructs to the items that the latent construct *causes* the scores on items.

Path analysis, the structural component of SEM (in bold arrows above), aims to provide the estimates of the magnitude and statistical significance of hypothesized causal connections among a set of variables using a set of regression equations. The path analytic is used when researchers *do not* complete a full SEM (measurement and structural) but only focus on the structural component. The path diagram is an illustration wherein the variables are identified and arrows from the variables are drawn to other variables to indicate theoretically based causal relationship. The

FIGURE 7.3
SEM graphical example

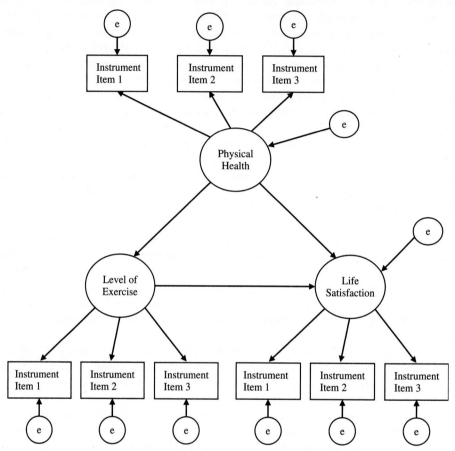

diagram in Figure 7.3 is also a mediated model (Baron & Kenny, 1986). That is, the relationship between level of exercise and life satisfaction is mediated by physical health. In path analysis, you may see the latent constructs drawn without the items (the measurement component). It is common, but not necessarily appropriate, for researchers to create a composite score out of the items and analyze the structural component using the composite score and skip the measurement analysis.

Confirmatory factor analysis (CFA) is used when the researcher's goal is to evaluate a number of well-articulated theories about the underlying structure for a set of variables. In Figure 7.3, the measurement structure is the specific relationships between the three latent variables (ovals) and the specific observed items (small rectangles). When using CFA, you are testing specific hypotheses about the number of factors and the items that are associated with those factors.

Exploratory Factor Analysis

The goal of **exploratory factor analysis (EFA)** is to analyze patterns in a correlation matrix in order to reduce a large number of variables to a smaller number of components or factors. EFA can be seen through the work of Spearman (1904, 1927, 1933). (See also Pohlmann's (2004) and Mulaik's (1987) historical essay on factors analysis.) Exploratory factor analysis holds the odd distinction of being a statistical technique that does not test a hypothesis (Mulaik, 1987).

Within exploratory factor analysis, there are two aspects that are important to understand: dimensionality (the number of components or factors to interpret) and rotation (transitioning the factors to a simple structure). The number of factors the individual items combine into is not known, and the researcher must eventually decide how many factors to allow. After the number of factors are chosen based on the analysis, the rotation or allowed relationship among the factors has to be determined. There are two general types: orthogonal and oblique. Orthogonal rotation restricts the factors, forcing them to be uncorrelated after rotation. Oblique rotation does not have this restriction and allows the factors to be correlated.

Hierarchical Linear Modeling

Hierarchical linear modeling (multilevel modeling) allows researchers in the social sciences confronted with data that have multiple levels, or nested data, to appropriately analyze the data. (See the discussion on unit of analysis above in quasi-experimental design.) Examples include individuals within families within neighborhoods, employees within divisions within companies, and students within classrooms within schools. Traditionally, data was either aggregated down or up a level and a multiple regression analysis was conducted. This was problematic because it calculated certain values incorrectly. Over the past 20 years, the software and computing power, along with the mathematics needed, have developed so that dealing with this nesting effect is much easier than it used to be through the general linear model of analysis of variance.

One strength of multilevel modeling is the fact that one can deal with the nesting effects. From a sociological perspective, you can examine the "big fish small pond, or small fish big pond" issue (Werts & Watley, 1969), such as when you have a participant who scores quite high in a small group of low-scoring participants or the reverse. A second strength of multilevel analysis is the cross-level interaction. A cross-level interaction tests whether the relationship between an independent variable and the dependent variable is affected by a variable at another level. For example, does attitude toward mathematics affect math achievement? Well yes, but it is affected by the size of the school the student is in. In smaller schools, the relationship between attitude and achievement is less pronounced than in large schools (Schreiber, 2002).

The above techniques are grouped together as multivariate statistical techniques and have a large number of rules and procedures to follow. This is evident by the fact that individual textbooks have been written on each of these techniques.

Therefore, it is advisable to complete a great deal of reading before embarking on these techniques. It is just as important to be a scholar of your methodology and statistical methods as it is to be a scholar concerning your area of interest. For many of us, methodology and analysis are our scholarly area of interest.

Latent Semantic Analysis

Latent semantic analysis (LSA) is a relatively new analysis technique for examining the meaning of words. Therefore, it is also a theory of meaning model, but it is not a complete model of language or meaning, and it needs the help of humans to work properly. Meaning is estimated through linear algebra (matrix mathematics; just like multivariate techniques) that is applied to a large body of text material (Landauer & Dumais, 1997). Currently there are five analysis components: Near Neighbors, Matrix, One-to-Many, Sentence, and Pairwise.

- Near Neighbors allows the examination of terms in relation to a body of text to examine which terms in the text are semantically near.
- Matrix allows the examination of multiple text or terms.
- One-to-Many allows the examination of one text to many other texts.
- Sentence allows the examination of the coherence between sentences.
- Pairwise allows the examination of pairs of text.

LSA is in its infancy from a technique perspective. Very few have used the technique for presentation or in social science research (e.g., Schreiber & McCown, 2007). Most of the articles we found deal with technical issues. We took a section of the chapter, formatted it properly, and then examined it using the Sentence component. We obtained a coherence value of .30. At this point, we do not have a good comparison to judge that, but knowing that the value can range from zero (no coherence) to one (perfect comparison), we decided to go back and make some adjustments to the text and boosted the value to .46 by changing sentences that had value near zero because, we felt, of a poor transition between topics.

TYPES OF DATA

Quantitative designs typically have numbers but that is not necessarily how the data began. Much of the data is qualitative at first and converted either by the participants or the researcher. For example, when you fill out a questionnaire that asks yes/no questions, you might circle yes or no and the researcher changes the responses to 1 or 0. Or you might fill in 0 or 1 for a no or yes response as you complete the questionnaire. Other conversions are possible because data can be transformed. Research purists, as we call them, will disagree with that statement, but data is transformed from words to numbers and numbers to words all the time. The map research Jim conducted in graduate school had students recall as much information about the maps and test material as possible in writing. The responses were then graded and assigned a numeric score, which was then analyzed quantitatively.

JUSTIFYING YOUR RESEARCH DESIGN

At the end of the day, you have to justify your research design within the previous literature and the questions you are trying to answer. Though it is not the best writing, you should be able to use the word *because* a great deal. For example, Jim chose a multilevel model for his dissertation *because* the data was nested, and he was interested in testing cross-level interactions that had been discussed in the literature, but not actually tested.

CASE STUDY

Ginette has created a factorial design for the undergraduate population. For example, she has manipulated the scale of the bar charts related to decreases in crime. This is her first independent variable, scaling. The basic graphs are shown in Figure 7.4. She is considering a third graph with different scaling so that she has three levels to this independent variable.

FIGURE 7.4
Crime levels between 2001 and 2007

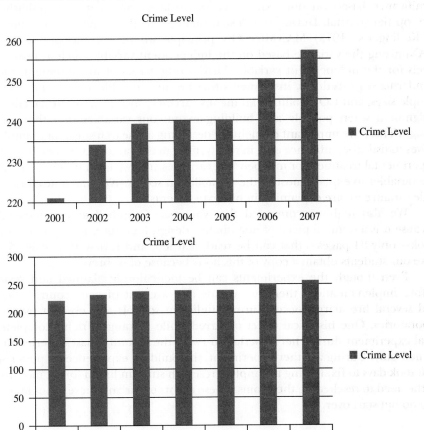

The question she is considering asking is: "Has there been a large increase in crime over the past seven years?" She is also concerned about the wording because of research conducted by Elizabeth Loftus in the 1970s. She is also considering manipulating one word, *large*, and using *significant*. This would give her a 3 × 2 factorial ANOVA with graph scale by word choices. This would help answer some of her questions about how graph design affects comprehension, but does not get at how people use these graphs if at all in daily life.

ARMCHAIR MOMENT

Designing a research experiment should lead you to minimize the number of weaknesses or limitations in your study. It's easy to forget this core idea of design. We have all made experimental mistakes at one point in time or another. Sometimes they are stupid mistakes. Jim once forgot to counterbalance a set of instruments before participants completed them. Other times, they are more serious, such as when a variable is collected improperly or not manipulated in a way that will illuminate the differences. Too often, we (researchers) focus on statistical significance based on our experience of working toward getting published in the top tier journal. During the design phase, though, we need to be reminded of Kerlinger's (1973) MAXMINCON principle where our thoughts center on MAXimizing the variance based on the independent variable, such as using three levels for the independent variable; MINimizing errors of measurement, such as standardized procedures, instruments that produce reliable scores, and adequate sample sizes; and CONtrolling extraneous variance, such as random selection and assignment when possible and building extraneous variables into the research design. These are important elements of designing a research study, but sample size drives statistical significance and, in reality, most of the variability is not explained by experimental treatment or independent variables, and we need to return to getting the variables to explain most of the variability in scores. We sometimes forget how little variance we are explaining in our experiments.

We also highly recommend that you read Campbell and Stanley (1963) because it is a seminal piece of quantitative design literature. It is a short, concise book—only 84 pages—that can be read, learned, and reviewed quickly. We still have our students obtain a copy of this book because of its brevity.

Even though the experiments can be meticulously planned and reviewed before implementation, there are events that are out of your control. Jim has had several fire alarms occur during studies in schools and even in psychology laboratories. One historical effect occurred while helping a friend complete the final experiment during her dissertation (well, the second to last experiment as it turned out). During another experiment, the building experienced a power surge that took days to fix, leaving a complete research study in limbo for six months due to the need to reschedule the rooms. These events occur and there is not much you can do but start over.

KEY WORDS

A-B-A design
A-B-A-B design
baseline period
cohort design
comparative design
compensatory equalization
   of treatment
compensatory rivalry
confirmatory factor
   analysis (CFA)
convenient random
   sampling
correlation design
counterbalanced design
dependent variable (DV)
design experiments (DEs)
developmental studies
diffusion or imitation of
   treatment
ecological validity
experimental design
experimenter effects
   (Rosenthal)
experimental treatment
   period
exploratory factor
   analysis (EFA)
ex post facto design
extended group time series
   design
external validity
factorial design
Hawthorne effect
hierarchical linear
   modeling

historical effect
independent variable (IV)
instrumentation threat
internal social
internal validity threats
John Henry effect
latent semantic analysis
Latin square design
maturation
meta-analysis
meta-ethnography
mortality
multiple treatment
nested data
nonexperimental design
nonrandomized
   control pretest-posttest
   design
novelty
observational studies
one group pretest-posttest
   design
one shot group case study
path analysis
placebo
posttest-only control
   group
preexperimental design
pretest-posttest control
   group
pretest treatment
   interaction
quasi-experimental design
random assignment
random selection

reactive or participant
   effects
regression analysis
regression discontinuity
regression to the mean
resentful demoralization
rival hypotheses
selection threat
selection-history
selection-maturation
selection-mortality
selection-regression
selection-testing
selection-treatment
simple time series
single-subject design
single-subject time series
   design
Solomon four-group design
specificity of your
   variables
static-group design
statistical validity
structural equations
   modeling (SEM)
survey studies
testing effects
true experimental design
validity

REFERENCES AND FURTHER READINGS

Armstrong, E. J. (1955). A note on Latin squares. *The Mathematical Gazette, 39*(329), 215–217.

Asner-Self, K., Schreiber, J. B., & Marotta, S. (2006). A cross-cultural analysis of the Brief Symptom Inventory-18. *Measurement and Assessment in Counseling and Development, 12*(2), 367–375.

Baron, R. M., & Kenny, D. A. (1986). The moderator-mediator variable distinction in social psychological research: Conceptual, strategic, and statistical considerations. *Journal of Personality and Social Psychology, 51,* 1173–1182.

Brown, A. L. (1992). Design experiments: Theoretical and methodological challenges in creating complex interventions in classroom settings. *The Journal of the Learning Science, 2,* 141–178.

Brown, A. L., Campione, J., Webber, L., & Mcgilley, K. (1992). Interactive learning environments—A new look at learning and assessment. In B. R. Gifford & M. C. O'Connor (Eds.), *Future assessment: Changing views of aptitude, achievement, and instruction* (pp. 121–211). Boston, MA: Academic Press.

Campbell, D. T., & Stanley, J. C. (1963). *Experimental and quasi-experimental designs for research.* Chicago: Rand McNally.

Cobb, P., Confrey, J., diSessa, A., Lehrer, R., & Schauble, L. (2003). Design experiments in educational research. *Educational Researcher, 32*(1), 9–13.

Cohen, J. (1988). *Statistical power analysis for the behavioral sciences* (2nd ed.). Mahwah, NJ: Lawrence Erlbaum Associates.

Cohen, J. (1992). A power primer. *Psychological Bulletin, 112,* 155–159.

Collins, A. (1999). The changing infrastructure of educational research. In E. Lagemann & L. Shulman (Eds.), *Issues in education research: Problems and possibilities* (pp. 289–298). New York: Jossey-Bass.

Cook, T. D., & Campbell, D. T. (1979). *Quasi-experimentation: Design & analysis issues for field settings.* New York: Rand McNally.

Downes, J., & Goodman, J. E. (2003). *Barron's finance & investment handbook.* Hauppauge, NY: Barron's Educational Series.

Dunkin, M., & Biddle, B. (1974). *The study of teaching.* New York: Holt, Rinehart and Winston.

Gibson, J. J, & Walk, R. D. (1960). The visual cliff. *Scientific American, 202,* 64–71.

Glass, G. V. (1976). Primary, secondary, and meta-analysis of research. *Educational Researcher, 5,* 3–8.

Glass, G. V. (2000, January). Meta-analysis at 25. Retrieved from http://glass.ed.asu.edu/gene/papers/meta25.html

Hopkins, K. D. (1982). The unit of analysis: Group means versus individual observations. *American Educational Research Journal, 19*(1), 5–18.

Huck, S. W. (1991). True experimental design. *The Journal of Experimental Education, 58*(2), 193–196.

Hunter, J. E., & Schmidt, F. L. (1990). *Methods of meta-analysis: Correcting error and bias in research findings.* Newbury Park, CA: SAGE Publications.

Kenny, D. A. (1979). *Correlation and causation.* New York: John Wiley & Sons.

Kenny, D. A. (2004). *Correlation and causation* (Rev. ed.). Retrieved from http://davidakenny.net/books.htm

Kerlinger, F. N. (1973). *Foundations of behavioral research.* New York: Holt, Rinehart and Winston.

Kirk, R. E. (1995). *Experimental design: Procedures for the behavioral sciences* (3rd ed.). Pacific Grove, CA: Brooks/Cole.

Klein, R. B. (2005). *Principles and practice of structural equation modeling* (2nd ed.). New York: Guilford Press.

Krishef, C. H. (1991). *Fundamental approaches to single subject design and analysis.* Malabar, FL: Krieger Publishing.

Landauer, T. K., & Dumais, S. T. (1997). A solution to Plato's problem: The latent semantic analysis theory of the acquisition, induction, and representation of knowledge. *Psychological Review, 104*(2), 211–240.

Landauer, T. K., Foltz, P. W., & Laham, D. (1998). Introduction to latent semantic analysis. *Discourse Processes, 25*, 259–284.

Landauer, T. K., McNamara, D. S., Dennis, S., & Kintsch, W. (Eds.). (2007). *Handbook of latent semantic analysis.* Mahwah, NJ: Lawrence Erlbaum Associates.

Lazaruk, W. (2007). Linguistic, academic, and cognitive benefits of French immersion. *Canadian Modern Language Review, 63*(5), 605–627.

Levin, J. R. (1992). On research in classrooms. *Midwestern Educational Researcher, 5*(1), 2–6.

Messick, S. (1989). Meaning and values in test validation: The science and ethics of assessment. *Educational Researcher, 18*(2), 5–11.

Mulaik, S. A. (1987). A brief history of the philosophical foundations of exploratory factor analysis. *Multivariate Behavioral Research, 22*, 267–305.

Noblitt, G. W., & Hare, R. D. (1988). *Meta-ethnography: Synthesizing qualitative studies.* Newbury Park, CA: SAGE Publications.

Pohlmann, J. T. (2004). Use and interpretation of factor analysis in *The Journal of Educational Research:* 1992–2002. *The Journal of Educational Research, 98*(1), 14–23.

Prifitera, A., Saklofske, D. H., & Weiss, L. G. (2004). *WISC-IV clinical use and interpretation: Scientist-practitioner perspectives* (pp. 71–100). San Diego, CA: Elsevier Academic Press.

Raudenbush, S. W., & Bryk, A. S. (2002). *Hierarchical linear models: Applications and data analysis methods* (2nd ed.). Newbury Park, CA: SAGE Publications.

Schaie, K. W. (1994). The course of adult intellectual development. *American Psychologist, 49*(4), 304–313.

Schoenfeld, A. H. (2006). Design experiments. In J. L. Green, G. Camilli, & P. B. Elmore (Eds.), *Handbook of complementary methods in education research* (pp. 193–206). Mahwah, NJ: Lawrence Erlbaum Associates.

Schramm, W. (1962). Learning from instructional television. *Review of Educational Research, 32*, 156–167.

Schreiber, J. B. (2002). Institutional and student factors and their influence on advanced mathematics achievement. *The Journal of Educational Research, 95*(5), 274–286.

Schreiber, J. (2008). Core reporting practices in structural equation modeling. *Research in Social and Administrative Pharmacy, 4*(2), 83–97.

Schreiber, J. B., & McCown, R. R. (2007, April). *Evaluating university teaching in the context of tenure and promotion: Framing the argument.* A paper presented at the annual meeting of the American Educational Research Association, Chicago, IL.

Shadish, W. R., Cook, T. D., & Campbell, D. T. (2002). *Experimental and quasi-experimental designs for generalized causal inference.* New York: Houghton Mifflin.

Shadish, W. R., & Lullen, J. K. (2006) Quasi-experimental design. In J. L. Green, G. Camilli, & P. B. Elmore (Eds.), *Handbook of complementary methods in education research* (pp. 539–50). Mahwah, NJ: Lawrence Erlbaum Associates.

Spearman, C. (1904). General intelligence objectively determined and measured. *American Journal of Psychology, 15,* 201–293.

Spearman, C. (1927). *Abilities of man.* New York: McMillan.

Spearman, C. (1933). The uniqueness of g. *Journal of Educational Psychology, 24,* 106–108.

Tabachnick, B. G., & Fidell, L. S. (2001). *Using multivariate statistics* (4th ed.). Boston, MA: Allyn & Bacon.

Thompson, B. (2004). *Exploratory and confirmatory factor analysis: Understanding concepts and applications.* Washington, DC: American Psychological Association.

Trochim, W. M. K. (1984). *Research design for program evaluation: The regression-discontinuity approach.* Newbury Park, CA: SAGE Publications.

Trochim, W. (2000). *The research methods knowledge base* (2nd ed.). Cincinnati, OH: Atomic Dog Publishing.

Weiss, L. G., Saklofske, D. H., &, Prifitera, A. (2005). Interpreting the WISC-IV index scores. In A. Prifitera, D. H. Saklofske, & L. G. Weiss (Eds.), *WISC-IV clinical use and interpretation: Scientistpractitioner perspectives* (pp. 71–100). New York: Elsevier Academic.

Werts, C. E., & Watley, D. J. (1969). A student's dilemma: Big fish–little pond or little fish–big pond. (ERIC Document No. ED029559)

CHAPTER 8

Qualitative Design

KEY IDEA

Protecting your fort from attack: A well-thought-out qualitative design.

Understand the basic differences between interactive and noninteractive approaches.

Describe the key components of the approaches for ethnography, phenomenology, grounded theory, critical theory, case study, narrative inquiry, content analysis, and historical analysis.

Describe the differences among the approaches.

Describe issues related to research using human participants and to institutional review boards.

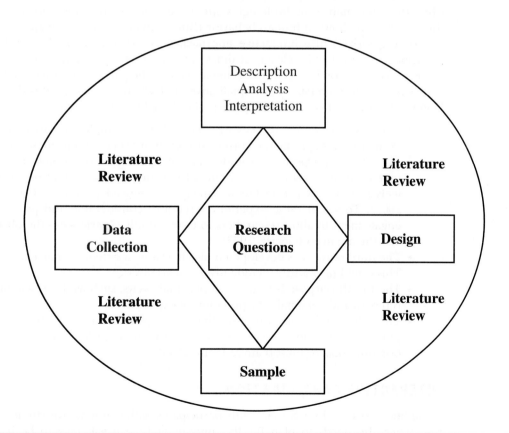

INTRODUCTION TO QUALITATIVE DESIGN

This chapter describes qualitative research methods, and then focuses on several types of traditionally designated qualitative research designs: ethnographic, phenomenological, grounded theory, case study, critical theory, narrative inquiry, survey, content analysis, and historical analysis. We could not discuss every type of qualitative methodology or the derivatives of each approach as they have evolved over the decades. Therefore, we chose to focus on a few that provide a variety and grounding for your initial introduction to these methods.

Qualitative research came out of the sociology and anthropology fields and describes the processes in which institutions, societies, families, and individuals engage. Qualitative research offers a way to dig deep into context, meaning, subjective experience, and other phenomena (Burke, 2005; Shaw, 2003). Qualitative research offers the opportunity to explore and discover hypotheses and theory, describe meaning (e.g., what an experience means to a person), and recognize multiple truths. Philosophically, qualitative research comes out of the postpositivist, postmodernist, and poststructuralist traditions (for a more detailed history, see Denzin & Lincoln (2005)). Qualitative studies cannot answer the what, where, and when that quantitative methodologies attempt to address, but they can focus on the whys and the hows of human behavior (Burke, 2005). Further, the approaches can be categorized into **interactive approaches**, where the researcher and the participants interact quite closely at times, and **noninteractive approaches**, where there is no interaction between researcher and the participants or person of interest. A succinct way to understand how qualitative methodology is best used is through Donmoyer's (2001) five overarching purposes of qualitative research:

- The first purpose is in seeking "Truth"; for example, researchers may wonder what might be the correct answer or answers to their question.
- The second purpose is to understand people's phenomenological interpretations; for example, researchers try to discover what depression truly feels like or how prison life is actually experienced (Bontra & Gindreau, 2005). To get at these experiences requires considerable and prolonged engagement to allow researchers to taste the full experience—the obvious and the nuanced (Geertz, 1973).
- The third purpose is developmental—how does a system change over time? This would necessarily include historical archives.
- The fourth purpose is to develop personal essays, such as the researcher's reflexive and personal interpretation of experience.
- The fifth and final purpose that undergirds qualitative research is praxis/social action research—the study of how we learn as people, as organizations, or both (Cho & Trent, 2006).

INTERACTIVE PARTICIPATION

In addition to the close contact with participants within interactive studies, the researcher also needs to plan for the amount of time it will take to be in the field. Many young researchers, who are trying to answer important questions, do not always realize the number of hours that are absorbed moving between sites, or scheduling interviews, and so on. As important as these methodologies are, they also absorb a great deal of research resources.

Ethnography

Ethnography arose primarily out of the cultural and social anthropological fields, which studied both how culture affected behavior and how cultural processes evolved over time. Ethnographers are interested in an entire group of people who share a common culture and have the goal of describing a culture in depth from an insider's perspective or reality. In other words, researchers are learning to think like a native or see from the natives' perspective (Geertz, 1974). As with all designs, there is an art and a science to it. The questions most likely to be posed that may lead to ethnographic research include functional and/or institutional change over time. For instance, questions in education may include: How does learning occur? How do high school cliques develop and what purpose(s) do they serve? How is abstract reasoning transferred (Patton, 1990)? In consumer behavior research, the interest could be on buying patterns or brand loyalty of certain groups (Schouten & McAlexander, 1995).

Therefore, ethnographers will observe a group in the natural setting for an extremely long time (e.g., months or years) with an open mind and an understanding of their own schemas of how they believe the world works. The focus for the researcher is the everyday occurrences and interactions of the individuals from the group, whereby the ethnographer can come to identify the norms, beliefs, values, structures, and behavioral patterns. The concept or boundary of "culture" has changed over time. Most people inherently think of culture as a large group of individuals (e.g., Italians), but culture can be a smaller group, such as an English department in a rural high school. If your research area appears to be centering around understanding a group of people in their natural setting (e.g., five-year-olds in kindergarten), then an ethnographic approach would be appropriate.

Cultural anthropologists such as Margaret Mead and Gregory Bateson lived with and interpreted the lives of the observed by learning to think like the people they were observing. This participant observation allows the researcher to enter into people's worldview, the **emic**, to describe these worldviews without the bias and judgment of the researcher's worldview. Unfortunately, observations can be biased by the dominant educational and scientific worldview of the researcher, which represents the **etic**, that is, the external social scientific perspective on reality.

The major design component of ethnography is fieldwork. The first step is to gain access to the site and the people you are interested in. This is easy for us to write, but not so easy to accomplish. You will most likely deal with a gatekeeper, and you must have already developed your informed consent materials and procedures (see Institutional Reviews Board in the Armchair Moment). The site you have chosen should be one in which you are a stranger and have no conflict of interest in the observations from the study, though this is not always the case. You might know a site well and be able to get easy access, but having a detached perspective to begin with is probably a better approach for someone new to this method. Once you have access, you need to determine your key informants, those who have information and are willing to provide that information to you. In the field, you are a participant-observer; there is no way to "make yourself invisible" and for people to go on about their normal daily lives. That is one of the reasons it takes a long time for a good ethnography to be completed. As you spend more time at the site, you will move in a trajectory path from the periphery toward the center and eventually outbound (Wenger, 1998). During your time in the field, you will be collecting extensive field data, including notes, maps, concept maps, and frequency counts (Leech & Onwuegbuzie, 2007). Field notes are not necessarily written as you are observing; sometimes you will complete them after the observation period. Other data collection techniques (e.g., interviews) and equipment (e.g., audiotapes), artifacts, and records are all common in ethnography. Now, watching as you are in the field or collecting artifacts is harder than it sounds. If you are new to research, the amount of information that can be collected from watching individuals in the field is enormous. We suggest you obtain more experience and understanding of ethnographic research before embarking.

In ethnographic research, and qualitative research in general, you will read or hear the term *thick description*, coined by Geertz. **Thick description** is the rich information that brings to life the scene you are describing. Geertz (1973) argued that the researcher constructs a reading of what happened and must include the time, the place, what specific people said and did, and what was done to them based on the world around them. To ignore this rich information would make the interpretation meaningless. In ethnography, thick description includes

- direct, firsthand observation of daily behavior;
- interviews (in-depth and informal, with people from all hierarchical positions in the society as well as identified key consultants);
- genealogy (as understood and valued by the group being observed); and
- local beliefs and perceptions.

How Counselors Use Thick Description.   In some ways, counselors use thick description in their practice without necessarily recognizing the term.

- A counselor often describes the issue on which the client reports and how he, the counselor, then interprets what he has seen, heard, and felt.
- The counselor also records his own observations and responses (cognitive and affective) to the client's report and interpretation. This includes, but is not limited to, behavioral observations regarding voice tone, body position, eye contact, and dress as followed with interpretations of said observations.
- Finally, the counselor uses these notes and his theoretical orientation to interpret what he believes is occurring and what therapeutic intervention might be useful. (This is similar to Subjective, Objective, Assessment, Plan [SOAP] notes for client care.)

If the counselor and the client become stuck, the counselor may request for either individual or group supervision. The notes allow others to offer perspectives and interpretations, depending on the clinical supervisor's history, orientation, culture, and experience. For example, Kim and her colleague once ran a psychoeducational group for immigrants and refugees to the United States addressing issues related to acculturation by using poetry (Asner-Self & Feyissa, 2002). In one session, participants read a poem titled "Yes or No." The interpretations of what "yes" and "no" meant differed by gender, country of origin, age, social standing, tone of voice, and body language. A "no" uttered by a woman in response to a request for a social engagement could be interpreted by a man as a "no, but try asking me later," "maybe," or a "never in your life." However, a "yes" from a girl to her parents' request to do a chore might mean "I will do it now," "I will do it when I am finished doing what I am doing now," "I will do it because you will not stop bugging me," or "I will not do as you have asked, however, I must say 'yes' because I may not respond otherwise."

Many social workers observe clients in their homes; many counselors, with the exception of school counselors, do not. Counselors in community agencies observe clients engaging in activities with other staff and clientele; family and couple counselors can observe familial interaction in their offices. However, for the most part, counselors tend to see the clients out of their natural settings. Despite this professional separation, counselors as researchers do engage in ethnographic research to gain a better grasp of the clients' shared histories, realities, worldviews, beliefs, and values (Vontress & Epp, 1997).

Finally, as Wolcott (1994) has noted, it is more important to be a listener and not a social talker. It also helps if you present yourself as someone who needs things explained over and over because you get a great deal of information and multiple examples.

Ethnographers are Not Value-Free.   In recent years, ethnographers have struggled with the recognition that their techniques are not value-free; rather, they are infused with Western philosophical thought representing, sometimes, colonialistic power differentials that assume a superiority of Western civilization over non-Western civilizations and cultures. To avoid this type of bias, researchers must bring to the table as much information as possible about their personal perspectives so that readers and practitioners can make their own interpretations.

Phenomenology

Phenomenology, as we will discuss, is based on current North American work in social sciences, such as sociology and education. This is the empirical approach to the study of the immediate lived experience before one has had time to reflect on the experience. The reflective is the study of the meaning of something, such as *friend*. Phenomenological methodology answers research questions aimed at describing the *essence* of a phenomenon. Phenomena are considered observable events that a person experiences rather than intuits. The essence of the phenomena refers to the

IN-TEXT ACTIVITY

1. Consider your day-to-day peer group. Who are you around most of the day? What are your beliefs as a group?

2. Visit a site where you believe their beliefs will be quite different from yours. For example, being born and brought up as a Christian, you attend a function at a non-Christian religious organization (e.g., Buddhism, Hinduism, Islam, Judaism, Sikhism, Wiccan), or go to the mall and observe a group you might not understand (e.g., tweens, children aged 8–12).

3. Just watch and listen.

4. Ask yourself: What do I see and hear? Write down what you observe in great detail. Did I hear something many times? What are their beliefs or values? What are my beliefs about this?

_____

_____

_____

_____

_____

_____

_____

_____

_____

''individual, real, or ultimate nature of a thing'' (Merriam-Webster, 2007). What is the essence and ultimate nature of the experience of, say, depression? Childbirth? Homelessness? Graduating? A Pittsburgh Steelers' home game? For women? Men? In Japan? Rural southern Illinois? New York City? Brownsville, Texas? How does a woman, man, Japanese, rural, or urban American experience these phenomena and intersubjectively (personally) construct meaning? Phenomenological research cannot be used to explain why people become happy; rather, it is used to describe how people experience content. Questions that will lead to a phenomenological study tend to focus on the essence of experience. What is the essence of being happy? Or, how do prison inmates experience rehabilitation programs?

The goal of phenomenological research is describing the phenomenon from the person's (or persons') perspective with as few preconceived notions or influence from the researcher as possible. Paradoxically, phenomenologists recognize, and actually embrace, the belief that no researcher can be fully objective or fully divorced from assumptions (implicit and explicit), and to purport to be able to do so is foolishness (Hammersley, 2000).

Phenomenological research can be done in a single-subject case study design or can include interviewing and/or observing multiple persons (Groenewald, 2004). Phenomenology defies specific techniques (Groenewald, 2004; Hycner, 1999), as use of techniques inherently detracts from the thick description of the inter-subjectively constructed meaning. Having said this, there are some generally accepted patterns of implementing phenomenological research. Moustakas (1994) suggests that researchers approach the phenomenological analysis in three phases:

1. The first phase is *epochè*, during which the researcher purposefully examines his or her own assumptions about the phenomenon to be studied.
2. The second phase is *phenomenological reduction* or *bracketing*, during which the researcher removes the phenomenon from the environment in which it occurs, takes it apart, and analyzes it in its purest form.
3. In the third phase—*structural synthesis*—the "true" essence of the experience for the participants is described.

Keep in mind that phenomenological research does not attempt to answer why people may experience the particular event as they do; its strength is in describing that event as one that involved experience and derive meaning from the interaction with the phenomenon. The approach does not offer causal explanation or interpretive generalizations. The results of such description may lead to further research into investigating "why," "how many," "what leads to this," and "what prevents/promotes this." The focus is the direct description of a particular event or situation as it is lived.

Grounded Theory

What if, in the process of trying to step into a client's worldview, you experience a jolt in your own worldview? You experience genuine doubt (Peirce, 1877). What if you found that what you had previously held to be unquestioningly "true" and "right" and "good" in certain situations was not necessarily so? This is an experience with which social scientists who have worked and lived in other countries are familiar. Different cultures may have considerably different ways of defining what is true, right, and good. And these "truths" are relevant and essential. As social scientists, we grapple daily with the need to understand the complexity of human interactions and behaviors. The primary purpose of **grounded theory** is focusing on situations or incidents and generating core concepts that help to explain people's behaviors (Glaser & Strauss, 1967).

Grounded theory, as a qualitative research method, was introduced by two sociologists, Barney Glaser and Anselm Strauss, in their book *The Discovery of Grounded Theory* (1967), in which they went over the methodology they used when conducting a research study on dying in California hospitals (see Glaser & Strauss 1965). Grounded theory emerged as a way to wed elements of good quantitative methodology (logic, systematic analysis, and scientific rigor) with the richness of qualitative methodology (Glaser & Strauss, 1967; Walker & Myrick, 2006). It was designed to allow researchers to reason inductively (though we would argue, abductively!) to generate hypotheses and theories about how people "create and respond to experiences" (Broussard, 2006, p. 215) from their own interactions with the data, rather than begin *a priori* with hypotheses and theories to be systematically confirmed or disconfirmed. Such resultant theories would "grab, would fit the data, and would work in the real world" (Walker & Myrick, 2006, p. 548). Grounded theory is not intended to be descriptive; rather its primary purpose is to focus on situations or incidents and generating core concepts that explain people's behaviors (Glaser & Strauss, 1967).

Collecting Data and Forming a Theory.   Theories and core stories emerge from the data. Data consist of the words, phrases, sentences, paragraphs, and meanings people ascribe to them in their response to situations. The researcher collects data and develops or forms what are called concepts. The concepts are not static but are dynamically developed as the data are collected. The data are constantly and continually compared, analyzed, and categorized. As the data collection and analysis continue, insight increases. As a result of increased insight and understanding, the concepts are adjusted and new ones are generated.

After a point of **saturation** is reached, when new data do not generate new concepts or aid in the modification of established concepts, the researcher goes to the literature to determine how that literature fits the generated concepts. A grounded theory is developed and findings are reported professionally. Grounded theory, then, is fundamentally a process designed to aid in the development of a specific theory that describes human interactions and informs practice (Broussard, 2006).

Variations on Grounded Theory.   Since the 1970s, grounded theory has evolved, with Glaser and Strauss going in different directions in three areas, including

1. concerns that researchers are using grounded theory either to generate "emerging" theories or "forcing" theories to emerge by the manner in which questions are asked;
2. how or whether to verify data and its meanings; and
3. how, specifically, to code and analyze the data generated.

(see Walker and Myrick (2006) for a discussion, or delve into the primary sources yourself: Glaser (1978, 1992) and Strauss and Corbin (1990, 1998)). Glaser (1992) argues heavily for immersing oneself in the data and over time allowing the data to offer up an emerging theory that could explain the human interactions involved. Strauss and Corbin (1990) argue that, to be as clean as possible from professional biases, researchers should not conduct a prestudy literature review. Rather, they should take the time to determine what they think and feel about the human situation to be studied in an attempt to recognize the cognitive filters through which analysis will occur. This transparency is necessary to ensure research rigor.

Briefly, in pure Glaser grounded theory, interviews are not audiotaped or videotaped, nor are notes taken. Rather, the researcher (or analyst) remains integral to the interview, writing down his or her memory of the content in field notes. Relevant data may also be collected through the popular press, seminars, informal discussions, professional conferences, and oneself. The researcher simultaneously engages in inductive reasoning through what Glaser calls **substantive coding**. Line by line of field notes are coded to define the situation and to determine how the person attempted to resolve the situation. Again, simultaneously, the researcher drafts memos to record his or her evolving thinking as the coding and conceptualization continue. Through this *open* substantive iterative *coding*, wherein categories generated from one situation or incident are compared incident by incident, together with the researcher's probing with **neutral questions**, a core concept emerges. This core concept is then used to selectively code data with the core concept as the researcher's filter, discarding and setting aside data that pertain to other concepts as irrelevant for his or her current purposes (**selective coding**). For example, when Jim was coding data on what counted for teaching excellence from faculty handbooks, he set aside all the comments about scholarship or service.

Glaser then moves on to the deductive phase of the research, the **theoretical sampling**—all subsequent data are both selected and analyzed with the core concept front and center. At all times, grounded theory researchers use **theoretical sensitivity**, the capacity to simultaneously conceptualize data intellectually as impartial observers and maintain a sensitive understanding of the research process and the researcher's role within that process. This process is similar to what the skilled professionals, such as counselors, develop to be effective with their clients.

Strauss and Corbin's manner of conducting grounded theory differs from Glaser's by using theoretically derived dimensions (factors based on previous research) during open coding, thereby *forcing*, rather than *emerging*, the theory earlier in the coding process. Timing on the use of theoretical sensitivity is another difference. Glaser believes that one attains theoretical sensitivity through in-depth immersion into the data. Strauss and Corbin, however, specifically offer techniques to improve theoretical sensitivity, such as **flip-flop**, where you turn the concept inside out (or upside down) in order to get a different perspective (see Chapter 4; Corbin and Strauss (2008)). Another difference between the two grounded theories is the process of **axial coding** introduced by Strauss and Corbin (1998). We believe that differences are so great that they are really two different approaches within the overall framework of grounded theory.

More recently, Bryant (2002) and Charmaz (2000, 2005) have brought forward a more constructivist grounded theory approach. They have retained the major components from the Strauss and Corbin approach 'but acknowledge the researcher's role in the development of the codes and categories. They have added in the issues of reflexivity, personal schemas, and the existing research base that affect the process.

IN-TEXT ACTIVITY

Learning the functional aspects of grounded theory can be difficult for those new to the method (Huehls, 2005). Below is an activity you can work through to give you a taste of this method.

1. First, obtain several issues of a magazine. We use relatively current issues of *TV Guide*, because you will be familiar with the shows.
2. Take the issues of *TV Guide* and create categories for the shows. For example, begin to create comedy, drama, male lead, female lead, cable (Basic), cable movie channel (e.g., HBO), and night of the week. If you have film and television experience, you might add things such as "arcing show," dramedy, or political drama.
3. Look up Neilson ratings or some sort of guide for popularity or success.
4. Next, examine the connections among the categories. What do you see?
5. Now, see if anyone else has done this from your class, or if you are reading this on your own, ask someone else to complete the activity.

In a grounded theory study, Moore (2005) studied five women with severe physical and/or psychiatric disabilities and how they "attributed meaning to their lives, experiences, and decisions" (p. 344). Moore found their core story to be a relational one—one of belonging and contributing to something larger than themselves, such as family, school, work, or church. The emerging theory from the data is consistent with discussions with theorists known as "self-in-relation" theorists who have argued that traditional ways of conceptualizing non-mainstream persons (people with disabilities, ethnic minorities, rural citizens, the indigent, immigrants, sojourners, religious and sexual minorities) through the rubric of West-ernized, individualist, positivistic thinking are necessarily detrimental to the healthy psychological development of said persons (Ivey, Ivey, & Simek-Morgan, 1997; Jordan, Kaplan, Miller, Stiver, & Surrey, 1991; Sue, Ivey, & Pedersen, 1996).

Critical Theory

Critical theory in research includes a wide swath of thought focusing on the examination of power within a culture. Secondarily, critical theory works to emancipate those in the culture who are oppressed. Central to the approach is the critique of the culture through a systematic and thorough analysis of the phenomenon in the culture, with the critique being the outcome of the approach. Finally, the rich examination of the unexamined assumptions of the culture is a crucial part of this analysis.

Within critical theory, there are three historical phases. The first phase can be traced to Max Horkheimer and the social theoretic school, along with Theodor Adorno and Herbert Marcuse at the University of Frankfurt am Main. They are the foundation of critical theory. After the Frankfurt period, Jürgen Habermas used communication and language as an analytic tool. In the third phase, some of Habermas's students transformed the approach by focusing on people in specific situations and how they developed over time.

Methodologically, historical analysis is used where the focus is on societies' actions and the policies set into place and how they affect individual behavior. The data that is gathered for the historical components is derived from documentation. For example, documents related to how the taxation structure was developed for the Commonwealth of Pennsylvania for public education can be obtained to examine inequality of access and quality of education. A researcher using this approach will examine the data with a focus on those individuals in the documentation who have the least ability to influence the policy. Observation is used in the normal course of the approach and the data gathered is examined to see which factors restrict or allow for emancipation of the individual. During the observation of an event, a researcher may track who speaks or who is allowed to speak, the relationship with their counterparts and their interests, and how these comments and actions may affect some negatively and some positively. Interviews are a necessity because observation alone will not provide the perspective of the individual. Most importantly, this allows the researcher to examine what people say and how they say it.

There are several types of critical theory, of which we briefly discuss three. **Critical race theory (CRT)** is an approach that places race and racism at the center of the analysis. The focus of U.S.-based race and racism is examined in reference to how it causes inequality. Researchers examine systemic issues that are a normal part of life in the United States versus random behaviors that would be categorized as racist. In the end, the goal is to remove the systemic inequality by bringing attention to it. **Critical humanism** attempts to identify and understand cultural differences that explain underlying human nature. Unlike many techniques in research, there is no path for **reductionism**, the reducing of data to categories or factors, which makes it a difficult approach to undertake. **Critical ethnography** uses the methods of traditional ethnography, but examines the oppression that occurs in social, cultural, political, and economic issues.

Case Study

Case studies are used when a program, organization, or individual is studied in depth for a specified period of time. The case study is very useful when a given situation or context is not understood well or there are changes over time. For example, a researcher might be interested in the success of a nonprofit organization as it grows over time. The level of analysis (like unit of analysis in quantitative) is part of the decision making process on what defines the "case." Time is just one way the case study may be bounded. For example, an educational researcher might study just the principal and only the principal of the school for one year. A marketing researcher might study a brand group, such as Corvette owners. Therefore, the focus of the study defines the case and sets the boundaries.

The choice of the case can be made for a variety of reasons, such as uniqueness or typicality, with the goal of maximizing information (Stake, 1995). Choosing a case can be problematic, and Stake (1995) recommends that researchers select cases that will allow them to maximize the amount of information to be gathered. A case that can provide information may be a better choice than the exact case you desire if that case will take a great deal of time or other resources to obtain.

A case study can be a single case or several cases. When the approach uses several cases, the focus is on replicating the conclusions. Multiple cases strengthen the observations because the researcher is able to test the patterns and inferences, that is, support the believability and credibility of the ideas or theory. This is discussed in experimental research, but the focus is on the sampling process and not necessarily on replication.

Case studies can be discussed based on the overall goal: exploratory, explanatory, or descriptive. The focus of **exploratory cases** is the collection of data in order to develop or further refine research questions and hypotheses and can be implemented as a precursor to other studies. This is where theoretical innovation occurs; pilot studies are a natural example of this type of work. **Explanatory cases** focus on the development of a causal argument. **Descriptive cases** focus on the examination of the case with reference to a previously developed theory.

Yin (1994) provides the following basic protocol for a case study:

- Overview of the project (project objectives and case study issues)
- Field procedures (credentials and access to sites)
- Questions (specific questions that the investigator must keep in mind during data collection)
- Guide for the report (outline, format for the narrative) (p. 64)

The researcher will obtain a large amount of data in the process of the case study. The data can be from interviews, documents, records, video, audio, or any other artifacts that can be used to understand the context of the case. The researcher will be at the case study site for an extended period of time interacting with the individual or individuals given the level of the case study. One goal of a case study is to provide a holistic picture for the reader, which also allows the reader to examine the case in comparison to a case or cases they are interested in (i.e., generalization). But, depending on the researcher, the goal will vary across a naturalistic, positivistic, or constructivist perspective.

Narrative Inquiry

Narrative inquiry can be described as the act of storytelling. As Connelly and Clandinin (1990) state, "Humans are storytelling organisms who, individually and collectively, lead storied lives. Thus, the study of narrative is the study of the ways humans experience the world'' (p. 2). Bruner (1984) wrote that ''[a] life lived is what actually happens....A life as told...is a narrative, influenced by the cultural conventions of telling, by the audience, and by the social context'' (p. 7). As humans, we have a purpose to tell each other our stories, the expected and unexpected, as we live our lives (Bruner, 2002).

Some argue that all research is narrative (Hendry, 2010) and therefore categorizing it as qualitative or quantitative is inappropriate. We have placed narrative inquiry in this chapter because the researchers using this method tend to focus on non-numeric data. Finally, at the core of all research, as we have focused in this book, is asking questions. Narrative inquiry is a useful method in this pursuit because it is based on doubt, which drives the questions we have (Hendry, 2010).

You can find narrative inquiry used in many disciplines, such as history (Carr, 1986), anthropology (Geertz, 1995), business (Swap, Leonard, Shields, & Abrams, 2001), drama (Peter, 2003), art (Bochner & Ellis, 2003), psychology (Coles, 1989), education (Bell, 2002), politics, nutrition, and medicine (Doyle, Hanks, Cherny, & Calman, 2009), but you may not always see the term *narrative inquiry*. You may see narration, story, oral history, lived experience, or lived life. Though the method is used in a variety of domains and has existed for quite some time, the field of narrative inquiry is still developing and the boundaries of narrative inquiry are being pushed (Barone, 2010).

Narrative researchers are focused on the lived life, the study of experience as story (Connelly & Clandinin, 2006). This is the one main constant across narrative researchers (Clandinin, 2006). When we try to make sense of our experiences and understand them, narratives provide a way for people to record these experiences.

Narrative inquiry is also a method for researchers to obtain stories and provide a representation of those stories for readers. The data from the stories that are developed into narratives are the evidence of these experiences. According to Connelly and Clandinin (2006), there are four key terms: living, telling, retelling, reliving. Participants are asked to provide information on their lives, the living. These tellings come in the form of data such as personal journals, stories, photographs, video, documents, interviews, notes, and so forth. The data are then constructed into a narrative to retell their living. The reliving after the retelling (writing out one's life) may be the most difficult to complete because one is now living out as a new person after the retelling (Connelly & Clandinin, 2006).

Further, Clandinin and Connelly (2000) developed a three-dimensional space in which narrative inquirers work: interaction, continuity, and situation. Interaction concerns the personal and social lives, continuity concerns the past, present, and future lives, and situation concerns the specific location of place. In this space, the researcher is not ''out of'' this space but must focus on the participants' experiences, their own experiences, and those experiences that are co-constructed during the research process (Clandinin, 2006). Silko (1997) describes this as a landscape where the researcher is part of the landscape, shapes the landscape, and is shaped by the landscape.

The starting point for narrative inquiry is an individual's experience (Clandinin & Rosiek, 2006), but it also will explore the social, cultural, and institutional stories that affect the person's life and the people involved with that life

(Clandinin, 2006). A narrative inquiry may begin by simply engaging in the life of the person or may start by telling stories; in both instances, the researcher is now in the landscape.

A key factor in the storytelling is the development of the relationship with the person. This is an inbound trajectory (Wenger, 1998). The relationship is negotiated and intentional and includes the relationship itself, the role and purpose of the research, and the transitions into and out of the relationship. As the life is experienced and told in the specific locations, a wide variety of data can be collected, such as photographs, field notes, interviews, and other artifacts. At some point, the researcher begins an outbound trajectory where she negotiates exiting the life of the participant—and the exit may involve returning as the narrative is developed.

A narrative of a day of a boy, "Raymond," was conducted in the late 1940s in a small town in Kansas. Raymond was one of several children studied, and the book by Barker and Wright (1966) details the behavioral events of a single day in Raymond's life when he was seven years old. We recommend you track down a copy of one of the two versions of the book; it is a great narrative.

Survey

We would be remiss if we did not add survey research in this chapter. Clearly, survey research can and does encompass non-numeric data collection. As described in Chapter 6, the general purpose of a **survey** is to examine the current state of something. For example, one semester, we had students take pictures of signs, posters, and so forth in the hallways of the different buildings on campus. The pictures were our artifacts and as a group we examined what types of materials were posted and in essence what appeared to be valued. For example, in the engineering building a large number of items posted were research posters or technical reports on studies occurring among students and faculty. In the education building, a large majority of posted items concerned teaching or presenting content.

NONINTERACTIVE PARTICIPATION

Though as the researcher you are not in direct contact with the participants, there is still a great deal of resources that can be absorbed. For example, there is just one resource issue in collecting pictures taken during a photographer's career to study them, and that is time. There is also the work that needs to be done in organizing the materials for easy access and analysis. Software programs have made this a bit easier, but they can be expensive. In essence, as with all studies, one component may be easier, for example, not having to identify and interview participants, but another, in this case, tracking down all relevant documents or pictures, is more difficult.

Content Analysis

Even though it has a rich history in mass communication, **content analysis** can be found across a wide spectrum of research programs in the social sciences (e.g., history, education, political science). Content analysis is not aligned to one methodological approach (e.g., qualitative or quantitative or grounded theory or case study) and can be based on a variety of data types (e.g., pictures, film, audio, text, memorandums, or Christmas letters to friends) (Banks, Louie, & Einerson, 2000). An example of content analysis for television is the review of stereotype and nonstereotype behavior in Jim Henson's *The Muppet Show* (Schildcrout, 2008). Out of all the approaches in this chapter, content analysis might have the greatest amount of upfront thinking and planning time. Many decisions must be made about the material before any coding can occur. With content analysis, the researcher typically has a well-developed, specific question before the study begins. For example, "Do doctoral-granting institutions as defined by the Carnegie categories use the same criteria for evaluating teaching in the tenure and promotion process?" (Schreiber, McCown, & Perry, 2008). A major reason for the specificity of the research is that the amount of information gathered can be daunting and the boundaries give the researcher the ability to answer the desired question in a more efficient manner.

The content can be analyzed in terms of clusters or codes that are used to create themes. These themes can be developed before the study begins or during the content analysis. When analyzing text material over a long time frame or an extensive number of documents, the researcher may identify conscious or unconscious messages, the frequency of topics or ideas, or the degree of something across a continuum (e.g., joy to sadness). Once the research question has been established, the researcher must make his or her coding choices. With respect to coding issues, we provide some topics to think about as provided by Carley (1992) and as a result of our own experience with content analysis:

1. Decide on the level of analysis. If you are examining text, you need to think about phrases, paragraphs, chapters, and so on. If you are examining video or audio, your concerns may be the amount of time to spend listening or the sections to listen.
2. Decide on how many concepts to code. If you have codes *a priori*, how many do you want to code for? If you are developing codes along the way, how many will you need to reach a saturation point?
3. Decide whether to code for existence or frequency of a concept. You may also want to code for connections of codes or concepts.
4. Decide on how you will distinguish the various concepts. Are some of your concepts similar theoretically or pragmatically?
5. Develop rules for coding your text. Are you coding right on copies of the text, using a software package, note cards, or some other system? This needs to be operationalized so that you can stay organized and be able to quickly retrieve information. If more than one person is coding, this is absolutely crucial to have developed.
6. Decide on the level of concept generalization. Are you coding the exact word or phrase, or some altered or condensed form of the material? You must also be concerned with whether tense or proper nouns are important for your text material. We agree with Carley (1992) that there is an art to this.

7. Decide on what to do with "irrelevant" information. There will be information that you will decide subjectively (which is fine) is not part of your study. You need to decide how to deal with such information. For example, you might want to categorize the information as completely irrelevant, irrelevant, appears irrelevant, looks irrelevant now but should be reviewed later (i.e., KIV). This is also part of selectively reducing the amount of material to code.

8. Decide how much to sample and how to sample. How much material are you going to sample? For example, are you going to read all of the writings of Shakespeare or just the first five years, or maybe just the comedies? Do you watch every episode of *South Park* to examine social commentary, or do you randomly sample episodes and time marks? This too is part of **selective reduction**.

9. Because of the amount of material we have previously come across, we suggest that you spend adequate thinking time working through this issue.

IN-TEXT ACTIVITY

You can conduct this activity on your own or with others. Again, your background and experience will come into play (e.g., music majors tend to complete this activity slightly differently than we do).

1. Choose your favorite 10 songs (variations: 10 songs from your favorite band, of all time, etc.)
2. Obtain the lyrics.
3. Decide on the level of analysis (word by word, line by line, only choruses/verses, or general theme of song).
4. Choose some codes *a priori* (e.g., love, sadness, escape, social commentary/critique). (We find this helps with students vs. *complete versus just leaving the students to decide on their own.*)
5. Start coding; we usually just start with basic frequency counts to see whether the word or concept is there.
6. Put your codes into a system where you can rearrange them, such as an Excel sheet or note cards.
7. Do you notice any other topics or themes? Are there many words, phrases, and so on that do not fit into your *a priori* codes?
8. Analyze for trends. Do you see your original codes a great deal? Do you see new codes or concepts that need to be included and the data reanalyzed?

Another version of this activity is to use wordle.net. Wordle is a Web site by Jonathan Feinberg, where you can insert a segment of text and it makes a word cloud. During the last Presidential Election, people took the text of the speeches and made word clouds.

Historical Research

Historical research, like *ex post facto* in quantitative research, is the examination of data that already exists. Though we have put historical research in the qualitative section, you will most likely have both numeric and non-numeric data. A current oral history project is the Story Corp project. This project focuses on people interviewing each other about a topic of interest. For example, you could interview your parents on how they met and decided to get married. One of our favorite historical research projects, which could also be an ethnography, is ''An Infinity of Little Hours'' by Nancy Maguire. This story is about five men who entered the Carthusian order and is set as a mystery about who remains in the order. It is a historical analysis of their entry, but the story is much later than when the events occurred. One could argue that it is an ethnography because there appears to be a concerted effort to understand the values, attitudes, beliefs, and behaviors of the order and the individuals in the order.

As a historical researcher, though, you are really an archeologist trying to piece together a narrative about something that has already occurred. Let us give you an example from Peircean abductive reasoning work in education (Table 8.1; Shank & Cunningham, 1996). You are typically in the hunch stage where you might have a possible idea of what could be going on. At some point you might be looking at symptoms, because they resemble something familiar. Given enough symptoms, you might create a metaphor to generate a possible rule or pattern. This allows you to make some meaningful connection with what you are seeing. As you get to a more general narrative of the data, you might determine that some information provides clues that will let you build a scenario. A scenario can then be tested to see whether it stands. This is not a linear process. You will have stops and starts and think you have some clues but the scenario fails to mature and you end up working with a different hunch.

A key component of historical research is the attainment of documented facts in relation to your historical question. Though commonly discussed within the non-numeric literature, historical research can include all types of data. One of our

TABLE 8.1
Abductive process

Open Iconic Tone (or Omen/Hunch) deals with the possibility of a possible resemblance.
Open Iconic Token (or Symptom) deals with possible resemblances.
Open Iconic Type (or Metaphor/Analogy) means the manipulation of resemblance to create or discover a possible rule.
Open Indexical Token (or Clue) is characterized as reasoning used to determine whether our observations are clues of some more general phenomena.
Open Indexical Type (or Diagnosis/Scenario) means the formation of a possible rule based on available evidence.

Source: Shank and Cunningham (1996).

favorite shows is *History Detectives* on PBS. Yes, we love research of all kinds. PBS's Web site has a nice set of guidelines. The Film Study Center at Harvard University on the DoHistory.org Web site, which is maintained by George Mason University, also provides a list for conducting a historical research project (Table 8.2). These checklists are a good starting point for thinking about a historical research project and can be also be used to evaluate the historical research systems and methods that you already use.

Primary and Secondary Sources. One of the greatest issues in historical research is dealing with primary and secondary resources. In general, primary sources are the data sources you want. A **primary source** is the original document, picture, audio, video, and so on. For example, the diary of a person you are interested in researching is a primary source, whereas the summary or book about the diary is a **secondary source**. Another example of a primary source would be the large number of sermons Jim has from his father-in-law who is a Lutheran Pastor. Reading across time, specific themes emerge and reading within religious celebrations provides different but related themes. Given the time period you are interested in, you may or may not be able to interview or read current interviews with people involved in your topic of interest.

Reliability and Validity. Historical projects create an extra level of concern about the believability of the data or data source and being able to understand that document or artifact in context. The researcher must be careful of counterfeit or heavily biased documents! Even once you have determined that a document is authentic (reliability) you also must understand it in context of the time period (validity). Within the reliability component (also termed external evidence), you may need to deal with paper analysis, textile analysis, or other document analysis. If you are working through a library or museum collection, the assumption is that all of this work has been completed. If you find a piece you think is important, but you do not know whether this reliability work has been completed, you may need to search for an expert. From the validity perspective, you need to be careful of the biases of the writers in primary and secondary sources. The "facts" presented are the facts from the perspective of the writer and may have other interpretations or other facts that were not included.

Data Collection. Lucky for you, technology has changed tremendously, so getting access to original documents is much easier than it used to be. We highly recommend that you invest in a good digital camera because many places will let you take pictures of documents, but will not let you photocopy. We have done this with original copies of texts that are under Plexiglas where you put your hands in with gloves and use a device to turn pages. You can take good pictures through the Plexiglas! You should also create a collection instrument to record where you have collected all of these pictures. Being organized takes time, but this will save you time if you ever needed to return to

TABLE 8.2
How-to list for historical research from DoHistory.org

1. **Decide what you want to know**. Why are you doing this? What do you want from it? Sometimes pure curiosity will drive your research. Sometimes you will have a primary source such as a diary or a trunkful of family papers and simply want to find out more. Explore the sources and reasons that you have and formulate a central question or issue.

2. **Find out what has been done already** to answer your question. You probably want to avoid reinventing the wheel, although much can be learned by retracing the steps of a seasoned researcher. Reformulate your question until it satisfies you.

3. **Envision the overall research project**. What will be the general overall look of your project? How big or small will it be? What will be the big goals of the project?

4. **Consider possible end products**. What do you want to have in your hands when you finish? Do you want to create a collection of related papers, write a book, give a report, write teaching materials, or make a film? Your end product will affect what kinds of sources and information you need to collect. A filmmaker, for instance, may need to collect and view many more visual sources than someone writing a book.

5. **Make a list of necessary equipment, people, and materials** that you will need to carry out your research.

6. **Estimate how long your project will take** from beginning to end. (I always allocate at least 30% to 50% more time on top of this.) Decide if you want to spend that much time and amend your plan accordingly.

7. **Make a sequence of tasks and list when you will need to complete them**. This sequence will not be the one you end up following exactly, but thinking ahead will help you foresee pitfalls.

8. **Estimate the costs** of your research. Include travel expenses, telephone and Internet fees, photocopying, meals, new equipment you must acquire, user's fees for libraries, and wages for helpers. Do you want to spend that much? Amend your plan accordingly.

9. **Identify and contact possible sources of funding**. If you will be depending on grants, you must find out about forms, deadlines, and when funding periods begin. Develop contingency plans to cover yourself if grant applications fail.

10. **Look at** Using Primary Sources in the History Toolkit. Move flexibly amongst steps (10), (11), (12), and (15).

11. **Conduct background research** to learn as much as you can about your source and the time and place from which it came.

12. **Conduct primary source research**. Explore the Doing History section of this site to see actual examples of how to explore and use sources.

13. **Periodically review what you have found, where you are in your budgeting of time and funds**, and amend your original research plan if warranted. For example, perhaps the sources that you thought were easily available don't even exist. Perhaps you have discovered a great new source that no one knew would be useful to you. Perhaps you have run out of money. Perhaps your commitment to your project has grown as you have discovered more and more.

14. **Keep citation information, and file everything** according to a system that fits your question and sources.

15. **Evaluate** your research findings and cycle back or go on to the next step (16). You may need to ask for evaluation and help from colleagues or experts to decide whether to go back and do more or to go forward. Please remember, however, that if you feel what you are doing is valuable and fulfilling, then it doesn't matter so much what other people think. Learn about accepted skills and standards of historical research, be accurate and thorough, build within a historical context, and then do what you think is best.

16. **Create an end product**. Organize and present your results.

17. **Store your primary sources and a copy of your end product archivally**. Ask your local historical society or librarian about archival storage materials and conditions. Avoid excess handling, dust, dirt, damp, acidic or corrosive storage materials, and extremes of temperature. Make two copies of everything, if possible, and store them in separate locations. If you do not wish to keep your results, inquire at local archives to see if they are interested in storing your work or making it accessible to other researchers. If you are doing family history, give copies of your findings to others in the family.

Source: *History Toolkit, Do History* http://dohistory.org/on_your_own/toolkit/index.html (accessed January 9, 2009). Reprinted with permission from the Center for History and New Media, George Mason University.

a location. There are also many online sites where you can get data in electronic format, such as the following:

The Making of America (http://quod.lib.umich.edu/m/moagrp/) focuses on books and articles published in the 1800s. One example is the curriculum from the Chicago Public Schools from 1869.

The New York Times Digital archive (http://query.nytimes.com/search/query?srchst = nyt&&srcht = a&srchr = n) now has every issue of the paper from 1851. We did a quick search of college costs and quickly found articles from 70 years ago about budgeting college costs.

Accessible Archives (http://www.accessible.com/accessible/) focuses on periodicals from the 18th and 19th centuries. For example, their Civil War collection has over 2,500 newspaper articles dating from 1860 to 1865.

Ancestry Plus is a genealogical database where you can trace the ancestry of your family or other people you are researching.

The Library of Congress is a wonderful place to conduct historical research. You can begin your search online at www.loc.gov.

IN-TEXT ACTIVITY

We have our students conduct an intellectual history project that is adapted from Dr. Myrtle Scott (Emeritus Indiana University). In the project, students are to interview four to six people who were influential in how they view the world and what they believe. Then they are to research the people who influenced those whom they interviewed. The project typically takes a full semester to complete, but at the end students have a great deal of experience collecting and managing a wide variety of primary and secondary data and a wonderful history project for themselves. You can experience a mini-version of this by interviewing one person who you feel has been influential in how you view the world. During the interview, ask the person to name one individual who has influenced his or her beliefs. If you can, interview that person; if not, try to find out as much as you can about that person through public records or Web searches.

CASE STUDY

Ginette is really interested in how people use the graphs they see in papers or in their daily lives. She is interested in graphs they make for work, but is most interested in how people discuss any of those graphs they use. Since she is interested in mistakes, she is wondering whether examining C-SPAN tapes of legislators using graphs to make a point make the same mistakes. She has walked through the congressional buildings—Russell, Dirksen, Hart, Rayburn, Longworth, and Cannon—for the

Senate and the House of Representatives and noticed many graphs and how they are scaled and presented. She is currently thinking that there will be a component of historical research because of the examination of old tapes. She would like to go back many years. She thinks that her problem area is: What makes one graph more persuasive than another? Because of this, she also thinks that the overall design of this component will be a grounded theory study because she is not sure what would make the most persuasive graph and if that might change over time or content. As she works through the idea of looking at these graphical displays, she realizes that her schema about graphs being "correct" will crash up against the reality of what makes a graph persuasive. In some cases, they may be overlapped, but really she thinks that they may be separate.

ARMCHAIR MOMENT

Research Study Procedures

Students using both quantitative and qualitative designs can have issues related to implementing the designs. We have put this discussion in the qualitative section, but many of the same issues arise with quantitative designs. We discuss those issues below and choose to put it here because interactive studies typically have to be concerned with all of these issues. This does not mean that because you are running an experiment, you are not violating participants' rights or on the brink of creating an unethical situation. Many undergraduate and graduate students do not participate in research activities as heavily as we did in our undergraduate and graduate studies. Some are quite nervous about actually conducting the study. We provide some of our experiences below so that students do not make the same mistakes we did.

Gaining Permission

No matter what you do, research-wise, you have to get permission. At the very least, you usually have to get permission from the organization that is funding you, such as your university, agency, business, or grant institution (e.g., the National Institute of Mental Health [NIMH] or the John D. and Catherine T. MacArthur Foundation), as well as the people you are studying. The organizations want to make sure that what you propose doing is a good use of their money, does much more good than harm, and treats participants ethically. As for the people you want to study, you should understand that most people dislike being observed or studied without their knowledge and consent, and in most professions, doing research without getting people's agreement is considered unethical. Well then, who determines whether what you are doing is ethical enough? Well, this leads us to the **institutional review board (IRB)**, sometimes called a **human subjects committee (HSC)**.

Institutional Review Boards

Institutional review boards and human subject committees exist today to address some serious ethical concerns in research that occurred in the not-so-distant past (e.g., studying the effects of untreated syphilis for over 40 years on the health of African American men (Jones, 1981; Loue, 2000). For a better overview and some computer-based training, see the National Institutes of Health's Web site. Review boards consist of a variety of key people such as social scientists, medical personnel, attorneys, community members, and prisoner advocates. Usually, the IRB is designed to help you, the researcher, make sure that you do not conduct research in a manner that could be considered unethical at the very least, fatal at the most extreme (Parvizi, Tarity, Conner & Smith, 2007).

The underlying ethical principles we're talking about are the basic ones that most social science professions base their ethical codes on: the five principles of *nonmalfeasance, beneficence, autonomy, fidelity,* and *justice* (U.S. Department of Health, Education, and Welfare, 1979; Kitchener, 1984). Basically, **nonmalfeasance** means "to do no harm." Research studies in the past that have not considered, or have not heeded, this principle have perpetrated heinous effects on the people involved. The Tuskegee Syphilis study mentioned above left men and their families ravaged with the effects of syphilis, and the men were denied treatment that could have alleviated or remitted the disease. The risks covered by nonmalfeasance are not limited to physical ones; they include psychological harm as well. In the Milgram study on the nature of obedience conducted in the early 1960s, participants were ordered to punish a confederate whom they believed to be another participant (Milgram, 1964). The participants were to shock the confederate for each failed response. Researchers told the participants that the shocks increased in painfulness and could cause harm and even death at a certain level. When participants hesitated, they were told they could not disobey. Participants who administered what they believed to be high levels and fatal levels of electrical shock were found to have suffered high levels of psychological distress that affected their quality of life considerably. As a result, IRBs look at study proposals with an eye to determining the intended and unintended risks inherent in a study.

Beneficence means to "to do good." If the research you are conducting doesn't do something good—say, add to the research literature in political science, improve the lives of clients, or lead to a more effective teaching style—then why are you doing it? Despite the incredible positive impact we believe you will have on your profession, doing your research just so you can get your degree and get out into the real world is generally not considered a good enough reason. We know—we've tried that reasoning ourselves. So, you will need to consider the quality of the reasoning for doing what you are doing, because the IRB will be determining whether the benefits of your research outweigh the risks and potential for harm.

Autonomy refers to respecting people's right to self-determination. That is, people get to choose whether or not they want to participate and/or stay in your study. They get to make their choice based on good information you have provided them about the benefits and risks of the study. They have the right not to feel pressured by you or anyone else to make their decision. Finally, they have to be capable of making such an informed choice. People can be considered incapable of making such a decision for a variety of reasons:

1. They may have what is called "diminished mental capacity." This means anyone who has limited cognitive functioning. Commonly, people who have

diagnoses of mental retardation, psychiatric disorders, and neurological disorders come under this category. It's pretty clear that someone who is in a coma would have a hard time being able to consent to a medical experiment. For social scientists, though, it's not always so clear as to who would be considered cognitively impaired. A counselor studying about depression would need to address whom she would be asking to participate and whether they are capable of choosing. A currently severely depressed person has far less ability to consent to a study than a middle management administrator who has had one depressive episode five years ago.

2. Minors (anyone under 18 years old) are considered incapable of giving reasoned consent to participate in a study. Usually, children under the age of 12 can only be a part of studies that their legal guardians agree to. Adolescents 12 to 17 may assent to the study; however, their legal guardians still have to consent as well.

3. Anyone who is currently involved with the legal system is protected. We don't mean you can't study attorneys or judges; we mean people who are prison inmates or currently addressing criminal sanctions. The potential for abuse and coercion is very high for prisoners, so it is assumed that they will have difficulty being able to choose whether to participate in a study or not.

4. People in some sort of residential program such as a hospital, boarding school, nursing home, or group home may not be able to give consent to participate in a study. Similarly, outpatient clinic participants are also considered possibly unable to make such a decision.

Well then, how does anyone get any research done that can inform our work with kids, inmates, or hospital patients? You, as the researcher, have to show that what you are doing and how you are explaining and designing your study will enable the above people to determine whether or not they wish to participate and/or continue in your study. You do that through your written protocols, statements, flyers, and interactions. Just know that the IRB has to believe that you are addressing the participants' autonomy.

The IRB wants to know that you have **fidelity**—that you are trustworthy, that as a researcher, you have the participants' safety and well-being firmly in mind, and that you provide clear and readily accessible ways in which a participant who would like to discuss any element of the research with you or your superiors (such as a dissertation or thesis chair, the chair of the IRB, your agency supervisor, school principal, or school board president), may do so. You must also provide documentation that tells the participants specifically who will have access to the data, in what form, and what will happen to the data after it is used. Finally, you must tell the participants exactly what your research entails, how much time and what sort of effort you expect of the participation, and what sort of incentive you will or will not offer them for completion.

The IRB also wants to recognize how you handle the **justice** elements of research ethics. The board wants to see that, in your research proposal, you are treating all participants fairly. One common area of fairness the IRB wants to see is in your stated inclusion/exclusion criterion. Who are you including or excluding in your study and how have you justified these decisions? Until the passage of the Women's Health Equity Act of 1990, the only breast cancer research that had ever been funded by the NIH were two studies that excluded women!

Now that you have some idea what the IRB will be looking for, you'll have to put together a research proposal that will be approved! There are three tiers of IRB review depending on how much risk is involved in the research design. The first level, sometimes called **Category I Review**, is considered to pose either minimal or no risk whatsoever and therefore is considered "exempt" and not reviewed by the full board. Instead it is reviewed by one or two members and accepted or rejected. Let's say our counselor wanted to determine the Masters-level mental health professionals' attitudes toward depression using an already published questionnaire. The participant pool is assumed to be capable of making their own decisions, and the survey used is assumed to trigger no risky responses. This would likely be a Category I Review.

What if, though, a counselor wants to study the effects of incarceration on inmates who are currently diagnosed with major depression? This study includes two vulnerable populations: the inmates and people with active psychiatric disorders. This type of study has the potential for greater-than-minimal risk of harm and will generally be best reviewed by all members of the IRB. This will be a full **Category III Review** and tends to take a great deal more time and patience for all involved. Kim, who is a member of an IRB, remembers that one proposed study set in the prisons took over a year to be approved by the committee! Getting a Category III Review through the IRB takes practice and may require the researcher to implement considerable adjustments to his or her design in order to address all of the committee's concerns. Be prepared to be asked to come to committee meetings to discuss your project, and never forget that the members of the committee are charged with participant safety first and foremost. If your motivation is only to get your research started, there can be considerable tension. Remember that you, too, care deeply about the participants and their well-being. Approaching the IRB from a mindful framework can help considerably.

There is a middle ground in IRB reviews when a proposal is determined to be of minimal risk. A **Category II Review**, or an expedited review, is usually done by a subcommittee of the IRB. An example of an expedited review is a counselor who wants to access her agency's archived files of formerly depressed clients to see whether there might be any connection between their socioeconomic status, early exposure to trauma, family structure, and subsequent diagnosis of depression. There is potential for risk, yet it is likely to be minimal, so the subcommittee determines first whether the study is a Category I or Category III review and acts accordingly. Doubtless, you are wondering whether you need to start from scratch or whether there are any written protocols or guidelines to help you put together your proposal.

For all types of research that involve participants, you should thoroughly read and understand your research organization's standards for research. We use the *Ethical Standards of the American Educational Research Association: Cases and Commentary* book by Strike (2002). The format and structure of the book allow you to become well versed in ethical issues surrounding research and how they are associated with your research.

Creating Written Protocols/Statements

You should create protocols for gathering data in the field and any statements or written documents that you need participants to read or have in advance. For you, there is a great number of previously developed protocols and other information accessible through your research office if you are at a university, from the people you are working with, and from research organizations, such as the American Educational Research Association or the American Psychological Society. You can also search the Internet for examples. If you are going to enter the field, you need consent forms for the participants to read and sign. But, you may have other information you would like to provide them. The protocol will also help you plan the steps for collecting data. For example, when using an intact classroom of students for a study, we randomly handed different packets of materials to the students as they walked to their seats. We realized during the planning stage that if we waited for them to sit first and then distributed the packets, we would lose the randomness we wanted and would have created one more transition to deal with. And as any teacher will tell you, transitions are where the problems occur. Jim's review board forms can be obtained at http://www.duq.edu/research/human-subject-irb.cfm and Kim's at http://www.orda.siuc.edu/human/.

The Field

Before **field entrance**, you need to determine criteria related to the site and the interviewees. By criteria, we mean how you will choose which sites, social scenes, or participants you are going to observe. The actual **site selection** is a negotiated process that allows the researcher to gain access to a site (and eventually people) that is suitable based on the research questions or problem areas and is feasible. It is negotiated because you will work with individuals who will agree to grant you varying levels of access. As a researcher, you should collect information (documents, networks, Web pages, or other information available to the public) to help you make the decision about which site or sites you would like to observe. The actual process is not formalized in any agreed upon manner; therefore, you must make your decisions transparent for the reader, so the reader understands what you have done or will do. This is a trustworthiness issue. Finally, this is heavily dependent on your good judgment about timing and tact in the process. For **participants criteria**, profiles of individuals to be sampled for in-depth interviews are what needs to be completed, but may not be possible until you are on site. You may not have access to information about individuals about the individuals before entry into the site.

After a possible site is identified, contact should be made with a person who can grant permission to work at the site. You need to provide the gatekeeper with a written statement concerning the project, such as your qualifications, desired scenes to observe, participants you would like to interview, activities you will engage in, timelines, and your role along with the roles of any colleagues (or others) working with you. As stated above, this may expand given what you learn after you enter the field and learn more.

Once you have been granted access, you should map the field. By mapping the field, we mean that you need to develop a rapport and trust with the participants. They need to believe in your ability to keep comments confidential. Second, you need to develop and obtain information concerning the social, spatial, and temporal relationships in your site or sites. Flexibility in examining to whom you have and want to have access is important. We have learned not to ignore someone willing to talk. This person may not be the exact person you want, but that does not mean that he or she does not have believable data that is important to you. We have been stunned by how many interns are the ones who understand the big picture of what is going on because they are always copying memorandums and hearing conversations because of the cross-assignment to many people. Traditionally, there is a basic process to determining which people you want to interview or observe. As stated above, you need to determine the criteria (i.e., desired attributes) of potential participants. Next you need to locate the people who appear to meet those criteria, and then screen them to make sure they meet the criteria.

Interacting with Participants

It seems obvious, but you must remain professional at all times while engaging with participants. A major component of this is to clearly articulate your level of engagement with the people or organization. A **complete observer**, in the purest form, simply takes notes and does not engage in any fashion with the people or the scene. You do not interact physically or psychologically with the participants or organization; however, you should realize that your existence is an interaction. **Full participants** are completely engaged with everyone and the scenes as they unfold. The researcher is essentially trying to live the experience of the people. **Participant-observers** are a blend where they are participating at some level, but are not fully engaged. You may also be an **insider-observer** where you as the researcher also have a formal position in the organization.

Issues in Data Gathering

Actual data collection can be overwhelming for the new researcher. Often, the data collection is the first time the person has had to deal with a set of data this large. Many courses, such as a course that would use this book, will have you practice with small data sets to learn the skill along with the conceptual knowledge. But, even interviewing people creates a massive amount of data. Jim interviewed 48 third-graders and then had them complete a task, which was videotaped. Transcribing, not analyzing, the data took weeks to complete. Therefore, you need to plan for data gathering and how to store and handle it. We also warn that plans on collecting data do not always go as planned. For a good deal of our research, fire alarms and weather delays have wreaked the most havoc on the data collection process.

Physical Data Collection.   We commonly use field journals in which we comment about observations, conversations, behaviors, artifacts, and so on, and write ideas about possible themes, interpretations, and questions. This is a skill that takes time. We recommend that you practice at a mall or coffee shop where you can sit, write and develop a format for your field journal that is comfortable and useful for you. In addition, once you are done, write summaries of observations and interviews after a field visit. We tend to scan all of our data for the day, then write the summaries, and then scan our previous data and summaries. We are looking for recurring ideas or meanings that may become themes. If you have provided participants with a survey, we suggest that you test it first for the amount of time it takes to complete and ease of use. Like our field notes, we scan the responses before we code them into a database to get a feel of what is there. For Likert-style surveys, it also gives us a chance to identify potential surveys that were filled out incompletely or incorrectly before we spend time coding the data for that survey. Dealing with the incomplete or incorrect survey becomes an analysis issue later. We do put those responses into that database, but do so at the end so that we can automatically code that there is a problem. If you are giving a survey and are using photocopies, make sure all pages are photocopied and scanned properly. Forgetting a back page or a page not properly scanned can destroy a research study and waste resources. We suggest that you make one copy, examine it thoroughly, and then make the remainder of the copies.

Electronic Data Collection.   With all electronic data collection techniques, you must make sure that the equipment is working by setting it up early to test it. You want close to a zero-failure policy or a working backup policy. We carry two tape recorders with us, extra tapes, and a load of batteries. Cameras have advanced so much and obtaining pictures is now so easy that they are a staple of fieldwork. Thousands of pictures can be saved on a camera or hard drive at any time. The worry about trying to save film and still obtain all the pictures needed to tell the story is no longer an issue. With this advancement is the overwhelming task of examining all those pictures. Jim worked in Italy a few years ago and while there he and his family took several thousand pictures to document their experiences. They still have not finished examining all of the pictures. Video has the same issue and can be even more overwhelming because coding data from video takes a great deal of time. If you are looking for the big picture or scenes, it is not as daunting; but if you have to examine small details (e.g., all the small mistakes, such as the gun switching hands between scenes, in hours of films), it can kill your eyes. As we discussed in the analysis section, you need to make some decisions early on.

If you are only collecting audio, take some notes when you are recording. It lets you get the big picture of the conversation. You cannot keep up with everything said. It will also allow for some space between speakers, which can help you later when transcribing (see following page). Participants, even in focus groups, can feel awkward at the beginning of the taping session. We advise having a basic conversation about the day or current events that will allow them to become accustomed to talking when the tape is running. We also suggest the following:

1. Do not try to hide a tape recorder. It is unethical, and you can't use the information you obtain.

2. A professional microphone is more important than the type of recorder. Jim learned this from recording in a studio. The microphones made a huge difference. Good microphones do not hiss and cause you problems later during transcription. We also recommend that you put the microphone on a small table stand with a bit of foam underneath the stand. We have used a small carpet that we put on a table, because all tile rooms bounce (reflect) sound all over the place and recording is problematic. Some people like "flat" microphones that can lie on a piece of foam. We recommend you test this to make sure people sitting at different spots are still picked up well. Again, show up early and test. With focus groups, either get an omnidirectional microphone or multiple ones.

3. During the recording, especially when you are in a focus group format, you need a way to identify who is talking. You can do this while taking notes. Each person can sit at a specific spot. Each spot has a number. When they talk, they state their number and then talk, or you can just list which number is talking and match it to the recording later. Some participants are comfortable with the number statement; others are not. You might consider using speaker identifiers, which look something like this in your notes: UGF5, representing an undergraduate from focus group 5, or GRM6, representing a graduate Masters-level student from group 6. Using the identifier this way will allow you in data software programs (see Chapter 10) to search the text for comments from a specific participant. For the interview, though, you do not have to interrupt in order for people to identify themselves. In the end, you must determine a way to understand who is talking during the transcription time period.

4. Recording: It is often a good idea to give your groups a feel of their progress during the session. This can be done through using a flip chart to record ideas as you go along. We like a visual method, because you can focus the discussion, and what is written can help the respondents agree with your interpretations, correct them, or provide more detail or nuance. It also allows the whole group to agree or disagree with an interpretation without it focusing on the person who said it, because they are focusing on your interpretation.

5. Transcription: We suggest that you transcribe your own tapes because you are most likely to be collecting the data at the time and will remember the scene more clearly than anyone else. Sometimes you need to contract the transcription out, but that can create problems and you end up listening through all the tapes anyway. Most players have a speed play button, which can help you find a certain time period on the tape. There are also a host

of speed devices you can use to slow down or speed up the tape while you transcribe. Most of the software packages originally designed for text analysis now let you upload audio and video and block certain segments for later analysis. They are actually quite sophisticated.

Computers/Internet.   Many data collections occur on computers, Palm Pilots, Blackberries, or the Internet in general. If you create a survey (e.g., Zoomerang) or other instrument to collect data and desire to have people use a variety of devices, versus sitting in a computer lab where you have more control, you have to test the collection on every device multiple times under a variety of situations. Even with all of this, you can still have problems. Jim had tested a handheld device over and over again in all the situations the students could find themselves! They still had problems here and there, leading to data integrity issues.

KEY WORDS

autonomy
axial coding
beneficence
bracketing
case study
Category I Review
Category II Review
Category III Review
complete observer
content analysis
critical ethnography
critical humanism
critical race theory
critical theory
descriptive case
emic
epoché
ethnography
etic
explanatory case
exploratory case

fidelity
field entrance
flip-flop
full participants
grounded theory
historical research
human subjects committee
   (HSC)
insider-observer
interactive approaches
institutional review board
   (IRB)
justice
narrative inquiry
neutral questions
noninteractive approaches
nonmalfeasance
Open Iconic Token
Open Iconic Tone
Open Iconic Type
Open Indexical Token

Open Indexical Type
participant-observer
participants criteria
phenomenological
   reduction
phenomenology
primary source
reductionism
saturation
secondary source
selective coding
selective reduction
site selection
structural synthesis
substantive coding
survey
theoretical sampling
theoretical sensitivity
thick description

REFERENCES AND FURTHER READINGS

Amatea, E. S., & Clark, M. A. (2005). Changing schools, changing counselors: A qualitative study of school administrators' conceptions of the school counselor role. *Professional School Counseling, 9,* 16–27.

Asner-Self, K. K., & Feyissa, A. (2002). The use of poetry in psychoeducational groups with multicultural-multilingual clients. *Journal for Specialists in Group Work, 27*(2), 136–160.

Banks, S. P., Louie, E., & Einerson, M. (2000). Constructing personal identities in holiday letters. *Journal of Personal and Social Relationships, 17*(3), 299–327.

Barker, R. G., & Wright, H. F. (1966). *One boy's day: A specimen record of behavior.* Hamden, CT: Archon Books.

Barone, T. (2010). Commonalities and variegations: Notes on the maturation of the field of narrative research. *The Journal of Educational Research, 103*(2), 149–153.

Bell, J. S. (2002). Narrative inquiry: More than just telling stories. *TESOL Quarterly, 36*(2), 207–213.

Bochner, A. P., & Ellis, C. (2003). An introduction to the arts and narrative research: Art as inquiry. *Qualitative Inquiry 9*(4) 506–514. doi: 10.1177/ 1077800403254394

Bontra, J., & Gindreau, P. (2005). Reexamining the cruel and unusual punishment of prison life. *Law and Human Behavior, 14*(4), 347–372.

Broussard, L. (2006). Understanding qualitative research: A school nurse perspective. Journal *of School Nursing, 22*(4), 212–218.

Bruner, E. M. (1984). The opening up of anthropology. In E. M. Bruner (Ed.), *Text, play, and story: The construction and reconstruction of self and society* (pp. 1–18). Washington, DC: The American Ethnological Society.

Bruner, J. (2002). Narratives of human plight: A conversation with Jerome Bruner. In R. Charon and M. Montello (Eds.), *Stories that matter: The role of narrative in medical ethics* (pp. 3–9). New York: Routledge.

Bryant, A. (2002). Re-grounding grounded theory. *The Journal of Information Technology Theory and Application, 4*(1), 25–42.

Burke, C. (2005). Comparing qualitative research methodologies for systemic research: The use of grounded theory, discourse analysis and narrative analysis. *Journal of Family Therapy, 25,* 237–262.

Carley, K. (1992). Coding choices for textual analysis: A comparison of content analysis and map analysis. *Sociological Methodology, 23,* 75–126.

Carr, D. (1986). *Time, narrative and history.* Bloomington: Indiana University Press.

Charmaz, K. (2000). Grounded theory: Objective and constructivist methods. In N. K. Denzin & Y. S. Lincoln (Eds.), *Handbook of qualitative research* (2nd ed., pp. 509–535). Thousand Oaks, CA: SAGE Publications.

Charmaz, K. (2005). Grounded theory in the 21st century. In N. K. Denzin & Y. S. Lincoln (Eds.), *Handbook of qualitative research* (3rd ed., pp. 507–535). London: SAGE Publications.

Cho, J., & Trent, A. (2006). Validity in qualitative research revisited. *Qualitative Research, 6,* 319–339.

Clandinin, D. J. (2006). Narrative inquiry: A methodology for studying lived experience. *Research Studies in Music Education, 27,* 44–54. doi: 10.1177. 13211103X060270010301

Clandinin, D. J., & Connelly, F. M. (2000). *Narrative inquiry: Experience and story in qualitative research.* San Francisco: Jossey Bass.

Clandinin, D. J., & Rosiek, J. (2006). Mapping a landscape of narrative inquiry: Orderland spaces and tensions. In D. J. Clandinin (Ed.), *Handbook of narrative inquiry: Mapping a methodology* (pp. 35–75). Thousand Oaks, CA: SAGE Publications.

Coles, R. (1989). *The call of stories: Teaching and the moral imagination.* Boston, MA: Houghton Mifflin.

Connelly, F. M., & Clandinin, D. J. (1990). Stories of experience and narrative inquiry. *Educational Researcher 19*(5), 2–14.

Connelly, F. M., & Clandinin, D. J. (2006). Narrative inquiry. In J. L. Green, G. Camilli, & P. Elmore (Eds.), *Handbook of complementary methods in education research* (3rd ed., pp. 477–487). Mahwah, NJ: Lawrence Erlbaum.

Corbin, J., & Strauss, A. (1990). Grounded theory research: Procedures, canons, and evaluative criteria. *Qualitative Sociology, 13,* 3–21.

Corbin, J., & Strauss, A. (2008). *Basics of qualitative research* (3rd ed.). Thousand Oaks, CA: SAGE Publications.

Denzin, N. K. (1989). *Interpretive biography: Vol. 17. Qualitative research methods.* Thousand Oaks, CA: SAGE Publications.

Denzin, N. K., & Lincoln, Y. S. (2005). *The SAGE handbook of qualitative research* (3rd ed.). Thousand Oaks, CA: SAGE Publications.

Donmoyer, R. (2001). Paradigm talk reconsidered. In V. Richardson (Ed.), *Handbook of research on teaching* (4th ed., pp. 174–197). Washington, DC: AERA.

Doyle, D., Hanks, G., Cherny, N., & Calman, K. (Eds.). (2009). *Oxford textbook on palliative medicine* (3rd ed.). New York: Oxford University Press.

Geertz, C. (1973). Thick description: Toward an interpretive theory of culture. In C. Geertz (Ed.), *The interpretation of cultures: Selected essays* (pp. 3–30). New York: Basic Books.

Geertz, C. (1974). "From the native's point of view": On the nature of anthropological understanding. *Bulletin of the American Academy of Arts and Sciences, 28,* 26–45.

Geertz, C. (1995). *After the fact: Two countries, four decades, one anthropologist.* Cambridge, MA: Harvard University Press.

Glaser, B. G. (1978). *Theoretical sensitivity: Advances in methodology of grounded theory.* Mill Valley, CA: Sociological Press.

Glaser, B. G. (1992). *Basics of grounded theory of theory analysis.* Mill Valley, CA: Sociological Press.

Glaser, B. G., & Strauss, A. (1965). *Awareness of dying.* Chicago: Aldine Transaction.

Glaser, B. G., & Strauss, A. (1967). *The discovery of grounded theory: Strategies for qualitative research.* Chicago, IL: Aldine Transaction.

Groenewald, T. (2004). A phenomenological research design illustrated. *International Journal of Qualitative Methods, 3*(1). Article 4. Retrieved from http://www.ualberta.ca/~iiqm/backissues/3_1/pdf/groenewald.pdf

Hammersley, M. (2000). *Taking sides in social research*. London: Routledge.

Hendry, P. M. (2010). Narrative as inquiry. *The Journal of Educational Research, 103*(2), 72–80.

History Toolkit, Do History. Retrieved from http://dohistory.org/on_your_own/toolkit/index.html

Holloway, I. (1997). *Basic concepts for qualitative research*. Oxford: Blackwell Science.

Huehls, F. (2005). An evening of grounded theory: Teaching process through demonstration and simulation. *The Qualitative Report, 10*(2), 328–338.

Hycner, R. H. (1999). Some guidelines for the phenomenological analysis of interview data. In A. Bryman & R. G. Burgess (Eds.), *Qualitative research* (Vol. 3, pp. 143–164). London: SAGE Publications.

Ivey, A., Ivey, M., & Simek-Morgan, L. (1997). *Counseling and psychotherapy: A multicultural perspective* (4th ed.). Needham Heights, MA: Allyn & Bacon.

Jones, J. (1981). *Bad blood: The Tuskegee syphilis experiment: A tragedy of race and medicine*. New York: The Free Press.

Jordan, J., Kaplan, A., Miller, J. B., Stiver, I., & Surrey, J. (1991). *Women's growth in connection: Writings from the Stone Center*. New York: The Guilford Press.

Kitchener, K. S. (1984). Intuition, critical evaluation and ethical principles: The foundation for ethical decisions in counseling psychology. *The Counseling Psychologist, 12*(3), 43–55.

LeCompte, M. (2002). The transformation of ethnographic practice: Past and current challenges. *Qualitative Research, 2*, 283–299.

Leech, N. L., & Onwuegbuzie, A. J. (2007). An array of qualitative data analysis tools: A call for data analysis triangulation. *School Psychology Quarterly, 22*(4), 28–43.

Loue, S. (2000). *Textbook of research ethics: theory and practice*. New York: Kluwer Academic/Plenum

Merriam-Webster's Collegiate Dictionary (11th ed.). (2007). Springfield, MA: Merriam-Webster.

Milgram, S. (1964). Group pressure and action against a person. *Journal of Abnormal and Social Psychology, 69*, 137–143.

Moore, D. L. (2005). Expanding the view: The lives of women with severe work disabilities in context. *Journal of Counseling & Development, 83*, 343–348.

Moustakas, C. (1994). *Phenomenological research methods*. Thousand Oaks, CA: SAGE Publications.

National Commission for the Protection of Human Subjects of Biomedical and Behavioral Research. (1979). The Belmont Report: Ethical principles and guidelines for the protection of human subjects of research. *OPRR Reports*.

Parvizi, J., Tarity, D., Conner, K., & Smith, J. B. (2007). Institutional review board approval and why it matters. *The Journal of Bone and Joint Surgery (American), 89*, 418–426.

Patton, M. Q. (1990). *Qualitative evaluation and research methods* (2nd ed.). Newbury Park, CA: SAGE Publications.

Peirce, C. S. (1877). The fixation of belief. *Popular Science Monthly, 12*, 1–15.

Peter, M. (2003). Drama, narrative, and early learning. *British Journal of Special Education, 30*(1), 21–27. doi: 10.1111/1467-8527.00277

Schildcrout, J. (2008). The performance of nonconformity on *The Muppet Show*—or, How Kermit made me queer. *The Journal of Popular Culture, 41*(5), 823–835.

Schouten, J. W., & McAlexander, J. H. (1995). Subcultures of consumption: An ethnography of the new bikers. *The Journal of Consumer Research, 22*(1), 43–61.

Schreiber, J. B., McCown, R. R., & Perry, S. (2008, March). *Accounts of university teaching: Auditing the auditors*. A poster presented at the annual meeting of the American Educational Research Association, New York.

Shank, G., & Cunningham, D. J. (1996). *Modeling the six modes of Peircean abduction for educational purposes*. In MAICS 1996 Proceedings. Online address for Proceedings: http://www.cs.indiana.edu/event/maics96/Proceedings/shank.html

Shaw, I. (2003). Qualitative research and outcomes in health, social work and education. *Qualitative Research, 3,* 57–77.

Silko, L. M. (1997). *Yellow woman and a beauty of the spirit: Essays on the Native American life today*. New York: Touchstone.

Stake, R. (1995). *The art of case research*. Thousand Oaks, CA: SAGE Publications.

Strauss, A., & Corbin, J. (1990). *Basics of qualitative research: Grounded theory procedures and techniques*. Newbury Park, CA: SAGE Publications.

Strauss, A., & Corbin, J. (1998). *Basics of qualitative research: Grounded theory procedures and techniques* (2nd ed.). Newbury Park, CA: SAGE Publications.

Strike, K. A. (2002). *Ethical standards of the American Educational Research Association: Cases and commentary*. Washington, DC: American Educational Research Association.

Sue, D. W., Ivey, A. E., & Pedersen, P. B. (Eds.). (1996). *A theory of multicultural counseling and therapy*. Pacific Grove, CA: Brooks-Cole.

Swap, W., Leonard, D., Shields, M., & Abrams, L. (2001). Using mentoring and storytelling to transfer knowledge in the workplace. *Journal of Management Information Systems, 18*(1), 95–114.

U.S. Department of Health, Education, and Welfare. (1979). *Belmont Report*. Retrieved from http://www.hhs.gov/ohrp/humansubjects/guidance/belmont.htm

Vaughn, M. J. (2004). Creating ''Maneuvering Room'': A grounded theory of language and influence in marriage and family therapy. *Contemporary Family Therapy: An International Journal, 26,* 425–442.

Vontress, C. E., & Epp, L. R. (1997). Historical hostility in the African American client: Implications for counseling. *Journal of Multicultural Counseling & Development, 25*(3), 170–184.

Walker, D., & Myrick, F. (2006). Grounded theory: An exploration of process and procedure. *Qualitative Health Research, 16,* 547–559.

Ward, E. C. (2005). Keeping it real: A grounded theory study of African American clients engaging in counseling at a community mental health agency. *Journal of Counseling Psychology, 52,* 471–481.

Wenger, E. (1998). *Communities of practice: Learning, meaning, and identity*. New York: Cambridge University Press.

Wolcott, H. F. (1994). Transforming qualitative data: Description, analysis, and interpretation. Thousand Oaks, CA: SAGE Publications.

Yin, R. (1994). *Case study research: Design and methods* (2nd ed.). Beverly Hills, CA: Sage.

WEB SITES

History Detectives
http://www.pbs.org/opb/historydetectives/techniques/index.html

National Institutes of Health Ethics
http://ohsr.od.nih.gov/researcher/intro.php

Phenomenology
http//www.phenomenologyonline.com

Story Corps Project
http://www.storycorps.net/

Wordle
http://www.wordle.net

Analysis Techniques: Descriptive and Inferential Statistics

KEY IDEA

I am a pattern tester or a pattern searcher—the essence of analysis.

POINTS TO KNOW

Describe different types of data and levels of measurement.

Describe the appropriate analysis techniques for the different types of data.

Identify which descriptive statistics to use based on your data.

Explain inferential statistics.

Define hypotheses, null hypothesis testing, and probability.

Define statistical significance and compare to error types and other types of significance.

Describe standard error of the mean and sampling error.

Explain the basic interpretations of different inferential statistics tests.

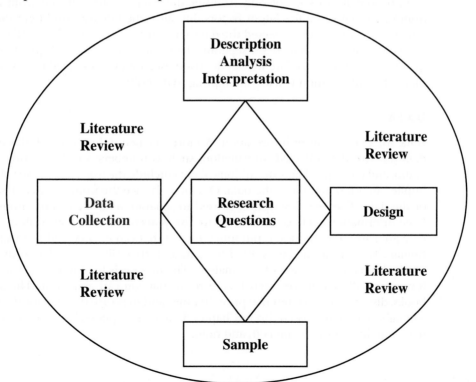

WHY CHOOSE AN ANALYSIS TECHNIQUE NOW?

The choice of the analysis technique is just as important as all the other components of research design. The technique must answer the questions while simultaneously taking into consideration the research design, sample, and type of data collected. Mistakes made early in the design and execution of a study are magnified at the analysis point. In reference to our overarching figure at the start of each chapter, we stated that as you make changes along the way you pull and tug on the different components and have to make adjustments. This is the point where pulling and tugging could snap the connections, because previous mistakes cannot be solved with statistical analysis.

This chapter focuses on the description of your data and inferences made from your data. Essentially, either you are searching for a pattern in your data or testing a pattern (that is, trying to confirm a pattern) or you are out exploring. As a species, we love patterns. You might use the terms *consistency* or *stability*, but they are all patterns. You most likely have said to yourself, ''But if I do this again, will I see the same thing?'' You are hoping or not hoping for a pattern given the situation. When you bake something, you follow a recipe and believe that you will get the same result at the end each time. In education, some teachers believe that if they were to replicate an activity the same way with the students, they could expect the same outcomes. In statistical analysis, such as exploratory factor analysis, you are looking to see not only whether the data can be reduced from a large number of items to a few latent factors, but also whether you would get the same few latent factors if you collected the data again and reran the analysis. All research has descriptive possibilities; we separate them into the traditional qualitative and quantitative patterns. Before we can discuss these, however, we need to examine the data—the information you are attempting to describe.

DATA

Data are a collection of information. A more detailed definition includes types of data that are the collected information, such as numbers, words, pictures, video, audio, and concepts. Many definitions of data include the word *fact*, or *facts*, but this implies an inference about the data. One may also see the word *raw* as a descriptor of the data. This *raw* description is used to separate data such as the number 42 from information such as ''At 42 you are five years older than your sibling.'' Once data are gathered, they are input into a format that can be analyzed by machine or human. The format can be a spreadsheet, note cards, or literary analysis software, all of which increase the ease of the analysis. The process is the same as in Chapter 3: formatting all of your research literature so that you can analyze it. The articles, books, dissertations, conference presentations, and so on are the data for the review. Though we have discussed this in Chapter 5, we review quickly the numeric types of data: nominal, ordinal, interval, and ratio.

Nominal

Nominal scale classifies objects or characteristics into categories that have no logical hierarchy or order. Here you can distinguish between categories but *cannot* conclude that one is more or less than the other. Examples include gender, religious affiliation, political affiliation, and ethnicity.

Ordinal

Ordinal scale classifies objects or characteristics into categories that have a logical order; therefore, you can distinguish between categories that have an order. Examples include order of finish in a race (1st, 2nd, 3rd), letter grades (A, B, C), college classification (freshman, sophomore, junior, senior), or law school rank.

Interval

Interval scale classifies objects or characteristics into categories that have a logical order and reflect equal differences in the characteristic being measured. Now you can distinguish, decide order, and know that the difference between categories is equal. Examples include course averages, test scores, temperature Fahrenheit, and temperature Celsius.

Ratio

Ratio scale classifies objects or characteristics into categories that have a logical order, reflect equal differences in the characteristic being measured, and have a "true zero," where zero indicates the absence of the characteristic being measured. Ratio has all of the qualities: order, equal distances, and a true zero. Examples include height, weight, age, temperature Kelvin, speed in miles per hour, and salary.

Qualitative data are non-numeric and have a greater variety. The data are generally categorized as verbal and nonverbal. Data are verbal if the majority of what is being analyzed is words. **Verbal data** include items such as personal diaries, letters, press reports, surveys or interviews, and field notes. Within the group of interviews, the data can come from in-depth/unstructured interviews, semi-structured interviews, structured interviews, questionnaires containing substantial open comments, and focus groups, for example.

Nonverbal data include items such as student concept maps, kinship diagrams, pictures, video, film, art, or print advertisements. Each type of data and how it was collected has different strengths and weaknesses in relation to the research questions and analysis techniques. For example, nonparticipant observations from video collected through surveillance cameras potentially allows the researcher to collect data without influence in the field of observation, but there are potential problems with the ethics of these observations.

IN-TEXT ACTIVITY

If you are designing your study while reading this, stop for a few minutes and take some notes.

1. What type of data from your variables of interest do you have?

2. Is it numeric or non-numeric?

3. Does it fit within the four types typically associated with quantitative research?

DESCRIPTIVE STATISTICS

Statistics are methods and rules for organizing, summarizing, and interpreting information. In general, when we talk about statistics, we are discussing a value, a **statistic**, that describes a sample (descriptive statistics). A **parameter** is a value that describes the population. We infer from our sample statistics to the population (inferential statistics). For example, suppose you are interested in the types of games third graders in the United States play at recess (that is, if their school still has recess). You randomly sample 30 third graders and watch their play at recess. You observe that the highest frequency game over the six months you watched is "tag." That frequency is a sample statistic. You do not know the population parameter (highest frequency based on every third grader), but infer that for other thousands of third graders, tag is the most common recess game.

Descriptive statistics are a set of procedures to summarize numerical data where a large number of observed values is reduced to a few numbers. The data do not have to start out as a number, but the descriptive procedure will be based on a numeric form. Descriptive statistics can be numerical, which includes measures of central tendency and measures of variability, or graphical, which includes histograms, bar charts, and scatterplots, to name a few. Again, descriptive statistics are *different* from inferential statistics. Descriptive statistics describe the data you have, whereas inferential statistics infer from the sample to the population of interest.

Univariate Descriptive Statistics

In addition to numeric and graphical categories, descriptive statistics can be separated into univariate and bivariate form. **Univariate descriptive statistics** examine one variable at a time, such as the average of a class of students' final exam scores. **Bivariate descriptive statistics** analyze two variables at a time, such as graphing pairs of test scores of students to explore whether students who scored well on the first test, also scored well on the second. With the increase in computer chip processing speed, you can now conduct trivariate graphical analyses. We do not discuss them below, but examining three variables at once is much faster than it used to be.

Measures of Central Tendency. Measures of central tendency allow you, the researcher, to describe numeric data that are *interval* or *ratio* in a limited space. The three measures of central tendency are mean ($\bar{x}$, M), median (Mdn), and mode (Mo). The **mean** is the average score from a distribution (group) of scores. For example, on the *Jay Leno Show* a group of participants answered a set of elementary-school-based questions where the possible scores were 0, no answers correct, to 10, all questions correct. The individuals scored 6, 2, 4, 5, 0, 10, or in mathematical order 0, 2, 4, 5, 6, 10.

The mean, or average value, would be 4.5. To calculate the mean mathematically, use the formula

$$\frac{(x_1 + x_2 + x_3 + x_4 + x_5 + x_6)}{N}$$

With the numbers from our example, it looks like

$$= \frac{0 + 2 + 4 + 5 + 6 + 10}{6} = \frac{27}{6} = 4.5$$

In the equation, each x represents a score and the N represents the total number of scores. This is commonly reduced to look like this:

$$\frac{\sum x_i}{N},$$

where Σ means add (sum) each item in the set (in this case quiz scores) together, the x indicates numbers (the participants' responses to be added), the subscript i means there are many numbers, and N represents the number of scores being summed. The subscript i is a common shorthand for mathematicians.

The **median** is the middle value in the ordered distribution of scores. By ordered, we mean the scores have been organized highest to lowest or lowest to highest. In this case, the median actually occurs between 4 and 5 (0, 2, 4, 5, 6, 10) because that is where the exact middle of the set or distribution of scores occurs. Think about the middle of a divided highway. In this small data set, the center is 4.5, exactly between the 4 and the 5. There is a more technical computation for determining the median when the data have repeating values at the median point,

FIGURE 9.1
Normality and skewness

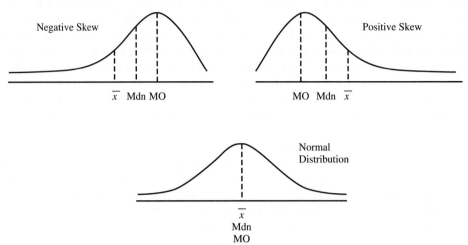

such as 0, 2, 4, 4, 4, 6, 10 (Gravetter & Wallnau, 2007), though statistical packages such as SPSS do not use this method.

The **mode** is the most common value in the distribution. In this example, the mode does not exist because each value has the same frequency of observation (once). In a group of numeric values, there can be no mode, one mode, or more than one mode.

The measures of central tendency are calculated when the data is considered continuous (interval or ratio). If the data are categorical or discrete (ordinal or nominal), such as gender identity or political affiliation, proportions or percentages are the traditional descriptive statistic used. For example, if you have 55 females in your study and 45 males, stating that the mean gender is .55 does not make sense. However, stating that 55 percent of the sample is female does.

Measures of Variability.   When you graph a distribution of numbers, you are examining how spread out they look (or variability) and what shape the numbers make. **Skewness** concerns the degree of asymmetry of the distribution, the shape (Figure 9.1). Positively skewed distributions occur when most of the values are at the lower end with some at the higher end. Negative skew is the reflected image of positively skewed. **Kurtosis** describes the flatness or peakedness of the distribution. A strongly peaked distribution is leptokurtic, whereas a flat distribution is platykurtic (Figure 9.2).

In Figure 9.1, notice that the mean, median, and mode are all at the same central location for the normally distributed set of values. As the distribution becomes asymmetrical, the mean, median, and mode begin to separate indicating a positive or negative skew. A negatively skewed distribution has one or more values "pulling"

FIGURE 9.2
Kurtic distributions

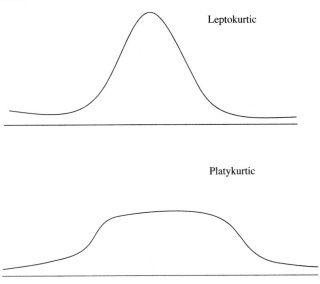

Leptokurtic

Platykurtic

the mean lower than the median and the mode. The positively skewed distribution has one or more values "pulling" the mean higher than the median and mode.

Variability, also known as **dispersion**, describes how the values from a set of numbers are spread out. Three common dispersion measures are range, standard deviation, and variance. The **range** of values for a distribution is calculated by subtracting the largest value from the smallest value. **Standard deviation** (*SD*) is the average distance the scores are from the mean. The more dispersed the values, the larger the standard deviation. In a normal distribution, 68.3% of the values will be within one standard deviation above or below the mean (Figure 9.3). You may also see this stated as 68.3% of the area under the curve is within one standard deviation of the mean. The standard deviation is more commonly provided because

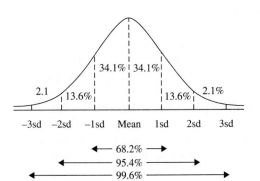

FIGURE 9.3
Normal distribution (normal curve or bell curve) with area percentages

FIGURE 9.4
Similar means, different distributions

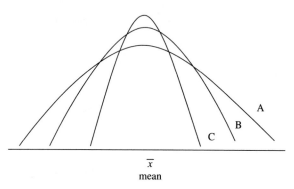

it is easily interpreted, whereas the variance simply indicates that variability in the observed values exists. Variance and standard deviation are mathematically related because the standard deviation is the square root of the variance ($SD = \sqrt{var}$). A fourth, though less commonly provided, dispersion descriptor is the interquartile range (IQR). The interquartile range is the distance between the 25th and 75th percentiles and indicates where the middle 50% of the values are.

Figure 9.4 displays three distributions with similar means but different dispersions. Distribution A has a great deal of variability, B has less, and C has the least amount of variance to the values.

An example of univariate descriptive statistics is provided in Table 9.1 with two groups of data to highlight the basic descriptive statistics that are expected in research articles.

In the example, group B has two modes (bimodal) because both 8 and 11 occur three times; however, we display only one (8) in the table. The skew for group A is negative, indicating that a few lower values are pulling the mean to the left of the median and mode. For group B, the distribution is considered platykurtic (more flat) because the kurtosis value is greater than 0. For group A, the distribution is leptokurtic, more peaked. The standard deviation for group A is 4.16, indicating that 68.3% of the values are between 3.55 and 11.87 (i.e., 7.71−4.16 and 7.71 + 4.16). The interquartile range for group A is 6.75 (10.25−3.50; see percentiles at the bottom of Table 9.1).

Categorical data (ordinal and nominal), such as terminal degree granted, gender, or liked/did not like the movie, are typically described by frequency of occurrence counts. The raw frequencies or percentages provide the description of the data. With ordered categorical data (lowest to highest), the frequencies or the median and mode can be displayed. For example, 326 participants (45%) had a high school degree, 291 participants (40%) had an associate or bachelor degree, and 109 (15%) had a graduate degree. Table 9.2 shows an example from a university fact book, showing the age group of the students, the raw number of students, and the percentage of the total group.

TABLE 9.1
Descriptive statistics example

Group A: 1, 2, 2, 4, 6, 7, 9, 9, 10, 10, 10, 11, 13, 14
Group B: 5, 6, 6, 7, 7, 8, 8, 8, 9, 10, 11, 11, 11, 15

		Descriptive Statistics	
		A	**B**
Mean		7.71	8.71
Median		9.00	8.00
Mode		10.00	8.00
Standard deviation		4.16	2.67
Variance		17.30	7.14
Skewness		−0.33	0.86
Kurtosis		−1.01	0.87
Range		13.00	10.00
Percentiles	25	3.50	6.75
	50	9.00	8.00
	75	10.25	11.00

TABLE 9.2
Categorical frequency and percentage data example

Age Group	Undergraduate	Percentage of Undergraduates
<18	76	1.3
18–19	2,255	39.5
20–24	2,324	40.7
25–29	124	2.2
30–34	93	1.6
35–39	65	1.1
40–44	53	0.9
45–49	35	0.6
50–59	26	0.5
> = 60	0	0.0
Not reported	660	11.6
Total	5,711	100

For measuring central tendency, mode can be used for nominal data and median can be used for ordinal (Table 9.3). There is no variability measure for nominal data, but the IQR or simply discussing the highest and lowest value can work for ordinal data.

Finally, if you happen to get hold of an older textbook on descriptive statistics, you may see the term *mathematical moments*. The mean, variance, skewness, and kurtosis are the first four mathematical moments of a distribution.

TABLE 9.3
Summary table of data type and typical univariate descriptive statistic

Level of Measurement		Central Tendency	Variability
Nominal		Mode	None
Ordinal		Mode, median	IQR
Interval or ratio	If the data are skewed, open ended, or have extreme scores ->	Median	IQR
	If not ->	Mean, median, and mode	Standard deviation

Bivariate (Two Variable) Descriptive Statistics

Correlation tables are bivariate descriptive statistics. A **correlation** is a standardized mathematical description of the linear relationship between two variables. By **linear** we mean that the true relationship between two variables approximates a straight line. That may not always be the case. The true relationship between the two variables may be curved. For example, the relationship between anxiety and performance are curvilinear. Anxiety is related to higher test scores up to a point, and then there is so much anxiety that performance starts to drop.

There are two components of a correlation: the magnitude and the direction. The magnitude describes how large the relationship is and ranges from 0 to 1 [0,1]. A value of 0 indicates no relationship and a value of 1 would indicate a perfect linear relationship. The direction of the relationship can be positive or negative. A negative relationship occurs when high values on one variable are related to low values on the second variable. For example, scores on a happiness scale are negatively related to scores on a depression scale. Or, the amount of money earned at a golf tournament is negatively related to your score at the tournament. In many correlation tables, a hypothesis test is included (see Inferential statistics in page 244) where a correlation will be designated as statistically significant. This is a bridge between descriptive and inferential statistics. The correlation is simply a description. Once it is tested against the null hypothesis that the correlation is zero, then it is inferential.

Each type of data (in this case, pairs of data points) has a specific type of correlation that should be conducted.

1. Pearson product-moment correlation: both variables are continuous (interval or ratio)
2. Spearman rank-order correlation: both variables are rank-ordered (ordinal)
3. Biserial correlation: one variable is continuous and the other is an artificial dichotomy (i.e., a high or low score on a measure) (interval/ratio and ordinal)
4. Point biserial correlation: one variable is continuous and the other is a true dichotomy (i.e., a score of right [1] or wrong [0] on a test item) (ordinal data)
5. Tetrachoric correlation: both variables are artificial dichotomies (ordinal)

6. Phi coefficient: both variables are true dichotomies (ordinal)
7. Contingency coefficient: both variables reflect two or more categories (nominal or ordinal)
8. Correlation ratio, eta: both variables are continuous but reflect a curvilinear relationship (interval or ratio)

Univariate Visual Descriptions

There are many types of univariate visual descriptions. A few common ones are discussed below. As with mathematical descriptions, the type of data affects the type of visual description that can be properly utilized.

A **bar chart** provides a visual description with ordinal data values. A common use of this visual description is for frequency counts of categorical data, such as gender or political affiliation.

The bar chart in Figure 9.5 indicates the number of males and females from a survey study. Notice that the bars are not connected, indicating no continuous linear relationship (e.g., highest to lowest) between the responses. **Histograms**, which are visually similar to bar charts, are used with data that are continuous or have an implied continuity to them; the bars are connected. The histogram in Figure 9.6 shows respondents' income for a given year.

Other univariate pictorial representations of data are frequency polygon, box plot, and stem-and-leaf plot. A **frequency polygon** is similar to a histogram but connects the data by points and lines instead of bars (Figure 9.7).

A **box plot**, or box-and-whisker plot, provides the lowest value, then the lower whisker (which is the bottom 25% of values), the middle 50% of values (the box), the

FIGURE 9.5
Example of a bar chart

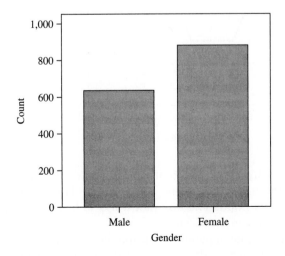

FIGURE 9.6
Example of a histogram

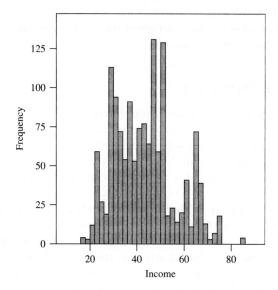

FIGURE 9.7
Example of a frequency polygon

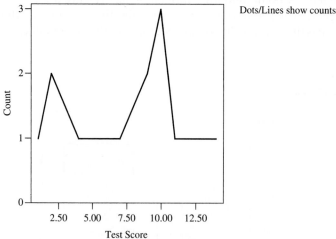

upper whisker (which is the top 25% of values), and the highest value (Figure 9.8). The horizontal line in the box is the 50% marker. There are 50% of the scores above and below that point. The box plot works well (compared to a histogram) when there is a small amount of data.

A **stem-and-leaf plot** separates each number into a stem and a leaf (Tukey, 1977). In Figure 9.9, income data is displayed. The 1.79 means that 1 is the stem

FIGURE 9.8
Example of a box plot

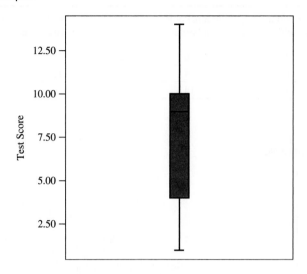

FIGURE 9.9
Stem-and-leaf plot

```
1 . 79
2 . 01222222223333444
2 . 5556777888888888889999999999
3 . 00000000001111111112222222223333344444
3 . 555555666666666666666778899999999
4 . 00000000000111122222222222333344444444
4 . 5555566666666666666677777777777888889999999
5 . 0000011111111111111111111112223444
5 . 556778899
6 . 000000111234444444444
6 . 5555666666689
7 . 1344
7 . 5
```

and 7 and 9 are each leaves. Therefore, these two numbers from the income are 17,000 and 19,000 because the numbers are actually in ten thousands. Turn the stem-and-leaf plot vertical and it will look like a histogram.

Bivariate Graphic Displays

In addition to univariate displays, there are two common bivariate descriptive displays. The first, **cross-tabulation**, creates a table where two variables can be crossed and, for example, the frequencies can be examined. Table 9.4 is an example of a 2 (gender) by 6 (race/ethnicity) frequency table. As can be seen, there are 10 Asian/Pacific Islander female faculty members.

TABLE 9.4
Example of cross-tabulation

Gender	Black Non-Hispanic	American Indian/Alaskan Native	Asian/Pacific Islander	Hispanic	White Non-Hispanic	Unknown	Total
Female	8	2	10	2	227	7	256
Male	5	1	4	1	160	2	173
Total	13	3	14	3	387	9	429

FIGURE 9.10
Example of a scatterplot

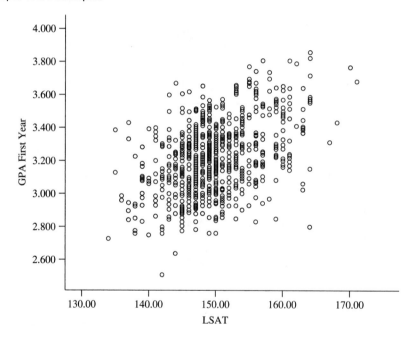

The second bivariate description is a **scatterplot** or scattergram. A scatterplot is used with continuous data and displays the relationship between two variables. The scatterplot in Figure 9.10 displays law school admission test (LSAT) scores by grade point average (GPA) in the first year for a sample of law school students.

The scatterplot demonstrates a positive relationship between LSAT scores and first-year GPA for these law students, that is, the higher a student's LSAT score, the higher the first-year GPA of that student, in general.

Descriptive statistics are used to provide a brief summary of your data or to explore the data you have. They can be based on mathematical computations, such as those for central tendency, or they can be a graphical representation, such as a histogram or scatterplot. A thoughtful use of descriptive statistics can inform the reader and highlight important information related to your overall research questions. Don't ignore descriptive statistics; they can greatly increase the quality of the argument you are making. You may not be able to publish all statistics you want due to space limitations, but with the increase use of online journal distribution, space issues are disappearing.

Qualitative Description: Non-Numeric Data

The line between describing data and explaining it is thin and grey. This is true with quantitative data also. People tend to explain data and even make inferences from that data based simply on the descriptions. Miles and Huberman (1994) state that there is no clear boundary. One can discuss the physical description of the data, such as hours of videotape. The summarizing of that data into a smaller verbal or visual space (similar to quantitative descriptive statistics) is a process of developing the data to work with, implementing a coding system, and displaying examples from the coding system to the reader. At this point, you are beginning your analysis (Carney, 1990). You have not tried to make connections among the data. Description also includes the setting and participants in order to provide a thorough picture for the reader. For qualitative researchers, the description is an extremely important component, and they often discuss this in terms of "rich or thick" description of the data. Do not forget that there may be times when some of the traditional quantitative descriptive techniques discussed above may be of great use to you as you develop your qualitative narrative.

IN-TEXT ACTIVITY

Which descriptive statistics might work for your study and why? Could you tell your research story through descriptive statistics alone and convince people? Again, write out a few thoughts below related to these questions.

_____

_____

_____

_____

_____

_____

_____

_____

INFERENTIAL STATISTICS

Inferential statistics are used when making an inference from your sample to the population. This is termed *generalization*. We actually do this all the time in daily life, but in research we must be more careful and exact. Remember, descriptive statistics allow you to describe the data you have. Nothing more, nothing less.

Hypotheses

In Chapter 1, we discussed hypothesis testing. Within hypothesis testing, you must understand the null hypothesis and alternate hypothesis. A **null hypothesis** simply states there is no difference between two groups or there is no relationship between two variables. For example, there is no mean difference in lifetime earnings between people who attended small private liberal arts colleges and those who attended large research universities.

The symbolic written expression of this looks like

$$H_o: \mu_1 = \mu_2,$$

where H_o indicates the null hypothesis, μ_1 is the population mean for group 1, μ_2 is the population mean for group 2, and $=$ indicates they are equal, no difference. But we rarely, if ever, obtain the whole population, so we use the sample mean designations and infer that they represent the population means, which looks like this:

$$H_o: \bar{x}_1 = \bar{x}_2,$$

where the sample means of groups 1 and 2 are said to be equal.

Notice that the symbols have changed. The reason for this is that we are now discussing the sample statistics and not the population statistics. It seems tricky, or at least many students have told us that. But in actuality it is about being precise with the information you are presenting.

The **alternate hypotheses** are traditionally your research hypotheses, what you think is going to happen. They can be separated into directional and nondirectional.

Directional hypotheses state which direction you think the results will demonstrate. For example, those who attended small private colleges earn more on average than those who attended large research universities. The representation looks like this:

$$H_a: \bar{x}_1 > \bar{x}_2$$

It is more common, however, for researchers to test nondirectional hypotheses, and this is the default in most of the statistical analysis packages. For example, there is a difference between average lifetime earnings for those who attended small private colleges and those who attended large research universities.

$$H_a: \bar{x}_1 \neq \bar{x}_2$$

The not-equal symbol simply indicates that the means are not the same. Not overly informative from our standpoint. Null and alternative hypotheses are the entry-level basics of hypothesis testing. The next phase is the actual testing. Below, we go into more detail about probability and the different analysis techniques related to the actual testing.

Probability

Every year, Jim introduces the birthday problem to his classes, both undergraduate and graduate, because it highlights the misconceptions about probability theory and rational thinking. The birthday problem is simple: given the size of class X, what is the probability that two students have the same birthday? Students and the public in general tend to focus on the number of days in a year, 365 (ignore leap years). That is the wrong focus, which is typical of how people think about probability. The focus should be on the number of ways (mathematically, combinations) that a match can occur. In a class of 30, the probability is .70.

A **conditional probability**, a probability with an extra condition to consider, is the next step; more specifically, the probability of event x given event y. Berry and Chastain (2004) provide a great example of conditional probabilities with illegal drug use (i.e., doping) in sports. The way most people think of this is "What is the probability of getting a positive test?" And that is the wrong way to think about it. The correct way to think about it is, "What is the probability that an athlete with a positive test is using illegal drugs?" Based on the Berry and Chastain's (2004) article, we can create our own contingency table (Table 9.5).

In the example, there are 1,000 athletes tested for illegal drug use. One-hundred (100) athletes are actually using performance-enhancing drugs. The test will positively identify 50 of the 100, true positive cases. The test will fail to identify 50, false negative cases. The test will identify nine as positive when in reality the athletes are not using the drugs, a false positive. Finally, the test will identify correctly 891 as negative. To answer the question of what is the probability of an athlete testing positive given that they are using performance-enhancing drugs is not .50 (50/100). In this case, it is 50/59 or .847. Now, the sensitivity of the test [sensitivity = correct positive test/(correct positive test + false negatives) = 50/(50+50) = .50] is a different issue. Probability in inferential statistics is also based on a conditional probability due to our sampling from a population.

TABLE 9.5
Conditional probability: doping example

	Reality		Total
Test Result	**No**	**Yes**	
Positive	9	50	59
Negative	891	50	949
Total	900	100	1,000

As stated previously, we sample from a population, therefore, variability exists in our sampling process. The descriptive statistics discussed above are based on data from a sample. If we were to proceed through the sampling process again and collect more data, most likely we would get slightly different results. We are just not sure how much of the values we have deviate from are the actual population values (called population parameters). We need to feel confident, or at least have a range of confidence, about the values we have.

Why do we worry about the values we have calculated? Remember, we sample from a larger population. For researchers, obtaining the whole population is quite rare. In the larger picture, we do not know whether our collected sample is representative—that is, how much we might be wrong if we collect, analyze, and make inferences from the data from this sample. For example, let us say the whole population contains 10 participants and their individual scores on our purchasing survey are 3, 5, 2, 8, 6, 9, 6, 4, 1, and 7. The mean value is 5.1. Now, if we randomly sample six participants of our population whose scores are 3, 6, 9, 1, 7, and 8, the mean score is 5.67. The difference between the population and the sample means is error associated with sampling, **sampling error**. If we do not know the population mean, we can still calculate an expected error value based on the sample called the standard error of the mean (*SEM*). The *SEM* provides a value that indicates how different another sampling mean from the population might be. The calculation of the value is easy because all you need is the standard deviation and the sample size. The equation is

$$\text{Standard error of the mean} = \frac{\text{standard deviation}}{\sqrt{N-1}},$$

where N is the sample size. For our sample of six numbers, the *SEM* is

$$\frac{3.08}{\sqrt{10-1}} = 1.26.$$

If we were to sample again, we would expect that 68.3% of the scores (remember the normal curve discussion from above) would fall between 4.41 and 6.93 (5.67+/−1.26).

We also know, in this example, that our population mean is 5.1. If we take the sample mean and subtract the population mean (5.67−5.1), we obtain the value of .57. Now, we can take that value (.57) and divide it by our *SEM* value of 1.26 to obtain a value of .45, indicating our sample mean is .45 standard deviations above our population mean.

STATISTICAL SIGNIFICANCE

A common statement among statisticians is "Statistics is never having to say you're certain," adapted from the quote from Eric Segal's novel *Love Story*, "Love means never having to say you are sorry." This is crucial to remember and understand; you are making an argument, hopefully persuasive, but at the end of the day, it

TABLE 9.6
Decision error matrix for null hypothesis testing

Researcher Decision	Null Hypothesis in Reality	
	True	False
Reject Null	Type I error (false positive)	Correct decision (true positive)
Do Not Reject Null	Correct decision (true negative)	Type II error (false negative)

is not proof, just probability. **Statistical significance** is based on the comparison of calculated values with a critical value from a specific shape of numbers (i.e., theoretical distribution of numbers), such as t, F, or chi-squared distributions. That comparison cannot tell anyone how important that calculated value is. Many studies have statistically significant observations, but are not all that important or meaningful. We agree with Ableson (1997), though, that even if there were no significance tests, we would create them or reinvent them, as the case may be. They do serve a purpose and have a role (Mulaik, 1987). Therefore, the balance is in using them appropriately (Frick, 1996), understanding and discussing their assumptions and limitations (Carver, 1993), and not using them past what the tests can actually do.

Error Types

Since statistical significance testing is probability and not proof and we have sampling process error, statisticians worry about risk: How much is acceptable? This risk level is associated with error, so we need to talk about risk level and error at the same time. We discuss two types of error: type I and type II (Table 9.6), but there are arguments for more types (Newman & Newman, 1994). **Type I error** occurs when we decide to reject the null hypothesis when we should not (Table 9.5). In our performance drug example, these are the nine false positives and we would reject the null, no drug use. We usually assign a risk value of .05 (also called alpha or the Greek symbol, α) and discuss it as the risk level for incorrectly rejecting a true null hypothesis. (Note that this alpha is different from Cronbach's alpha from Chapter 5 on score reliability.) **Type II error** is associated B, or really $(1-B)$, the probability of correctly rejecting a false hypothesis. The error is not rejecting when you should, our false negatives from above. B, the type II error level, is typically set at .20 and, therefore, $1-B$ is .80. Type II error is also discussed in terms of power for the study. That is, do I have enough power to detect a departure from the null hypothesis being tested? Again, type I error probability is typically set at .05 for incorrectly rejecting a true null hypothesis, and statistical power is typically set at .80 for detecting a moderate deviation from the hypothesis being tested.

Table 9.7 provides the null hypothesis testing language with the illegal doping example.

Another way to view this is through the distribution of scores for two groups (Figure 9.11). The dark shaded (on the left) distribution in Figure 9.11 is acting as

TABLE 9.7
Null hypothesis: Athletes not using drugs

	Reality		Total
Test Result	No (Not Using)	Yes (Using)	
Positive (reject null)	9	50	59
Negative (do not reject null)	891	50	949
Total	900	100	1,000

FIGURE 9.11
Error type with distributions

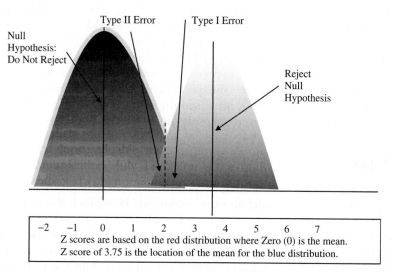

the null distribution of scores in this example. The distribution is set up by z scores, with a mean of zero and standard deviation of one. The light shaded distribution of scores is the group we are interested in knowing whether their average score is different from the null group. In the example, the mean of the light-shaded blue distribution has a z score of 3.75 in comparison to the null group.

The critical z value of 1.96 is the dashed line separating the overlap areas for type I and type II errors. If we did not reject the null hypothesis, especially with the distance between the means and the very little overlap, we clearly would be making a type II error. If we reject the null, which we should because our z-score distance of 3.75 is clearly greater than 1.96, we would be making a correct decision.

Finally, in contrast to null hypothesis testing, we like the idea of point estimate testing. Point estimate testing is the process of testing your obtained value against a specific value, not just whether it is different. When you know the population parameter, such as the population mean, you can complete a test of your sample value against that population parameter value. When you do not know the population parameter, you can test against the average values obtained from the literature review you have already conducted. For example, we examine a body of literature that uses the same instrumentation for two variables. We notice that the relationship between variables across the studies is .31 (a correlation in this case). After we collect our data, we test our value against the .31 to see whether our obtained value is different from the currently observed average.

What Statistical Significance Is and Is Not

The reasons for the critiques, which date back to the 1930s, we feel, are rooted in our belief that most people have a fundamental misunderstanding of probability, inductive reasoning, and statistical inference, thereby misusing or misinterpreting null hypothesis testing. This in turn leads to the critiques. At the core, statistical significance testing is a process for determining the likelihood of a result *assuming* null hypothesis is true given a random sampling *and* random assignment process with a sample size, n (Shaver, 1993). Therefore:

1. The test is a probability statement.
2. The two choices allowed are reject and do not reject the null hypothesis.
3. The test assumes that null hypothesis is true.
4. Random selection and assignment are required; therefore, it is a conditional probability.

We notice that most people understand, to some level, numbers 1 and 2. Number 3 is typically forgotten. People focus on what they believe (the alternative or research hypothesis). Number 4 is completely ignored or irretrievable from long-term memory. Randomization is a major assumption because it is supposed to ensure the independence of observations or errors (Glass & Hopkins, 1984). Independence in this case means that the scores from the participants in the sample are not related in some way, such as students in the same class. Yet, most researchers ignore this and plunge in to analyze the data. Examining independence is extremely difficult because one would have to examine all potentially relevant variables in relation to the dependent variables (Shaver, 1980); however, we should not ignore the assumption either. Shaver (1993) wrote that without random selection *and* assignment, the conditional probability question is "What would be the probability of the obtained result *if* random samples had actually been drawn?" (p. 299).

The test of the null hypothesis will not tell you whether you would see the same results if you repeated the sampling process and ran the study again. Tukey (1969) wrote that statistician R. A. Fisher's "standard of firm knowledge was not one of extreme significant results, but rather the ability to repeatedly get results significant at 5%" (p. 85). It is much more valuable for your field if you replicate your result than if you get one statistically significant result.

A test of statistical significance does not indicate the probability that the null hypothesis is true or false (Table 9.8). The same thing can be said for the alternative hypothesis. The test simply provides you with information in reference to the likelihood of a result given that the null hypothesis is true. Rejecting the null

TABLE 9.8
Common misstatements concerning statistical significance testing

The probability of the null hypothesis is <.05.
The probability that the results are due to sampling error (chance) is <.05.
The probability that the decision taken to reject the null hypothesis as a type I error is <.05.
The probability of the alternative hypothesis is >.95.
The probability of replication is >.95.

based on one result is a very strong statement and probably too strong. The test cannot tell you how important or large your results are—that is where effect sizes and measures of association help.

As has been demonstrated may times over many decades, a large enough sample with relatively reliable scores will provide statistically significant results almost every time (e.g., Meehl, 1954). We demonstrate this with an example of correlation and sample size below. Statistical significance tests are not going away, but understanding what they do and not do is important. Most importantly, understanding that they are a conditional probability and have limits of what can be stated will help you be a thoughtful researcher and data analyst.

INFERENTIAL TESTS

Inferential tests of statistical significance come in two popular flavors: parametric and nonparametric. **Parametric tests** assume that the data you have is normally distributed, or follows a normal bell curve (see Figure 9.3). Second, the data are interval or ratio scaled. In social science research, we assume that much of the data is interval scaled. Next, the participants in the sample are independent. That is, every participant in the study have had the same chance of being chosen. Finally, we assume that the variances of the groups' data are equal—that is, they have the same dispersion. Violating these assumptions is problematic and can cause a researcher to make an incorrect decision. Overall, minor violations such as slight skewness do not cause great problems, but if the data is extremely skewed, you need to move to nonparametric statistics.

Nonparametric tests are used when the data is considered nominal or ordinal. More commonly, they are used when interval data is extremely skewed because nonparametric tests do not assume that the data distribution must be a specific shape. The negative side of these techniques is the requirement of a larger sample size (i.e., more power) because of an increased difficulty in rejecting the null hypothesis. Finally, not all parametric statistics have a companion in nonparametric statistics.

We would be remiss at this point if we did not mention three other significance types: practical significance, clinical significance, and economic significance. **Practical significance** analyses and discussions have grown over the past 30 years since Gene V. Glass's work on effect size. An effect size provides an indication of how big a difference (or relationship) is. For example, two commercials are run for a company in two different but very similar regions. The company wants to see how much of an increase in sales occurs. A test of the null hypothesis will only tell them whether a difference exists statistically, but won't tell them how much; the effect size will help to provide evidence of how much. For the company, commercial A was associated with average sales of 1,254 units per store and commercial B was associated with 1,097. Now that looks like a big difference, and with 100 stores in each commercial area, it is probably statistically significant. But how big is that difference? One way to measure the practical difference is **effect size**, which is the averages of the groups in relation to the pooled standard deviation (the standard deviation of both groups combined). The equation looks like this:

$$ES = \frac{\overline{x_2} - \overline{x_2}}{sd_{pooled}}$$

If the average for commercial A sales is 1,254, commercial B sales is 1,097, and the pooled standard deviation is 173 units, our effect size is

$$ES = \frac{1,254 - 1,097}{173} \text{ or } = .91$$

The .91 value is interpreted as .91 standard deviation difference between the groups. This is a large effect size in reference to the difference between two groups. There are generic rules of thumb for comparing your effect size to a standard. In our example, with the differences of two means, 0.2 is considered a small effect, 0.5 medium, and 0.8 large (see Cohen, 1992).

Clinical significance measures provide data regarding the extent to which the intervention makes a real difference to the quality of life of the participants or to those with whom they interact (Kazdin, 1999). In contrast to traditional null hypothesis testing, it is possible to have clinical significance without statistical or practical significance. **Economic significance** is the examination of the economic value of a program or intervention in reference to the effects of the study both long and short term (Leech & Onwuegbuzie, 2004). One example of this type of significance examination is the HighScope Perry Preschool Study, where students were randomly assigned to a treatment group (preschool) and a control group (Schweinhart, Barnes, & Weikart, 1993). By the time the groups of students reached the age of 40, the financial return to the economy was $244,812 per participant (3% discount rate using year 2000 dollars).

Correlation: Different from Zero

A correlation alone is simply a description of the linear relationship between two variables. When someone writes that the correlation was statistically significant, that is an inferential test. The actual hypothesis being tested is whether the magnitude of the correlation is different from zero: H_o: $r_{xy} \neq 0$. Verbally, we would state for the null hypothesis: There is no relationship between the variables.

In reality, for interval and ratio data, once you have a sample size of 30 (degrees of freedom = 28), any correlation (nondirectional) over .35 is statistically significant

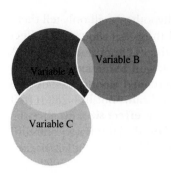

FIGURE 9.12
Shared variance

with alpha set at .05. By nondirectional, we mean that the value correlation could be positive or negative; we are only interested in how large the correlation is.

At a sample size of 100 (98 degrees of freedom), a correlation over .20 is statistically significant. However, this is not much **shared variance**, your correlation squared. A correlation of .20 means that the two variables share 4% (.04) of variance. Alternatively, they don't share 96%. From a "measure of association" perspective, that is not very much. In Figure 9.12, we diagram shared variance among three variables, A, B, and C. The shared variance between A and C is about .30, or a correlation around .55. The shared variance between A and B is about .10, or a correlation about .30. Finally, the shared variance between B and C is zero with a correlation of zero also. You really want the correlation to be much higher between variables, so that if you know the value for one of the variables of interest, you have a very good idea what the value will be for the variable you do not know.

Degrees of freedom—the number you need to use in the table and match with the alpha level you have chosen—is a difficult topic for students to grasp because it is an abstract idea and a technical issue in statistical analysis. We notice that many people have a misunderstanding of it. One of the best nonstatistical discussions of degrees of freedom is the dinner party example by Burns (2000). You decide to have a dinner party for you and nine of your classmates. Given that there are 10 of you and you want prearranged seating, you begin to set the table and get to the last one. There is only one spot left, so you have no more degrees of freedom of where to place the 10th person.

Regression

Bivariate **regression** is the examination of a dependent variable regressed on an independent variable. Multivariate regression is the examination of a dependent variable regressed on multiple independent variables. Bivariate regression can be thought of as the next step after a correlation analysis that takes into account error. When you look at a scatterplot of two variables (see the Descriptive Statistics section above), the more the plot looks like a straight line, the closer the magnitude is to one. For regression, that indicates there will be less error. The equation for a bivariate regression model is

$$Y = B_0 + B_1 x + \text{error},$$

FIGURE 9.13

Scatterplot of percent male by motor vehicle thefts

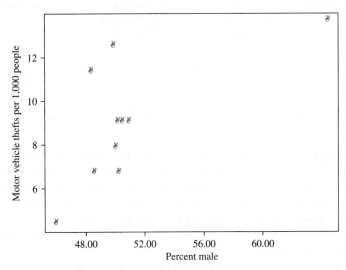

where Y is the dependent variable and x is the independent variable. B_0 is the intercept (constant) where the regression line crosses the y-axis and can be thought of as the starting point, or the mean of Y, the dependent variable. B_1 is the slope, the steepress of the regression line, and the rise over the run that you were taught in high school. Another way to think about slope is how fast or slow the values rise or fall. A slope of 0 would look like a flat horizontal line, a slope of 1 would look like a vertical line, and a slope of .50 would look like a 45-degree line.

Suppose you have the number of car thefts in an area and the percentage of males living in that area, along with other variables. This data can be obtained at the DASL Web site hosted at Carnegie Mellon University. The scatterplot for this data is in Figure 9.13.

Now, if we were to run a regression model with percent male as the independent variable and auto thefts as the dependent variable with

$$\text{Auto thefts} = B_0 + B_1\,(\textit{Perc. Male}) + \textit{error}$$

as the regression equation, we would obtain the results in Table 9.9. Dependent Variable: motor vehicle thefts per 1,000 people

In the table, you see many pieces of information. First is the two types of coefficients. The unstandardized estimates (B) are based on the raw data and can be used to compare with other studies that have collected the same data using the same instruments. It indicates a prediction of how much the dependent variable Y (car thefts) would change based on a 1-unit increase in X (percent of males). The raw data scale range for thefts is 0 to 14.

Standardized coefficients (Beta) allow you to examine which independent variables appear to be the most important within the study. In this case, we only

TABLE 9.9
Regression results

	Unstandardized Coefficients		Standardized Coefficients	*t*	Sig.
	B	Std. Error	Beta		Std. Error
Intercept	−9.711	7.499		−1.295	.231
Percent male	.370	.148	.663	2.504	.037

have one independent variable. Standardized estimates range between −1 and 1 and indicate the magnitude of the slope. Notice that in a bivariate regression the standardized estimate is the same value as the correlation between independent variable (percent males) and the dependent variable (number of car thefts per 1,000 people). Once you begin adding more independent variables, the correlation values between the independent and dependent variables will be different from standardized coefficients.

If you divide the unstandardized coefficient by the standard error value (e.g., .370/148), you will obtain the t(t value). Notice that for the percent male, the variable is 2.504. This result is statistically significantly different from zero at the .05 level because .037 is less than our risk level of alpha at .05. If we had chosen a more stringent risk level of .01, this result would not be statistically significant. You can also obtain an estimate of the amount of variability accounted for in the dependent variable by the independent variables commonly written as R^2. You may also see R^2, called the coefficient of determination or measure of association. In this example, the variance accounted for in auto thefts by the percent male variable is .44. Or, 44% of the variance in thefts is explained by the percentage of males living in the theft area. The value is one indication of study's result size, commonly termed effect size. For your research area, it is important, as a scholar, to understand the common study result sizes that have been observed in the literature. For many research areas, .44 would be considered quite good and others quite poor. Please note that in the scatterplot there is an outlier (top right corner). Take that point out of the analysis and see what happens.

Independent vs. Paired *t*-Tests

To examine whether two groups (distributions) of scores are statistically significantly different, researchers use *t*-tests. Essentially a *t*-test answers the question, "How far apart are the means of the distributions?" The *t*-test can be traced back to Student (1908) who was actually, W. Gossett, a worker at the Dublin Guinness Factory. It can also be seen in the work of Green and Swets (1966) on signal detection theory (see Chapter 4).

There are two types of *t*-tests: independent or dependent (paired). In **independent *t*-tests**, the scores are independent of each other. In social science research, this generally means that the scores are from two different groups of participants. For example, group A, which took a test after being in an experimental session, and group B, which took the same test and are serving as the control/nonexperimental group. The null hypothesis for the independent *t*-test can be written as

$$H_0\colon \overline{x}_1 = \overline{x}_2,$$

which indicates that the test will examine whether the means of the two groups are

statistically significantly different.

A **paired** or **dependent** *t*-test examines the difference between two observation periods for one group. For example, you provide students with an essay exercise and grade the essays for grammar. After a discussion and practice on grammar, you provide the same essay exercise and grade them again.

Within the *t*-test, there are several categories:

- One Group: Used when testing your sample mean against the known population mean.
- Two Groups/Independent/Same Sample Size: Used when testing the difference between two groups that are not related to each other.
- Two Groups/Independent/Different Sample Size: Used when testing the difference between two groups that are not related to each other, and each group has a different number of participants.
- One Group/Dependent: Used when you have only one sample but have collected the data twice (or maybe more) from them, such as a pretest-posttest for a training exercise.

Each calculated *t* value is compared to the *t*-distribution using a critical value based on the study's degrees of freedom, the *t*-distribution, and your risk (alpha) level. If the value you calculated is larger than the comparison from the *t*-distribution, your value is considered statistically significant and you would reject the null hypothesis that the means are the same.

Table 9.10 provides an example of an independent *t*-test using two groups of randomly assigned participants: normal physical rehabilitation (group 1) or normal physical rehabilitation plus playing the Wii (group 2). At the end of two months, participants were given a physical fine motor skill test. This would be a two independent groups *t*-test.

Group Statistics

	Wii Group	*N*	Mean	Std. Deviation
Fine Motor Skill Score	Wii	3	5.0000	1.00000
	No Wii	8.5000	1.29099	.64550

TABLE 9.10
Independent *t*-test example

Fine Motor Skills Score	Wii Group Status
4	1
8	2
6	1
9	2
10	2
5	1
7	2

For the score, 10 is a perfect score. Group 1 = no Wii; Group 2 = Wii

Because there were two independent groups, with different participants in each group, we conducted an independent *t*-test. The results in Table 9.11 indicate that if we assumed that the variability across the two groups is the same or different, there is a statistically significant difference between the average values of each group at the .05 level, the *p*-value is .012.

Another example of an independent *t*-test is the study released by Mathematica Policy Research Inc. on the effect of abstinence-only programs, which recently reported that no statistically significant difference was observed between participants in the program (group A) and participants not in the program (group B). Therefore, they did not reject the null hypothesis and the calculated *t* value was less than the critical *t* value needed to reach statistical significance.

Analysis of Variance (ANOVA) and Covariance (ANCOVA)

Analysis of variance (ANOVA) is the examination of variability in scores when you have more than two groups. Essentially, one is attempting to test whether there are differences in means between groups. With ANOVA, we usually discuss the between

TABLE 9.11
Independent samples test

		t-Test for Equality of Means						
		t	df	Sig. (two-tailed)	Mean Difference	Std. Error Difference	95% Confidence Interval of the Difference	
		Lower	Upper	Lower	Upper	Lower	Upper	Lower
Fine Motor Skills Score	Equal variances assumed	−3.873	5	.012	−3.50000	.90370	−5.82302	−1.17698
	Equal variances not assumed	−4.041	4.959	.010	3.50000	.86603	−5.73171	−1.26829

FIGURE 9.14
Pie chart example of between and within variance

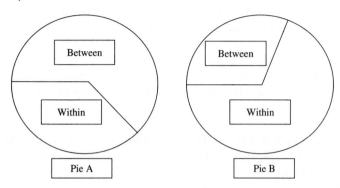

variance and the within variance. This type of research question, along with the analysis, can also be conducted using linear regression, because ANOVA is part of the general linear model (see McNeil, Newman, & Kelly, 1996).

The between variance is a mathematical description of how much of the variability in scores can be attributed to the difference in the groups. The within variance is the amount of variance within each group. If you have three groups that work with the Wii—groups A, B, and C—and want to know whether they are statistically significantly different in their motor skills at the end, you would complete an analysis of variance. The ANOVA would answer this question: ''Is there a statistically significant difference between the group means?'' It will *not* tell you which means are different from each other—that is a different analysis.

A way to visualize this is through a pie chart that contains all the scores, variability (Figure 9.14). In Pie A, most of the variability is between the groups and in Pie B it is within the groups. The separation of variance in Pie A is preferred because it demonstrates that most of the difference is between groups. That is, most of the variability in the outcome variable is explained by the group to which the participants were assigned.

If we added a group to the Wii study, such as half-time Wii, we would have three groups. The analysis for three groups is an ANOVA and the results are in Table 9.12. In the table, the F value at the end, like the t value, is compared to a critical F value to determine statistical significance.

TABLE 9.12
Variance source table for analysis of variance

Variation Source	Sum of Square	df	MS	F
Between (Groups)	1238.34	2	619.17	11.46
Within	5673.91	105	54.04	
Total	6911.25	107		

The observed F value of 11.46 would be compared to a critical F value based on the degree of freedom between, within, and our risk level (e.g., .05). In this case the critical F value is 3.09. Given that our observed F value is greater than the critical F value, we would argue that this result is statistically significant and would reject the null hypothesis that there is no difference between the groups. Though you will learn this in future statistics courses, F and t are related. F is the squared value of t. Though the test can indicate a difference between groups, it does not tell you which group has statistically significantly better fine motor skills. To answer that question, you must complete a post-hoc (multiple comparisons) test such as Scheffé's method (Kirk, 1995).

Analysis of covariance (ANCOVA) is ANOVA with one or more variables that the researchers are trying to control or to increase power. Extraneous variables could be prior knowledge as examined on a pretest or experience with a product. But ANCOVA is a statistical procedure used to equate groups on one or more variables so that they "start" at the same point. It is not a solution for a problematic design. Essentially, it adjusts the postexperiment score for initial differences in the preexperiment scores. The greatest irony of ANCOVA is that it is commonly used for intact group designs (quasi-experimental) when a major assumption within the technique is that the participants have been randomly assigned.

A major benefit of ANCOVA is that it can increase power by reducing within-groups (error) variance. This increase in power provides the researcher with the ability to correctly reject the null hypothesis, given that all the statistical assumptions of ANCOVA have been met. MANOVA and MANCOVA are multivariate versions of ANOVA and ANCOVA. **MANOVA/MANCOVA** are used when the researcher is examining more than one dependent variable and the dependent variables are correlated with each other.

Factorial ANOVA

Factorial ANOVA is an extension of ANOVA where more than one main effect (e.g., the difference among Wii groups) is examined along with interactions between the main effects (see Chapter 7). Suppose we have three different versions of a commercial we want to use on the Internet and are interested in the number of clicks each will receive. We are also interested in two different music types. This gives us a factorial model of 3 (ad types) by 2 (music types), for a total of six combinations. The most interesting component of factorial designs is the interaction. We are interested in the interactions between the music and the ad types; that is, "Do the number of clicks vary by the combination of ad and music types?"

There are three types of interactions: no interaction, ordinal, and disordinal. Below are the three examples based on the above study. Figure 9.15a has no interaction; they move at the same rates. The lines for M1 and M2 are parallel between groups A and B and between groups B and C. Figure 9.15b has an ordinal interaction where the two lines are no longer parallel, which indicates that the number of clicks is moderated by both the music and advertisement. Figure 9.15c is a disordinal interaction not only because the lines cross, but more importantly because the number of clicks is moderated by the combination of the music and the advertisement.

FIGURE 9.15
Three interaction types

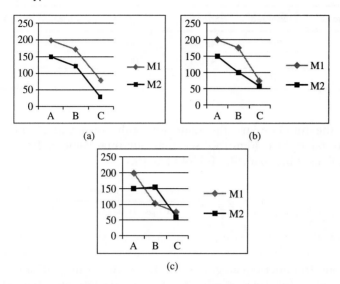

(a)   (b)

(c)

Parametric/Nonparametric Chart with Research Questions

Nonparametric analyses used with the data are nominal or ordinal or the data are very skewed. The group of tests is also described as "distribution-free" tests because the values or scores are independent of a population distribution such as F or t, where we assume the data follow a specific distribution. **Chi-square** is a good introduction to nonparametric analysis, because there are many examples students naturally understand. A basic way to think about chi-square is, "What did you expect to see and what did you actually see?" For example, does a liberal Supreme Court take more liberal or conservative cases? Shipan and Moffett (2004) conducted a study similar to this question with an initial research hypothesis of: The Supreme Court is more likely to hear a higher proportion of liberal cases as the median justice becomes more liberal. You can also reverse this hypothesis for a conservative court. If there were no difference, the null hypothesis, we would expect about the same proportion of liberal versus conservative cases.

In a basic chi-square analysis, we need to know or decide what we expect to see and then what we actually observed. The difference between those will be tested. In this case our expected proportion is .50 or an even number of cases. Now, how many decisions for cases did liberal Supreme Courts give? Using Shipan and Moffett's data from 1953 to 2000, there were 7,265 cases with 2,866 liberal and 4,399 conservative. Now we need to set up our chi-square table. Let us simplify the numbers a bit for the example and say there are 999 cases total, with 600 conservative and 399 liberal, which is close to the split (see Table 9.13).

In the table, you need to start by subtracting the expected value from the observed value, then squaring that number. Next, you must divide the squared number by the original expected value. In our case because we expected a

TABLE 9.13
Court decision by political ideology

Cases/Decisions	Observed	Expected	Obs-Exp	(Obs-Exp)^2	(Obs-Exp)^2/Exp
Liberal	399	499.5	−100.5	10100.3	20.220721
Conservative	600	499.5	100.5	10100.3	20.220721
Total	999				40.441441

50-50 split, the numbers are the same for both conservative and liberal decisions. In the far right column, we see that our total value is 40.44. That is our chi-square value. Mathematically, it looks like this:

$$X^2 = \sum \frac{(\text{Observed} - \text{Expected})^2}{\text{Expected}}$$

The value of 40.44 will be compared to a critical value of chi-square based on the degrees of freedom. In our case, since there are two categories, the degree of freedom is one (number of categories−1). If our risk value is .05 and we have one degree of freedom, our critical value is 3.841. Is 40.44 greater than 3.841? Yes, so we would reject the null hypothesis that there is an even distribution of liberal and conservative decisions. Shipan and Moffett concluded that "liberal Courts are more likely to hear conservative cases and conservative Courts are more likely to hear liberal cases" (p. 18).

Within nonparametric analyses you are still trying to answer research questions. For example, if you are interested in group differences:

1. Two Groups Independent Samples (Ordinal Data): Mann–Whitney U Test or Kolmogorov–Smirnov test
2. Two Groups Independent Samples (Nominal Data): Chi-square test
3. More than Two Groups Independent (Ordinal Data): Kruskal–Wallis one-way ANOVA
4. More than Two Groups Independent (Nominal Data): Chi-square test for *k* independent samples

If you are interested in repeated measures or change:

1. Two Dependent Samples (Ordinal Data): Wilcoxon matched-pairs signed ranks test
2. Two Dependent Samples (Nominal Data): McNemar test for the significance of change
3. More than Two Groups Dependent (Ordinal Data): Friedman two-way analysis of variance
4. More than Two Groups Dependent (Nominal Data): Cochran Q test

The crucial point to remember is that the data you actually collect will affect the choice of analysis you need to conduct in order to make a solid argument.

Advanced Analyses

The previous analyses are the traditional ones students learn in quantitative research courses. There are several analysis techniques that are considered more advanced, but over the past few years they are becoming more traditional with newer techniques being more advanced. The level of detail needed for the explanation of analyses in these techniques is beyond the scope of this text. At the end of the chapter is a list of Further Readings for Advanced Analyses. These are listed by topic, with some literature that can be used to familiarize yourself with the techniques for your specific analysis.

CASE STUDY

Ginette's main research questions in this area are: "Does scaling affect the inference made from the graph?" and "Does wording affect the inference made?" Given these two questions, what analysis do you think she will conduct? She is also interested in the question, "Does the type of wording used interact with scaling of the graph?" Knowing this, what analysis do you think she will conduct? She is pretty sure that scaling that highlights differences along with wording that emphasizes differences will have the most responses stating that there are significant differences. She has chosen a factorial design and will conduct an analysis of variance with two main effects and the one interaction based on her factorial design (Chapter 7).

   She will also conduct a chi-square analysis for males versus females on the frequency of mistakes overall and a more detailed one for categories of mistakes. Since she is interested in the frequency of mistakes based on typology, nonparametric analysis is appropriate for her here. She has access to a convenience sample of undergraduate students who will be randomly sampled and then randomly assigned. She knows that this is not completely a random sample of all undergraduates in the nation, but she feels better that she is allowed to randomly sample from the undergraduate student population before she randomly assigns. Her expected sample size is 150, and she has enough power given a moderate to small effect size for the analyses she wants to conduct.

ARMCHAIR MOMENT

We have included here a basic flow chart from research question to analysis (Figure 9.16). We have a more detailed one that is available online. When you are designing your research, you need to plan what the appropriate analysis will be based on all the other work you have conducted. We have seen, even from experienced colleagues, great studies with the wrong analysis. We have quietly told them later to change the analysis. We have noticed that most of these instances occur because their training in statistical analysis is limited to a few courses many years ago. It is a reminder to us that being a scholar all the way through the design, implementation, and analysis components is crucial. This chapter has provided an overview of analysis techniques, but you need to read in detail all of the nuances

FIGURE 9.16
Basic flow chart for core quantitative research question to analysis

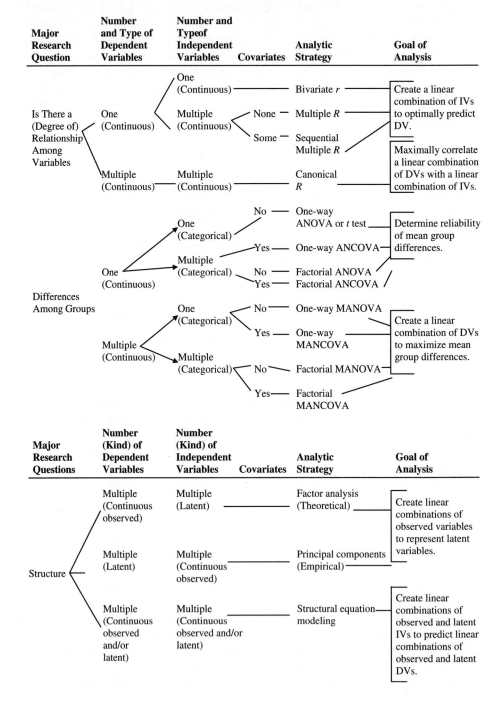

and assumptions that are associated with each technique. We recently have had students come to us with research questions that can only be answered using a path analytic analysis, but they are trying desperately to use a *t*-test. If the question you want to answer has a technique that will answer the question, that is the one to use even if you need to do a great deal of work to understand it. We must also note that many research organizations, even ours, state that you should use the simplest technique possible to answer the question. We agree, but too often we see people operationalize that statement by using the simplest technique that has nothing to do with the question, but matches the type of data they have. Therefore, take the time and do it right. You will be happier in the end.

Now it is time for you to practice with the flow chart in Figure 9.16. A fellow student comes to you and says:

> I am interested in understanding whether a program I have developed will make a difference—that is, improve achievement scores in mathematics—and I am also interested in the differences between boys and girls.

What would you tell the fellow student? After you answer, if your fellow student says, "I also have mathematics grades from the previous year." What would your answer be? The same? Different? Use the flow chart and see what you think. After the references, we provide our answer.

KEY WORDS

alternate hypotheses
analysis of covariance
   (ANCOVA)
analysis of variance
   (ANOVA)
bar chart
bivariate descriptive
   statistics
box plot
categorical data
chi-square
clinical significance
conditional probability
correlation
cross-tabulation
data
descriptive statistics
dispersion
economic significance
effect size

frequency polygon
histogram
independent *t*-test
interval scale
kurtosis
linear
MANOVA/MANCOVA
mean
measures of central
   tendency
median
mode
nominal scale
nonparametric tests
nonverbal data
null hypotheses
ordinal scale
paired/dependent *t*-test
parameter
parametric tests

practical significance
range
ratio scale
regression
sampling error
scatterplot
shared variance
skewness
standard deviation
statistic
statistical significance
stem-and-leaf plot
type I error
type II error
univariate descriptive
   statistics
variability
verbal data

FURTHER READINGS FOR ADVANCED ANALYSES

Multivariate Analysis

Tabachnick, B. G., & Fidell, L. S. (2001). *Using multivariate statistics* (4th ed.). Boston: Allyn & Bacon.

Factor Analysis

Thompson, B. (2004). *Exploratory and confirmatory factor analysis: Understanding concepts and applications.* Washington, DC: American Psychological Association.

Structural Equation Modeling

Byrne, B. M. (1994). *Structural equation modeling with EQS and EQS/Windows.* Thousand Oaks, CA: SAGE Publications.

Kline, R. B. (2005). *Principles and practice of structural equation modeling* (2nd ed.). New York: The Guilford Press.

Multilevel Modeling

Raudenbush, S. W., & Bryk, A. S. (2002) *Hierarchical linear models: Applications and data analysis methods* (2nd ed.). Newbury Park, CA: SAGE Publications.

REFERENCES AND FURTHER READINGS

Ableson, R. P. (1997). A retrospective of the Significance Test Ban of 1999 (If there were no significance tests they would be invented. In L. L. Harlow, S. A. Mulaik, & J. H. Steiger (Eds.), *What if there were no significance tests?* Mahwah, NJ: Lawrence Erlbaum Associates.

Berry, D. A., & Chastain, L (2004). Inferences about testosterone abuse among athletes. *Chance, 17*(2), 5–8.

Burns, R. B. (2000). *Introduction to research methods.* London: SAGE Publications.

Carney, T. F. (1990). *Collaborative inquiry methodology.* Windsor, Ontario: University of Windsor, Division of Instructional Development.

Carver, R. P. (1993). The case against statistical significance testing, revisited. *Journal of Experimental Education, 61,* 287–292.

Cohen, J. (1988). *Statistical power analysis for the behavioral sciences* (2nd ed.). Hillsdale, NJ: Erlbaum.

Cohen, J. (1992). A power primer. *Psychological Bulletin, 112,* 155–159.

Denzin, N. K. (2004). Reading film. In U. Flick, E. V. Kardorff, & I. Steinke (Eds.), *A companion to qualitative research* (pp. 237–242). London: SAGE Publications.

Frick, R. W. (1996). The appropriate use of null hypothesis testing. *Psychological Methods, 1,* 379–390.

Glass, G. V, & Hopkins, D. (1984). *Statistical methods in education and psychology.* New York: Prentice-Hall.

Gravetter, F. J., & Wallnau, J. B. (2007). *Statistics for the behavioral sciences* (7th ed.). Belmont, CA: Thompson Wadsworth.

Green, D. M., & Swets, J. A. (1966). *Signal detection theory and psychophysics.* New York: John Wiley & Sons.

Harper, D. (2004). Photography as social science data. In U. Flick, E. V. Kardorff, & I. Steinke (Eds.), *A companion to qualitative research* (pp. 231–236). London: SAGE Publications.

Heath, C., & Hindmarsh, J. (2002). Analysing interaction: Video, ethnography, and situation conduct. In T. May (Ed.), *Qualitative research in action* (pp. 99–120). London: SAGE Publications.

Henry, G. T. (1994) Graphing data: Techniques for display and analysis. *Applied Social Research Methods.* Thousand Oaks, CA: SAGE Publications.

Kazdin, A. E. (1999). The meanings and measurement of clinical significance. *Journal of Consulting and Clinical Psychology, 67,* 332–339.

Kirk, R. E. (1995). *Experimental design: Procedures for the behavioral sciences* (3rd ed.). Pacific Grove, CA: Brooks/Cole.

Kirk, R. E. (1996). Practical significance: A concept whose time has come. *Educational and Psychological Measurement, 56,* 746–759.

Leech, N. L., & Onwuegbuzie A. J. (2004). A proposed fourth measure of significance: The role of economic significance in educational research. *Evaluation and Research in Education, 18*(3), 179–198.

Levin, H. M., & McEwan, P. J. (2001). *Cost-effectiveness analysis: Methods and applications* (2nd ed.). Thousand Oaks, CA: SAGE Publications.

McNeil, K., Newman, I., & Kelly, F. J. (1996). *Testing research hypotheses with the general linear model.* Carbondale, IL: Southern Illinois University Press.

Meehl, P. (1954). *Clinical versus statistical prediction: A theoretical analysis and a review of the evidence.* Minneapolis: University of Minnesota Press.

Miles, M. B., & Huberman, A. M. (1994). *Qualitative data analysis* (2nd ed.). Thousand Oaks, CA: SAGE Publications.

Mulaik, S. A. (1987). A brief history of the philosophical foundations of exploratory factor analysis. *Multivariate Behavioral Research, 22,* 267–305.

Newman, I., & Newman, C. (1994). *Conceptual statistics for beginners* (2nd ed.). Lanham, MD: University Press of America.

Prior, L. (2003). *Using documents in social research.* London: SAGE Publications.

Schweinhart, L. J., Barnes, H. V., & Weikart, D. P. (1993). *Significant benefits: The High/Scope Perry Preschool study through age 27* (Monographs of the High/Scope Educational Research Foundation, 10). Ypsilanti: High/Scope Press.

Shaver, J. P. (1980, April). *Readdressing the role of statistical tests of significance.* Paper presented at the annual meeting of the American Educational Research Association, Boston, MA.

Shaver, J. P. (1993). What statistical significance testing is, and what it is not. *Journal of Experimental Education, 61*(4), 383–387.

Shipan, C. R., & Moffett, K. W. (2004). *Liberal justices, conservative cases? Explaining the ideological nature of the Supreme Court's agenda.* A paper presented at the Annual Meeting of the American Political Science Association, September 2–5, Chicago, IL.

Student (W. Gossett). (1908). The probable error of a mean. *Biometrika, 6*(1), 1–25.

Tukey, J. W. (1969). Analyzing data: Sanctification or detective work. *American Psychologist, 24*(2), 83–91.

Tukey, J. W. (1977). *Exploring data analysis.* Reading, MA: Addison Wesley.

Wright, D. B., & London, K. (2002). *First steps in statistics.* Thousand Oaks, CA: SAGE Publications.

WEB SITES

At Carnegie Mellon University DASL
http://lib.stat.cmu.edu/DASL/

Mathematica Inc. Abstinence Study
http://www.mathematica-mpr.com/publications/pdfs/impactabstinence.pdf.

Answer for practice question on flowchart Figure 9.16:

Fellow student scenario:

We initially think that the student would conduct an ANCOVA because the student wants to know whether achievement is different for the students in the program compared to something else, though this is not directly stated. Given that there will probably not be random selection and assignment, having a baseline, a covariate, is a good place to start. Therefore, we assume that there are experimental and control groups along with a pre-test. The experimental group gets the new program and the control group gets nothing, or just the traditional lecture. For those who have had more statistics courses, instead of the ANCOVA, one could conduct a one-within one-between analysis. A one-within one-between would more accurately answer the change question. Once the student announces the existence of last year's scores, that implies a covariate, with those scores as the covariate, the new achievement scores as the dependent variable, and the group membership (experimental or control) as the independent variable. If the student is really interested in the gender differences, then this is still a "difference between groups" question, with multiple categorical independent variables. Those criteria, push this toward a factorial ANCOVA. Or, a factorial ANOVA with a pre- and post- test treated as a repeated within measure. Finally, for those who have had a few statistics courses, you will probably recognize that this could be analyzed using a linear regression since all of these analysis techniques are part of the general linear model.

CHAPTER 10

Data Analysis: Non-Numeric Data

KEY IDEA

I am a pattern tester or a pattern searcher—the essence of analysis.

POINTS TO KNOW

Understand the general analysis patterns.

Understand the difference between coding, data reduction, and connecting codes.

Describe the concept of study validity in qualitative terms.

Understand descriptive, interpretive, and theoretical validities.

Explain the threats of researcher bias and reactivity.

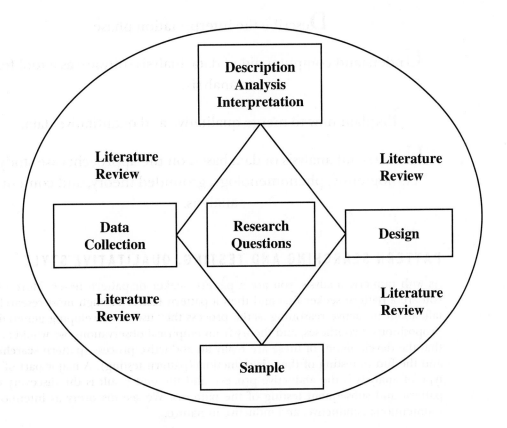

POINTS TO KNOW

Understand the methods used to handle these threats.

Understand generalization from a qualitative perspective.

Understand the description phase of analysis, including researcher focus and current capability.

Describe the data coding phase.

Understand the methods to code data.

Understand the concept categorization phase.

Describe the interpretation phase.

Understand computer-aided data analysis software as a tool for analysis.

Explain how to merge qualitative and quantitative data.

Understand analysis of data based on the approach: case study, ethnography, phenomenology, grounded theory, and content analysis.

PATTERN SEARCHING AND TESTING, QUALITATIVE STYLE

As with numeric analysis, you are a pattern seeker or pattern tester. More often you are a pattern seeker first and then a pattern tester. Though most researchers talk about inductive reasoning as the process they use for developing generalized propositions, hypotheses, and theory from empirical observations, we would argue that the development of these are really an abductive process (**pattern searching**) and the future testing of them is induction (pattern testing). A major part of this type of analysis is the abductive process, and the end result is the discovery of a pattern and subsequent testing of the patterns. We see discovery as intentional, unintentional, abductive, and inductive in nature.

In qualitative research, your data are often in the form of words—lots and lots of words—in formats such as transcripts of interviews, archival writings, observations in field notes—the documentation goes on and on. Qualitative research generates a considerable amount of different types of data. Your role is to make sense out of this plethora of information. Qualitative analysis requires researchers to look at words, phrases, and observed behaviors that will lead them to some sort of meaningful discovery or conclusion. Unlike quantitative analysis, there is, necessarily, a dearth of pure uniformity. In fact, qualitative analysis thrives in a more relative and less standardized atmosphere than quantitative analysis. It also tends to generate so much data as to become utterly overwhelming (Patton, 1980). This has, at times, meant that researchers become so beleaguered with the data that they lose their way, or lose their ability to report to others, or miss the forest for the trees. One significant criticism of qualitative work, which has been leveled at quantitative work: studies have been published that have been found to be poorly designed, analyzed, and discussed. Good qualitative analysis is highly organized, systematic, focused, and disciplined in order to clearly and honestly report one's own reflections.

The general cadence of qualitative analysis is different from quantitative analysis. First and foremost, the data is typically described chronologically so that anyone reading the information may be brought on board with the same picture. Next, the data are organized by importance. This may be by person or by event. Third, the settings where the data collection took place and/or the people interviewed or observed needs to be described. In many ways, these become case studies. Fourth, the processes need to be described. Finally, the coding, cross analysis, and interpretation may begin (Patton, 1980). In Table 10.1 we provide three general patterns by three different qualitative researchers or research partnerships.

Cresswell (1998) has a data analysis spiral (Figure 10.1) as a general model that can be used with a variety of non-numeric data analyses. The spiral is a good visual description because a common component of qualitative data analysis is the iterative nature of analysis, collection, and reasoning during the research process. The first stage is to organize the data in some format such as note cards, folders, or computer programs. You need to make it functional, organized, and accessible for you. If you have a team, you need it functional for everyone. The second phase is to constantly examine the data set as a whole so that you are familiar with what is in your data set. At this point, memos are created in order to develop some early categories. These can be written in the margins or on Post-it Notes, or using Stickies that are colored coded. We have seen and used many types. Memos can be pattern guesses (hunches) at this point and may provoke some questions to be answered along the way. Next, categories and themes are developed. Given the nature of the study and the data, some subcategories or subthemes may also be developed. At this point, the researcher will be developing patterns in the data, which is a coding phase. We all have personal analytic habits: line by line or section by section. Because of the size of some data sets, the researcher must decide how much and what is coded and what is not. There will be parts

TABLE 10.1
General patterns of analysis

Tactic	Miles and Huberman (1994)	Wolcott (1994)	Van den Hoonaard and Van den Hoonaard (2008)
Noting hunches	Margin notes in field journal	Focus on specific information in description	
Note taking	Reflective comments in notes		Initial insights
Summarizing notes from field/elsewhere	Summary sheet created based on field notes		Memoing
Scenario development	Metaphor creation		Ideas about what is going on from memo data
Data display	Comparisons and contrasts	Display findings in graphic form and compare cases against a standard	
Coding	Write out codes and memos		How much to code based on previous ideas
Data reduction	Pattern searching	Identify pattern regularities	
Quasi-stats	Frequency counts of codes, etc.		
Category connections	Develop relations among patterns and themes/ building a logic model		
Specific tactics for specific inquiry mode (e.g., ethnography)		Follow traditional fieldwork procedures	Colored pencils, not cards, computer software
Examine within current literature		Contextualize observations within current literature	
Next steps		Next study or redesign this study	

of the data that are not related to your problem area of interest. As the coding becomes saturated, propositions, scenarios, or hypotheses develop. The next step is to integrate the data, categorize it in a logical framework (e.g., graphic logic model, see Chapter 11), and summarize all of it for the reader.

STUDY VALIDITY IN QUALITATIVE ANALYSIS

Validity and reliability are just as important in qualitative research as they are in quantitative research. Confusion occurs when these terms are used, but have slightly different meanings in the different venues of qualitative and quantitative

FIGURE 10.1
Cresswell's analysis spiral

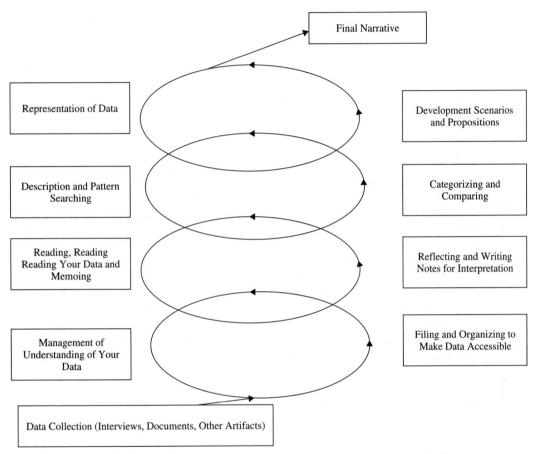

Source: Adapted from Cresswell (1998).

(Agar, 1986). Because qualitative researchers tend to use both sets of terminology, we will do our best to help organize these terms in ways that will allow you to understand and effectively evaluate your study and the studies you are reading.

Validity can also be understood as *authenticity:* Is the author and the author's work plausible, credible, and trustworthy? (See Chapter 5 also.) If so, we as the readers may be more comfortable with the authenticity of the work (Agar, 1986). Like quantitative researchers, qualitative researchers are concerned with threats to their study design that would undermine the readers' willingness to accept the work conducted and the conclusions proposed. Without validity, in quantitative research, we really can't make any inferences about the scores we receive. Without validity, in qualitative research, we really can't make any inferences about the data analysis to which we are exposed.

In quantitative design, we are provided a great deal of information about internal, external, and statistical validity. In qualitative-based studies, the focus is not the same, but validity is still an important concept when viewed from the perspective of believability and trustworthiness. Essentially, the readers and participants think you "got it right." We placed the discussion in the analysis section, because most of the validity discussion deals with the description, analysis, and interpretation of the data and not always with the design of the study. You can still think of it as rival hypotheses (Huck & Sandler, 1976) as we discussed in Chapter 7. Maxwell (1992) uses a category system to discuss validity-related issues and topics for traditional qualitative research.

Description Phase

The **description phase** consists of describing what you see, hear, read, and so on. The threat with your description occurs when you do not have complete information. For example, during an evaluation of a manager, dean, or other superior, the researcher uses focus groups to collect data but only takes notes during the interviews; therefore, not all of the data is captured and a missing data threat occurs. The same issue can occur when only people who are disgruntled show up to the interviews. Part of the data, from biased sampling, is missing. The researcher might have chosen to not record the interviews because he or she felt that people would not be open if it was recorded, but the problem still persists.

In the description phase of any qualitative study, readers have to be convinced that they can trust the filters (i.e., the researchers) through which they are receiving the description. This is harder than it sounds. Think about the times you and a friend have gone to see a movie. If you were to describe the movie afterward, it would not be surprising that both of you had focused on similar scenes. However, you both were also likely to remember different scenes and even attributed different meaning to the scenes. In many cases, you knew your friend's preference well and were not surprised that she remembered all the car chase scenes first, whereas she was not surprised that you were entranced by the planning scenes for, say, a robbery.

Interpretation

Interpretation threats occur when you map your own meaning onto the data and not the perspective of the interviewees and what they had meant by what they said. This occurs when you do not "bracket" your own thoughts off to the side or write your assumptions. We have also seen it happen when a leading question is asked because the interviewer is hoping to get a desired answer. Asking participants, or member checking, to review your interpretations is one way to handle this threat.

Theoretical

The greatest threat is the failure to search for and examine discrepant data. Some of the data will not fit the scenario you have developed, and you will need to investigate those discrepancies. In addition, you must put forth alternative explanations and determine whether those alternative explanations are better than the ones you have abductively reasoned to.

Specific Threats

Researcher bias is the selecting of data to support inferences or preconceptions and the subsequent selective data choices. Clearly, this is an issue because the researcher is the main instrument through which data is filtered. Note that bias is everywhere in research regardless of methodology, choice of items to test, decisions on which stimuli to present; all are based on beliefs and values that can bias the inferences made. The researcher comes fully equipped with various examined and unexamined biases (see Chapter 8). That researcher bias must be accounted for in all stages of the research. That being said, and knowing as we do that the richness of qualitative work eschews rigidity, qualitative researchers, over the years, have what might be considered generally accepted procedures to aid in addressing a study's validity.

To address researcher bias initially, the researcher may engage in different reflexivity exercises. Some, such as *bracketing* and *epochè* (Chapter 8), are specifically designed to help the researcher report what filters and biases she or he may be bringing to the design. Others, as previously described in Chapter 6, such as *reflexivity (memos), triangulation (data, investigator, method, theory, member checking), pattern matching, peer review, negative case sampling,* and *extended fieldwork,* are strategies designed to address researcher bias in the descriptions, interpretations, theory choice, as well as internal study validity.

Reactivity is the affect the researcher has on the situation, the setting, or the people involved. You might understand this as the "white lab coat syndrome" where your blood pressure goes up when you see the doctor. You cannot eliminate this problem, but you must determine it and use it to help you understand the phenomenon you are studying. Becker (1970) stated that in natural situations the researcher is not as influential as the situation. In interviews, though, the researcher is very influential because the response is always a function of what is asked and how it is asked. Therefore, understanding how you are influencing the responses is important.

Handling the Threats

To increase the credibility of descriptions and interpretations offered, many qualitative researchers rely on **triangulation.** The concept of triangulation is a familiar one for sailors who use two known data points to triangulate to a third point in order to navigate the oceans. In qualitative analysis, it refers to using multiple data sources, investigation, methods, and/or the literature to navigate the meaning of the data across settings and people. **Data triangulation** is the gathering of data from multiple viewpoints. For example, in exploring the meaning behind a congressional district's most recent election, a political scientist may interview some voters who participated in the event. To triangulate the data, the political scientist might decide to interview both registered males and females, and Democrats, Republicans, and other affiliations in the district. The researcher might collect data on local economic conditions, creating a variety of data to describe and interpret. Therefore, the researcher is triangulating the data by learning how the district's registered voters of either gender and political persuasion voted, to attribute meaning to the recent election. But, as Fielding and Fielding (1986) have noted, just collecting a variety of data from people and situations does not mean you have solved the threat. Any one of those pieces could be problematic and weaken your inferences. You must look for error and bias in all the data collected in order to harness the strength of triangulation. Think back to the counselor and the comedian study in Chapter 7. Consider how the researcher came up with the idea of the comedy study. How might the researcher triangulate the data sources to come up with the idea for a comedy study?

Investigator triangulation happens when there is more than one researcher collecting, analyzing, and interpreting the data. Presumably, multiple investigators offer more opportunity for checks and balances in researcher bias. Each investigator would also use self-reflective techniques to avoid the possibility of group think bias. If multiple researchers, with different acknowledged biases, observing the same behaviors, can come to similar conclusions, then readers like you are going to be much more likely to take the research and observations seriously! Let's say your consulting firm is contracted by a regional, rural university to help them determine the process the current generation of local college-bound teenagers go through to decide which university to apply to, with many it seems to be leaving the area. Your team might design a study where you videotape (after having cleared all of this work with an institutional review board, of course!) a group of high school juniors who have been brought together by one of your group facilitators to talk about their approach to the college application process. Your team consists of three research observers (you and two others); each researcher watches the videotape, describing the interactions observed, coding, and interpreting the meaning of the students' discussion. How does this help promote the authenticity of the study? What are some problems that you can see in using this technique with the above example?

Method triangulation means mixing and integrating numeric and non-numeric data and methods. You know enough about research methodology to be aware that, in reality, there just is no such thing as a perfect research method. If you know the strengths and limitations of several methods, then you can certainly pair two or more methods that complement one another. For example, in Chapter 7 we wrote about some of the strengths and weaknesses of the research designs used with the comedian Denis Leary. Well, suppose we want to know how people's experiences of sadness and happiness change while listening to Denis Leary. In addition to developing a grounded theory research design, we could strengthen this by surveying people with the BDI-Short Form before and after listening (or not listening—i.e., the control group) to Denis Leary's act. The pretest-posttest research design could help us measure change in the construct of depression as defined by the BDI-SF and allow us to control history and maturation threats. The grounded theory design would allow the process of emotional change to emerge from the words of the participants. This method of triangulation offers multiple ways to gather data and to understand. Completing an appropriate method triangulation can add to the authenticity (or validity) of your study. Now in addition to presenting the rich description of your observations and participants' responses, your descriptive phase would likely include demographic information, the mean scores, intercorrelations, and alphas on the pretests and posttests of the BDI-SF for both groups. Becker's (1970) argument for **quasi-statistics** works well here because the researcher uses descriptive statistics to bolster the description or inferences being made. For you, it is important during the design to think about these questions: What kind of research question(s) might lead to the inclusion of quasi-statistics? What limitations in the grounded theory section of the design are strengthened by the pretest-posttest quasi-experimental design in terms of the descriptive phase? What limitations in the quasi-experimental design are strengthened by the grounded theory design in the descriptive phase?

Member Checks.   Member checking is when you have the participants examine your descriptions and interpretations (Guba & Lincoln, 1989). It is the best way to rule out misinterpretation of respondents' statements. The goal is to determine that you have interpreted their comments properly. For example, Jim's son Jakob is in a narrative creation stage where the basic laws of physics are not important. Jim can ask Jakob, "So, if I understand what you said, the penguin did X, Y, and Z, interesting. Is that what you meant?" And Jakob replies, "Yes, Dad, that is what I said." Well, Jim has ruled out a misinterpretation about what he meant by what he said, but penguins can't fly themselves to space after morphing into a rocket ship.

Feedback.   Having a colleague, friend, or partner examine what you are saying for consistency or logic—feedback—is another way to handle these threats. Jim finds that during a study, having a colleague, a student, and his wife read what he has written and provide feedback is helpful. He gets three different frames of feedback. All three are important and improve the writing, but their ideas or comments rarely converge.

Rich or Thick Data.   Rich or thick data (Ryle, 1949; Geertz, 1973) allow the reader to get a full picture of the phenomenon, situation, or people. For interviews, this means a detailed account to make the readers feel as though they were there. A fine example of a rich description is Barker, Wright, and Barker's (1966) description of Raymond's day from waking up and getting dressed while hiding behind his mother, to going to bed that night.

Generalization

Generalization is not quite the same as external validity in quantitative, but it is analogous. Maxwell (1996) breaks generalization into two types: internal and external. **Internal generalization** refers to the interpretation within the study settings or people. It is the descriptive, interpretive, and theoretical inferences within the study. If you study an organization but only talk to the executives, you have greatly weakened your internal validity. In relation to quantitative design, internal generalization is analogous to statistical conclusion validity. In the big picture, **external generalization** is not the goal, and the interpretations do not typically generalize outside the study. That does not mean that they won't or that the descriptions and interpretations cannot be generalized, but it is not the goal. More importantly, in quantitative design, the goal is to generalize from the sample to the population. In qualitative research, the tradition is to generalize the theory or inferences and not the sample or to let the *reader* generalize from the study.

DATA ANALYSIS TECHNIQUES, PHASES, AND ISSUES

Description Phase

The description phase needs to be "thick" (Geertz, 1973)—rich in observable detail, participants' words, and researchers' reflections of their own experiences. This description stage is essential in qualitative analysis. It allows readers to enter into the event as much as possible and to generate their own interpretations. Remember, philosophically, qualitative inquiry supposes that there are many ways to construct meaning out of the same data (Lincoln & Guba, 1984). As such, the description phase needs to be as inclusive as needed, yet exclusive enough so that readers can develop their own understanding. It is also an area in which a careless, untrained, or unwitting researcher's bias, knowledge, and experience may inadvertently affect what data are described. In Chapter 8, we talked about *epochè* and bracketing. On the one hand, given the transparency of the researcher's work, description of self-perceptions, and orientation, the reader can account for biases in the descriptive phase. On the other hand, the researcher in naturalistic inquiry is not considered value-free. By the very nature of interacting and observing an event and/or participant, the researcher becomes inextricably bound into the data. No human being is fully self-aware and capable of clearly describing himself or herself so that others might clearly recognize all the filters through which meaning is being ascribed. As a result, the data description phase tends to be affected by the researcher in terms of focus and current capability.

Researcher Focus.   Sir John Lubbock is quoted as saying "What we see depends mainly on what we look for." Qualitative researchers know this and begin the description phase by returning to their research questions to regain focus. Researchers describe in great detail the data generated from their research questions. The amount of data is generally quite large and can lead to two potential problem spots for the researcher: one, including every detail, and two, selectively parsing data to support interpretation.

New qualitative researchers can be so afraid that they will inadvertently lose some data that will prove to be salient that they try to describe every bit of detail they can. However, they find that there is always more data to be described, that the job will end. To maintain focus, Patton (1980) recommends returning frequently to the research questions, to the notes one has kept while formulating the questions, and to the goals one has for the data.

In qualitative analysis, interpretation and data description are understood to be occurring simultaneously. However, to aid in organizing the data, many researchers attempt to note when they are describing data and when they are interpreting. It is not unusual for a researcher to follow a train of thought through the data (Strauss & Corbin, 1998). In this way, the unwary researcher can unwittingly parse data too much in an attempt to support later interpretation. As a result, researchers keep memos to themselves to help them recognize, as much as possible, their own evolutionary process within the data description and interpretation phases. This also helps researchers return to the data over time, with new insights, experiences, and viewpoints that may result in alternative interpretations. This leads us to the recognition that qualitative inquiry allows for human development over time.

Current Capabilities. "The eye sees only what the mind is prepared to comprehend" (Henri Louis Bergson). In one of her classes, Kim works to help counselors-in-training grasp the concept of "privilege" so that they may be better able to step into their clients' realities. Borrowing heavily from McIntosh's (1988) work on identifying 46 privileges that many White people in the United States are often unaware that they have, and that many Black people are aware they do not have, Kim offers her students statements representing privileges they each have based on skin color, gender, sexual orientation, religion, and ability. In each class, the female students become aware of the privileges they have that many men do not (e.g. sitting next to each other at a movie versus keeping a seat between them, and able to stay at home with their children without friends and family asking about their "real" occupation); White students become aware of the privileges they have that Black students do not (e.g. not having to teach their children how to handle intentional and unintentional racism on a daily basis, and rarely considering the color of the bandages they apply to a cut on their skin); and heterosexual students become aware that they have privileges they did not recognize that homosexual students may not have (e.g., they can hold their partners' hand in public without fear of provoking physical or verbal violence). The exercise is to help counselors-in-training see the world through another's perspective—to recognize that, whether or not they have chosen to embrace their privileges, they do have them in certain arenas, and they do not have them in others. Their capacity to step into their clients' circumstances is essential in the counseling process. Prior to truly grasping the concept of "privilege," students are often simply unable to comprehend some fundamental differences in the daily existence of others. A quote attributed to Henri Bergson summarizes this nicely: "After, their eyes can actually see what their minds can now comprehend." This is true for qualitative inquiry, too. As researchers develop, as their thinking and comprehension evolve, so does the manner in which they see their data. This means that conclusions based on interpretations from description in naturalistic inquiry are by their very nature fluid.

Data Coding Phase

After researchers describe the data, they move on to the next phase of analysis—**data coding**. What a researcher codes takes experience and, dare we say, intuition (Merriam, 1998). A researcher must code anything that is meaningful or even potentially meaningful. How do you tell? A well-coded data unit generally has two characteristics. First, it ought to pertain to the study question, specifically helping to uncover a kernel of information that actually kindles both the researcher's and the reader's understanding, interests, and musings about the study question. Second, it needs to be the smallest, most efficient and parsimonious bit of data that it can be (Lincoln & Guba, 1984). The unit of data coded could be one word, a paragraph, or two pages long. It has to stand on its own.

Coding Is a Process.   How and when a researcher codes his or her data can depend on the kind of qualitative research methodology employed. For example, in action research, the researcher is probably coding continuously, using the insights gathered from the patterns emerging from the data to inform the next data collection. Let's look at different techniques for coding.

Manual, Brute Force, or Reams of Paper, Highlighters, Note Cards, and Caffeine. The down and dirty way to code data is by hand. Kim has colleagues who swear that this is the most valuable way to get to know the data well (Stinchfield, personal communication, July 11, 2008). One of Kim's doctoral students, Ino Amarante, conducted a phenomenological study interviewing inmates in a supermax prison (Amarante, 2008). The interviews were taped and then transcribed. Once transcribed, Ino spent hours upon hours reading the transcripts, highlighting phrases in different colors, jotting notes in the margins, rereading transcripts, all to try to get a feel for the data. What were Ino's participants trying to tell her? How could she give a voice to the essence of their experiences? The highlighted phrases became her data coding. As she read and reread the transcripts and her jottings, she began to find patterns emerging from the data coded. While Ino used highlighters, Kim has used both highlighters and note cards with archival analysis pertaining to adult survivors of childhood sexual abuse, jotting notes onto 3 by 5 index cards and coding the cards with different colored highlighters. Some cards were coded only pink (characteristics), others were coded with two or three, even four colors: pink, green (empirical study), yellow (effects), and blue (conceptual). Either way, the actual experience of mucking around in the data can be invaluable. It isn't anything anyone else can do for you, is a daunting task, and can lead to exhaustion, boredom, and eventual error. Many qualitative researchers opt for getting some help.

Softwar – The Knight in Shining Armor?   There are several free and commercial **computer-assisted qualitative data analysis software (CAQDAS)** packages available. Some work better for some methodologies than others; but all have their advantages

TABLE 10.2

Common CAQDAS search functions

Simple searches	These find specific text strings either from the data document or from a coded data document. Many will highlight the results within the text so that you can see the information in context.
Placeholder searches	These searches give you the opportunity to use "placeholders" to widen the search.
Boolean searches	We talked about these in Chapter 2. Booleans searches let you combine your simple searches in a variety of ways using logical operators (AND, OR, NOT, XOR)
Proximity searches	Using the Boolean operators, proximity searches help you combine whole text strings and codes that are close to each other.

and disadvantages, and for some researchers they are a knight in shining armor. The more you know about each software program the better decisions you can make about choosing one technique or another addressed in this chapter.

All CAQDAS have search and coding functions, as well as the ability to organize the codes in some sort of visual or conceptual network. Search functions range from the fairly simple to the more complex. You're already familiar with many of these functions if you've been on the Internet, using a search engine for information about, say, Ethiopian restaurants in Kansas City, Missouri. Closer to home, you've already used search functions when you've gone to the library and accessed the computer to look for articles for this book. Table 10.2 provides a basic overview of search functions. Keep in mind that not all CAQDAS have all these functions.

Coding is, by far, the major function of CAQDAS. In addition, most of the commercial software programs, to remain competitive, are always being updated and improved. Coding functions include free coding, automatic coding, multimedia coding, and memos (annotations, personal notes).

Free coding is the simplest form of coding and entails a nonhierarchical, nonconceptually linked list of coded text. This sort of coding requires merely identifying those bits of text that the researcher believes represent a concept. Later, these codes may be considered for patterns and connections to form nodes that may branch hierarchically like a tree. Some CAQDAS offer nice graphics that present **nodal interconnections**, relationships between coded text, in a visual format.

Autocoding is coding generated by the CAQDAS. One way in which it occurs is by automatically coding any data coming in according to a previous set of codes. For example, our counselor has interviewed four people so far about their experiences of depression. As mentioned before, she may begin coding the data while she is still interviewing. She's transcribed the interviews and gone through them looking for text to code. One thing she notices is that the interviewees all discuss physical responses to depression. She codes those bits of text as "physical symptoms." Were she to do this by hand, she might highlight these in blue. However, using the CAQDAS, she merely codes those bit of text as she notes them. Autocoding, however, allows the CAQDAS to comb through any new data coming in, or any prior data, using the "physical" code as a type of filter. Think about how a spell check works. Every word in a text is considered against a filter containing the appropriate spelling of millions of words. Should the word not fit, it is highlighted and, often, suggested spellings are made. The writer now has to determine whether to keep the spelling as is, change it according to the suggestion, or change the word entirely. Autocoding is as helpful or harmful as spell checking. It would be easy for our counselor to hire someone to transcribe her interviews. If she just runs a spell check, then her transcript might very well read something like this:

> Depression is really tough, your really hurting. Its not allot of stuff people can see, but still . . . .its bad, and worse when your own parents get on you because your so out of it and the kids are being notty. . .

The same problem exists for autocoding. It is a terrific tool, but not a substitute for the amazing mind. Some CAQDAS actually offer coding suggestions based on earlier coding hierarchies. If our counselor links all the text she coded as "physical symptoms" with text she coded as "perceived pain," and "emotional symptoms" with "perceived pain," then the CAQDAS might suggest a new code connecting both the physical and emotional symptoms and call it "pain symptoms." She might agree and keep the new code, she might completely disagree and toss it, or she might modify the code. In this case, she might modify the code to "depressive symptoms."

While all this coding is going on, it is likely that the counselor from the example is starting to engage in some abductive reasoning. Before things crystallize in her mind, she continually records her thoughts in terms of her research on what can be called *memos*. Memos are used as a reflective tool. The researcher, while reading the data, jots a memo to herself about her current thoughts, reflections, concerns, wonderings, and meaning. These memos, when done by hand, might be written in the margins of the transcripts. When conducted using a CAQDAS, the memos can be anchored to a particular passage and/or compiled in a research process file (Weitzman & Miles, 1995).

What makes CAQDAS nice is that, as a tool, it offers researchers some advantages. These programs can provide a way to rapidly access and shuffle coded data to observe potential links. They can cut down on the tedium of going through hundreds (even thousands) of papers and files multiple times. Such tedium can lead to a decrease in researcher attention and to an increase in coding errors. As usual, tools have their down sides, too. First, not all qualitative methodologies lend themselves readily to CAQDAS. For example, let's say you are trying to build a playhouse and need to divide some planks in half. Because you are very competent and confident in your ability to use a hammer, you decide to use it on the boards. Using a hammer to whack through the 2 by 4 board is certainly possible, but it's ugly, and the resulting splitters and cracks may be so pronounced that the two pieces of wood can't be used. No matter how skillful you are using a hammer, it's not likely to give you the results a saw could give you when cutting a 2 by 4 board in half.

Like the hammer and saw, each CAQDAS is usually designed with a certain purpose in mind, and it can be helpful to know the original purpose of the software. Grounded theory, ethnographic research, qualitative content analyses, and phenomenological methodologies tend to fair well with CAQDAS. Conversation analyses can also be a good fit. These methodologies do tend to allow for a chunking of relative data into a type of standardized box or code that can be analyzed with quantitative data analysis techniques. Remember, though, too much parsing of the data could mean not seeing the forest for the trees. In other words, it's easy to focus so much on reducing the data that you find yourself losing the essence, the big picture, the richness of the study, for the minutiae. This means that you've strayed from your research design and need to regroup. Remember what the study purpose is. If your purpose is to examine mental health by counting healthy thinking versus unhealthy thinking in response to certain scenarios, so be it; this is a quantitative design—go back to Chapter 7. If your purpose is to examine mental health by describing how people experience a certain scenario, then you are looking at a qualitative design and need to get back on track. Much of what is called **discourse analysis** and **hermeneutics** is not really well suited to CAQDAS. By its very nature, discourse analysis focuses completely on a holistic explanation of the data under review. Hermeneutics is the ability to interpret data from the participant's point of view while being mindful of the historical and sociocultural factors that affect that person's worldview.

At one time, Kim visited a hospital founded in 1913 in Lambaréné, Gabon, Africa, by a doctor named Albert Schweitzer. Dr. Schweitzer wrote extensively about a number of topics beyond medicine, including the meaning of life, faith, music, peace, and civilization. His work in Gabon, which continues to this day, was lauded and admired to such an extent that he was awarded the Nobel Peace Prize in 1952. Twenty years later, though, Dr. Schweitzer's writings were considered racist, and his attitude toward his African patients, offensive (Dungan, 1975). Writings, thoughts, and actions that warranted high praise in one era, can be met with disdain in another time and place. The hermeneutic researcher would need to be able to study Schweitzer's works within their historical context. She would need to be able to step into his worldview, aware of the forces that helped to shape him, and interpret the data from his time. Hence, most hermeneutic researchers might find CAQDAS to be no more useful than a search engine.

Conceptual Categorization Phase

As the researcher codes data, becoming intimately familiar with the data, he or she begins to notice the coding clumping into concepts. Codes are routinely checked with each other and with all the categories to determine whether, as new data emerge, the fit is still a good one. What the researcher is hoping for is *saturation*, that is, there are enough codes to describe adequately the categories and subcategories. These categories and subcategories are compared continually with one another to determine the uniqueness of their concepts (Strauss & Corbin, 1994). Again, this is not a linear process, but an iterative one that continues throughout the study. One example of a category emerging from the data is Hylander's (2003) use of 150 codes clumped into 11 categories and five subcategories in her grounded theory study. She examined how change occurs in consultee-centered consultation used in Swedish schools between teachers and psychologists who work with students with behavioral difficulties. One of the categories she called **false turning** to describe what happened when teacher-consultees either no longer wanted to work with the psychologist-consultants or wanted to talk about something other than the students.

Researchers wonder how these concepts, once they become saturated, hang together. How do the concepts interconnect to represent the complexity of the phenomenon being studied? Again, keeping reflexive memos helps the researcher in monitoring bias. To triangulate the categories and subcategories here, the researcher might show just the codes to other people and ask them how they might organize them. Any discrepancies need to be discussed, noted, and clarified. Once agreement is reached, the researcher moves to the pattern searching phase.

Pattern Searching Phase

During the **pattern searching phase**, the researcher looks for ways that the concepts might interact. In an ethnographic or a phenomenological study, the patterns emerge to help describe the essence of the person's experiences. Although the concepts may be interrelated, we can't really talk about cause and effect because we just don't know *how* the concepts are interrelated, just that they may be. In a grounded theory study, we ask questions to help us understand cause and effect among concepts. We look for the patterns to emerge to help describe a process. For grounded theory, we are looking for a model or theory that will help describe the observed process. In action theory, we are looking for less hardened models that we can respond to immediately to inform our next actions, and then the process begins again. In any case, it is common to graphically represent the categories in what is called a **concept map** (see, for example, Novak & Cañas (2008)). Figure 10.2 is an example of a concept map of elements that influence readiness for change.

Throughout this phase, the researcher is trying to determine how all the data fit together. At the same time, she's still jotting notes to herself in the form of reflective memos, while bracketing her thoughts and emotions to help her winnow out bias. She also wants to triangulate the concepts and the concept maps. Again, she could have another person or two create concept maps from her earlier data. Remember, we want to tell a trustworthy story with the research.

Interpretation Phase

Reading the story is quite an art. We want to be able to interpret (the **interpretation phase**) the concept maps in ways that give voice to the people we studied. In ethnographic studies, we want to make sense of other people's worldviews and see the

FIGURE 10.2
Concept map example

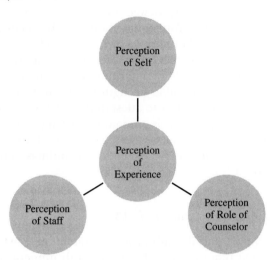

event(s) studied through the participants' eyes, minds, ways-of-being, and society. Our interpretation has to make sense to the participants. In phenomenological studies, we want our story to accurately convey the essence of the shared experiences the participants expressed. Again, our interpretation has to feel right to the participants. In a grounded theory study, we want to integrate all the patterns and concepts in the prior phases into a way to understand the process under observation.

A great way to find out whether your interpretations of what you observe and/or hear are, in fact, what you observed or heard, is to do a member check. Kim has served on dissertation committees and attended presentations where researchers have assumed that a member check is merely transcribing an oral interview and giving it back to the participant to say: "Yup, I said that" or "No, I didn't say that." This is not a member check. In one case, the researcher allowed the participants to change their words on the transcripts and did his analysis on the changed interviews! What kinds of threats does that create?

Formal member checks allow the participants to check your perceptions. Although you may do member checks at several points in the study, most participants are not as invested in the research as you are, and if your timing is off, it's not uncommon to get very little back from your member check. Remember, in ethnographic, phenomenological, grounded theory, and action research, you are often engaging in what could be called informal member checking through your iterative process. For example, let's say that in your phenomenological study, you interviewed several people about their experience listening to Denis Leary. During the interview, you might paraphrase what you heard the participant say. The participant then naturally corrects you, agrees with you, and/or adds to the paraphrase. This informal check is a part of the qualitative validity process.

Formal member checks are more specific. In the above example, you might write a two-page summary of what you heard each interviewee say. You would then run the summary back by the interviewee and ask the person in what ways the summary is or is not accurate. You would then use the feedback you received to clarify each summary. Another sort of member check can occur during the interpretation phase. You might contact the interviewees with your thematic results and ask them to comment how well the interpretations fit them. This triangulation from the members lends considerable strength to the study because it allows the people being studied the opportunity to attest to the accuracy of the findings.

In the interpretation phase, it is common to triangulate the interpretation to the research literature, as discussed earlier. The counselor studying the essence of the experience of depression would likely tie her findings to the mental health literature on depression.

Merging Numeric and Non-numeric Data

More and more studies, especially with program evaluation (see Chapter 11), have research questions that require the collection of both numeric and non-numeric data. Most of this is discussed within the mixed-methodology literature (Tashakkori & Teddlie, 2003). What is most important from an analysis perspective is the merging and synthesis of the multiple types of data. Onwuegbuzie and Teddlie (2003) provide a multistep process for integrating numeric and non-numeric data from your study after you have made a series of decisions. Below we focus only on the analysis process.

> Step 1: **Data Reduction**. During this step, the researcher reduces the numeric and non-numeric data. For numeric data, descriptive statistics are computed. The researcher may be exploring the data and conducting an exploratory factor analysis here. For the non-numeric data, memos, initial codes, and summaries would be in the reduction stage.
>
> Step 2: **Data Display**. Once reduced, the data need to be displayed into understandable formats such as tables, logical diagrams, networks, or lists. The displays should foreshadow the interpretations that the researcher will make later. Remember, a believable narrative is being built.
>
> Step 3: **Data Transformation**. At this stage, the researcher can qualitize or quantize data (Tashakkori & Teddlie, 1998). Once data are transformed, a variety of statistical or other techniques can be applied. For example, categories from text can be coded in binary fashion and an exploratory factor analysis can be completed. This really is not that different from taking strongly agree to strongly disagree endorsements and turning them into the 1 through 5 numeric system that is so common in survey data analysis.
>
> Step 4: **Data Correlation**. Data that have been transformed can be correlated if in numeric format and you should still have two sets of data for each individual. This can help aid in data triangulation (Greene, Caracelli, & Graham, 1989).

Step 5: **Data Consolidation**. The researcher may choose to combine the data and create new composite variables or data sets (Caracelli & Greene, 1993) instead of correlating the data. For example, the researcher may have perceptions of a product from users and employees. The researcher would average the users' and employees' responses into a summarized value for perception of the product.

Step 6: **Data Comparison**. The researcher may not want to or be able to correlate or consolidate the data and therefore chooses to compare the data. The researcher compares the two types of data. For example, the researcher could have comments about the climate of working with a manager from focus groups and responses from a Likert-type scaled survey. The researcher may compare the mean values on the workplace climate and comments concerning such climate from the focus groups in order to triangulate the data.

Step 7: **Data Integration**. In this step, the data are integrated into a coherent whole or possible two wholes (numeric and non-numeric). The researcher, though, is developing a coherent, complete narrative developed from the data where inferences can be made. At the integration point, the data may not create a coherent narrative and more data may need to be collected; the process can start all over again.

Finally, Onwuegbuzie and Teddlie (2003) argue for the researcher to focus on the purpose of the study, confirmatory or exploratory, and then the type of analysis. The type of analysis can be concurrent, where the types of data can be analyzed together simultaneously; sequential, where one type is analyzed first, followed by another; or parallel, where the data are analyzed next to each other at the same time. Finally, the researcher needs to decide which data type is dominant in the analysis, numeric or non-numeric (see Onwuegbuzie & Teddlie, 2003, Table 13.3).

WHICH SOFTWARE TO CHOOSE, IF YOU GO THAT ROUTE

There are too many software packages for us to discuss them all. We recommend that you obtain a copy of Lewins and Silver's (2006) book. It is important that you ask yourself some questions before you decide on a software package, if you have a choice. Here are a few from Lewins and Silver (2006) that you should answer:

- What type and how much data do you have, and how do you want to handle it?
- Do you like working on the computer?
- What is your theoretical approach to analysis and how well developed is it at the outset?
- Do you have a well-defined methodology?
- Do you want the software to help you manage *your* thinking and *thematic* coding?
- Are you more concerned with the *language*, the terminology used in the data, the comparison and occurrence of words and phrases across cases, or between different variables?

- Do you wish to consider tools that offer suggestions for coding, using *artificial intelligence* devices?
- Do you want both thematic and quantitative content information from the data?
- Do you want a multiplicity of tools (not quite so simple) which will enable many ways of handling and interrogating data?
- How much time do you have to "learn" the software?
- Will you use the software again?
- How much analysis time has been built into the project?
- Are you working individually on the project or as part of a team?
- If you are part of a team, does the team need to learn the software?
- Is this just one phase of a larger project—do you already have quantitative data?
- Is there a package—and peer support—already available at your institution or place of work?

Brief Review of a Few Software Packages

ATLAS.ti.   Atlas.ti is a flexible software program that lets you complete easily not only basic content analysis, but also more complicated mapping of quotes and other material (Lewins & Silver, 2006). We have worked with ATLAS.ti and have found it to be quite easy to use from the start, but we are also learning how the software can help with more in-depth analysis. We agree with Lewins and Silver (2006) that the external database system tends to make moving data around a bit cumbersome.

HyperRESEARCH.   We have only used HyperRESEARCH sparingly. We do like how easy it is to use for beginners, and some students have liked the easy startup learning curve. The main problem with the software is the inability to move project files from one computer to the next (Lewins & Silver, 2006).

MAXqda2 (MAXdictio & MAXmaps).   Because of the positive comments we have heard from colleagues about the ease of use, we suggest this program for researchers beginning their first study with qualitative data. There appears to be some difficulties with the autocoding function, but we do not traditionally autocode our data, so this is not that big of an issue for us. We hear that the coding process is fairly fast and flexible. This program also has a user-defined weighting system, where the relevance of a code can be assigned.

N6, NVivo2, NVivo7.   We are most familiar with QSR software because it was introduced to us first as graduate students and we have been using the different versions for over a decade. We have noticed, as we learn new software programs, that the coding process is not as flexible and reports can take time to arrive. We really like the new NVivo program because it can do so much, and we enjoy the ability to code our thoughts "next to" the data as we are analyzing data. Lewins and Silver (2006) note that beginners may need more support to use the NVivo2 software.

They also note that the merge tool is not integrated into the main software, so early planning is needed if you have to use this function.

QDA Miner.   QDA is unique because it was designed to mix numeric and non-numeric data from the outset of its design. Our experience with QDA is quite limited, because we can't afford to buy all the software; the demos are great but don't let you really dive in. Lewins and Silver (2006) state that the interactivity between the windows is quite good and that the code analyzer is excellent and quite a useful tool within the software.

Qualrus.   Qualrus, like QDA, is different than the rest of the CAQDAS packages. It really is a different generation of software because it helps the researcher analyze the data along the way through easy co-occurrence searchers and other computational strategies (e.g., artificial intelligence). We have not had the chance to completely use Qualrus as of this writing, but we do know from discussions with colleagues that you need to learn the scripting language that it uses, and the coding process is a bit involved. Our limited experience with the software has been positive, and we see the potential strength of the design. We are particularly keen on the hypothesis-testing tool (probably due to our Peircean backgrounds).

   As we stated previously, you should be a scholar, and in this case a scholar of the software package you want to use, as much as you were a scholar of the literature you read. Each software package has a history of development and original purpose for the development. Because of this history, some packages may be more useful to you than others. Many students and researchers are trapped by the packages supported by their school. We have found that in the long run it is better to research the programs and "save up" or write a grant where the appropriate program can be purchased.

A Basic ATLAS.ti Example

We are not promoting this software program over any other. This program is the one with which we have the most current experience due to the desire of some graduate students to use it. ATLAS.ti is a qualitative software program that enables researchers to analyze data from a traditional textual perspective while offering other features to extend its use as a knowledge management tool (Piecka, 2008). The ATLAS.ti acronym stands for "Archiv fuer Technik, Lebenswelt und Alltagssprache" or loosely translated "archive for technology, the life world and everyday language" (Scientific Software Development, 2004). The "ti" extension at the end of the name is pronounced "tee eye" and means "text interpretation" (Scientific Software Development, 2004). The software originated at the Technical University of Berlin as the Project ATLAS (1989–1992). Since its inception, the software has undergone multiple iterations to meet the changing demands of the 21st century Lebenswelt or life world (Uexküll, 1957) and is intended for interdisciplinary analysis.

The ATLAS.ti software supports both textual and conceptual processing levels. On the textual level, ATLAS.ti assists in many ways: coding of all types of data, organization of data volumes, search and retrieval capabilities, comparison of texts, and identification of themes. Many of these attributes also help the researcher on a conceptual level to represent and form links with his data. The conceptual resources in the ATLAS.ti software include visualization of the codes and their relationships in the network view of the software, the creation of concept maps, the comparison of codes and their relationships, and the reading into or probing of hidden meanings in the textual data.

To begin working with ATLAS.ti, all data is stored in a project or "hermeneutic" unit. Data is imported into the project and saved as a primary document. ATLAS.ti provides great flexibility in the type of files used for primary documents and includes formats such as text files (e.g., field notes, transcriptions, journal entries, or e-mails), picture formats, audio tracks, and even videos. Each primary document receives a unique number for the project. Once the primary documents are loaded and associated with the project, coding begins.

Coding with ATLAS.ti.   ATLAS.ti permits four different alternative methods for coding primary documents: open coding, *in vivo* coding, coding by list, and quick coding. While coding, the data appears on the left portion of the computer screen, and the linked coding names are listed on the right-hand side of the window. Thus, the researcher always views both the data and the codes simultaneously while coding. **Open coding** is used to create a new code name. Once the data to be coded is highlighted, an open coding window allows one to enter code names. Multiple names may be entered at the same time. For ***in vivo* coding**, the software inputs the actual name of the highlighted data as the *in vivo* code. Figure 10.3 displays the *in vivo* code "That's where I am from."

Another popular method of coding, especially after multiple codes have been entered, is the code by list feature. When coding by list, it is easy to view all of the code names previously entered in the code manager (Figure 10.4). After highlighting the intended data, the researcher can opt to use one or more of the previously created code names by dragging them from the code list onto the data that is already selected. Quick coding uses the currently selected code name and applies it to newly selected data. The **code editor** (Figure 10.4) keeps track of their coding definitions and descriptions. ATLAS.ti further facilitates axial coding through efficient means of locating and viewing multiple file types (e.g., video and text) for extended comparison and contrast of code names.

Data Display.   The ATLAS.ti **network editor** provides a slate for researchers to form and manipulate visual images of their data including quotations, codes, and pictures. In the **network view**, the researcher may create semantic networks, also known as concept maps (Jonassen, 2001), consisting of nodes representing codes and labeled links delineating relationships between the nodes that provide an "intuitive graphical presentation" (Muhr, 2004, p. 217). Multiple network views or graphical representations may be generated which selectively minimize

FIGURE 10.3

Four coding options highlighting *in vivo* coding

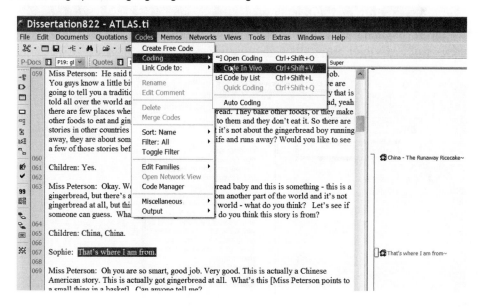

FIGURE 10.4

List of codes in the code manager and code editor with code description

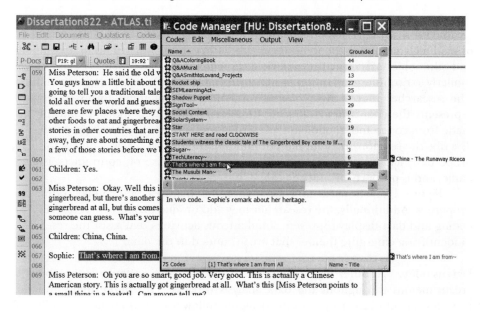

FIGURE 10.5
Concept maps made up of codes and quotations

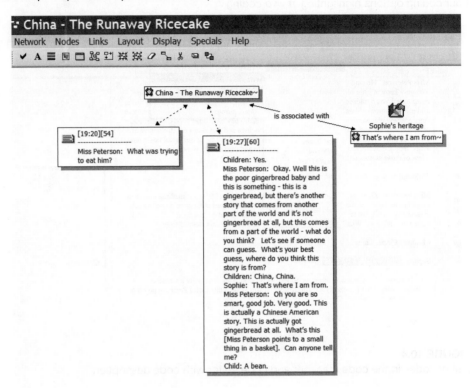

or explode the data to be scrutinized. After importing codes, memos, quotations, and other objects into the network view, these items may be physically manipulated similarly to dropping and dragging a picture or graphic file on a personal computer. The researcher moves these objects until their arrangement forms patterns or represents the data in a visual representation. Figure 10.5 shows a concept map made from codes and quotations. ATLAS.ti uses the term ''**network properties**'' to describe the relationship between the nodes in the network view. Choices for these properties include ''is associated with, is part of, is cause of, contradicts, is a, no name, and is property of'' (Muhr, 2004).

Figure 10.6 shows a concept map using pictures of planets, codes, and properties. Additionally, the researcher may add unique property names. ATLAS.ti coding and data display represent simultaneous activities that assist the researcher in identifying emerging themes that are grounded in the data.

Defensibility. Another useful function of the ATLAS.ti software is the ability to create memos throughout the data analysis process. This **defensibility** function provides an interface to jot down ideas for follow-up or to create an audit trail

FIGURE 10.6
Concept map using codes from text and photographs and relationships between codes

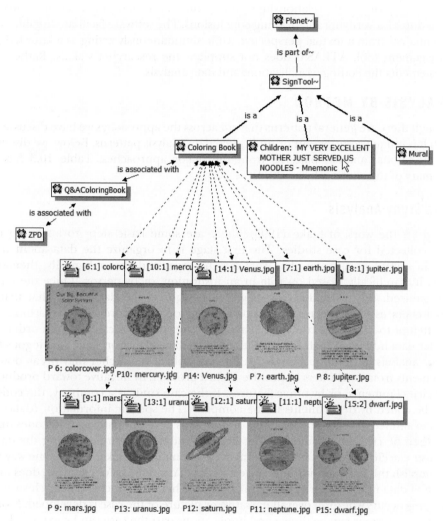

about coding decisions or other clarifications, and this provides a way to defend the researcher's inferences. Whether coding a sequence of text or watching movies, the software affords the opportunity to note items requiring further refinement or review. The software also possesses multiple methods of searching for and querying the data and includes many interfaces for importing and exporting the results. ATLAS.ti's resources to document and disclose decisions about data reduction, coding, and relationships add to the methodological rigor and analytical defensibility of qualitative data analysis using the software (Piecka, 2008).

Summary. ATLAS.ti is a multifaceted tool that aids researchers in several ways: staying close to their data, centralizing all data sources, coding data, refining codes, visualizing code relationships and themes, and following a set of rigorous procedures for verifying and drawing conclusions. The software facilitates qualitative data analysis from a textual perspective while simultaneously acting as a knowledge management tool. ATLAS.ti does not supplant the researcher's skills. Rather, it supplements the coding, visualization, and data analysis.

ANALYSIS BY METHOD

Though there are general patterns that cut across the approaches we have discussed, each has unique components or traditional data analysis patterns. Below, we discuss the traditional analysis patterns from the major approaches. Table 10.3 has a summary of the analyses by method.

Case Study Analysis

Based on the work of Stake (1995), there are some basic steps to analyzing of data collected for case studies. The first stage is to organize the data about the case in some logical order. The data may be organized chronologically, thematically, hierarchically, based on role in an institution, or by person. Once the data is organized, the researcher can begin to categorize the data. Note that many researchers use this process during data collection in a more iterative fashion in an attempt to triangulate the data. The researcher develops categories in order to cluster data into meaningful units. This is also a data reduction stage (analogous to factor analysis in numerical analysis). For example, a researcher may break down statements from consumers by positive toward product, by negative toward product, by price comments, or by other features. If the case study is a company, the codes may be coded by departments in the company. The specific information (data) is then examined in relation to the case overall. This develops patterns and codes that can then be critically examined. This is also a moment for triangulating the data to ensure accuracy and examine alternative explanations (Stake, 1995). One way to accomplish this is to use multiple sources of data (Yin, 1984). For example, does this piece of data fit the pattern or is it discrepant? When this process is near closure, a synthesis occurs where an overall narrative or picture of the case is developed. From there, conclusions can be drawn and implications past the case can be explored.

Ethnography Analysis

Based on the work of Wolcott (1994), there are some generic patterns to ethnographic analysis. It is important to remember that it is virtually impossible for a researcher to be objective in the analysis and interpretation stage. Wolcott argued that we must practice rigorous subjectivity, where we focus on balance, fairness, and completeness. Ethnographers use a variety of data organization patterns, such as time, a typical day, a critical event, or a story narrative. The data are categorized in order to develop patterns and regularities. From these patterns and regularities, the culture is inferred and described.

TABLE 10.3

Summary of analyses by design

Stage	Phenomenology	Grounded Theory	Ethnography	Case Study	Content Analysis
Data organization	Create useful files for the researcher	Create useful files for the researcher	Create useful files for the researcher	Create useful files for the researcher	Create useful files for the researcher
Reading/memos	Read through the text/margin notes/early codes	Read through the text/margin notes/early codes	Read through the text/margin notes/early codes	Read through the text/margin notes/early codes	Identify the specific body of information; define it precisely; read through the material and codes
Description	Describe meaning of the experience for the researcher		Describe the social setting, actors, events; draw picture of setting	Describe the case and its context	Describe the data in terms of frequency of each characteristic observed
Categorizing/ Scenario building	Identify those statements of meaning for individuals that relate to the topic; group these statements into units	Engage in axial coding, causal condition, context, etc.; engage in open coding, categories, etc.	Analyze data for themes and patterned regularities	Use categorical aggregation; establish patterns of categories	Identify patterns in the data and begin to build the scenario and narrative
Interpretation	Develop a textual description, "What happened"; develop a structural description of how the phenomenon was experienced; develop an overall description of the experience, the essence	Engage in selective coding and development of stories; develop a conditional matrix	Interpret and make sense of the findings	Use direct interpretation; develop naturalistic generalizations	Interpret the scenarios and narrative in context
Representing data and narrative	Present narration of the essence of the experience; use tables or figures of statements and meaning units	Present a visual model or theory; present propositions	Present narrative presentation with tables, figures, and sketches	Present narrative with tables and figures	Present observations in tables and narrative form that focuses on themes and trends observed

At this point, the researcher may or may not include and discuss other existing work, such as theories, for building the interpretation process.

Phenomenological Analysis

Cresswell (1998) states that once the interviews are transcribed, the researcher begins with the identification of statements that relate to the phenomenon of interest. This is where the subjectiveness of separating relevant and irrelevant data occurs. Once this stage is complete, the remaining information is separated into parts that contain a single, specific thought. As these thoughts are developed, the researcher begins the grouping of the thoughts into some meaningful categories. Next, instead of converging on a specific overall theme, which would be a more quantitative approach, the researcher looks for ways people diverge on the perspective of experiencing the phenomenon. Finally, the researcher creates an overall narrative to describe how people experience the phenomenon with a goal of a general description through the eyes of the participants.

Grounded Theory Analysis

As we stated in Chapter 8, there are two views of grounded theory. Below we discuss Strauss and Corbin (1998), though we agree with Charmaz (2000) that this approach can be too structured. As with all qualitative techniques, we recommend that you be a scholar and read a variety of sources about grounded theory analysis.

The first stage is open coding where the data are divided and examined for common components that can be possible categories. Once the categories are completed, the data is then reviewed for specific attributes (properties) that define each category. After the open coding is completed, *axial coding* occurs, which creates interconnections among categories and properties. The key is to determine more detail about each category. This is not a linear process as researchers move between the raw data and open and axial coding in order to refine the categories and their interconnections. Additional data can also be collected during this time. Once the categories and interrelationships are refined or saturated, the researcher begins to form a story narrative about the phenomenon being studied. This is similar to a scenario in Shank and Cunningham's (1996) abductive reasoning model. At the end of the story, a theory about the phenomenon is put forward which can take many forms, such as verbal, visual, or hypotheses. The key is that the theory is developed completely from collected data.

Content Analysis

The analysis of data for content analysis is presented in Chapter 8 as part of the discussion of content analysis as a design. Similar to certain techniques in quantitative analysis, content analysis rolls over that line between design and analysis.

As we have stated many times in this book, you must be a scholar all the way through your research study. When it comes to the analysis stage, you must continue that scholarly endeavor. We hear colleagues complain that non-numeric analysis can change drastically depending on who is completing the analysis. We know the same is true with numeric analysis. For example, in exploratory factor analysis, there is an infinite number of possible factor solutions because of the mathematics involved.

In regression, depending on which variables you include, called *model specification*, the results can change. In all analyses, you are building an argument that the reader must find believable. Therefore, you need to analyze your data in a way that the readers—and in many qualitative designs, your participants—believe that you have the narrative correct. Just take this piece of advice: Just about everything you observe will be observed to be incorrect at some level by the time you are done or after you have retired. Even Einstein might be wrong (Albert & Galchen, 2009).

CASE STUDY

Ginette initially thought she was conducting an historical study, using content analysis. As she began to sift through the videotapes, pictures, and other artifacts she collected, she realized that what she needed to conduct the study was a grounded theory approach to this idea of graphical and pictorial usage in the halls of Congress. At the initial stage of her analysis, her hunch was that correctness of the graph did not matter, but how persuasive it was. She had created a coding scheme to use before she began coding in CAQDAS. In many instances, this procedure works well and provides a solid study. In other instances, it creates tunnel vision that takes time to break so that one sees that the data does not fit. She noticed that many of her fellow students seemed to get stuck with the software; they can't break free of the codes they had created. This is where discrepant data analysis helps. Ginette began to notice in her side notes written in the memoing component of the software that her coding was not working. More and more, the correctness of the graph did not matter because some other point or ideological issue was the message. Sometimes the graphs were correct and at other times, they were not. Yet, in other situations the correctness of the information did matter, and her new hunch had to do with the feelings of the population and the nearness of a major election. Therefore, she had to go back and recode for those pieces of information in order to develop a richer theory of how accuracy of the graphs did or did not play a role.

ARMCHAIR MOMENT

With qualitative analysis we always hope that the narrative reported provides us with new insight or a unique perspective on a phenomenon we think we understand at least from our perspective. We try in our own work to find the nugget of experience or understanding that provides a perspective we are not expecting. This is partly to do with not letting our coding run away with us. Most of the work we do has a theoretical framework, which lends itself to the development of *a priori* coding. Like Ginette, it takes time to let the coding go. We have become better at this over the years and tend to run two analyses at once on our non-numeric data. We open "free" code in parallel with *a priori* concepts based on our own research and that of others. The disparities in codes are the most exciting to us because we have to spend time reconciling those discrepancies. The negotiation between us along with discussions with colleagues tends to lead to wonderful insights and pushes us intellectually. We also have enough experience with the note cards and color-coded ideas taped to our walls, and with software analysis generation. We see strengths and weaknesses in both. Our wall allows us to see everything at once, and the software lets us make and remove relationships easily to test scenarios. We do not have a recommendation of which you should choose. It is a personal choice. We just ask that you do a thorough job and work diligently to take what you have and illuminate the area of interest for your readers. We also ask that you be as transparent as possible in your collection and analysis procedures—well, as transparent as you can, given the page limitations you might have with the journal to which you submit your work for publication. That transparency will help your readers believe and trust what you have to say, and in that way your work can have a positive effect in the field of study.

KEY WORDS

autocoding	data triangulation	member checking
code editor	defensibility	method triangulation
concept map	description phase	network editor
computer-assisted qual-	discourse analysis	network properties
itative data analysis	external generalization	network view
software (CAQDAS)	false turning	nodal interconnection
data coding	feedback	open coding
data comparison	free coding	pattern searching
data consolidation	hermeneutics	pattern searching stage
data correlation	*in vivo* code	quasi-statistics
data display	internal generalization	reactivity
data integration	interpretation	researcher bias
data reduction	interpretation phase	rich or thick data
data transformation	investigator triangulation	triangulation

REFERENCES AND FURTHER READINGS

Agar, M. H. (1986). *Speaking of ethnography: Qualitative research methods* (vol. 2). Newbury Park, CA: SAGE Publications.

Albert, D. Z., & Galchen, R. (2009). Was Einstein wrong?: A quantum threat to special relativity. *Scientific American, 300,* 32–39.

Amarante, M. I. (2008). Rehabilitative counseling: A qualitative analyses of inmates in a super-maximum security correctional institution. *Dissertation Abstracts International Section A: Humanities and Social Sciences, 68*(10–A), 4210.

Barker, R. G., Wright, H. F., & Barker, L. S. (1966). *One boy's day: A specimen record of behavior.* New York: Archon Books.

Becker, H. S. (1970). *Sociological work: Method and substance.* New Brunswick, NJ: Transaction Books.

Caracelli, V. W., & Greene, J. C. (1993). Data analysis strategies for mixed-method evaluation designs. *Educational Evaluation and Policy Analysis, 15,* 195–207.

Charmaz, K. (2000). Grounded theory: Objectivist and constructivist methods. In N. K. Denzin & Y. S. Lincoln (Eds.), *Handbook of qualitative research* (2nd ed., pp. 509–536). Thousand Oaks, CA: SAGE Publications.

Cresswell, J. W. (1998). *Qualitative inquiry and research design: Choosing among five traditions.* Thousand Oaks, CA: SAGE Publications.

Dungan, D. L. (1975). Reconsidering Albert Schweitzer. *The Christian Century, 92,* 874–877.

Fielding, N., & Fielding, J. (1986). *Linking data.* Beverly Hill, CA: SAGE Publications.

Geertz, C. (1973). *Interpretation of cultures.* New York: Basic Books.

Greene, J. C., Caracelli, V. W., & Graham, W. F. (1989). Toward a conceptual framework for mixed-method evaluation designs. *Educational Evaluation and Policy Analysis, 11,* 255–274.

Guba, E. G., & Lincoln, Y. S. (1989). *Fourth generation evaluation.* Newbury Park, CA: SAGE Publications.

Huck, S. W., & Sandler, H. M. (1976). *Rival hypotheses: "Minute mysteries" for the critical thinker.* London: Harper & Row.

Hylander, I. (2003). Toward a grounded theory of the conceptual change process in consultee-centered consultation. *Journal of Educational & Psychological Consultation, 14*(3/4), 263–280.

Jonassen, D. H. (2001, September 26–28). *Computers as mindtools for engaging learners in critical thinking.* Paper presented at the 3° Simpósio Internacional de Informática Educativa, School of Education of the Polytechnic Institute of Viseu, Viseu, Portugal.

Lewins, A., & Silver, C. (2006). *Using software for qualitative data analysis: A step-by-step guide.* Thousand Oaks, CA: SAGE Publications.

Lincoln, Y. S., & Guba, E. G. (1984). *Naturalistic Inquiry.* Newbury Park: SAGE Publications.

Maxwell, J. A. (1992). Understanding and validity in qualitative research. *Harvard Educational Review, 62*(3), 279–300.

Maxwell, J. A. (1996). *Qualitative research design: An interactive approach.* Thousand Oaks, CA: SAGE Publications.

McIntosh, P. (1988). *White privilege and male privilege: A personal account of coming to see correspondences through work in women's studies.* Working paper no. 189. Wellesley College Center for Research on Women, Wellesley, MA.

Merriam, S. B. (1998). *Qualitative research and case study applications in education.* San Francisco, CA: Jossey-Bass Publishers.

Miles, M. B., & Huberman, A. M. (1994). *Qualitative data analysis* (2nd ed.). Thousand Oaks, CA: SAGE Publications.

Muhr, T. (2004). *User's manual for ATLAS.ti 5.0.* Berlin: Scientific Software Development.

Novak, J. D., & Cañas, A. J. (2008). The Theory Underlying Concept Maps and How to Construct and Use Them, Technical Report IHMC CmapTools 2006-01 Rev 01-2008, Florida Institute for Human and Machine Cognition, 2008. Retrieved from: http://cmap.ihmc.us/Publications/ResearchPapers/TheoryUnderlyingConceptMaps.pdf

Onwuegbuzie, A. J., & Teddlie, C. (2003). A framework for analyzing data in mixed methods research. In A. Tashakkori & C. Teddlie (Eds.), *Handbook of mixed methods in social and behavioral research* (pp. 351–384). Thousand Oaks, CA: SAGE Publications.

Patton, M. Q. (1980). *Qualitative evaluation and research methods* (2nd ed.). Newbury Park, CA: SAGE Publications.

Piecka, D. C. B. (2008). Show and tell: Learning with interactive videoconferencing in kindergarten. *Dissertation Abstracts International.*

Ryle, G. (1949). *The concept of mind.* London: Hutchinson.

Scientific Software Development. (2004). ATLAS.ti version 4.2 legacy site: Frequently asked questions (atlas.Ti4). Retrieved from http://www.atlasti.com/A4/faq.html

Shank, G., & Cunningham, D. J. (1996, April). *Modeling the six modes of Peircean abduction for educational purposes.* Paper presented at the annual meeting of the Midwest AI and Cognitive Science Conference, Bloomington, IN.

Stake, R. (1995). *The art of case research.* Thousand Oaks, CA: SAGE Publications.

Strauss, A., & Corbin, J. (1994). Grounded theory methodology: An overview. In N. K. Denzin & Y. S. Lincoln (Eds.), *Handbook of qualitative research* (pp. 1–18). London: SAGE Publications.

Strauss, A., & Corbin, J. (1998). *Basics of qualitative research: Techniques and procedures for developing grounded theory.* Thousand Oaks, CA: SAGE Publications.

Tashakkori, A., & Teddlie, C. (1998). *Mixed methodology: Combining qualitative and quantitative approaches* (Applied Social Sciences Research Methods, No. 46). Thousand Oaks, CA: SAGE Publications.

Tashakkori, A., & Teddlie, C. (2003). *Handbook of mixed methods in social and behavioral research.* Thousand Oaks, CA: Publications.

Uexküll, J. von. (1957). A stroll through the world of animals and men. In C. H. Schiller (Ed.), *Instinctive behaviour.* London: Methuen.

Uexküll, J. von. (1982). The theory of meaning. *Semiotica, 42,* 25–82.

van den Hoonaard, D. K., & van den Hoonaard, W. C. (2008). Data analysis. In L. M. Given (Ed.), *The Sage encyclopedia of qualitative research methods.* Thousand Oaks, CA: SAGE Publications.

Weitzman, E. A., & Miles, M. B. (1995). Choosing software for qualitative data analysis: An overview. *Cultural Anthropology Methods, 7*(1), 1–5.

Wolcott, H. F. (1994). *Transforming qualitative data: Description, analysis, and interpretation.* Thousand Oaks, CA: SAGE Publications.

Yin, R. (1994). *Case study research: Design and methods* (2nd ed.). Beverly Hills, CA: SAGE Publications.

WEB SITES

ATLAS.ti
http://www.atlasti.de

HyperRESEARCH
http://www.researchware.com

MAXqda2 (MAXdictio & MAXmaps)
www.maxqda.de

N6, NVivo2, NVivo7
http://www.qsrinternational.com/

QDA Miner
http://www.provalisresearch.com/

Qualrus
http://www.qualrus.com

Program Evaluation

KEY IDEA

How does it work? Does it work? Do people think it works the same way? Is it worth anything?

POINTS TO KNOW

Describe what evaluation is and what it is not.

Identify the agreed-upon standards for program evaluation.

Describe the key components of each approach.

Describe the questions posed with each approach.

Describe the methods used with each approach.

Understand the strengths and weakness of each approach.

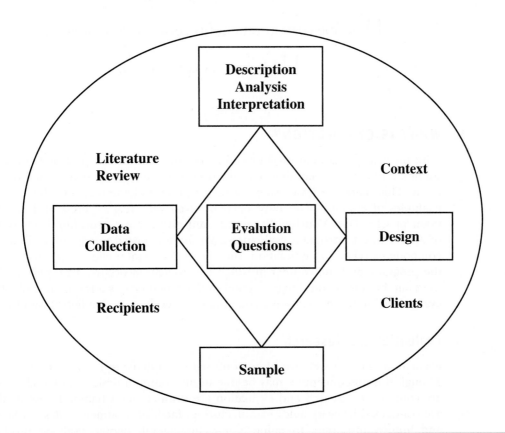

POINTS TO KNOW

Describe summative versus formative evaluation.

Describe need for contract detailing the evaluation.

Understand what an evaluand is.

Describe the development of criteria.

Explain logic models.

Describe claims and evidence.

Describe information needed for reporting evaluation observations.

Describe costs and benefits concepts to evaluation.

Understand exportability.

WHAT IS EVALUATION?

With many students interested in evaluation and the current push for evaluation studies, a basic understanding of evaluation is required for research methods students. This chapter will describe several program evaluation approaches, provide examples of evaluation we have been involved with (e.g., Cleveland Tutor Program or Cleveland Voucher Program), and give a basic procedural description of approaches to program evaluations. We have adjusted our graphics to add in components related to evaluation, such as the evaluation client, the recipients of the program, and the context in which the evaluation occurs. The graphics look the same because good design is good design whether it is a research study or an evaluation, but there are unique components to evaluation that must be addressed.

Evaluation and Research

Evaluation and research are often confused by students to be one and the same. Though this misconception may be due to the common designs and analyses that are conducted, research and evaluation are distinct (see Chapter 1). Evaluations are conducted in every field: manufacturing, medical treatment, sales marketing, and human resources, to name a few. In general, people evaluate products, processes, other people, ideas, and so on, in order to make a quality judgment or to make a decision on what to buy or implement as policy.

Many domains of knowledge, **evaluation** being one of them, have a variety of definitions and purposes based on who is writing the definition and the epistemological (ism) tradition in which they were trained. Even our key idea is laden with "ism" tradition. We personally like Scriven's (1991) definition that professional evaluation is defined as the systematic determination of the quality or value of something. Stufflebeam (2001) writes that program evaluation is "a study designed and conducted to assist some audience to assess an object's merit and worth" (p. 11). Both of these evaluation definitions have a final conclusion of merit or worth, though as you study the various approaches, you will see that not all do. Scriven specifically states and Stufflebeam implies that the evaluations are systematically conducted. A well-designed evaluation study will be systematic and will allow the reader, other evaluators, and interested parties to understand the who, what, where, why, and how of the evaluation.

Standards for Evaluation

The *Program Evaluation Standards* (3rd ed.) (Joint Committee on Standards for Educational Evaluation, in press) are presented in Table 11.1. There are 30 standards that are embedded within five content areas: Utility, Feasibility, Propriety, Accuracy, and Evaluation Accountability. Each of the five components is operationalized through the indicators. For example, in the Utility components, **Explicit Values** is the evaluator's description of the perspectives, procedures, and rationale that he or she used to interpret the observations, which allows the reader to understand why certain decisions or conclusions were made. The need for standards in evaluation is obvious from the perspectives of technical quality (how well the evaluation was carried out); sensitivity to the people, group, or institution being evaluated (morality); and the potential for corruption in the process (ethics). Finally, with standards being set, the field and those in the field can be seen to be more professional, where their work can be judged independently and compared to the standards by those outside of the evaluation field.

MODELS/APPROACHES TO EVALUATION

It is not possible in this chapter to cover in depth all the approaches to evaluation. Instead, we provide a description of several approaches that appear to be very good across many different indicators of quality (Stufflebeam, 2001). We provide an overview of the approach, the questions asked, the methods used, the strengths and weakness, a specific approach (if appropriate), and a checklist (if available). Web sites concerning the evaluation approaches are presented after the References and Further Readings section. The material presented is based on our experiences with, reading about, and Stufflebeam's (2001) summary work on these approaches.

TABLE 11.1
Summary of the 2009 evaluation standards

UTILITY

U1 Evaluator Credibility	*Evaluations should be conducted by qualified people who establish and maintain credibility in the evaluation context.*
U2 Attention to Stakeholders	*Evaluations should devote attention to the full range of individuals and groups invested in the program and affected by its evaluation.*
U3 Negotiated Purposes	*Evaluation purposes should be identified and continually negotiated based on the needs of stakeholders.*
U4 Explicit Values	*Evaluations should clarify and specify the individual and cultural values underpinning purposes, processes, and judgments.*
U5 Relevant Information	*Evaluation information should serve the identified and emergent needs of stakeholders.*
U6 Meaningful Processes and Products	*Evaluations should construct activities, descriptions, and judgments in ways that encourage participants to rediscover, reinterpret or revise their understandings and behaviors.*
U7 Timely and Appropriate Communicating and Reporting	*Evaluations should attend to the continuing information needs of their multiple audiences.*
U8 Concern for Consequences and Influence	*Evaluations should promote responsible and adaptive use while guarding against unintended negative consequences and misuse.*

FEASIBILTY

F1 Project Management	*Evaluations should use effective project management strategies.*
F2 Practical Procedures	*Evaluation procedures should be practical and responsive to the way the program operates.*
F3 Contextual Viability	*Evaluations should recognize, monitor, and balance the cultural and political interests and needs of individuals and groups.*
F4 Resource Use	*Evaluations should use resources effectively and efficiently.*

PROPRIETY

P1 Responsive and Inclusive Orientation	*Evaluations should be responsive to stakeholders and their communities.*
P2 Formal Agreements	*Evaluation agreements should be negotiated to make obligations explicit and take into account the needs, expectations, and cultural contexts of clients and other stakeholders.*
P3 Human Rights and Respect	*Evaluations should be designed and conducted to protect human and legal rights and maintain the dignity of participants and other stakeholders.*
P4 Clarity and Fairness	*Evaluations should be understandable and fair in addressing stakeholder needs and purposes.*

(continued)

TABLE 11.1

Summary of the 2009 evaluation standards (*Continued*)

P5 Transparency and Disclosure	*Evaluations should provide complete descriptions of findings, limitations, and conclusions to all stakeholders, unless doing so would violate legal and propriety obligations.*
P6 Conflicts of Interests	*Evaluations should openly and honestly identify and address real or perceived conflicts of interests that may compromise the evaluation.*
P7 Fiscal Responsibility	*Evaluations should account for all expended resources and comply with sound fiscal procedures and processes.*

ACCURACY

A1 Justified Conclusions and Decisions	*Evaluation conclusions and decisions should be explicitly justified in the cultures and contexts where they have consequences.*
A2 Valid Information	*Evaluation information should serve the intended purposes and support valid interpretations.*
A3 Reliable Information	*Evaluation procedures should yield sufficiently dependable and consistent information for the intended uses.*
A4 Explicit Program and Context Descriptions	*Evaluations should document programs and their contexts with appropriate detail and scope for the evaluation purposes.*
A5 Information Management	*Evaluations should employ systematic information collection, review, verification, and storage methods.*
A6 Sound Designs and Analyses	*Evaluations should employ technically adequate designs and analyses that are appropriate for the evaluation purposes.*
A7 Explicit Evaluation Reasoning	*Evaluation reasoning leading from information and analyses to findings, interpretations, conclusions, and judgments should be clearly and completely documented.*
A8 Communication and Reporting	*Evaluation communications should have adequate scope and guard against misconceptions, biases, distortions, and errors.*

EVALUATION ACCOUNTABILITY

E1 Evaluation Documentation	*Evaluations should fully document their negotiated purposes and implemented designs, procedures, data, and outcomes.*
E2 Internal Metaevaluation	*Evaluators should use these and other applicable standards to examine the accountability of the evaluation design, procedures employed, information collected, and outcomes.*
E3 External Metaevaluation	*Program evaluation sponsors, clients, evaluators, and other stakeholders should encourage the conduct of external metaevaluations using these and other applicable standards.*

Source: Joint Committee on Standards for Educational Evaluation (in press).

Improvement/Accountability

There are three general approaches in the area of **improvement/accountability**: decision/accountability, consumer oriented, and accreditation/certification. The three approaches focus on improvement by assisting in program decisions, providing consumers with assessments of optional programs and services, or helping the consumer to determine the quality of competing institutions and programs. Overall, the goal is to make a judgment on the merit or worth of the product or program (Stufflebeam, 2001).

Decision/Accountability Approach. The purpose of a **decision/accountability approach** is to improve the programs and judge the merit of the program. The underlying philosophy is **objectivist**—an objective reality can be determined. A key defining attribute is the engagement with **stakeholders**, those affected by the evaluation, in determining questions to be answered. In the end, a final judgment is made concerning the quality of a program, implementation, or who is accountable for an outcome. This model is quite popular at all levels of education at this time, though value-added approaches (see below) dominate elementary and secondary education in the United States.

Questions. The traditional questions revolve around quality, merit, or effectiveness. For example, did students who were eligible for and took the educational vouchers score higher on the Stanford 9 achievement test than those who were eligible for the vouchers but did not take them? In essence, did the program work based on statistical analysis?

Methods. The methods typically used are surveys, needs assessments, case studies, advocate teams, observations, interviews, resident evaluators, and quasi-experimental and experimental designs. This is a wide variety of methods used with both non-numeric and numeric data possibilities. We have traditionally seen this approach used with numeric data along with inferential statistics. Jim's work on the Cleveland Tutor Program while at the Indiana Center for Evaluation (now known as the Center for Evaluation and Education Policy, CEEP) is one area where a merit decision was the goal within a quasi-experimental design using surveys and standardized achievement tests.

Strengths/Weaknesses. The decision/accountability approach utility is best seen in the evaluation of personnel, students, long-term projects or programs, manufacturing facilities, and products. Stufflebeam (2001) states that a major advantage of the approach is that it encourages program personnel to use evaluation continuously and systematically to plan and implement programs that meet beneficiaries' targeted needs. This approach, when properly implemented, can assist decision makers or teams at all levels in a program and has the added benefit of focusing on continuous improvement. The decision/accountability approach is applicable in cases where program staff and other stakeholders want and need both formative and summative evaluation. It can provide the evaluation framework for both internal and external evaluation.

There is a great need for a close collaboration between the evaluator and stakeholders. This collaboration can introduce the possibility for individuals to block certain components of the evaluation or introduce bias into the data, thus creating validity problems in the inferences made from the results. Clearly, this is at its highest potential when there is a politically charged environment. Evaluators who are providing information from a continuous improvement perspective are actually influencing the program's path and can become so closely tied to the success of the program that they lose their independent, detached perspective. Finally, many times this approach focuses too much on formative evaluation (improvement or progress along the way) and very little on summative evaluation (final overall decision).

Example of Decision/Accountability: CIPP.   The **CIPP (Context, Input, Process, and Product) model** is an accountability evaluation approach that has developed over several decades. Stufflebeam (2003) describes it as a "coherent set of conceptual, hypothetical, pragmatic, and ethical principles forming a general framework to guide the study and practice of evaluation" (p. 2). **Context evaluations** are used to assess needs or problems and help those who have to make decisions define the goals and priorities and help other users evaluate those goals, priorities, and outcomes. **Input evaluations** are used to evaluate alternative programs or plans and budgets from feasibility and cost-effectiveness perspectives. Input evaluations are quite important because they allow one to examine competing opportunities as to how to schedule worker hours or assign faculty to courses. **Process evaluations** are used when one needs to examine how a plan was implemented in order to later evaluate the performance and quality of the program. In education, we discuss the robustness of program implementation, which answers the core question: "Did the teachers use the material or present the material in the correct manner?" **Product evaluations** are used to identify and evaluate the outcomes. **Outcomes** are both short and long term and examine both intended and unintended consequences. This evaluation works well when you are helping those working on the product or program to keep the important outcomes in focus, and when later you need the larger user group to determine the success of the program or product in meeting needs. All four of these evaluations are occurring in a solid evaluation. Jim is currently working on a program where several school districts have been brought together under a set of specific overarching goals. The organization that is putting this program together is being evaluated along with the program. The problems have been identified to a certain extent but some work is still needed because many are focused on the symptoms and not the actual problem. Input is being examined by how competing ideas of ways to work in this large group is playing out over time. Process is the heart of this evaluation at this moment, because they have implemented their plan and are judging it along the way. The product evaluation has been more difficult for organizations to keep their finger on; at times they feel that they have the outcome they are really interested in, and at other times they do not.

CIPP also focuses on both formative and summative components. Formative evaluation assists in guiding the project and according to Stufflebeam (2001) asks these questions:

Context—What needs to be done?
Input—How should it be done?
Process—Is it being done?
Product—Is it succeeding?

As information is gathered concerning these questions, reports are filed and submitted to the stakeholders. In Jim's case, his first report is being written that covers these areas.

A final or summative report would provide all obtained information and will have answered the questions:

Context—Were important needs addressed?
Input—Was the effort guided by a defensible plan and budget?
Process—Was the design executed competently and modified as needed?
Product—Did the effort succeed?

Stufflebeam (2001) crosses the components of CIPP with formative and summative evaluation. For example, from a formative assessment perspective, the product is examined for improvement, modification, or termination of the effort; and from the summative assessment perspective, the product is examined in reference to positive and negative effects with a related merit judgment. Stufflebeam (2001) also states that the product evaluation over the long term can be divided into **impact**, **effectiveness**, **sustainability**, and **transportability**. For impact, you want to determine whether the people who were supposed to benefit from the program or product actually did. Did the gains for the beneficiaries last over time or did they end when the program ended? The program also needs to be assessed to determine whether it can be transported to other venues; that is, can it be implemented or adapted for effective use beyond the original site? Finally, the CIPP model is a values model. By values, we mean the range of beliefs that are held by an individual, a group, an organization, or society. The evaluator, in this approach, must determine with the client the values that will drive the evaluation. One example of a value is "No student will fail."

Consumer-Oriented Approach.   The **consumer-oriented approach** focuses on protecting the consumer from fraudulent or dangerous programs and products. Evaluation in this approach is the determination of the merit or worth of the product. You have most likely read a Consumer Reports analysis before you made a major purchase of a durable good (a product that lasts a long time such as a refrigerator). The focus is the combining and synthesizing of reliable (stable or good) information that the consumer can use to make a valid (correct) inference about the product. In essence, this approach is used to help with the "common good" for all. Evaluators do not just evaluate the final product but help people produce and deliver high-quality products that are useful to the consumer. Because the consumer-oriented approach is part of the decision/accountability family, it is an objectivist perspective that the reality can be determined and the best product or answer found. According to Stufflebeam (2001), this approach uses a wide variety of assessment topics, such as program description, background and context, client, consumers, resources, function, delivery system, values, standards, process, outcomes, costs, critical competitors, needs assessment, and practical significance.

Questions.   The central question associated with this approach is, "Which of several alternative programs or products is the best choice given the different costs, the needs of the consumer, the values of the society, and positive and negative outcomes?" Jim is in the middle of examining several alternatives for replacing his television. He does not really watch television, but has a Wii system, a digital video recorder, a digital cable system, and a desire to hook the computer up to the screen at times. Finally, the cabinet will only accommodate a 26-inch screen or smaller. Now is the point where he has to decide which is the best alternative given the dozens of brands out there with a wide variety of options; therefore, he needs an independent evaluator for the best choice given the parameters in which he must work.

Methods.   This approach utilizes design methods such as checklists, needs assessments, goal-free evaluation, experimental and quasi-experimental design, and cost analysis (Scriven, 1974). Typically, an external evaluator is used and who is highly competent, independent, thorough, and essentially a surrogate for the consumer of the product (Stufflebeam, 2001). Every approach needs a competent evaluator, but the consumer-oriented approach is unique because of its role as a surrogate for the consumer.

Strengths/Weaknesses.   A strength of this approach is the opportunity for rigorous independent assessment that is designed to protect consumers and help them find the best option for their needs at the lowest cost. A major weakness is that a summative evaluation occurs too early in the product or program development and the results, essentially, scare personnel or companies from further development or eliminates the inherent creativity associated with new programs and products. If the evaluation occurs too late, then there is difficulty in obtaining enough quality evidence to provide a credible evaluation of the product's merit.

Key Evaluation Checklist.   Michael Scriven's (1991) key evaluation checklist (KEC) can be used for a summative evaluation to determine the merit or worth of the product or program. The checklist can be found online with the Web address at the end of the chapter. We briefly describe the components of the checklist next. Scriven separates the checklist into four parts: Preliminaries, Foundations, Subevaluations, and Conclusions and Implications. The preliminaries include an executive summary with the rationale for the evaluation, methodology, and overall observations. Foundations covers the background of the study, any descriptions that are required for the reader, the consumers of the report, the people the report affect, along with resources and the values of the study. Subevaluations concern areas such as process of the evaluation and the outcomes. In addition, the generalizability of the evaluation is provided. Finally, in the discussion, a summary and most importantly an evaluation of the evaluation are provided.

Accreditation/Certification Approach.   The accreditation/certification approach is used for many organizations, such as hospitals, universities, or other social service programs that provide a function for society. The accreditation demonstrates to clients of the service that the personnel, the programs, and the institution have met basic requirements for the field. This approach does not compare one institution with another; the focus is a comparison of the institution against the criteria for accreditation/certification. Essentially, any field that could put the public at risk if services are not delivered by highly trained specialists should have an accreditation system. In education, there are multiple accrediting organizations based on the content area and level of the institution. Kim has been heavily involved with the Council for Accreditation of Counseling and Related Educational Programs (CACREP) for the counseling program she teaches, and Jim has been involved with the National Council for Accreditation of Teacher Education (NCATE), the National Board for Professional Teaching Standards (NBPTS), and the Teacher Education Accreditation Council (TEAC). One requirement for CACREP is that the program faculty members have earned doctoral degrees in counselor education or doctoral degrees in a closely related field. For TEAC, faculty members in the program must be qualified to teach the courses in the program by having an advanced degree in the content area, scholarship and contributions to the field, and professional experience.

Questions.   Three generic questions used in this approach are:

1. Should the institution and/or the personnel in this institution be allowed to deliver this service?
2. How can the institution and the personnel improve their performance?
3. Where are the strengths and weaknesses?

More specific questions are derived based on the institution, the programs offered, and the specific accrediting body.

Methods.   The core method used is a **self-study** by the organization. A self-study is a process and a final document produced by the institution under review where the institution examines itself according to the standards, criteria, and evidence needed for accreditation. In general, during the accreditation process, a group of experts from the field are assigned by the accrediting organization to review the document and evidence provided, along with a visit to the institution to verify the self-report that the institution submitted. The committee also has the added responsibility of gathering additional information it feels is necessary. The committee commonly holds meetings with stakeholders (focus groups and individual interviews) in private to obtain personal perspectives of the organization, the process, and the evidence in the document. The committee members will also examine previous and current internal institution documents, which is a historical approach.

Strengths/Weaknesses.   The greatest strength of an accreditation study is that it provides the client or consumer with a "seal of approval" that the organization and the people are qualified to deliver the service, thus reducing the amount of time the client must spend researching the organization. One weakness is that accrediting bodies tend to focus on the inputs and processes of the organization and not the final outcomes, though this is changing. Second, there is also the potential for corruption in the process; therefore, an independent evaluator (not associated with the institution or the accrediting body) could be employed to oversee the evaluation that the accrediting body completed.

Social Agenda/Advocacy

The overarching goal of **social agenda** approaches is to improve society through evaluation. The focus of these approaches is to give power to those who are disenfranchised or marginalized. The disenfranchised have a strong role to play in the evaluation because of the underlying current of democracy, fairness, and equity within the approaches. The downside is the potential to focus so heavily on the social mission that the need for a solid evaluation is lost. Finally, this family of approaches can be categorized as postmodern and, more specifically, a multiple reality view of knowledge and understanding.

Utilization-Focused Evaluation.   Utilization-focused evaluation (U-FE) is based on the idea that evaluation should be judged on the utility of the results (Patton, 1997, 2000, 2002). The utility is based on functional aspects of the results: Can they be used? That is, how are people actually using the observations and experiencing the whole evaluation process? Because of this focus, the values of the evaluation are aligned with the end users, making the evaluation process highly personal and situated. In the end, the evaluator is helping those end users decide the evaluation that is needed. In essence, the evaluator hands authority over to the end users in order to increase the likelihood that the evaluation observations are implemented. Finally, there is no overall judgment of merit or worth at the end of the evaluation. That is, no final statement such as excellent, fair, or poor is made.

Questions.   The questions developed through the interactive process with the end users are as varied as the methods that can be used. If an experimental design is used, the questions will invariably revolve around an independent variable causing the outcome variable. If the focus is on cost-benefit analysis, the questions will focus on whether the money spent on the program resulted in the desired observations or effect. A process evaluation may ask questions dealing with how the program was implemented and how that implementation was experienced and completed by the participants.

Methods.   According to Patton (2002), U-FE does not subscribe to any one type of evaluation content, model, method, theory, or use. The goal of the method is to assist intended users in deciding the evaluation that would be appropriate in the given context. U-FEs can be formative, summative, or developmental; collect numeric and non-numeric data; use one or many designs (e.g., mixed, naturalistic, experimental); and focus on the process, outcomes, impacts, costs, benefits, and so on. As Patton (2002) wrote, "Utilization-focused evaluation is a process for making decisions about these issues in collaboration with an identified group of primary users focusing on their intended uses of evaluation" (p. 1). The checklist can be found online with the Web address at the end of the chapter. Patton's (2002) checklist contains 12 categories. The first six categories concern foundational components for an evaluation, such as the people who want the evaluation need to be invested in the evaluation, the evaluator is ready and has the capability to complete the evaluation, and the purpose and focus of the evaluation are identified. Categories 7 through 11 focus on the design, the data to be collected and how the data might be used, and analysis of the data. Different from most evaluations, the end users are involved in the interpretation process; therefore, the interpretations serve the end users' purposes. Because of this active engagement, the evaluator must balance the utility focus with concerns about validity. Finally, a metaevaluation is completed where the use of the evaluation by the stakeholders is examined.

Strengths/Weaknesses.   The strength of the U-FE is the increase in the probability that the intended users will implement the evaluation observations and recommendations if they have a sense of ownership of the evaluation process and findings. By actively involved, Patton (2002) means that the evaluator is training the intended users to actually implement the information and focusing on the intended utility of the evaluation at each step in the process. A major limitation is the fact that users leave the environment, teachers change schools, and employees switch companies, so the new members may desire that the program evaluation be examined and new goals and questions developed. Therefore, a great deal of work that was completed previously may need to be recreated in order to sustain or renew the prospects for evaluation impacts. This renegotiation can derail or greatly delay the process. Second, there is always the potential for the process to be corrupted by the users because they have a great deal of control over what will be examined, the questions that are asked, the methods used, and the data actually gathered. By corruption in these areas, we mean that the end users may limit the evaluation scope or work to ignore certain questions. Because of these limitations, an evaluator, who is an expert in multiple methodologies, both qualitative and qualitative in nature, and a skilled negotiator, is necessary. The evaluator must ethically balance the standards of professional evaluation and bring all stakeholders into an agreement of what should be completed and in what time frame during the evaluation process. An experienced, well-trained evaluator who is politically savvy would fit the bill here.

Client-Centered/Responsive Approach.   Based on Stake (1983), the responsive evaluation is so labeled because the evaluator must work with a diverse client group. Therefore, the **client-centered/responsive approach** is best used when there is a highly complex program being evaluated and there are multiple stakeholders with clearly different perspectives on what the program should accomplish. This is not the same as the consumer-oriented approach. In many education programs, there are multiple clients that are affected, such as the funding agency, the school board, district administration, school administration, teachers, staff, students, and parents. Each client group has needs or questions it desires to be answered by the evaluator's work. Therefore, the evaluator is in constant contact with the clients and other stakeholders (e.g., businesses that hire students from the school system). This approach is quite different from the previous approaches discussed because philosophically it rejects the concept of objective truth and does not come to a final merit decision. As Stufflebeam (2001) cogently summarized, "the evaluation may culminate in conflicting findings and conclusions, leaving the interpretation to the eyes of the beholder" (p. 63). Because of this, the client who requested the evaluation must be able to accept ambiguity and forgo anything that resembles a controlled experimental study in the field.

Questions.   The client-centered approach does not have a specific set of questions because the evaluator is continually searching for key questions the client is interested in. If there is a general focus, it is to understand the program in its current state, determine the satisfaction level of the people in the program, determine what the program has achieved, and understand how those involved in the program and experts view the program. As the evaluation progresses, more specific questions will develop from the interactions between the evaluator and stakeholders.

Methods.   The common methods for this approach are case study, purposive sampling, observation, and narrative reports with the goal of determining stable observations and interpretations. Within the method, a common tactic is to be redundant in the data collection phase, such as completing two cases studies in an attempt to replicate the original inferences. This approach will utilize any data or design that will provide information to get at the program's complexity even if in the end it makes the final "decision" about the program difficult to grasp.

Strengths/Weaknesses.   The greatest strength of this approach is in helping clients learn how to conduct their own evaluation and use the data gathered to improve their own decision-making processes. The use of multiple information sources or design methods allows the evaluator to triangulate inferences being made from the data collected, which allows the researcher to examine unintended outcomes. Finally, it gives interested stakeholders a voice in the evaluation process by incorporating their views and concerns.

Those external to the evaluation tend to see the approach as less "objective" or "rigorous" because people involved in the program or product being evaluated are involved in the process. Evaluators may also lose their outsider perspective because they are working so closely with the people. Finally, because there is no final decision made on the merit or quality of the program, problems can occur among the stakeholders on what decision should be made.

Deliberative Democratic Approach.   The focus of the deliberative democratic approach is the development of political practices and institutions that affect the power imbalances evident across citizens so that the citizens can experience free and equal participation. In addition, the conclusions reached after this process must be defensible; that is, they must provide reliable and valid claims (Stufflebeam, 2001). To achieve this, participants must experience and engage in genuine deliberation where the goal is the common good (House & Howe, 1998, 2000a, 2000b; Howe & Ashcroft, 2005). House and Howe (1999) describe three general principles for this approach: inclusion, dialogue, and deliberation.

Inclusion requires that all groups that are considered stakeholders—those with significant interests in the evaluation—be included in the evaluation (Howe & Ashcroft, 2005). Inclusion is not a one-size-fits-all prospect; some may be passively involved by simply filling out a basic survey, whereas others are heavily involved by participating in face-to-face discussions about the evaluation. Inclusion leads to dialogue because those who are included are given an opportunity to dialogue. **Dialogue** is categorized as elucidating and critical. **Elucidating dialogue** allows for the clarification of views and self-understanding of the participants, how they see and comprehend the situation (Howe & Ashcroft, 2005). There are limitations to clarifying the views and self-understandings of research participants. **Critical dialogue** includes elucidating dialogue and examining these views from a rational perspective. Critical dialogue includes not only clarifying the views and self-understandings of research participants, but also subjecting these views and self-understandings to rational scrutiny. This dialogue allows rationally based decisions to develop (Howe & Ashcroft, 2005). Dialogue then leads into deliberation. When participants enter into a dialogue about a program or policy, they can have misconceptions. An example of a misconception is the benefit or detriment the program can have on participants (Howe & Ashcroft, 2005). Clarifying these misconceptions is one part of the dialogue; the most important part is coming to an evaluative conclusion or conclusions that are based on evidence (Howe & Ashcroft, 2005). Overall, equity and changing power imbalances are the focus, where those who are powerful parties are not allowed to dominate the evaluation.

Questions.   The evaluators develop the questions that are answered after dialogues and deliberations with the stakeholders. Within the approach, a core question is developed which addresses judgments about the program's worth or value to the stakeholders.

Methods.   Evaluators typically use discussions with stakeholders, surveys, and debates to gather data. Clearly, the dialogue and deliberations are central to the evaluation from the design to the final write-up and presentation of the observations of the evaluation.

Strengths/Weaknesses.   The greatest strength of this approach is the focus on obtaining democratic participation of stakeholders at all stages of the evaluation. The incorporation of all interested parties with a focus on equity increases the likelihood that even those who are marginalized in traditional settings will see the evaluation observations useful and implement them. A second strength is that this approach allows the evaluator to have the right to refuse any inputs that are considered incorrect or unethical. This responsibility is not left to a vote from stakeholders who may or may not have conflicts of interest. This also allows for a final decision to be made. The major weakness with this approach is that it is often difficult to completely implement. As Howe and Ashcroft (2005) state in their evaluation of the school choice issue in Boulder, Colorado, the school board was not interested in their approach because it would not qualify as "objective" (p. 2,279). Even though this approach is difficult to implement, we agree with Stufflebeam (2001) that attempting to reach this ideal is something we should keep in mind.

Deliberative Democratic Evaluation Checklist.   The complete checklist can be found online with the Web address at the end of the chapter. In the checklist there are three major categories: inclusion, dialogue, and deliberation. Inclusion considers who is represented in the evaluation, the stakeholders who are included and those who are not. Dialogue considers the power structures of those involved with the evaluation and how the power differentials might distort the dialogue and interactions that occur. Finally, deliberation examines how the deliberation is organized, whether the deliberation is reflective and considered in-depth, and the cohesiveness of the data (does it all fit together?). Again, as with all checklists, it prompts the evaluator to be focused, but does not provide all the nuanced information one needs to conduct this approach in the field.

Constructivist Evaluation.   In constructivist evaluation, there appears to us an expectation that the evaluator will empower those who are disenfranchised. This is accomplished by having those involved consider how they can improve and transform their society and the world in general. There are some basic assumptions according to Guba and Lincoln (2001). Epistemologically, the approach is constructivist; more specifically, it is relativistic, where making sense of the world by humans is an organized experience that is comprehensible, understandable, and communicable. This community-based understanding is also independent of any reality that may or may not exist. Therefore, there is no "truth out there," but this does not mean that anything goes, either. We have agreed-upon understandings of how the world works. Included in this epistemology is **transactional subjectivism**, which means that reality depends on the current meaning that individuals bring to the table with an agreed-upon understanding that not all individuals will have the same level of understanding. Methodologically, the assumption is **hermeneutic-dialecticism**, which is a process of understanding the constructions of reality that stakeholders have and examining them for similarities and differences.

Questions.   The questions are not determined ahead of time but developed during the process of determining why this evaluation will occur, the planning stages, and the initial discussions with individuals about how the program will be evaluated. Essentially, the evaluator and the stakeholders identify questions. More questions will also emerge in the development phase of the evaluation plan. As the hermeneutic and dialectic process occurs, more questions will develop. Finally, the questions are never considered set or fixed, and, therefore, will evolve.

Methods. This constructivist methodology approach is unique because it diverges at first and then converges. During the hermeneutic process, the evaluator collects and describes alternative constructions related to the current evaluation question or issue. The key is that the participants approve the description. This assumes communication channels are continually open during this process. Next, the evaluator begins the dialectical process where the goal is to achieve as much agreement as possible among the different constructions. The participants review all of the constructions (understandings and inferences from the evaluator), and the evaluator has the participants study and contrast the current constructions with the goal of getting consensus. While this is occurring, the differences must be reasoned out. The process can continue indefinitely because there is always something else to learn; an ultimate answer is not philosophically attainable within this approach. Finally, the approach makes no comment on the use of a quantitative or qualitative approach because all constructions are discussed and compared.

Strengths/Weaknesses. The strength of the constructivist approach is the openness of the evaluation process and the observations. This approach, as with other approaches, directly involves a wide range of stakeholders who might be harmed or helped by the evaluation. In our view, we appreciate the fact that it helps everyone involved in understanding causal arguments and uses participants' understanding, values, and experiences as instruments in the evaluation process. Finally, we personally like the focus on triangulating observations from a variety of sources. The major problem with this approach is the difficulty in reporting observations because of the divergent and convergent stages. Those who make decisions want information at a specific time with a specific recommendation, and this approach does not necessarily fit within that time environment. Plus, stakeholders have to be responsibly involved, which is not always the case, and when there is stakeholder turnover, the situation degrades. There can be problems with openness of participants. One of our evaluations is currently experiencing this because participants in the evaluation are clearly not providing their private thoughts, and therefore getting a consensus on the issues is difficult. Others in this evaluation are not well informed on certain issues and are unwilling to compare and contrast their constructions of reality with other stakeholders. Finally, there are some who do not want competing constructions reported and believe that only one construction should be presented at the end.

Fourth Generation Evaluation. An example of the constructivist evaluation can be seen in fourth generation evaluation (Guba & Lincoln, 1989). This approach is carried out through a series of steps, though not necessarily linear. Initially, the focus in the checklist is the identification of stakeholders, with a specific examination of those who will benefit from or be hurt by the evaluation. Time is also taken to engage stakeholders from each audience to construct their understanding of the evaluand, that which is to be evaluated. With a negotiated understanding as the goal, the evaluation moves into sorting out the constructions and then prioritizing any unresolved items. The evaluation continues with the gathering of further information and constructions. Not all stakeholders will have their particular items negotiated, and those items can be considered as the process cycles. As the evaluation continues, reporting will occur, most often in several forms tailored to the specific concerns of the different stakeholding groups. The report is to be organized around the original purpose of the evaluation, specifically whether it was a formative or summative assessment and a "merit or worth" focus. The evaluation may occur in iterative waves or be reiterative as the time within the evaluation processes and the constructions discussed above evolve through dialogue and evidence gathering.

Questions/Methods Approaches

The questions/methods approaches typically begin with a narrow set of questions that are matched with a set of methods and data to answer those questions. As Stufflebeam (2001) notes, the focus is not on whether these questions or methods are appropriate to answer the merit or value aspects of a program. The questions are typically derived from the objectives of the program or from the funding agency. Stufflebeam (2001) categorizes them as quasi-evaluation because, at times, the approaches provide evidence that can be used to assess merit and worth.

Case Study.   A case study is a focused, rich, and in-depth description, analysis, and synthesis of a specific program, policy, or product. Evaluators do not engage in the program, but examine it as it is unfolding or after it has unfolded. The focus is holistic in that the evaluator examines inputs, outputs, and processes along with a range of intended and unintended outcomes. The goal of the case study approach is to illuminate what did or did not occur. It is not an approach to help develop or make a value judgment about merit.

Questions.   The questions addressed by the evaluator are developed from the questions of the main audience members. According to Stufflebeam (2001), some typical questions are:

> *What is the program in concept and practice?*
> *How has it changed over time?*
> *How does it work and create the desired and undesired outcomes?*
> *What has it produced?*
> *What are the shortfalls and negative side effects?*
> *What are the positive side effects?*
> *In what way and to what degree do various stakeholders value the program?*
> *At what level does the program effectively meet beneficiaries' needs?*
> *What are the most important reasons for the program's successes and failures?*

Methods.   Case studies employ a wide range of qualitative and quantitative methods. The data collected are is quite wide ranging because of the potential for a historical examination. Some of the analyses from the data collected may be historical in nature, for example, a map analysis, testimony, photographs, videos, a collection and examination of artifacts such as products produced, a content analysis of program documentation, independent and participant observations, interviews, a logical analysis of operations, focus groups, tests, questionnaires, rating scales, hearings, or forums. Quite a variety of data is available. Therefore, given the nature of the case study, an evaluator that is experienced in multiple methodologies and data analyses is valuable.

Strengths/Weaknesses.   A major strength of the case study approach is that the wide variety of methods used and data collected allow triangulation of multiple perspectives, which increases accuracy. This approach looks at programs holistically and in depth that allows a solid description for how the program works and produces outcomes. The focus on the audiences' questions adds to the potential use of the evaluation observations later. Because the case study can occur while the program is running or as a historical analysis, the approach is quite flexible. Finally, multiple case studies can be conducted simultaneously, which increases the strength of this approach. The main weakness of the case study approach is the evaluator. An evaluator can allow the open nature of the approach to take over and miss critical steps to achieve a sound evaluation. Evaluators also can overly focus on the description and not provide enough information to allow a final judgment to be made.

Outcomes Monitoring/Value-Added Models.   Value-added models (VAMs) analyze the change in students' test scores from one year to the next through complex statistical analysis. Through this analysis, for example, teacher effects are calculated to see how much "value" a teacher adds to a student's change in scores. Each teacher is assigned a number at the end of the analysis that is either positive or negative. A positive value is interpreted as the teacher having a positive effect on student scores, and a negative value is interpreted as a teacher having a negative effect on student scores. Epistemologically, VAMs are philosophically objectivist. The approach has many statistical modeling assumptions, such as the teacher's effect is the same for all students in a given subject and year and that it goes forward into the future undiminished. It also assumes that teachers are assigned with the same academic goals for their classes and all have the same resources.

VAMs can also be categorized as VAM-P or VAM-A. **VAM for Program Evaluation (VAM-P)** is used to evaluate educational programs and identify the characteristics of effective teachers. **VAM for Accountability (VAM-A)** is used to evaluate individual educational personnel, especially teachers. The goals of these two approaches are very different.

Questions.   In addition to asking whether the teacher or school has an effect on the student's scores, other questions include:

> Is (and by how much) the program adding value to students' achievements?
> What are the cross-year trends in outcomes?
> Where in the district or state is the program working the best and poorest?
> Are the program successes (or failures) related to the specific groupings by grade level (e.g., primary, middle or junior high, and high school)?

Methods.   A complex multilevel statistical regression analysis is conducted to determine the trends and effects over time based on tests and sometimes survey data about the students' and teachers' demographic variables. **Multilevel regression analysis** is briefly discussed in Chapter 7.

Strengths/Weaknesses.   The greatest strength, besides improvement in the technical aspects of trying to examine nested longitudinal test score data, is the fact that this approach is attempting to track student achievement over time. Researchers and policy makers have been discussing this for decades, and the approach works toward that incredible goal. Second, it is much better than adequate yearly progress (AYP), which is simply plagued by so many problems (such as the fact that it suffers from cohort changes each test administration) that it is practically useless. However, VAM suffers from many weaknesses. The causal interpretation from the number calculated for the teacher is not fully warranted because students and teachers are not randomly selected and randomly assigned, which is an assumption within inferential statistics. Teachers get to select where they work and have seniority choices, and no statistical model can solve this problem. There is also the problem of construct shift (Martineau, 2006). Vertical scales are used in VAM, which is sound; but the problem is that the test scales span wide content and developmental ranges. This massive shift makes the interpretation of the results less than stable. With VAM-A specifically, it is hard to say that one teacher is clearly better than another; in one year a teacher can seem to add value and the next year he does not—this is termed *persistence* (Harris, 2007). Finally, the value added by an individual teacher can vary depending on how the statistical model is specified, that is, what variables are included.

Concluding Comments on the Approaches

The approaches presented above were chosen because they appeared to score well in a comparison to the 1994 Standards for Program Evaluation based on an analysis by Stufflebeam (2001). They are all very different in their focus, and evaluators tend to stick with one approach though they may use different methods within that approach. The information above is quite brief and the approaches have been discussed in a large volume of associated articles. We suggest that before you attempt an evaluation you should read indepth the related documents for each approach, obtain formal training in the profession, and if at all possible, engage in an apprenticeship with a professional evaluator who is highly engaged in the field.

OUR MODEL AND EXPERIENCE WITH EVALUATIONS

We have a general framework that has developed from working with clients. You will see pieces of each of the above approaches, but overall, most people tend to classify us as client centered (without letting the client run amok). We truly enjoy our evaluative work, and in a sense it keeps us grounded, given that most of our days are filled with theoretical arguments or examining that of others.

Getting to Know Clients and Stakeholders

Determining the main purpose(s) of the evaluation in the eyes of the stakeholders and working with the client has been critical to our success and provides our largest learning curve. Most of the evaluations we work on are small, and the client and stakeholders understand the need for the evaluation, but are not fully sure what they are interested in understanding at the end of the evaluation time frame. The client typically has not thought about who the full range of stakeholders are. This is an opportunity to work through this issue.

During this initial phase, we work with the client to examine whether the evaluation is to determine merit and whether the focus is more on formative or summative evaluation. There are two types of merit the client and stakeholders could be interested in: **absolute merit** (Was it worth the money? How effective overall was the program?) or **relative merit** (Is it better than other programs?). For example, "How is it working right now compared with previously?" is a relative merit question; "After 40 years of watching the Ypsilanti Perry Preschool Project participants, was the program effective?" is an absolute merit question. Note that you need to define effective here. "Which high definition television should I buy?" is a relative merit question because you are comparing products.

We also discuss goal-free evaluations at this point. A **goal-free evaluation** is where the goals of the program or project are not the most important part of the evaluation. Let us explain. Many programs we have been asked to evaluate have multiple goals and objectives to meet. The problem is that some of those goals are hard to reach (e.g., school culture change), while others are easier (e.g., creating middle- and high-school transition teams). If we were to evaluate a program just on the goals, the goals may be reached and the program seems successful, but they were easy goals to meet. Whereas some goals were hard to reach and while the program made great progress toward the goal in the evaluation time frame, it did not meet the goal and seems unsuccessful. Therefore, the programs have goals, but the attainment or nonattainment of the goals is not the central focus of the evaluation.

It is important to remember that different audiences for the evaluation will have different views on what should come out of the evaluation and what is important. From our experience obtaining this divergent information is important and provides you an opportunity to interact with people who may hold information you need in order to answer the evaluation questions. For example, Jim was involved in a school of law evaluation for several years. The initial question was, "Why are our first-time bar exam test takers not passing the test at a higher rate?" Well, that was a wide open question. Jim interviewed several people in and out of the law school (and even a bar exam executive) and asked them for their views on the failures and what questions they wanted answered. There were statements about LSAT scores (which for this law school were essentially unrelated to passing the exam), grade inflation (evidence did surface related to that), the content in the courses (which was politically unanswerable because it affected academic autonomy), and a host of other issues. Only once during those conversations did bar-exam-related courses and student enrollment in those courses (which ended up being a major reason for the failures) come up—and that was a question from an alumnus.

Summative evaluations are desired when you need to decide how to implement a program or whether to buy a product, when you need to determine how to allocate resources, when you need to compare your product to the competition, or when you need marketing or sales data. The summative evaluation combines all the gathered evaluative data and typically provides a recommendation to the client and stakeholders. For many programs in business, this evaluation type is based on a return-on-investment (ROI) concern, but for school districts it may be a yes-no when deciding to implement the program for the district.

Formative evaluation occurs when the stakeholders are interested in determining areas of improvement. Many times, we have had clients who had already implemented a program and wanted information on how the program was working and needed to identify areas of improvement. Scriven (1991) stated that formative evaluations work well with new products, programs, policies, and staff members. In the department where Jim works, young faculty members go through a formative evaluation after the first two years. Formative evaluations can also work well with a program that has existed for a long time. With the changes in demographics, technology, and society in general, evaluating the performance of a current program is necessary. Just because performance has been superior in the past does not mean it is now or will be in the future. The law school also wanted formative evaluations along the way.

Initial Contractual Agreement

After an initial meeting to obtain a basic understanding of the client's needs and desires, we typically set up a basic contract for the development of the evaluation and not the evaluation in general. We don't always do this, but from our experience it has worked well because it takes a bit of time to completely understand the full scope of some evaluations and the true resources needed. We follow the contractual guidelines by Daniel Stufflebeam, which can be found at the Western

Michigan Evaluation Web site. This process and use of the checklist truly reduces misunderstandings between clients and evaluators.

Determining the Evaluand

The **evaluand** is what is being evaluated. The evaluand can be a product, person, tactic, process, or group. Depending on the purpose and questions to be addressed, there may be more than one evaluand. Clients have an idea of what they want evaluated, but conversations with them and stakeholders clarify the evaluand before any criteria development or data collection occurs. This does not mean that during the evaluation, questions, evaluands, or data collected will not be modified given the nature of the evaluation. Unlike a pure laboratory experiment, evaluations tend to be more fluid, especially as the length of time for the evaluation increases. The evaluand for the school of law was the pass rate, but once the pass rate increased, new evaluands began to be identified. After the determination of the initial evaluand, we typically develop a formal full contract for the evaluation period because we have a solid foundation on what this evaluation should constitute.

Criteria

Once you and the clients have a good grasp of the desired evaluation questions, evaluand, and the purpose of the evaluation, you can move on to developing the **criteria** or merit dimensions. "What is the criterion for the effectiveness of this program?" is a typical baseline question. For the school of law, they were not sure of the exact pass rate, but above 80% was the initial value. For a high definition television, one criterion is the angle at which the screen can still be seen.

Within the development of criteria, many clients of program evaluations love to develop goals. It is important to understand the implicit and explicit goals, or even specific targets a program may have. We like goals, but tend to move our clients toward a goal-free evaluation as stated earlier. This approach also allows us to examine both positive and negative effects during the investigation.

We use the medical model to discuss this issue with clients. When you see the doctor with **symptoms**, you have no idea what the real **"problem/issue"** may be. Now, Jim will be the first to admit that medicine has a huge database (e.g., Isabel) where symptoms can be submitted and potential causes provided. At other times, we conduct a needs assessment. A **need** is "something without which unsatisfactory function occurs" (Davidson, 2005, p. 53), which is different than a want. You can want something, and without it you are unhappy, but you can still function. Not all evaluations have a full needs assessment, but we find it to be a good exercise for you, the client, and stakeholders throughout the evaluation time frame. Understanding the needs of the users of the product or program is important. Therefore, who are the people you should be concerned with? Well, everyone. Really, it ranges from those who were involved in the design and implementation to immediate recipients to other audiences who might be directly affected by the program, process, or product.

For example, let us think of an after-school program that allows primary school students to take a laptop home. The stakeholders may include the computer company, a funding organization, the program staff, the students, the parents, the siblings, neighbors, teachers, schools, and classmates. As you move from the program staff to the actual recipients, the effect may diminish quickly, but it is important to understand the potential effect. A needs assessment can be necessary before and during an evaluation. What you thought were the needs at the design phase may not be the needs half way through.

Logic Model Development

At this point, we begin a **logic model**, which graphically depicts how the program should work and the outcomes stakeholders expect to see. This is the development of a cause-and-effect argument. It should tie the evaluand to the needs. For example, Jim is working on an educational intervention project that is designed to help single mothers leave public support (welfare) and get a job in the biological sciences field. From a goal perspective, that is considered to be quite a large goal. However, the evaluation of the program has been formative and needs based. In Figure 11.1, we have simplified the larger model. Key needs for the participants are childcare, funding, safe housing, counseling services, academic scaffolding, along with the content and skills necessary for the job market.

At some point, you will test the causality issue to see whether it works out. Within the design of the program, safe housing was initially not a need and was not considered in the causality model of success (graduating and job attainment). This activity also allows you to challenge assumptions and values that are embedded in the logic model and the program itself and acts as an internal check for which values are important and which assumptions might be biased.

Method: Sampling and Data Collection (Evidence to Warrant Claims)

We now begin the sampling process and data collection. Who and what needs to be sampled? How many or much? Given the purpose of the evaluation, the answers to these questions should make logical sense. The sampling process of

FIGURE 11.1
Dr. Michelle Zuckerman-Parker's logic model for educational intervention project

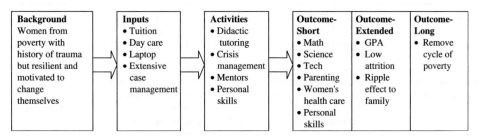

Background	Inputs	Activities	Outcome-Short	Outcome-Extended	Outcome-Long
Women from poverty with history of trauma but resilient and motivated to change themselves	• Tuition • Day care • Laptop • Extensive case management	• Didactic tutoring • Crisis management • Mentors • Personal skills	• Math • Science • Tech • Parenting • Women's health care • Personal skills	• GPA • Low attrition • Ripple effect to family	• Remove cycle of poverty

participants, documents, artifacts, and so on will help support your arguments or can undermine your claims depending on your method. Understanding that the experience of a cohort admitted to a new program will have different sampling and data collection processes compared to a new manufacturing process that reduces the number of improperly made products is important. Both may collect numeric and non-numeric data, but their design and sampling will look very different.

We always collect multiple lines of evidence that consist of numeric and non-numeric data in order to substantiate the claims we make. We are not talking about mixed methodology from a design perspective; we are talking about triangulating the claims with trustworthy data to make a stable claim that can be trusted by multiple audiences reading the report. This is integrating numeric and non-numeric data (see Chapter 10). We spend a good deal of time examining the evidence we have based on quality and importance. We have an iterative process where we look at the believability of the data we have and how important that data are in relation to the purpose of the evaluation. To examine our data and claims, we create a matrix with the claim on the left side and the evidence on the right. An example for the school of law evaluation is shown in Table 11.2.

We also look at the evidence gathered that was not planned but added to the understanding of the evaluation. Remember, you cannot plan to collect everything. You have to make decisions on what you will collect and what you will not. This is a completely subjective process, but it should be rational and logical to the clients and stakeholders.

Analysis

We typically are analyzing and reanalyzing data as the evaluation is in progress to check our biases, blinders, assumptions, and values. The analysis used depends on the questions, design, and data collected, as we have stated several times throughout this book. Again, the focus is to triangulate our interpretations across data sources and settings in order to obtain a coherent narrative of what is occurring or what has occurred. Sometimes, this data convergence does not occur, but that can be important for the evaluation and for the client to see.

TABLE 11.2
Claim and evidence example

Claim	Evidence
Failures due to lack of bar-exam-related course taken by students	90% of students, who took less than 70% of courses related to bar-exam content during their three years, failed the bar exam. Whereas 99% of students, who took more than 90% of the bar-exam-related courses, passed the bar exam
LSAT score not related to pass score or pass/fail categorization	Given a close to normal distribution of LSAT scores ranging from $-2\ SD$ to $2.5\ SD$ above the mean, the correlation between bar passage and LSAT scores for 10 years of tests average .18, which indicates that LSAT scores account for less than 4% of the variance in passing.

Reporting

When we begin the reporting process, we use Scriven's checklist, though we use this throughout an evaluation, and Gary Miron's checklist; both can be obtained online at the Western Michigan Evaluation Center. We use these checklists as our organizing format and begin filling in the specific information section by section. Since our evaluations have a unique part to all of them, we add a section or two that highlight the unique aspects of the evaluation. The checklists are good reminders as you are completing your evaluations and can be utilized to help the client understand how the information will be presented in the final report. In addition, there are typically three stakeholder audiences to which we present results. We typically write one report and create three different presentations and mini-reports. The focus of each presentation varies, but the checklists are a good tactic to make sure that all the required information a reader needs to make a judgment about the evaluation and the program under evaluation is included.

ADDITIONAL TOPICS

There are other well-known topics in program evaluation, which have not been discussed above. The two most common are the benefits generated in comparison to the costs of a program, project, or group. There are three ways to examine this group of evaluations. There is the cost analysis of program inputs, which tallies the financial cost of a program for the history of the program. The original costing out—**cost analysis**—of the program can be compared to the actual costs over time or to other similar programs. The greatest benefit is to stakeholders and decision makers within the organization. These reports rarely leave the organization, unless it is a government-based or government-funded report that must be released by law or contractual agreement.

Cost-effectiveness analysis also examines the cost of a program over time in relation to reaching the goal of the program. For example, a company may develop three products that are compared in reference to increasing market share. If one product is the least expensive to produce and increases market share the most, it would be considered the most cost-effective. In education, if three reading programs are compared over time and one is observed to cost about the same as the other two but has a much higher reading achievement level associated with student scores, that program would be considered cost-effective.

Cost-benefit analyses are an extension of the previous two. This approach goes beyond the basics of cost and goal achievement and examines such broad topics as positive and negative effects of the program in the context in which the program implemented won. It also includes benefits unrelated to the original costs of the program. For example, the Ypsilanti Perry Preschool Project cost-benefit analysis examined the long-term benefits of reduced social service needs to those who were in the experimental group as compared to those in the nonexperimental group. The defining attribute of the cost-benefit analysis is the placement of monetary values on a wide variety of inputs and outputs for a program. Jim has been involved in cost-benefit analyses of educational programs to examine the cost to taxpayers at program initiation in comparison to benefits to taxpayers in the future.

Exportability is the examination of the program being implemented in a different context or area. Many programs start small in one location to solve a problem. Once the program is successful, many ask, "Can this work anywhere else?" You will also see the term **scalability**, which means using the program with a larger number of people. As programs are exported, unique components of the new participants or geographical area are highlighted because they are not part of the original implementation and the program may not fit or work as well. As people try to include more participants in a program, the infrastructure to serve those people must increase. This is where potential problems begin because resources needed to export or scale-up a program can grow exponentially.

CASE STUDY

Looking at the previous designed studies from an evaluator's perspective, Ginette has decided to create a program that she will align with the National Council on Teaching Mathematics and the National Science Education Standards to help students learn and use graphing properly from K–12. She did some investigative work with teachers and heard from many teachers that students do a great deal of graphing up until sixth grade and then it trails off until they come across it again in high school. Thus, most students have trouble recalling what they have learned or the context has changed so much that they can't transfer their knowledge to a new situation.

Ginette's overall goal is to fill the gap that exists in the grades with the program. She is considering a traditional educational intervention program or a virtual environment where the students play characters who own a company that helps people develop graphics. She would like to incorporate the work Professor Tufte has completed into the program or game, so that a larger audience would be exposed to his work earlier in their graphic display experience. The type of evaluation approach she feels most comfortable with is CIPP, but with education she knows there will be many stakeholders she will have to bring into the mix.

ARMCHAIR MOMENT

We have had our share of wonderful and horrific evaluation experiences. Jim had one evaluation project in which the program really did improve the lives of the recipients, but the clients, after it was all over, had wanted it to fail because they disagreed with it philosophically. He has seen unethical requests on the part of the clients and has even requested that his name be removed from an evaluation. He has also had wonderful experiences in which the program essentially failed but the clients were happy to have all the information. The clients were appreciative for the examination of the unexpected costs of the program, which were not part of the original costing out estimate. Jim has learned from his evaluation experiences that keeping a moral compass on at all times is the most important. You never know who will try to chip away at your ethics.

If you are a young evaluator, a good sounding board, such as another evaluator, is a priceless resource. This should be someone who is not associated with or bound to any of the groups involved in the evaluation, who will give you an honest assessment of the situation. We are lucky to have colleagues who are very good at this.

From a day-to-day evaluation perspective, being well organized is also crucial. Taking detailed notes from clients' statements, along with those you are interviewing about the program, is crucial. Clients tend to forget what they have said or asked for, so you need to document, document, document. Remember that no one truly likes being evaluated. We appreciate it, but we do not like it. It makes everyone nervous. Being a good listener will help you through this. In the end, most clients want a sound, rigorous, and believable evaluation, regardless of the outcomes. If you are reading this book, most likely you are not in a program evaluation exercise. There are not that many. We suggest that you find a course or two specifically in program (or personnel or development) evaluation and take it. You will only enhance your skill set and the skills you will bring to your organization. Finally, join the evaluation wiki at http://www.evaluationwiki.org/index.php/Main_Page

KEY WORDS

absolute merit
accreditation/
    certification approach
case study
CIPP model
client-centered/responsive
    approach
constructivist
    evaluation
consumer-oriented
    approach
context evaluations
cost analysis
cost-benefit analyses
costs-effectiveness
    analysis
criteria
critical dialogue
decision/accountability
    approach
deliberative democratic
    approach
dialogue

effectiveness
elucidating dialogue
evaluand
evaluation
explicit values
exportability
formative evaluation
fourth generation
    evaluation
goal-free evaluation
hermeneutic-dialecticism
impact
improvement/
    accountability
inclusion
input evaluations
key evaluation checklist
    (KEC)
logic model
multilevel regression
    analysis
need
objectivist

outcomes
problem/issue
process evaluations
product evaluations
relative merit
scalability
self-study
social agenda
stakeholder
summative evaluation
sustainability
symptom
transactional
    subjectivism
transportability
utilization-focused
    evaluation (U-FE)
value-added model (VAM)
VAM for accountability
VAM for program
    evaluation

REFERENCES AND FURTHER READINGS

Baker, E. L, O'Neil, H. R., & Linn, R. L. (1993). Policy and validity prospects for performance-based assessment. *American Psychologist, 48*, 1210–1218.

Bhola, H. S. (1998). Program evaluation for program renewal: A study of the national literacy program in Namibia (NLPN). *Studies in Educational Evaluation, 24*(4), 303–330.

Boruch, R. F. (1994). The future of controlled randomized experiments: A briefing. *Evaluation Practice, 15*(3), 265–274.

Chelimsky, E. (1987). What have we learned about the politics of evaluation? *Evaluation Practice, 8*(1), 5–21.

Chen, H. (1990). *Theory driven evaluations.* Newbury Park, CA: SAGE Publications.

Cook, D. L. (1966). *Program evaluation and review techniques, applications in education.* Washington, DC: U.S. Office of Education Cooperative Monograph, 17 (OE-12024).

Cook, T. D., & Reichardt, C. S. (Eds.). (1979). *Qualitative and quantitative methods in evaluation research.* Beverly Hills, CA: SAGE Publications.

Cousins, J. B., & Earl, L. M. (1992). The case for participatory evaluation. *Educational Evaluation and Policy Analysis, 14*(4), 397–418.

Cronbach, L. J., & Associates. (1980). *Toward reform of program evaluation.* San Francisco, CA: Jossey-Bass.

Davidson, J. (2005). *Evaluation methodology basics: The nuts and bolts of sound evaluation.* Thousand Oaks: CA. SAGE Publications.

Davis, H. R., & Salasin, S. E. (1975). The utilization of evaluation. In E. L. Struening & M. Guttentag (Eds.), *Handbook of evaluation research, Vol. 1.* Beverly Hills, CA: SAGE Publications.

Eisner, E. W. (1983). Educational connoisseurship and criticism: Their form and functions in educational evaluation. In G. F. Madaus, M. Scriven, & D. L. Stufflebeam (Eds.), *Evaluation models.* Boston, MA: Kluwer-Nijhoff.

Ferguson, R. (1999, June). Ideological marketing. *The Education Industry Report.*

Fetterman, D. M. (1984). *Ethnography in educational evaluation.* Beverly Hills, CA: SAGE Publications.

Flexner, A. (1910). *Medical education in the United States and Canada.* Bethesda, MD: Science and Health Publications.

Flinders, D. J., & Eisner, E. W. (2000). Educational criticism as a form of qualitative inquiry. In D. L. Stufflebeam, G. F. Madaus, & T. Kellaghan (Eds.), *Evaluation models.* Boston, MA: Kluwer.

Glass, G. V. (1975). A paradox about excellence of schools and the people in them. *Educational Researcher, 4*, 9–13.

Glass, G. V., & Maguire, T. O. (1968). *Analysis of time-series quasi-experiments.* (U.S. Office of Education Report No. 6–8329.) Boulder, CO: Laboratory of Educational Research, University of Colorado.

Guba, E. G. (1969). The failure of educational evaluation. *Educational Technology, 9*, 29–38.

Guba, E. G. (1977). *Educational evaluation: The state of the art.* Keynote address at the annual meeting of the Evaluation Network, St. Louis.

Guba, E. G. (1978). Toward a methodology of naturalistic inquiry in evaluation. *CSE Monograph Series in Evaluation.* Los Angeles: Center for the Study of Evaluation.

Guba, E. G. (1990). *The paradigm dialog.* Newbury Park, CA: SAGE Publications.

Guba, E. G., & Lincoln, Y. S. (1981). *Effective evaluation.* San Francisco, CA: Jossey-Bass.

Guba, E. G., & Lincoln, Y. S. (1989). *Fourth generation evaluation.* Newbury Park, CA: SAGE Publications.

Guba, E. G., & Lincoln, Y. S. (2001). *Guidelines and checklist for constructivist (a.k.a. Fourth Generation) evaluation.* Retrieved from http://www.wmich.edu/evalctr/checklists/constructivisteval.pdf

Hambleton, R. K., & Swaminathan, H. (1985). *Item response theory.* Boston, MA: Kluwer- Nijhoff.

Harris, D. N. (2007). *The policy uses and "policy validity" of value-added and other teacher quality measures.* Paper prepared for the Educational Testing Service (ETS), San Francisco, CA, September 24–25, 2007.

Herman, J. L., Gearhart, M. G., & Baker, E. L. (1993). Assessing writing portfolios: Issues in the validity and meaning of scores. *Educational Assessment, 1,* 201–224.

House, E. R. (Ed.). (1973). *School evaluation: The politics and process.* Berkeley, CA: McCutchan.

House, E. R. (1980). *Evaluating with validity.* Beverly Hills, CA: SAGE Publications.

House, E. R. (1983). Assumptions underlying evaluation models. In G. F. Madaus, M. Scriven, & D. L. Stufflebeam (Eds.), *Evaluation models.* Boston, MA: Kluwer-Nijhoff.

House, E. R., & Howe, K. R. (1998). *Deliberative democratic evaluation in practice.* Boulder: University of Colorado.

House, E., & Howe, K. R. (1999). *Values in evaluation and social research.* Thousand Oaks, CA: SAGE Publications.

House, E. R., & Howe, K. R. (2000a). Deliberative democratic evaluation. *New Directions for Evaluation, 85* (Spring), 3–12.

House, E. R., & Howe, K. R. (2000b). Deliberative democratic evaluation in practice. In D. L. Stufflebeam, G. F. Madaus, & T. Kellaghan (Eds.), *Evaluation models* (pp. 409–422). Boston: Kluwer.

Howe, E. R., & Ashcroft, C. (2005). Deliberative democratic evaluation: Successes and limitations of an evaluation of school choice. *Teachers College Record, 107* (10), 2275–2298.

Joint Committee on Standards for Educational Evaluation. (1981). *Standards for evaluations of educational programs, projects, and materials.* New York: McGraw-Hill.

Joint Committee on Standards for Educational Evaluation. (1988). *The personnel evaluation standards: How to assess systems for evaluating educators.* Newbury Park, CA: SAGE Publications.

Joint Committee on Standards for Educational Evaluation. (1994). *The program evaluation standards: How to assess evaluations of educational programs.* Thousand Oaks, CA: SAGE Publications.

Joint Committee on Standards for Educational Evaluation. (in press). *The program evaluation standards: How to assess evaluations of educational programs.* Thousand Oaks, CA: SAGE Publications.

Karlsson, O. (1998). Socratic dialogue in the Swedish political context. *New Directions for Evaluation, 77,* 21–38.

Kee, J. E. (1995). Benefit-cost analysis in program evaluation. In J. S. Wholey, H. P. Hatry, & K. E. Newcomer (Eds.), *Handbook of practical program evaluation* (pp. 456–488). San Francisco: Jossey-Bass.

Kirst, M. W. (1990, July). *Accountability: Implications for state and local policymakers.* In Policy Perspectives Series. Washington, DC: Information Services, Office of Educational Research and Improvement, U.S. Department of Education.

Koretz, D. (1996). Using student assessments for educational accountability. In R. Hanushek (Ed.), *Improving the performance of America's schools* (pp. 171–196). Washington, DC: National Academies Press.

Levin, H. M. (1983). *Cost-effectiveness: A primer. New perspectives in evaluation.* Newbury Park, CA: SAGE Publications.

Lincoln, Y. S., & Guba, E. G. (1985). *Naturalistic inquiry.* Beverly Hills, CA: SAGE Publications.

Linn, R. L., Baker, E. L., & Dunbar, S. B. (1991). Complex, performance-based assessment: Expectations and validation criteria. *Educational Researcher, 20*(8), 15–21.

Madaus, G. F., Scriven, M., & Stufflebeam, D. L. (1983). *Evaluation models.* Boston, MA: Kluwer-Nijhoff.

Madaus, G. F., & Stufflebeam, D. L. (1988). *Educational evaluation: The classical writings of Ralph W. Tyler.* Boston, MA: Kluwer.

Martineau, J. A. (2006). Distorting value added: The use of longitudinal, vertically scaled student achievement data for growth-based, value-added accountability. *Journal of Educational and Behavioral Statistics, 31*(1), 35–62.

Messick, S. (1994). The interplay of evidence and consequences in the validation of performance assessments. *Educational Researcher, 23*(3), 13–23.

Miron, G. (1998). Choosing the right research methods: Qualitative? Quantitative? Or both? In L. Buchert (Ed.), *Education reform in the south in the 1990s.* Paris: UNESCO.

Mullen, P. D., Hersey, J., & Iverson, D. C. (1987). Health behavior models compared. *Social Science and Medicine, 24,* 973–981.

National Science Foundation. (1997). *User-friendly handbook for mixed method evaluations.* NSF 97–153. Arlington, VA: Author.

Nevo, D. (1993). The evaluation minded school: An application of perceptions from program evaluation. *Evaluation Practice, 14*(1), 39–47.

Patton, M. Q. (1980). *Qualitative evaluation methods.* Beverly Hills, CA: SAGE Publications.

Patton, M. Q. (1982). *Practical evaluation.* Beverly Hills, CA: SAGE Publications.

Patton, M. Q. (1990). *Qualitative evaluation and research methods* (2nd ed.). Newbury Park, CA: SAGE Publications.

Patton, M. Q. (1994). Developmental evaluation. *Evaluation Practice, 15*(3), 311–319.

Patton, M. Q. (1997). *Utilization-focused evaluation: The new century text* (3rd ed.). Newbury Park, CA: SAGE Publications.

Patton, M. Q. (2000). Utilization-focused evaluation. In D. L. Stufflebeam, G. F. Madaus, & T. Kellaghan (Eds.), *Evaluation models*. Boston, MA: Kluwer.

Patton, M. Q. (2002). *Utilization-focused evaluation checklist*. Retrieved from http//www.wmich.edu/evalctr/checklists

Platt, J. (1992). Case study in American methodological thought. *Current Sociology, 40*(1), 17–48.

Rogers, P. R. (2000). Program theory: Not whether programs work but how they work. In D. L. Stufflebeam, G. F. Madaus, & T. Kellaghan (Eds.), *Evaluation models*. Boston, MA: Kluwer.

Rossi, P. H., & Freeman, H. E. (1993). *Evaluation: A systematic approach* (5th ed.). Newbury Park, CA: SAGE Publications.

Sanders, J. R. (1992). *Evaluating school programs*. Newbury Park, CA: SAGE Publications.

Sanders, W. L. (1989). Using customized standardized tests. (Contract No. R-88–062003) Washington, DC: Office of Educational Research and Improvement, U. S. Department of Education. (ERIC Digest No. ED 314429)

Sanders, W. L., & Horn, S. P. (1994). The Tennessee value-added assessment system (TVAAS): Mixed model methodology in educational assessment. *Journal of Personnel Evaluation in Education, 8*(3), 299–311.

Schatzman, L., & Strauss, A. L. (1973). *Field research*. Englewood Cliffs, NJ: Prentice-Hall.

Schwandt, T. A. (1984). *An examination of alternative models for socio-behavioral inquiry* Unpublished Ph.D. Dissertation, Indiana University.

Schwandt, T. A. (1989). Recapturing moral discourse in evaluation. *Educational Researcher, 18*(8), 11–16.

Scriven, M. (1974). Evaluation perspectives and procedures. In W. J. Popham (Ed.), *Evaluation in education: Current applications*. Berkeley, CA: McCutchan.

Scriven, M. (1991). *Evaluation thesaurus*. Newbury Park, CA: SAGE Publications.

Scriven, M. (1994a). Evaluation as a discipline. *Studies in Educational Evaluation, 20*(1), 147–166.

Scriven, M. (1994b). The final synthesis. *Evaluation Practice, 15*(3), 367–382.

Scriven, M. (1994c). Product evaluation: The state of the art. *Evaluation Practice, 15*(1), 45–62.

Shadish, W. R., Cook, T. D., & Leviton, L. C. (1991). *Foundations of program evaluation*. Newbury Park, CA: SAGE Publications.

Smith, M. F. (1989). *Evaluability assessment: A practical approach*. Boston, MA: Kluwer Academic.

Stake, R. E. (1967). The countenance of educational evaluation. *Teachers College Record, 68*, 523–540.

Stake, R. E. (1971). *Measuring what learners learn* (mimeograph). Urbana, IL: Center for Instructional Research and Curriculum Evaluation.

Stake, R. E. (1974). *Nine approaches to educational evaluation* (unpublished chart). Urbana IL: University of Illinois, Center for Instructional Research and Curriculum Evaluation.

Stake, R. E. (1975, November). *Program evaluation: Particularly responsive evaluation.* Kalamazoo, MI: Western Michigan University Evaluation Center, Occasional Paper No. 5.

Stake, R. E. (1983). Program evaluation, particularly responsive evaluation. In G. F. Madaus, M. Scriven, & D. L. Stufflebeam (Eds.), *Evaluation models* (pp. 287–310). Boston, MA: Kluwer-Nijhoff.

Stake, R. E. (1986). *Quieting reform.* Urbana, IL: University of Illinois Press.

Stake, R. E. (1988). Seeking sweet water. In R. M. Jaeger (Ed.), *Complementary methods for research in education* (pp. 253–300). Washington, DC: American Educational Research Association.

Stake, R. E. (1995). *The art of case study research.* Thousand Oaks, CA: SAGE Publications.

Stake, R. E. (1999). Summary of evaluation of reader focused writing for the Veterans Benefits Administration. *American Journal of Evaluation, 20*(2), 323–343.

Stake, R. E., Easly, J., & Anastasiou, K. (1978). *Case studies in science education.* Washington, DC: National Science Foundation, Directorate for Science Education, Office of Program Integration.

Steinmetz, A. (1983). The discrepancy evaluation model. In G. F. Madaus, M. Scriven, & D. L. Stufflebeam (Eds.), *Evaluation models* (pp. 79–100). Boston, MA: Kluwer-Nijhoff.

Stufflebeam, D. L. (1966). A depth study of the evaluation requirement. *Theory Into Practice, 5* (June), 121–134.

Stufflebeam, D. L. (1967). The use of and abuse of evaluation in Title III. *Theory Into Practice, 6* (June), 126–133.

Stufflebeam, D. L. (2001). Evaluation models, *New Directions for Evaluation, 89,* 7–98.

Stufflebeam, D. L. (2003, October). *The CIPP model for evaluation.* Presented at the 2003 Annual Conference of the Oregon Program Evaluators Network (OPEN), Portland, OR.

Stufflebeam, D. L., Foley, W. J., Gephart, W. J., Guba, E. G., Hammond, R. L., Merriman, H. O., & Provus, M. (1971). *Educational evaluation and decision making.* Itasca, IL: Peacock.

Stufflebeam, D. L., Madaus, G. F., & Kellaghan, T. (2000). *Evaluation models* (Rev. ed.). Boston, MA: Kluwer.

Stufflebeam, D. L., & Shinkfield, A. J. (1985). *Systematic evaluation.* Boston, MA: Kluwer-Nijhoff.

Suchman, E. A. (1967). *Evaluative research.* New York: Russell Sage Foundation.

Swanson, D. B., Norman, R. N., & Linn, R. L. (1995). Performance-based assessment: Lessons from the health professions. *Educational Researcher, 24*(5), 5–11.

Torrance, H. (1993). Combining measurement-driven instruction with authentic assessment: Some initial observations of national assessment in England and Wales. *Educational Evaluation and Policy Analysis, 15,* 81–90.

Torres, R. T. (1991). Improving the quality of internal evaluation: The evaluator as consultant mediator. *Evaluation and Program Planning*, *14*(1), 189–198.

Tsang, M. C. (1997). Cost analysis for improved educational policymaking and evaluation. *Educational Evaluation and Policy Analysis*, *19*(4), 318–324.

Webster, W. J. (1995). The connection between personnel evaluation and school evaluation. *Studies in Educational Evaluation*, *21*, 227–254.

Webster, W. J., Mendro, R. L., & Almaguer, T. O. (1994). Effectiveness indices: A ''value added'' approach to measuring school effect. *Studies in Educational Evaluation*, *20*, 113–145.

Wholey, J. S. (1995). Assessing the feasibility and likely usefulness of evaluation. In J. S. Wholey, H. P. Hatry, & K. E. Newcomer (Eds.), *Handbook of practical program evaluation* (pp. 15–39). San Francisco, CA: Jossey-Bass.

Wiggins, G. (1989). A true test: Toward more authentic and equitable assessment. *Phi Delta Kappan*, *70*, 703–713.

Worthen, B. R., & Sanders, J. R. (1987). *Educational evaluation: Alternative approaches and practical guidelines*. White Plains, NY: Longman.

Worthen, B. R., Sanders, J. R., & Fitzpatrick, J. L. (1997). *Program evaluation* (2nd ed.). New York: Longman.

Yin, R. K. (1992). The case study as a tool for doing evaluation. *Current Sociology*, *40*(1), 121–137.

WEB SITES

Western Michigan Evaluation Center
http://www.wmich.edu/evalctr

Contract Checklist by Daniel Stufflebeam
http://www.wmich.edu/evalctr/checklists/contracts.pdf

KEC: Key Evaluation Checklist
http://www.wmich.edu/evalctr/checklists/kec_feb07.pdf

Deliberative Democratic
http://www.wmich.edu/evalctr/checklists/dd_checklist.PDF

Fourth Generation
http://www.wmich.edu/evalctr/checklists/constructivisteval.pdf

U-FE
http://www.wmich.edu/evalctr/checklists/ufe.pdf

Gary Miron's Evaluation Report Checklist
http://www.wmich.edu/evalctr/checklists/reports.xls

Writing the Proposal or Final Report

KEY IDEA

Telling your story: From design engineer to public relations.

POINTS TO KNOW

Describe the basic rules of thumb for writing theses, dissertations, and reports.

Describe APA format and organization.

Describe the keys to editing your own work.

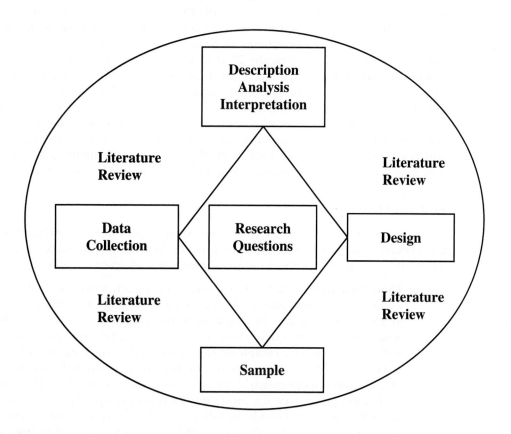

RESEARCH REPORT WRITING

This chapter outlines key components of a thesis and dissertation proposal or a final report. As stated in Chapter 2, our students typically need extra assistance in writing. This chapter is a continuation of that discussion with the focus now on the traditional first three sections of a proposal: introduction, literature review, and method. We also provide a differentiation of research report narrative for qualitative studies. Your role is changing though. For the majority of this book, we have wanted you to be a good design engineer and carefully design and plan your study based on what you want to learn. This at times can be very functional and one can get lost in the minutiae. Now, we are asking you to take everything you have planned and turn it into a narrative that can be easily read and understood by a wide variety of readers.

Research proposal and final report writing are not considered good literature, mainly because of the technical jargon. This is one of the reasons that research is not disseminated to a wider audience (Kennedy, 1997). Literature has a wonderful flow and rich characters. Empirical research studies only flow because we use headings (e.g., Method) to force the change in topic for the reader. Second, we have a limited amount of space, typically 25 double-spaced pages, for a manuscript to describe a study that may have taken a year to accomplish. Therefore, a great deal of information is lost, and the writer (you) must decide what should be included (or excluded). To that end, there are many previously developed reports that can be obtained through Internet searches to make sure you have included everything you need. We discuss some basic rules of thumb to follow based on our experience and that of others whom we have read. We also discuss formatting in terms of quantitative and qualitative studies, along with some specific issues for each.

Rules of Thumb

The following rules of thumb are from a mix of our experience, the Online Writing Lab at Purdue, and the University of California Berkeley writing proposal workshop. These sites have been helpful to our undergraduate and graduate students.

- **Think first, write second**. Before you can write clearly, you must think clearly. The more time you take to clean your ideas mentally, the easier it will be to get them on paper. By engaging in this cognitive activity, you will be answering the who, what, where, when, why, and how questions for your study. Once you have completed this activity, put your thoughts in writing. Then let it bake for a bit and return to check on it. Continually ask yourself, "Can I write it more clearly?" We agree with Thompson (1995) that "poor writing will doom even the most significant manuscript" (p. 73). Next, ask yourself, "Does this fit with the other words I have written and the current way I am thinking?" Finally, ask, "Can I explain my study and its relevance in less than 50 non-jargon words to a friend outside of my academic life?"
- **Draw it, if you can**. We like to have our students draw their ideas from point A to point Z. Some students like to use outlines, and they will work just fine,

too. Kim and I outline after we have drawn. Once we have an outline, we begin by filling in the key sentence for each term or phrase in the outline. Once we have done this, we begin to fill in the body of the text. This process allows us to examine the logic and flow of our arguments and the flow of content. Several outline sections for this book were changed during this process because the content no longer made sense logically. Plus, we had students read it, like a member check, to get their reactions to the flow and content.

- **Get to the point, now**. Your proposal should be easily read by your audience. A rule of thumb is not to assume that your reader understands what you mean or understands the journey you are taking them on. Specifically, make your goals, objectives, research questions, or hypotheses clear. Do not make the reader search whether it is for a grant, a dissertation, or an article.

- **Write simply: Be brief and minimize jargon**. Write as though you are writing for your parents or siblings who will not understand you unless you make it make sense. In short, to-the-point sentences are appreciated, along with paragraphs that begin with an informative sentence to tell readers where you are taking them. If you stay within active voice, the use of verbs next to the subjects will be easily recognizable and appreciated. You want to convey your meaning and not create multiple interpretations. This is easier to write than to do. We have written what we thought were perfectly simple sentences, only to have students interpret them in completely new and exciting ways. Headings, subsections, and verbal clues all help the reader remain oriented to your meaning.

- **Have peers critique your work**. We are past recommending that you have someone read your work. We usually demand **peer critiques**. Even our undergraduate students have to read and review each other's papers. The key is to have a variety of people read the manuscript (or a section or sentence). In education, we call this heterogeneous grouping. The benefit of this pattern of review is that each person brings a different strength or unique perspective to the narrative. These differences will help you "see" things right in front of your face.

- **Make sure your writing is coherent**. Any proposal or manuscript typically goes through has multiple versions before the final one is sent out. The problem is that during the editing stage, the original logic and flow, or **coherence**, is lost.

- **Check the interconnections in your study**. The interconnections among your theoretical concepts, questions of interest, rationale for the study, the study method, and the subsequent analysis will be critiqued like nothing you have ever experienced. As Jim has stated, when he was in graduate school, he was trained to review manuscripts and to begin the review with the Method section and then expand forward and backward in the text. If the alignment, or **interconnectedness**, among these is bad, nothing else matters. For every question you have, you need to plan out in great detail how you are going to gather the convincing evidence to answer that question.

- **Make sure your study is feasible**. Can you actually pull off this study or series of studies in any reasonable amount of time and on a limited budget? In other words, does it have **feasibility**? Novice researchers tend to try to solve all the problems in the previous studies all at once in their proposals. That is simply not possible. What most new researchers lack is experience in project management. Remember that having to travel distances or observe people individually or have multiple sites quickly adds on to the actual time it will take. As a rule of thumb, we tell students it will take you six months to a year to get a solid proposal defended and agreed to by the committee and six months to a year to collect, analyze, write, and defend the dissertation. A rushed dissertation never turns out well, and invariably the student takes the same amount of time dealing with all the problems.
- **Check the readability**. What we mean by **readability** is making sure that the words and ideas help guide the reader through the material. A colleague, Dr. Jill Stamm, once told Jim that she kept rearranging the ideas of her proposal until they made a smooth "s" shape on the wall of her house so that the reader would be gently guided into the reason for the study and the questions to be asked.
- **Attend to Details**. After all this, you are usually quite tired and want to skip paying attention to the citations, page numbers, and references. Do not. It leaves a bad impression. A mistake here and there will occur, but it becomes readily apparent when the writer has not double-checked references. Later in your career it is quite frustrating when reviewing manuscripts or proposals you have been cited incorrectly.

Writing Style by Research Organization

Each research organization and some research councils have their own style guides. Kim and I work under the American Psychological Association's style manual (APA, 2010). In Table 12.1, we provide the citations with their accompanying Web sites.

PROPOSAL REPORT/ORGANIZATION

The formatting and flow of information has some traditional patterns that go back to the time of Cicero, where he had the exordium (introduction), narration (statement of facts), division (where you disagree with others, rationale), proof (evidence from your study), and conclusion. We discuss the overall pattern for APA. Next, we provide a traditional quantitative design example, followed by one that is qualitative.

Formatting Highlights from APA

Below we provide some highlights from the APA style manual that we constantly need to review as we prepare manuscripts. You are not expected to remember

TABLE 12.1

Organizations and their related style manuals

Style	Citation	Web Sites
APA	*Publication manual of the American Psychological Association* (6th ed.). (2010). Washington, DC: American Psychological Association.	http://www.apastyle.org http://owl.english.purdue.edu/owl/resource/560/01/ http://www.wisc.edu/writing/Handbook/index.html
Chicago	*Chicago manual of style* (15th ed.). (2003). Chicago: University of Chicago Press.	http://owl.english.purdue.edu/owl/resource/557/01/ http://www.wisc.edu/writing/Handbook/index.html http://www.chicagomanualofstyle.org/home.html
MLA	*MLA style manual and guide to scholarly publishing* (3rd ed.). (2008). New York: Modern Language Association.	http://www.mla.org/style http://www.wisc.edu/writing/Handbook/index.html

every detail of your style manuals, but you should have a firm grasp on some basic components.

Headings.   Headings act as quick and hard transitions between topics in research reports. There are multiple levels with APA rules governing their placement. In Table 12.2, we have attempted to demonstrate the five levels through example.

The number and types of headings to use depends on the number of heading types needed. More specifically, if you are using,

- 1 type of heading, use Level 1
- 2 types of headings, use Levels 1 and 2
- 3 types of headings, use Levels 1, 2, and 3
- 4 types of headings, use Levels, 1, 2, 3, and 4
- 5 types of headings, use Levels 1, 2, 3, 4 and 5

TABLE 12.2

APA heading levels

Level 1
  Centered, Boldface, Uppercase and Lowercase Headings
Level 2
  Left Aligned, Boldface, Uppercase and Lowercase Headings
Level 3
  Indented, boldface, lowercase heading with period.
Level 4
  Indented, boldface, italicized, lowercase heading with period.
Level 5
  Indented, italicized, lowercase heading with period.

Page Layout.   The pages are to be set in a specific pattern, called **page layout**. There are five basic guidelines you should follow for APA:

1. Typed, double-spaced
2. Standard-sized paper (8.5" × 11")
3. 1" (inch) margins on all sides
4. 10–12 pt. Times New Roman or a similar font
5. Page header (short title and page number) in the upper, right-hand corner of every page
6. Two spaces after periods throughout the paper

Basic Sections.   Each manuscript will have five sections regardless of the type of design the study used. The five sections are listed below.

1. Title Page
2. Abstract
3. Body (varies by traditions within quantitative and qualitative)
4. References
5. Tables/Graphics

Voice and Point of View.   The voice of the verbs is to be active voice. We discuss this in the Armchair Moment section because it is a general guideline to good writing. For example, "John *was suspended* by the school" is in passive voice. "The school suspended John" is in active voice. Specifically, you should work on writing in active voice. We write in passive voice when we are tired or pressed for time. The point of view concerns first, second, and third person. You should write in the third person for your articles in general. Some researchers write in the first person due to the traditions in their field. For example, "The researcher interviewed each participant" versus "I interviewed each participant."

Tables and Figures.   As with all components of APA, there are some basic rules for tables and figures. For **tables**:

- All tables are numbered (e.g., Table 1, Table 2, Table 3).
- Each table is to have a title that is italicized and presented with each word capitalized (except *and, in, of, with,* etc.). See the example in Table 12.3.
- Horizontal lines are allowed for clarity but vertical lines are not.
- Each column must have a descriptive heading.
- Table headings in left column are set left, others are centered.
- The first letter of each heading is capitalized.
- The words, numbers, symbols, etc., are double-spaced.
- Each table is to be placed on a separate page.
- Each table must be referenced in the text (body) of the paper at least once.
- Tables are last, after your reference list and appendices.
- Abbreviations for standard terms (e.g., *M, SD*) do not need further explanation.

TABLE 12.3
APA formatted table

Sample Table for Study Descriptive and Inferential Statistics

	Group A		**Group B**	
Metacognitive	*M*	*SD*	*M*	*SD*
Score	35.71	5.21	48.92*	4.35

$p <. 05$ Note. The numbers are rounded to two decimal places.

FIGURE 12.1
Example of APA formatted figure

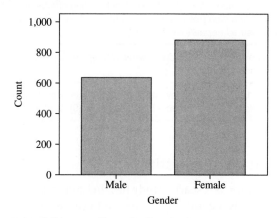

Figure 1. Frequency Count Bar Chart for Gender

- If an abbreviation or word needs further explanation, the explanation can be added to Note below the table.

For **figures**:

- The figure caption is set below the image. It should be double-spaced and the type set for *Figure* 1 (or 2 or 3 or 4, etc).
- The word *Figure* and the number are italicized and the alignment is flush left along with the caption.
- The first letter of the first word is capitalized. If there is a proper noun(s) in the caption, the noun(s) must also be capitalized.

Example References.   **References** follow the general pattern of authors, year of publication, title of work, and then the publication information (e.g., journal, book, Web site). In Table 12.4, we provide some common reference examples by type.

TABLE 12.4
Examples of APA reference formatting

Book	Kreft, I. G. G., & de Leeuw, J. (1998). *Introducing multilevel models*. London: Sage.
Chapter in an edited book	Secada, W. G. (1992). Race, ethnicity, social class, language and achievement in mathematics. In D. A. Grouws (Ed.), *Handbook of research on mathematics teaching and learning* (pp. 623–660). New York: Macmillan.
Article in a journal (where each volume is paginated)	Ethington, C. A., & Wolfe, L. M. (1986). A structural model of mathematics achievement for men and women. *American Educational Research Journal, 23*, 65–75.
Presentation	Kanyongo, G., Schreiber, J. B., & Brown, L. (2006, April). *Multilevel education model of Botswana data*. Paper presented at the annual meeting of the American Educational Research Association, San Francisco, CA.
Web-based article	Veal, W., & Schreiber, J. B. (1999). Block scheduling effects on state mandated test of basic skills. *Education Policy Analysis Archives, 7*(29). Retrieved from http://epaa.asu.edu/epaa/v7n29
Online encyclopedia and dictionaries	Scorer Reliability. (n.d.). In *Encyclopædia Britannica online*. Retrieved from http://www.britannica.com
Dissertation abstracts	Delgado, V. (1997). An interview study of Native American philosophical foundations in education. *Dissertation Abstracts International, 58*(9), 3395A.

Traditional Quantitative Formatting

Every quantitative empirical research study has the same basic set up. You have seen this in Chapter 2, but it is a good time to review because you have been exposed to and learned a great deal of content since that chapter. In Table 12.5, we review the basic components of a quantitative report.

Quantitative Example.   In Figure 12.2, we provide an example of the formatting and organization of a quantitative-based manuscript from a paper presentation by Kanyongo, Schreiber, and Brown (2006). For each page, we highlight specific formatting aspects in APA format.

Quantitative Formatting Special Issues.   Formatting statistical equations or just the symbols always seems to be a problem. We recommend using an equation writer to get the symbols correct. We have presented common examples with the words associated with them below.

   Mean and **standard deviation** are easiest to read when separated with parentheses:

The participants' average score was low ($M = 57.21, SD = 2.01$).
The average age of the participants was 23.45 years ($SD = 5.21$).

TABLE 12.5
Generic quantitative organization

Abstract	Provides a brief who, what, where, when, and why of the study. This should allow the reader to decide whether they want to read further.
Literature review	Provides information on previous studies, theoretical (and epistemological) bases of the study, and the research questions or problems area. Depending on the journal and the history of the field, this could be sparse or detailed.
Method	Describes the sampling process, final sample, data collection methods, data collected, and analytic techniques all in relation to the research questions or problem area of interest.
Results	Describes verbally or visually the observations from the analysis. When appropriate, inferences will be made based on the type of analysis completed. Can be organized by research question, which makes it easier for the reader to follow and make connections to previous components of the study read earlier.
Discussion	A review of the observations in the larger context of the previous research.

Note: This is a general format that is easily recognizable for most social science research articles.

Display **percentages** in parentheses without decimal places:

Almost half of the participants (49%) self-reported single as their marital status.

Chi-square statistics include the degrees of freedom and sample size in parentheses, the Pearson chi-square value (rounded to two decimal places), and the statistical significance level:

The percentage of participants who participated in illegal activities did not differ by location, $X^2(2, N = 55) = 1.03, p = .597$.

For **t-test statistics**, include the degrees of freedom in parentheses, two decimal places for the t value, and the statistical significance level:

The difference between genders was statistically significant, $t(93) = 7.21$, $p < .0001$, with women providing more positive statements than men.

ANOVA (both one-way and two-way) statistics include both the between- (first) and the within-group (second), separated by a comma. Next, state the F statistic value, with two decimal places, and the significance level. For example:

There was a statistically significant main effect for map order, $F(1, 127) = 8.07, p < .0005$, but no statistically interaction, $F(2, 127) = 1.12, p = .329$.

For readers who want to recreate the ANOVA table, it is nice to include the mean square error (*MSE*).

FIGURE 12.2
A brief APA formatted manuscript

Runninghead is shortened version of title. Set left and page number set right.

Running head: MATH ACHIEVEMENT IN BOTSWANA, NAMIBIA AND LESOTHO

Title is placed in the upper half of the page, centered. Then Name & Affiliation (e.g., university, etc.)

Math Achievement for 6th Graders in Botswana, Namibia, and Lesotho

Gibbs Yanai Kanyongo, James B. Schreiber, and Lancelot I. Brown

Duquesne University

MATH ACHIEVEMENT FOR 6TH GRADERS IN BOTSWANA, NAMIBIA, AND LESOTHO   2

Abstract

The researchers used the Wiley-Harnischfeger model of school processes to examine student and teacher variables associated with mathematics achievement. The participants for this study included 6th graders from Botswana, Namibia, and Lesotho. The researchers employed a multilevel regression model to analyze the three samples of data. For each data set, the regression models were the same. For the Botswana data, the researchers conducted a more detailed analysis after the first models. The most consistent result across all three countries was the higher the teacher's score on the test, the higher the class average mathematics score. Further discussion focuses on issues of using a Western model of school processes with international data.

Keywords: mathematics, achievement, multilevel modeling, Africa

Header
Abstract (Centered)
Then 120 word concise summary
Paragraph is not indented
Keywords after Abstract

Header

Title Centered

Body of with first
paragraph indented

The purpose of this study was to investigate the relationship among mathematics achievement and student, teacher and school variables of 6th graders in Southern Africa. The study uses data collected by the Southern and Eastern Africa Consortium for Monitoring Educational Quality (SACMEQ) during the period 2000–2002 under the auspices of the United Nations Educational Scientific and Cultural Organization's International Institute for Educational Planning (UNESCO-IIEP, 2004). Researchers involved with the second educational research policy project named SACMEQ II covering fourteen Southern African countries collected the data.

The study attempted to answer the following general questions:

1. Are there differences in 6th grade mathematics achievement among schools in Botswana, Namibia, and Lesotho?
2. What are the student characteristics that explain differences in mathematics achievement among 6th graders in Botswana, Namibia, and Lesotho?
3. What are the home background characteristics that explain differences in mathematics achievement among 6th graders in Botswana, Namibia, and Lesotho?
4. What are the teacher characteristics that explain differences in mathematics achievement?

Theoretical Framework

In this study, Wiley and Harnischfeger's (1974) model acted as the overall framework for choosing variables, dealing with the nested nature of educational data, and conceptualizing multiple components of education. In a similar study to the current one, in which he looked at institutional and student factors affecting advanced mathematics achievement, Schreiber (2002) examined the Harnischfeger-Wiley Model of school learning.

Method

Note the boldface
On Method,
Participants, and
Variables

Details what was
done, how it was
done, and the
analysis

Method

Participants

This study used the SACMEQ II data (UNESCO-IIEP, 2004) to examine the relationship between the student and classroom level variables and mathematics achievement among 3276 6th graders nested in 469 classrooms in Botswana, 5048 6th graders nested in 606 classrooms in Namibia, and 3155 6th graders nested in 250 classrooms in Lesotho. The study employed multilevel regression analysis using HLM 5.05 to answer the research questions, where the student level variables are termed Level 1 and teacher and school level variables are termed Level 2.

Variables

The Level 1 variables in this study are *Gender, Mother's education, Homework done, Livestock,* and *Math score.* The variable *Gender* codes are male students (1) and female

MATH ACHIEVEMENT FOR 6TH GRADERS IN BOTSWANA, NAMIBIA, AND LESOTHO   4

students (0). *Mother's education* is a measure of the mother's level of educational attained, and it is measured on a 1 to 6 scale with 1 being "no education," 2 being "some primary education," 3 being "all primary education," 4 being "some secondary education," 5 being "all secondary education," 6 being "postsecondary education," and 7 being "completed university." The variable *Homework done* is a measure of the number of times a parent checks to make sure that homework is done. It is measured on a 4-point scale from 1 to 4 with 1 being "no homework," 2 being "never," 3 being "sometimes," and 4 being "most of the time." *Class size* is simply the number of students in the teachers' class.

> Results summarizes the observations from the study.

Results

Table 1 provides the multilevel results for the Botswana, Namibia, and Lesotho data. We first ran null models (no predictor variables included) for each data set and determined the intraclass correlation values. All three null models indicated a good amount of variance between schools and, therefore, something to model. We provide deviance values due to the problems estimating R-squared in random coefficient models (Kreft & de Leeuw, 1998). We chose to have gender, mother's education level, and number of livestock (a proxy for the Western concept of SES) randomly varied due to empirical observations from previous research with similar variables (Schreiber, 2002) for our random coefficient (full) model. Checking homework was not allowed to vary randomly because theoretically it does not make sense that it should vary among classrooms, but would vary among parents.

Discussion

Overall, the predictor variables chosen did not explain much of the variability in student scores. The variables chosen are just a few of many from the data set that can be used and a further examination of the data set variables that fit the model is warranted. It may also be that a different model needs to be derived. A possible reason for this could be that we used a Western model of the teaching and learning process to try to account for variance in test scores in South African countries. Due to some obvious cultural differences, the other variables or an adaptation to

TABLE 1
Descriptive statistics level-1 Botswana

	N	Min	Max	M	SD
Mother's education	2900	1	7	3.37	1.76
Homework done	2900	1	4	3.36	.66
Livestock	2900	.00	7.33	3.11	1.71
Math score	2900	5	57	25.71	8.09

MATH ACHIEVEMENT FOR 6TH GRADERS IN BOTSWANA, NAMIBIA, AND LESOTHO   5

the Harnischfeger-Wiley Model need to be examined to gain a better picture of variables associated with mathematics achievement. We may also need to try and derive, at least empirically, a different model altogether.

References

American Association of University Women. (1999). *Gender gaps: Where schools still fail our children.* New York: Marlowe & Company.

Betts, J. R., & Shkolnik, J. L. (1999). The behavioral effects of variations in class size: The case of math teachers. *Educational Evaluation and Policy Analysis, Special Issue: Class Size: Issues and New Findings,* 21, 193–213.

Biddle, B. J., & Berliner, D. C. (2002). Small class size and its effects. *Educational Leadership,* 59(5), 2.

(End of APA formatted manuscript)

Correlations include the degrees of freedom (total participant size − 2) in parentheses and the statistical significance level:

> The correlation between Education Level and Job Responsibilities were statistically significantly different from zero, $r(156) = .49, p < .001$.

Regression analyses are easiest to read in table format. In the narrative of the Results section, it is appropriate to provide the standardized slope (beta), degrees of freedom, t value, and statistical significance level. Note that the degrees of freedom for the t-test is $N - k - 1$, where N is the total number of participants and k is the number of predictor/independent variables. Finally, you should present the variance accounted for and the related F test. For example:

> Teacher content knowledge statistically significantly predicted class average test score, $\beta = .78, t(1529) = 6.53, p < .0001$.
> Teacher content knowledge accounted for a statistically significant proportion of variance in student scores, $R^2 = .42, F(1, 1529) = 35.21, p < .0001$.

Qualitative Format by Design

Though we discussed in Chapter 1 a basic format for qualitative and quantitative research articles, there are traditions within qualitative research and how the information from a research study is presented. Below, we discuss the unique aspects of representing the information for ethnography, phenomenology, grounded theory, and case study.

Ethnography.   We have chosen Emerson, Fretz, and Shaw's (1995) somewhat strict format to discuss the organization of writing the narrative of an ethnography.

Though, we believe, some will disagree with the categorization, we realize that students learning about design need a bit more structure than more advanced students. The process described below seems to help that.

To begin, the writer provides an introduction that will capture the reader's attention and provides a central focus for the study. The reader should also understand why the researcher conducted this study and the research questions. Next, the researcher provides the connection between the interpretations and larger issues within the scholarly community about this topic. Second, the setting and the method for gathering the data are introduced to the reader. This is the point where the researcher provides the details of data collection, entry into the field, participation, and any other information that would provide understanding for the reader. The reader should be getting a thick description of the setting. For example, "He sat at his desk wondering what to do next" versus "With limited florescent lighting from above, the realization that his program was being eliminated, he tapped on his computer keyboard and appeared to be wondering whether he should continue working on the manuscript or start looking for a new job immediately."

In the third part, the researcher makes analytic claims about the culture being studied and provides patterns and themes that have been observed. Because claims are being made, evidence through the descriptions of artifacts, interviews, or other documentation needs to be provided. The researcher should use the participants' actual words along with his or her account and understanding. The quotes the researcher uses should directly relate to the claims being made. Finally, the observations are related to the research questions, the concepts and theories within the discipline, and the larger research community.

Phenomenology. Moustakas (1994) provides an overall organization for phenomenological studies where the researcher develops six chapters for the reader to follow. Chapter 1 is the introduction, statement of the topic, and outline. The researcher provides a personal background description that explains how the researcher ended up deciding to study this phenomenon. This could include a discussion of personal curiosity, some confusion about the phenomenon, and the new knowledge from the study that will contribute to the field. In a sense, the researcher is answering "the why" part of conducting the study for the reader. Chapter 2 is a review of the relevant research and literature. The researcher is to provide to the reader an introduction to the literature, how studies selected from the databases were used, how these studies were conducted and what was observed, a summary of all of the literature, and how the current study is different. The difference should be specific in relation to the research question, the model, the method, and the data collected.

Chapter 3 provides the conceptual framework of the model. The theoretical model used as well as the procedure for the design is to be explained. In Chapter 4, the method section is detailed. Note that Chapters 3 and 4 could be combined. Here the details of method, procedure, preparations, data collection, organizing the data, analyzing, and synthesizing are provided. As with all studies, readers should be able to replicate what the researcher did from reading this chapter. Chapter 5 is the presentation of the data. The researcher will discuss the themes that developed out of the analysis, provide verbatim examples, and provide a synthesis of the meaning and essence of the phenomenon that was studied. Finally, Chapter 6 provides a summary and implications of the study. The researcher will compare the observations in the current study with the observations discussed in the literature review. Limitations of the study and possibilities for future studies are also discussed. The overall goal of the write up of a phenomenological research study is to allow the readers to understand the phenomenon better than they did before they started reading (Polkinghome, 1989).

Grounded Theory.   Cresswell (1998) has five sections for a grounded theory manuscript. The first section includes the major research question, the evolution of that research question, and the definition of key terms. Remember, in a grounded theory study, the initial question is quite broad and will change over time as the theory is developed during data collection and analysis. Next, the writer provides a literature review that only discusses the gaps or biases within the existing literature base. The researcher does not provide theories, concepts, or hypotheses. The third part is the methodology, which is introduced early in comparison to quantitative studies and will provide a description of the evolution of the methodology during the study. This part will obviously provide detail on the procedures and types of data collected. Part four focuses on the theoretical model or scheme. Actual data will be provided in the form of a vignette (i.e., a short written or graphic scenario) or quotes. This allows the reader to evaluate how well the theory that is being claimed is grounded in the evidence of the data. Finally, the developed theory is discussed in context with other existing knowledge within the domain and the implications of developed theory for future research and practice.

Case Study.   Stake (1995) provides an outline for the flow of information and ideas for a case study report. They are as follows:

1. **Vignette:** The author provides a vignette so that the reader can get a feel for the time and place of the study. This is to be a vicarious experience to draw the reader into the case.
2. **Issue Identification:** The author describes the main issue, the purpose, and the method of the study so that the reader understands the development of the study, the writer, and the issues involved in this specific case.
3. **Description:** The description of the case is quite thorough at this point and focuses on data that are relatively stable or noncontroversial. The researcher provides enough information that if the reader were the one watching he or she would have provided a similar description. Stake (1995) states that if he has controversial data, he places it in the description section from the perspective of a contender or witness.

4. **Development of Issues:** Here the researcher develops and discusses a few key issues to frame the case and its complexity. The goal is not for generalization, but to get at the story. A veteran case study researcher will also draw from previous cases at this point to develop the issues.

5. **Data Evidence:** The researcher provides data as evidence to support the claims, typically through triangulation. The researcher will also discuss what was completed in an attempt to disconfirm the claims, such as searches for discrepant data.

6. **Assertions:** The researcher provides a summary of what is understood at this point in the case. The researcher will provide the evolution of the understanding of the case and his or her confidence level about the assertions.

7. **Closing Vignette:** The researcher closes with a vignette and highlights to the reader that the report is only one perspective of the case.

BEING YOUR OWN BEST EDITOR

When you are writing your proposal (or report), you should ask yourself a few questions along the way. Table 12.6 is just one of the many checklists you can use. We have specifically broken the questions into sections. The outline in Table 3.4 is also helpful.

SUMMARY

If you examine the research report structure across the studies you are reviewing, you will notice common components. Qualitative articles are heavily dependent on the data analysis component. There is less development of the theoretical framework as described earlier for quantitative research. Also note that the data collection procedures and materials can change over time for these studies, and because of that, the reader needs great detail in order to make a complete account and understanding of the study.

ARMCHAIR MOMENT

We want to take a moment to discuss grammar. Earlier we stated that a good manuscript is doomed if it is poorly written. Poor grammar takes all the energy out of the reviewers and typically upsets them. If you do not feel you are a strong writer, we suggest you obtain a copy of *Eats, Shoots & Leaves* by Lynne Truss or *Well-Tempered Sentence* by Karen Elizabeth Gordon and review it before writing. The book you choose does not matter as much as the decision to develop your writing skills. Below we provide common mistakes we see in manuscripts every day. This list is not complete, but reflects the most common errors Jim has seen in the past four years while editing a journal.

TABLE 12.6
Self-editing questions

Abstract:
Did I cover the five basic areas?
Background — Basic summary of the study
Objective — Purpose of the study
Method — Sample and design
Results — What was observed?
Discussion — How does this fits into the larger picture?

Literature Review:
Have I discussed the purpose of the review?
Did I try to put too much in the review?
Is anything replicated or redundant?
Did I focus on primary research articles and only support with secondary sources?
Are my citations from credible, widely accepted publications?
Did I highlight the most current thinking in this area?
Are there any irrelevant literatures that do not directly relate to questions or problems of interest?
Did I double-check the citation information for name spelling, pages, volume, title, and so on?
Is my review organized (by topic, theme, historically) and is it logical?
Has someone else reviewed it?
Did I include the most cited study and the most important theories in detail with empirical results?
Are contradictory observations and theories discussed?
Did I adequately critique what has been completed to date?
Did I compare results for similarities and differences?
Did I explain, if applicable, the theory that drives the study in enough detail?
Did I summarize the current research?
Did the literature review lead to the questions for this study?
Does the literature review adequately explain why these questions and this study need to be conducted?

Method Section:
Have I stated my questions, problem area, or related hypotheses?
Are the questions asked logically related to the sampling process?
Have I justified this sampling process?
Have I discussed the human participants issues and related internal review board clearance?
Are the questions asked logically related to the design?
Have I justified this design?
Are the questions asked logically related to the study procedures, data, and data collection processes?
Have I justified these procedures, data, and processes?
Have I adequately discussed reliability and validity or believability and credibility?
Do I have enough statistical power for quantitative studies?
Have I explained the independent and dependent variables?
Can a colleague run this study based on my description?
Have I discussed missing data?
Have I discussed any attrition (e.g., participants leaving the study, unreturned surveys)?

Results:
Have I provided the information needed to evaluate the observation?
Did I follow the AERA/APA/NCME reporting guidelines?
Did I provide an understandable interpretation of the results?
Did I present tables or figures that are understandable on their own?

Discussion:
Did I relate the observations to the literature I reviewed (if appropriate)?
Did I place the observations from the study in the larger research area?
Did I provide the limitations to this study in accurate detail?

The Comma and the Dependent Clause

The **dependent clause** needs to be connected to an **independent clause** to make it complete. Common "marker words" for dependent clauses are *after, although, as, as if, because, before, even if, even though, if, in order to, since, though, unless, until, whatever, when, whenever, whether,* and *while.* An example is provided below.

> *When Jim wrote this chapter*, he was very tired.

Please notice the **comma** linking the two clauses. Many of our reviewers are a bit put off by the lack of the comma in this situation. Other examples are provided below.

The Comma Splice Error

A **comma splice** error occurs when a comma is placed between two independent clauses.

> *Error:* I like this book, it is fun to read.
> *Ways to correct:*

1. I like this book. It is fun to read.
2. I like this book; it is fun to read.
3. I like this book, and it is fun to read.
4. I like this book because it is fun to read.

Finally, with a dependent clause at the beginning of a sentence:

5. Because it is fun to read, I like this book.

Run-on Sentence Errors

Run-on sentence errors are essentially a missing period, colon, or semicolon.

> *Error:* I like this book it is fun to read.
> *Ways to correct:*

1. I like this book. It is fun to read.
2. I like this book, and it is fun to read.

Sentence Fragment Errors

Sentence fragments are dependent clauses or other incomplete statements as a sentence.

> *Error:* Since I read the book.
> *Ways to correct:*

1. Since I read the book, I know what to say.
2. I read the book.

The Apostrophe: Possessive and Plural Examples

Paul's book (the book belongs to Paul)
Children's play lot (an area played in by more than one child)
Women's movement and it's (it is, it has)
It's cold outside. (It is cold outside.)
Thank goodness it's Friday. (Thank goodness it is Friday.)
The test looks appropriate, but I am concerned about its *(i.e., the test)* long-term
   validity.

Noun-Verb Agreement Examples

Data are analyzed using statistical methods.
Rodney and Jim are working on an ethnographic project.
Rodney is working on an ethnographic project.
The children are at recess.
The child is at recess.

Parallel Construction Errors

Error: Jim likes playing Uno, swimming, and *to walk.*
Correct: Jim likes playing Uno, swimming, and walking.
Error: The study was completed quickly, efficiently, and within budget.
Correct: The study was completed quickly, efficiently, and cost effectively.

Passive Voice

The "study" sentence above is in **passive voice**. To change it to **active voice**, you
typically need to change the initial noun or switch the noun and the direct object.
We are as guilty of this as everyone else.

The researchers completed the study quickly, efficiently, and cost effectively.

In addition, "studies" do not complete things, people do.

We recommend you read through the writing lab at Purdue University, specifically on grammar, punctuation, and spelling at http://owl.english.purdue.edu/
handouts/grammar/index.html

KEY WORDS

abstract	Chicago	correlations
active voice	chi-square statistics	data evidence
ANOVA	closing vignette	dependent clause
APA	coherence	description
apostrophe	comma	development of issues
assertions	comma splice	discussion

feasibility	noun-verb agreement	references
figure	page layout	results
headings	parallel construction	run-on sentence
independent clause	passive voice	sentence fragment
interconnectedness	peer critique	standard deviation
issue identification	percentages	table
literature review	possessive	*t*-test statistic
mean	plural	vignette
method	readability	
MLA	regression analysis	

REFERENCES

American Psychological Association (APA). (2010). *The publication manual of the American Psychological Association* (6th ed.). Washington, DC: Author.

Cresswell, J. W. (1998). *Qualitative inquiry and research design: Choosing among the five traditions.* Thousand Oaks, CA: SAGE Publications.

Emerson, R. M., Fretz, R. I., & Shaw, L. L. (1995). *Writing ethnographic fieldnotes.* Chicago: University of Chicago Press.

Kennedy, M. (1997). The connection between research and practice. *Educational Researcher, 26*(7), 4–12.

Moustakas, C. (1994). *Phenomenological research methods.* Thousand Oaks, CA: SAGE Publications.

Polkinghome, D. E. (1989). Phenomenological research methods. In R. S. Valle & S. Halling (Eds.), *Existential-phenomenological perspectives in psychology* (pp. 41–60). New York: Plenum.

Stake, R. (1995). *The art of case study research.* Thousand Oaks, CA: SAGE Publications.

Kanyongo, G., Schreiber, J. B., & Brown, L. (2006, April). Multilevel education model of Botswana data. A paper presented at the annual meeting of the American Educational Research Association, San Francisco, CA.

Thompson, B. (1995). Publishing your research results: Some suggestions and counsel. *Journal of Counseling and Development, 73,* 342–345.

WEB SITES

Purdue University's Online Writing Lab
http://owl.english.purdue.edu

University of California at Berkeley's writing workshop
http://globetrotter.berkeley.edu/DissPropWorkshop/style/

Author Index

Topic Index